The Chilterns

THE
CHILTERNS

Leslie W. Hepple and Alison M. Doggett

Phillimore

1992

Published by
PHILLIMORE & CO. LTD.
Shopwyke Hall, Chichester, Sussex

ISBN 0 85033 833 6

Printed in Great Britain by
CHICHESTER PRESS
West Sussex

To our families

Suzanne

Philip, Laura and Simon

This worke then is composed of *Geographie* (which is a description of the knowne Earth and the parts thereof) and Historie, which is (*Oculus Mundi*) the eye of the World. These two goe inseparably together, and as it were hand in hand ...

Preface to the first English edition of Mercator's *Atlas* (1636), by Henry Hexham, translator.

Contents

List of Illustrations

Frontispiece: Horse ploughing at Hambleden in the 1920s

Illustration and Copyright Acknowledgements

We are grateful to the following individuals and institutions for providing copies of photographs and giving us permission to reproduce them, or for permission to reproduce copyright material. All the other photographs (both colour and black-and-white) were taken by Alison Doggett.

The Warden and Fellows of All Souls College, Oxford: 98; Geoffrey Bles: 147; Lionel Brett (Viscount Esher) and Architectural Press: 155; Bodleian Library, Oxford: 52, 95, 116, 126; The Trustees of the British Library: 4, 6, 41, 46, 49, 53, 54, 59-62, 64-66, 75, 84; The Trustees of the British Museum: 39; J. P. Browne (*O.S. Map Cover Art*): 151; Buckinghamshire County Museum: 115, 121, 131, 159, 168; Buckinghamshire County Record Office: 144; Cambridge University, Committee for Aerial Photography: 11, 18, 25, 26, 48, 70, 145, 171; The Syndics of Cambridge University Library: 12, 118; Cambridge University Press: 51; Ministry of Defence (Crown copyright): 5, 17, 36, 69, 99; English Nature (Nature Conservancy Council for England): 88; Faber & Faber: 141; Mark Fiennes: 165; Simon Godden: 1, 3, 10, 35, 42-45, 47, 56-58, 63, 74, 83, 104, 112, 125, 127, 170; R. W. Hepple: 78; Hertfordshire Record Office: 111; High Wycombe Library: 37, 96, 146, 150; Hitchin Museum: 132; London Transport Museum: 138-40, 152, 153; Luton Museum: 7, 114a, 133, 134; Manshead Society, Dunstable: 40; National Motor Museum, Beaulieu: 149; National Railway Museum, York: 113; Oxfordshire Archives: 93, 100; Public Record Office (Crown copyright): 50, 55, 67, 117, 130; University of Reading, Institute of Agricultural History and Museum of English Rural Life, Reading: frontispiece, 120, 122, 124, 136, 148; Royal Commission on the Historical Monuments of England (RCHME) (Crown copyright): 71; Colin Seabright: 109, 110, 143, 164; Society of Antiquaries of London and Verulamium Museum: 27, 29, 31-33, 38; I. G. Sparkes: 114b; Victoria & Albert Museum: 97.

Preface

This book is about the Chilterns region, its landscape and its history. It sprang from our exploration of the Chilterns countryside: its winding lanes, beechwoods, remote hamlets and ancient flint churches. These explorations produced a whole series of questions and puzzles which sent us into the libraries searching for answers. Our very first enquiries yielded some gems: David Roden's work on the medieval period, Arnold Baines' papers on the Anglo-Saxon Chilterns, John Chenevix Trench on Coleshill, Oliver Rackham's work on the ecology of the woodlands, and John Evans' work on snails and early landscape. At this very early stage, it was apparent that the Chilterns stood apart as a special region at all of these various times in their history.

Further researches took us into the local record offices and libraries, and to the more rarified and beautiful reading rooms of the British Library, the Bodleian, and the Public Record Office, to look at the scholarly work on the region and to set about tracing the sources in old manuscripts, maps and documents. It was a joyful search, both because so much work had already been done, and because there was an inexhaustible supply of marvellous and often very ancient parchment to search through. But more than that, there was, for reasons that will shout out of the book, so much to see today on the ground. For anyone with an interest in landscapes and their history, the real thrill is to be able to make these connections in the field.

What became equally apparent was that this wealth of scholarship had never been gathered together and presented in a form that is both interesting to a wide readership and useful to those who, like us, have been drawn into further research. To this end, we have written this book: expressly to bridge the gap between academic writing and a more general readership. That is why we have included a large number of illustrations on the one hand, and careful footnoting with an extensive bibliography on the other. We have taken and included many photographs to capture the region in all seasons and lights over the two-year time-span of our work. And we have included samples of our favourite documents, old maps and photographs, many of which have not been published before, along with the specially-drawn maps and diagrams that you would expect where geographers are involved.

No one has previously attempted such a regional landscape history of the Chilterns. Our prime objective in writing the book is to share our enjoyment of the landscape and our fascination with its history and regional distinctiveness. But we also hope that its publication now may be timely, when there is a growing consideration of the Chilterns as a planning and conservation region, and perhaps a new awareness of regional self-identity and the environment. The Chilterns, as a region, may at last be coming into its own.

We are grateful to many academic colleagues and friends have helped us along the way, and have given us encouragement in our project. Many have been kind enough to read draft chapters and offer comments and corrections, though we remain responsible for all errors of fact or interpretation. We thank: Dr. Arnold Baines (chapter 4); Professor Keith Branigan (University of Sheffield), 3; Dr. Bruce Campbell (Queen's University of Belfast), 5 and 6; Ann Cole, 4; Professor Terry Coppock (University of Edinburgh) 11; Dr. John Evans (University of Wales at Cardiff), 2; Michael Farley (County Archaeologist, Buckinghamshire), 2, 3 and 4; Dr. Harold Fox (University of Leicester), 5 and 6; Dr. Michael Freeman (University of Oxford), 9; Professor Sheppard Frere (University of Oxford), 3; Dr. James Galloway (Centre for Metropolitan History, University of London), 5 and 6; Dr. Margaret Gelling (University of Birmingham), 4; Dr. Paul Glennie (University of Bristol), 5, 6 and 8; Oliver Green (Curator, Colchester Museum; formerly London Transport Museum), 12; László Gróf, 11; Professor Dennis Hardy (Middlesex University), 12; Professor Paul Harvey (University of Durham), 5 and 6; Michael Havinden (University of Exeter), 8; Dr. Sonia Chadwick Hawkes (University of Oxford), 4; Dr. Pamela Horn, 11; Dr. Jack Langton (University of Oxford), 9; Dr. David Matless (University of Oxford), 12; Professor W.R. Mead (University College, London), 8; Dr. Margaret Murphy (Centre for Metropolitan History, University of London) 5 and 6; Marian Nicholls (Luton Museum), 11; Patricia Preece, 7; Dr. Oliver Rackham (University of Cambridge), 7; Dr. David Roden (Eldoret Field Centre, Kenya), 7; Tim Schadla-Hall (Director of Museums, Leicestershire), 2 and 3; Ivan Sparkes, 10; Professor Michael Turner (University of Hull), 11; Eleanor Vollans, 7; Dr. Ross Wordie (University of Reading), 8 and 11.

Many archivists, curators and librarians have assisted us, both within the Chilterns and outside in Bristol, Cambridge, London, Oxford and Reading. Along the way, many Chilterns' residents, and staff of numerous planning and government departments, have always been willing to help. We thank them all. At the University of Bristol, we thank Paul Glennie for his enthusiasm and help throughout this project, Simon Godden for all the maps and diagrams, and Tony Philpott for help with photographic reproduction. Our gratitude goes to our parents, families and friends who have given us great encouragement and support. Our greatest debt is to our immediate families—to Suzanne in Bristol and Philip, Laura and Simon in Berkhamsted. Without them the book would never have been written, and we dedicate it to them with love and thanks.

LESLIE HEPPLE
ALISON DOGGETT

Berkhamsted
October 1992

Chapter One

Discovering the Chilterns

Setting the Scene

The scenery of the English chalklands needs little introduction, and the Chilterns make no secret of their chalky background. It is obvious as soon as we see the white-speckled escarpment rising proud of the Vale. We expect the gently-rounded, rolling downland scenery as the plateau dips towards the Thames, for this is familiar English countryside. The landscape of John Bunyan's *Pilgrim's Progress* was based on the Bedfordshire countryside, with the Chilterns as 'Immanuel's Land': '... a most pleasant mountainous country, beautiful with woods, vineyards, fruits of all sorts; flowers also with springs and fountains; very delectable to behold'.[1]

These hills are part of the calcareous backbone that underlies much of southern England to include the North and South Downs, Salisbury Plain and East Anglia and stretching northwards towards the Wolds of Lincolnshire and Yorkshire. The Chilterns form a discrete block rising between two gaps—the Goring gap near the Thames and the Hitchin Gap 60 miles to the north east. Along their length they invade four counties: Oxfordshire, Buckinghamshire, Hertfordshire and Bedfordshire. It is the northern edge which became the scarp, crenulated and pierced by coombe and valley and rising to a high point of 260 metres near Wendover. Behind it the dipslope trends south-eastwards divided by five long parallel troughs and numerous subsidiary valleys, many of them dry.

Whilst these hills are undeniably and recognisably chalk downlands, they are not typical of the scenery we may recognise elsewhere with vast open grasslands like those around Marlborough or on the South Downs. The Chilterns are predominantly crowned with woodland; they have somewhere near one quarter of their area covered with trees, numbering them amongst England's most densely wooded regions. Here you can walk through high beech forests with their carpets of spring bluebells and spectacular autumn tints, or search out the rarer juniper and box bushes on the steeper banks of the escarpment.

In addition to the woodlands, extensive areas of rough common and heathland still remain in the Chilterns since, unlike many other chalk regions, the plateau tops have a mantle of clay with flints producing heavy, acid soils. These are a legacy of the last Ice Age and provide some of the reasons for this region's distinctiveness; the commons such as those at Ibstone and Berkhamsted remind us of the once more widespread heathlands.

Exploring the countryside means venturing off the major roads, and entering a labyrinth of high-sided lanes winding up the valley sides and tumbling down the scarp slopes. The steep banks support a wealth of wild flowers and are topped by hedges, some so high that they meet overhead to form tree tunnels. The hedgerows extend to divide the patchwork of fields with their Jacob's coat of seasonal colours—the product of a mixed farming region. In the Chilterns one can still find old downland pastures containing twenty or more species of wild flowers, and acres of blushing poppies creating distant red horizons. So too, the more familiar neatly combed blue-green fields of winter wheat or irridescent yellow of oil seed rape in full bloom.

1

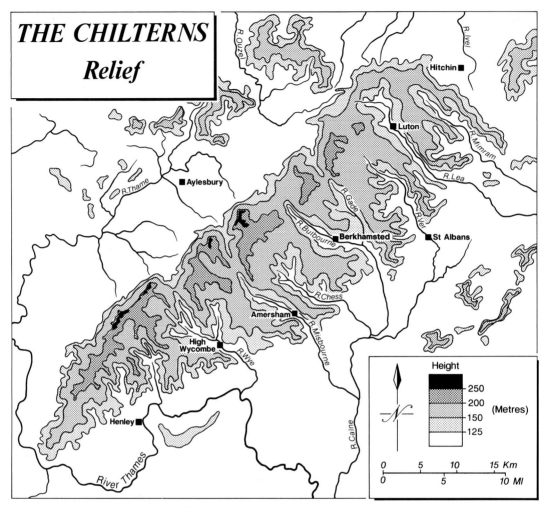

THE CHILTERNS
Relief

1. The relief and drainage of the Chilterns.

To describe the Chilterns as a predominantly rural landscape is not to deny their accessibility nor to underplay their towns and villages. Canals, railways and trunk roads penetrate and traverse the region, connecting Chiltern settlements to the surrounding area and to London in particular. Despite the growing pressure of commuter and dormitory populations the traditional hierarchy of places remains intact. The larger towns such as High Wycombe, Luton and Dunstable dominate the major gaps with smaller market towns such as Wendover, Berkhamsted and Princes Risborough spaced out along the valleys or lined up along the scarp foot. Picturesque villages, many built around traditional greens and ponds such as those at Cholesbury and Aldbury, are found dotted along the hilltops or nestling in dry valleys between the countless hamlets and farmsteads that are sprinkled throughout the entire landscape.

Gaining a Perspective
In this brief cameo we have introduced the Chilterns as a region which is distinctive, internally diverse and scenically attractive. If we are to progress from general observation to a more

inquisitive examination, then we must pose questions which will require us to investigate how this small region has developed through history. We are tempted to seek a fuller understanding and deeper appreciation of what is simply 'interesting' at a glance.

This book is about our search and charts the relationship between successive groups of people and the land on which they lived. For this ancient and long-settled corner of England contains a wealth of discoverable evidence for us to piece together. The legacies of the past survive in many forms and remain reflected in today's landscapes. They may be contained within the land itself as ancient barrows, buried villas, dykes and boundaries which can be studied using archaeological techniques and aerial photography. Other legacies survive in existing buildings: the Chilterns boasts churches dating back to the 12th century and beyond, medieval wall-paintings and tiles, and cruck-construction houses that speak of building techniques that are a relic of pre-Saxon times. Good fortune has provided us with a rich documentary record: ancient deeds and charters such as the cartulary of the monks of Missenden Abbey, as well as surviving grange accounts, wood books, old maps and the Domesday record.

Place-names tell their own story, and studied in conjunction with local topography, can provide new insights into the penetration of different groups of invaders and settlers. For instance, Ann Cole has recently shown how Anglo-Saxon settlers in the Chilterns recognised local differences in relief and water-supply in their use of suffixes such as *-den*, *-cumb* (coombe), *-bourne* and *-well*. It is also our intention to take the historical search one stage further and consider the ecological aspects which have recently revealed so much about the way in which people have been altering their environment ever since the first flint axe cut the first clearing in the virgin forest. The history of the countryside is embodied as firmly in the woodland trees and hedgerow shrubs we see today as it is in the archaeological remains and old buildings.

In discovering history in any region we are concerned with unearthing these many elements—often from obscure and disparate sources—and using them to build a picture. Such a synthesis inevitably draws on the work of many scholars who have poured over fusty documents and tramped the fields and hedgerows. We have gained much satisfaction from the discovery, selection, emphasis and linkage of our materials, and the final picture reflects our own field and archive studies and is inevitably our own interpretation of all this material.

First and foremost amongst our sources is the rich tradition of local history research and writing in the Chilterns as published through journals such as *Records of Buckinghamshire*, *Oxoniensia*, and *Hertfordshire Archaeology*. Among recent outstanding contributions are the work of Keith Branigan on the Roman period, Arnold Baines on the Anglo-Saxon Chilterns, John Chenevix Trench on the Coleshill area near Beaconsfield, and David Roden's work on medieval farming and settlement.

We have also discovered researches not primarily aimed at the local or regional historian, which have used Chilterns case studies and illustrations as part of classic archaeological and scientific investigations. One example is A. S. Watt's work on the ecology of English beechwoods using the Chilterns as his prime example. A second study is John Evans' pioneering work using snail shells as a method of investigating and dating the early environmental history of chalk regions for which pollen analysis had thus far proved unsatisfactory. Evans' initial work was done on Chilterns escarpment sites at Pitstone and Pink Hill. It has also proved rewarding to apply to our region ideas and approaches to landscape and ecological history developed in studies of other parts of the country, but so far largely unapplied to the Chilterns, notably Oliver Rackham's ecological approach to the history of ancient woodland and countryside.

Landscape historians wear many hats when attempting to fit together the pieces of this complicated jigsaw puzzle of historical evidence. They must concentrate on the links between several pieces if they are to connect properly what is seen with what has gone before. And the evidence must be weighted carefully—some is hard, heavy and convincing, whilst other evidence remains flimsy and circumspect, and sometimes completely untrue. Take for example the sometimes-quoted tale of the journey of the Italian poet Brunetto Latino through the Chilterns to Oxford in the 13th century:

> Our journey from London to Oxford was with some difficulty and danger made in two days. We passed through many woods considered here as dangerous places being infested with robbers, which is indeed the case with most of the roads of England. However as our company was numerous we had less cause to fear. Accordingly we arrived the first night at Shirburn Castle in the neighbourhood of Watlington, under the chain of hills over which we passed at Stocquinchurque.

In fact the whole tale is an early 19th-century literary hoax, and Latino was never in England at all.[2]

The Ancient Countryside
The Chiltern scarp is a dramatic boundary that divides the countryside emphatically into hill and vale. This is no mere break of slope; it marks a line which distinguishes two totally different kinds of landscape and as such is unsurpassed anywhere in England. The hills on one side form what contemporary historians call 'ancient countryside'. The Vale beneath them is a textbook example of a 'planned' or 'champion' landscape. This distinction is very important both because it serves to identify the Chiltern Hills as a special region, and also because it provides a framework for explaining these special features and what lies behind them. The differences between ancient and planned countryside—or in the older terminology between 'wooded' (referring to hedged enclosed fields as well as woods) and 'champion' countryside—have long been recognised and are also very much a part of current historical debate.

The distinction was one well recognised by the Tudor antiquarians and topographers. William Harrison in his *The Description of England* (1587) wrote of 'our soil being divided into champaign ground and woodland', and earlier John Leland had pinpointed the division very clearly as he journeyed through the Chilterns from Aylesbury to Uxbridge in the 1530s. From Aylesbury to Wendover he was on the low, wet claylands of the Vale:

> There a causey made almoste thrwghly to passe betwixt Aillesbery and it [Wendover], els the way in wet tyme as in a lowe stiffe claye grownde were very tedius and ille to passe by. The tounelet selfe of Wyndover stondythe partely apon one of the north-est cliffs of Chilterne Hills. The residew and north-est parte of the towne standyth in the rootes of the hills. Looke as the conterye of the vale of Aillesbyre for the moste parte is clene baren of woodde, and [is] champaine; so is all Chilterne well woodyd, and full of enclosures.[3]

In the 18th century the agricultural improver and writer William Ellis, who lived and farmed at Little Gaddesden in the Hertfordshire Chilterns, wrote his text on the difference and its agricultural implications, *Chiltern and Vale Farming Explained* (1733).

What is ancient countryside? To avoid confusion it may be better to start with what it is not. It is not a landscape which has necessarily been settled for longer than areas around it. The distinction lies in the way that it has been transformed and what has survived over the last thousand or more years. In an ancient countryside the sort of transformations that took place were different from the more familiar changes in planned countryside. Most of the 'ancient' countrysides are in wooded and often hilly regions and their history is one of piecemeal changes over small areas and over a long time. This has allowed them to retain characteristics from a much more distant past than planned countryside.

Planned or champion countrysides are dominated by the legacies of major landscape revolutions: first the creation of the medieval open field or 'champion' systems with nucleated villages (probably dating from the later Anglo-Saxon period), and secondly the replanning in the 18th or 19th century with the parliamentary enclosure of the open fields. Any evidence of what they were like before is largely buried as archaeological remains or briefly hinted at in the lines of roads.

In ancient countryside such drastic and all-encompassing farming and settlement practices were not imposed wholesale. Thus, as W. R. Mead's studies using air photographs have shown, the Chilterns are lacking the extensive ridge-and-furrow so characteristic of former open-field country in the Vale and north Buckinghamshire.[4] The topography and woodland vegetation of the Chilterns were not conducive to the rigid constraints of the three-field open system. Many places in the Chilterns were always suitable for agriculture, but the Hills did not have the same potential as lowland areas for farming. It was only below the scarp on the Icknield Belt with its easily workable loams that there were really first-class soils. Farming had been successful there for a very long time. Some parts of the Chilterns are physically marginal for agriculture, but the valleys contain pockets of good soils and the local diversity of relief and soils has encouraged a flexible farming system. 'Marginal' does not mean backward: such regions are often more flexible, efficient and innovative than their more fertile counterparts, and this was true of the medieval and early modern Chilterns. The Chilterns has a long tradition of arable and mixed farming, combining arable, pasture and woodland on different

2. Sunken lane at The Crong, Dancer's End. One of the ancient ways that descend from the Chiltern plateau to the lower ground.

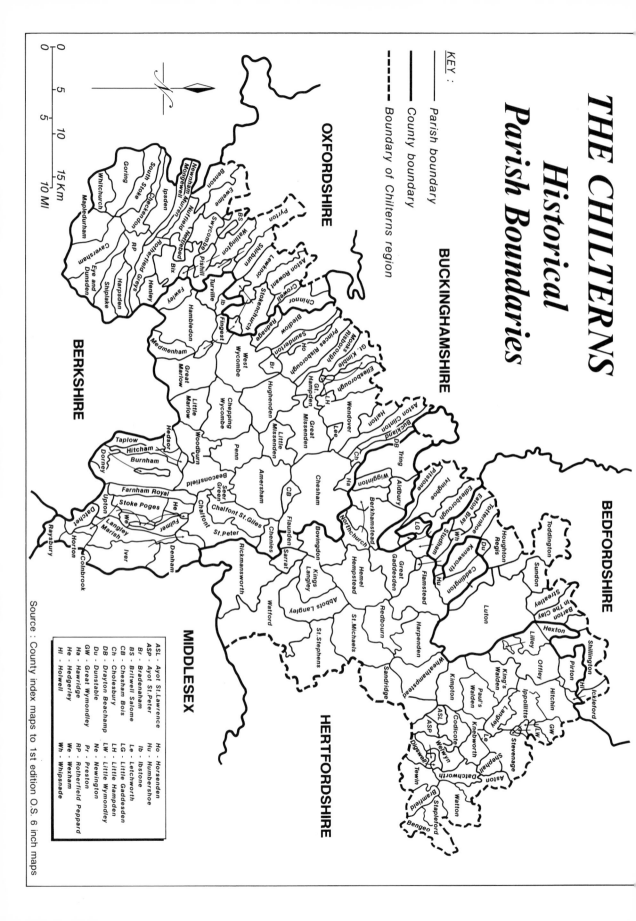

THE CHILTERNS
Historical
Parish Boundaries

KEY :

- - - - - Parish boundary
───── County boundary
– – – – Boundary of Chilterns region

OXFORDSHIRE

BUCKINGHAMSHIRE

BEDFORDSHIRE

BERKSHIRE

HERTFORDSHIRE

MIDDLESEX

ASL - Ayot St.Lawrence	Ho - Horsenden
ASP - Ayot St.Peter	Hu - Humbershoe
Br - Bradenham	Ib - Ibstone
BS - Britwell Salome	Le - Letchworth
CB - Chesham Bois	LG - Little Gaddesden
Ch - Cholesbury	LH - Little Hampden
DB - Drayton Beauchamp	LW - Little Wymondley
Du - Dunstable	Ne - Newington
GW - Great Wymondley	Pr - Preston
Ha - Hawridge	RP - Rotherfield Peppard
He - Hedgerley	We - Wexham
Hl - Holwell	Wh - Whipsnade

Source : County index maps to 1st edition O.S. 6 inch maps

soils up the valley slopes. The heavy clays of the plateau summits were less easily worked so more woodlands remained, and their economic usefulness added to the flexibility of the farming community.

An interesting sidelight is that it has been convincingly shown that the 13th-century agricultural writer Walter of Henley came from Kimble, with family holdings at East Marsh in the Vale section and Longdown (then 'La More') in the Hills.[5] Walter's *Husbandry* shows considerable sensitivity to the role of different soils, and in paragraph 49 we discover:

> Twoe sortes of groundes which are for lenton [Lent or spring] corne see that thow sowe theim tymelye; that is the chalkye and the Chilterne lande; and I will telle you whye.[6]

What this long-evolved farming tradition has meant in landscape terms is a wealth of features that we can see, such as winding sunken lanes, very old enclosures and thousand-year-old hedges. It is these that have been obliterated in the planned countryside. We must be careful, however, in our interpretations and not imagine that everything we look at in the countryside is ancient or fossilised. What we see are features which have characteristics that have persisted through time and hint much more strongly of their ancient past. It is these features which we will devote time and space to later. To search for them is not an easy task for the landscape is, and always has been, dynamic—fields and farms are in constant use, woods and trees are cut and regrow. The evidence must be scrutinised to see if we are looking at something which is old in itself or more recent but existing in an old pattern. It is easy to make mistakes. Some antiquities which appear very old turn out to be relatively recent. The 'White Crosses' of the Chiltern scarp at Whiteleaf and Bledlow have often been seen as ancient landscape features. Prehistoric, Anglo-Saxon and medieval origins have been suggested—the great Egyptologist Sir Flinders Petrie was convinced they were measured out in Etruscan feet. But no source can date them back before the 17th century, and they are probably one of our less ancient pieces of countryside.[7]

Defining the Region

To write about the Chilterns we must identify our region and give it boundaries, however flexible these may then be. The central core is easy to identify, but the outer boundary is more difficult. We have seen that the scarp edge marks a very visible topographical line between Chiltern and Vale, but on the dipslope such a delimitation is much harder, and writers have varied in where they include or exclude. The south Buckinghamshire area around Stoke and Burnham does not strictly have a Chiltern geology, and some leave out this part. Yet Stoke and Burnham Hundreds were part of the 'Chiltern Hundreds', and have intimate historical links with 'genuine' Chiltern country. As soon as we consider land-use and settlement, the boundary must be extended because the historical pattern of Chiltern parishes ties the Hills into these surrounding lowlands. This linkage applies along the scarp edge too, and we must constantly look at the interaction of Hill and Vale. These ties are an integral part of the landscape history of the region. We therefore take a fairly catholic view of the Chilterns as a region, and our elastic boundary stretches as necessary to bring in places which may be marginal but relevant in context.

The early references to the Chilterns do not really differ from our perspective. The Chilterns as a name first appears in a 7th-century document as *Cilternsaete*, 'the Chiltern dwellers'. A later Anglo-Saxon charter writes of Risborough *be Cilternes efese*, 'by Chiltern eves', a lovely description of the escarpment. Medieval uses include the Chiltern Hundreds of Buckinghamshire and Oxfordshire, which extend into the surrounding lowlands, and scattered references that accord with modern perceptions.[8] Thus a 1296 Dunstable Priory record notes

3. *(opposite page)* The Chilterns: historical parish boundaries.

4. Extract from an 11th-century charter for Risborough. The Latin version (reproduced here) describes Risborough *margine luci Ciltern*, 'by the edge of Chiltern wood', and the Anglo-Saxon version uses *be Ciltern efese*, 'by Chiltern eaves', a delightful and appropriate description. [BL: Cotton Claudius A iii, 2v.]

an abundant beech-mast 'in Ciltria', and means Shortgrave and Kensworth. Later the great Elizabethan age of topographical writing, map-making and the 'discovery' of England brought a renewed recognition of the Chilterns' regional distinctiveness. Writers such as Leland and Drayton marked off the Chilterns from surrounding areas, and in the 17th century Robert Plot spoke of 'Chiltern Country' in the same way that Walter of Henley had earlier written of 'Chilterne lande', a theme taken up by many writers such as William Ellis.

Yet although the Chilterns' identity and regional distinctiveness was recognised, virtually all historical and descriptive writing remained locked within the county system. The political and administrative importance of the counties, and the local loyalties they built up, has influenced almost all subsequent serious historical research and writing. The same is true of map-making: starting in Elizabethan times the county has been the dominant unit. Saxton's beautiful maps were 'County maps' although we have uncovered a rare three-county map which does give a full-length display of the Chilterns (plate 12).

The late 19th and early 20th century saw a rebirth of topographical writing, and the Chilterns attracted a new interest. Robert Louis Stevenson devoted an elegant essay to a walk from High Wycombe to Tring (where he hopped back on the train to London), calling the region 'the country of the larks'.[9] Rupert Brooke and Edward Thomas walked there and, as travel and rambling became more commonplace, so a series of topographical works appeared, most notably H. J. Massingham's *Chiltern Country* (1940). A popular novelist of the '30s, Cecil Roberts, found a picturesque cottage north of Henley after a car-breakdown on Bix Hill. He not only bought the cottage, but went on to write a series of 'Pilgrim Cottage' novels and three best-selling books about the south Chilterns.[10]

Historical writing (including landscape history) has, however, continued to be county-based. The county approach has many merits, but the price is relative neglect of regions that fall across county boundaries, as the Chilterns do. In Bedfordshire and Hertfordshire, the Chilterns are a minority portion. In Buckinghamshire the Chilterns are treated seriously, but only that county's part. In Oxfordshire the Chilterns tend to get rather short-shrift, subordinate to the Thames, the Cotswolds and the City of Oxford. A regional, rather than county, approach is needed to grasp the historical distinctiveness and character of the Chilterns. Every time the history of the area has been chopped into four something gets lost; without making undue and exaggerated claims for the Chilterns, they certainly deserve an overall treatment. It is an investigation using this different and very neglected perspective that lies at the root of this book.

The Leading Edge—the Icknield Way

There is no problem of where to start the search for the most ancient historical evidence in the Chilterns. We must return to the edge of the scarp that marks our previously discussed dividing line, because it is here that we can identify signs of prehistoric culture. Running right along the edge of the Hills is the Icknield Way. It was originally one of the flint-ways which scored the hillsides and it bridged the gap between Britain's two largest Neolithic centres in East Anglia and on Salisbury Plain in Wessex. Both of these were on chalky outcrops which contained the flints so vital as tools in this, the New Stone Age.

The importance of this area for so much of the subsequent history of the Chilterns merits its being singled out for a special examination. It was the frontier zone and its significance stemmed originally from its basic geology. The Icknield Way ran largely through a transition zone between the stiff heavy clays in the Vale with their impenetrable woods, and the steep

5. Icknield Way and scarp edge between Little Kimble and Coombe Hill. The line of the Upper Icknield Way can be followed across the foreground by the tree-lined road with Ellesborough church high on its mount and Coombe Hill and the monument behind. Lower right is Little Kimble, site of Roman villa and medieval earthworks. The pre-turnpike road ran closer to the scarp foot, following the base of the tree line. The centre right shows the Prime Minister's country residence of Chequers and its park.

chalk slopes and wooded summits on the glacial clay with flints. This zone is referred to as the Icknield Belt and it had much lighter loamy soils formed from greensands. It was a gently sloping band of well drained and easily worked soils below the scarp slope. This made it easy to keep clear and, with still primitive farming methods, more easily cultivated.

The Icknield Way would have been a broad community way which wandered across a wide area according to conditions. It had two forks—a summer track and a winter track. The Lower Icknield Way ran below the escarpment, and was a more direct route, making a good summer track, but it probably became muddy and waterlogged in winter. The Upper Icknield Way ran parallel but further up the escarpment side, and would have remained drier in winter. It was the lower route which became part of the Roman Icknield Way and still has several lengths in the present major road network. The Upper Icknield Way has tended to remain in the minor road and bridle-path system and is part of the Ridgeway. Some sections survive as delightful chalky lanes or wooded paths, as at Wain Hill near Risborough. The poet Edward Thomas travelled the Icknield Way in 1913, just before the First World War and also before the metalling of minor roads. Of this section he wrote:

> The way was some distance up on a steep slope, and in places so steep from side to side that there were two tracks, one two yards above the other. then it was a broad track of level turf, next a narrow and rough one, the ruts, as near the Horsenden road, mended with lemonade bottles and meat tins.[11]

It is thus not surprising that much of the earliest archaeological evidence comes from this line. Neolithic travellers would have found along this track places which begged to be settled: springs seeped from the scarp foot providing a ready water supply, the ground could be tilled, and flints were available for tools and arrowheads. Worked flints can still frequently be found on the surface of Chiltern fields. Barrows covering the burial chambers of tribal chieftains stood as sentinels above and visible from the route; at Whiteleaf above Risborough and at Maiden Bower and other sites near Dunstable these long barrows have been dated as Neolithic. The importance of the route increased into the Bronze Age some 2,500-3,000 years ago—long before the Iceni after whom it is supposed the Saxons later named it. The greatest number of barrows come from this period with examples such as those at Ellesborough, Wendover and Dunstable.

During the early and middle Iron Age, settlements seem largely to have remained along the routeway with concentrations around the heads of gaps through the hills. It was at this time that the hillforts—high and isolated on the summits—were constructed. The Ivinghoe fort is thought to be one of the earliest known anywhere in Britain. A variety of earthworks collectively known as Grim's Ditch may have arisen at this time although conjecture as to their origins and purpose rivals anything that Hans Christian Andersen might have conjured up! (Though, as we shall see, recent archaeological work is beginning to give a convincing dating and interpretation of these features.)

The Romans when they arrived had a sophisticated culture and have left us with a wealth of hard evidence—villas, roads, mosaics and personal artifacts from which historians and archaeologists have built up an increasingly accurate picture of their society and their impact on the landscape. The full story and enormous scale of this Roman impact on the Chilterns is only now emerging from recent research and excavation. We know that most of the early villa sites were next to the major routes and there are several verified scarp foot sites such as those Totternhoe, Terrick, Little Kimble, and Saunderton. The Romans extended the road network into and through the Chiltern valleys in an east-west direction and produced a new crop of villas in other parts of the region. There is evidence that some of the early villas were built on previously occupied sites, and it is here in the springline settlements, if anywhere, that we are likely to find continuity of occupation.

The Icknield Belt remained an important frontier long after the decline of the Roman empire. It is for the period after these people left that we choose to move up the scarp and eventually onto the plateau and dipslope. For it is these 'Dark Ages' after the Roman departure that have left their scattered imprint on the Chilterns landscape such that we can give local significance to the term 'ancient countryside'.

The Middle Ground—Tracing the Boundaries

There are many ways in which we can start to look for indications of past landscapes. One of the best is to search for boundaries. Tracing and exploring boundaries has always held a fascination and it is a theme that will thread its way through this book. They shed light on some of the more intriguing aspects of ancient countryside especially in an area such as this where we possess some extremely old boundaries which can be studied on the ground and also corroborated with documentary evidence.

Boundaries exist in many forms and they were usually designed to be permanent. Thus many have outlived their original purpose and remain quite out of context to remind us of a past era. Others remain for centuries and still affect the way that we organise our activities today. We must distinguish between those that are visible on the ground—the dykes and ditches, woodbanks, hedges and lanes—from those on maps and documents like the parishes and hundreds. These administrative boundaries often have features which can be traced in the field and they are sometimes the longest lasting features of an estate or settlement. This outer skin may remain intact long after its interior has disappeared or moved. The study of boundaries can give us insight into the extent of woodlands and how (and more importantly, when) areas were grubbed up. The ancient boundaries we see today reflect a long history of woodland clearance, settlement and changing field systems.

One important boundary is that which divides the Chiltern Hundreds from the three Aylesbury Hundreds. 'Hundreds' were groupings of estates and parishes for administrative and tax purposes, and the 'Stewardship of the Chiltern Hundreds' (a Crown office) remained in the public eye long after it had ceased to have any real function: Members of Parliament cannot hold royal appointments, so applying for this nominal Stewardship became a way of resigning as an M.P. John Chenevix Trench has suggested that the simple line dividing the two groups of Hundreds on the map marks a much more ancient frontier—that between Angle and Saxon, and speaks of the Chilterns as 'the last refuge of independent Britons in south east England'.[12] The evidence for such an assertion comes from many sources. The reconstruction of this critical period in the Chilterns' history is difficult, and we will encounter conflicting interpretations when we look at it. We do know, however, that the Saxons penetrated the Hills relatively late, leaving the resident Britons to their own devices until the late 6th century. The Britons were sandwiched between two rival groups—a recently arrived Anglian group collectively known as the *Cilternsaete* in the north west and a much longer settled mid-Saxon group to the south east. This Anglo-Saxon frontier line has had an enduring legacy, and has continued to be an important administrative boundary to the present day. This has created some peculiar results. The *Cilternsaete* had advanced beyond the natural watershed, capturing the upper reaches of the Chess river-basin. Because this same line still separated the two 20th-century water authorities, the people of Aylesbury Vale have continued to benefit from tapping the headwaters of the river Chess, entirely as a result of land-grabbing in the 7th and 8th centuries. Other anomalies also arose. Between Beaconsfield and Amersham—deep in south Buckinghamshire—is 'Hertfordshire House', so called because it lies in a small area around Coleshill

6. Anglo-Saxon boundary charter for Pyrton, a Chiltern strip-parish. This document dates from *c.*1070. The description begins with *To Peritun* in the margin, and *paes wudes gemeara*, 'the boundaries of the woodland holding'—followed by a clockwise description of the bounds of the detached upland portion including Stonor. In a separate hand, the bounds of the main Pyrton portion begin *XL hida land gemaeru*, 'the boundaries of 40 hides of land'. [BL: Cotton Claudius A xiii 32v and 33.]

that was a detached part of Hertfordshire until 1844, when Victorian bureaucrats 'tidied up' the administrative map of England.

A small number of Anglo-Saxon boundary charters have survived for Chilterns estates, and some of the boundaries can be traced out in the present landscape as parish boundaries and physical features. The charter for Monks Risborough with its 'Black Hedge' is studied later. This marvellous hedge is still visible today—a huge belt of scrubwood snaking between the fields and up Windsor Hill towards Great Hampden, described by Gordon Home as 'one of those deliciously out-of-the-way places in which the Chilterns are so rich'.[13]

Another boundary charter is that of the strip parish of Pyrton in the Oxfordshire Chilterns. Like Monks Risborough, this is one of the numerous long thin parishes which run perpendicular to the scarp, giving the inhabitants access to a wide range of soils and resources. The Pyrton charter puzzled scholars until they realised that it dealt with two distinct units, separated by a thin neck of land, and this is exactly how Pyrton parish remained—split by a piece of Watlington—until parish changes in 1896. The upland portion included Stonor, and *Stanora lege* or 'wood belonging to Stonor' is noted in the charter (Plate 6). It ran around the east side of the present Stonor Park, and then ran down the stony hillside (*innan stan beorh*) to what is now the road through the Stonor valley. This whole section still defines the county boundary between Oxfordshire and Buckinghamshire.[14]

Other boundaries reveal the later activities of medieval farmers and woodmen, legacies from the great period of expansion up to 1300. Colonisation and assarting (woodland or waste clearances converted into farmland) put their lasting imprint on the Chilterns, and the important woodland economy is seen in the woodbanks. These are quite easily distinguished as a raised bank often with coppiced trees on them. Woodbanks were designed as permanent structures to keep out grazing animals from neighbouring pasture. Growing coppiced wood for fuel and a multitude of other uses was a vital part of the Chilterns economy. In some places the advancing and retreating frontier of the woodland has engulfed the ancient woodbanks within later woods, but in many cases (as at 'Sampsonsbreche' in Coleshill) the boundary remains just where the medieval farmer left it.

Forging Ahead

The mid-16th century brought revived economic growth after the recession of the later Middle Ages, and this had dramatic consequences for the region. The rapid population expansion in London was the real engine of economic growth and this had a major effect on the whole of the south east including the Chilterns. A more efficient agricultural system was needed to provide foodstuffs for the growing numbers of people, and this led to a spate of enclosure from the middle of the century, reaching a peak during the 17th century. However enclosure in the Hills was very substantially different from that in the Vale. Most of it was achieved by piecemeal private agreements between a few men who gradually consolidated their holdings. By 1750 most Chiltern common fields had disappeared and parliamentary enclosure was only really concerned with fencing common woods and heaths. Thus the enormous changes that involved complete reorganisation in the Vale and the virtual destruction of previous field patterns did not happen in the Chilterns.

The period after the enclosure of irregular open fields in the Chilterns and before the parliamentary enclosure of the big open fields in the Vale was the period of starkest contrast between the two landscapes, especially because the Vale was almost totally woodless and had few hedges at all. When the Swedish agriculturalist Pehr Kalm visited Little Gaddesden in the 1740s, he was very struck by the vivid differences between open-field Ivinghoe in the Vale and enclosed Gaddesden in the Chilterns above.

The huge expansion in transport routes through the Chilterns in the 18th and 19th centuries produced a rate of growth and change that had no historical parallel. This process was staggered in time and started with the turnpikes—regarded by some as a necessary evil required to improve the generally appalling standard of the roads. The building of the Grand Junction (now Union) Canal in the 1790s was further to encourage the transport of goods and change accessibility in the Chilterns. Its construction was a mammoth undertaking, not without its problems; but it permitted barge traffic to travel from London to Birmingham. Today the canals provide attractive waterways in these otherwise poorly watered hills and one can still see evidence of the wharves that would once have been busy loading and unloading all manner of goods.

These transport changes reinforced the connection of the Chilterns to the demands of the London metropolitan markets. The effects could work in contradictory ways—the Chilterns landscape became much more vulnerable and at the mercy of large scale supply-cost and market price changes. The woodlands provide the best example of this. As London grew, sales of coppiced wood for fuel also grew, and preserved the profitability of woodland here at a time when agricultural improvers were grubbing up areas of woodland in other parts of England. Yet later the links worked in reverse: improved transport allowed not only coal from Newcastle to out-compete wood-fuel in London—so that Pehr Kalm in 1745 wrote that coal was almost entirely replacing billet as a fuel in the town—but the canals enabled coal to penetrate the Chilterns and out-compete wood-fuel in its very heartland. This collapse in the wood-fuel market, together with the growth of the Chiltern chair-making industries, was a principal factor behind the conversion of the woods to the high beech forest we know today.

The coming of the railways in the late 1830s produced similar effects and contradictions. One example was the way in which the farming recession of the 1870s affected the Chilterns. The increase in accessibility which the railways brought worldwide led to greater international competition, and home-grown wheat suddenly became unprofitable. In the Chilterns this meant an extension of the grass acreage, and contemporaries talked of fields 'that tumbled down to grass'. Through the intricate web of farming relations this was to have an impact that we can see today: the higher slopes with poorer soils were left to pasture but the number of sheep, previously so familiar a sight in the Chilterns, declined as fewer were needed to fertilise the remaining arable land. Between 1867 and 1904 the number of sheep in the Chilterns halved. The decline of grazing animals has a profound effect—previously open grassland is recolonised to become scrub and eventually reverts to woodland. Meanwhile farms favourably placed along the local railway network extended their dairying herds to supply the growing local towns.

The Chilterns and surrounding areas attracted a number of rural craft industries, such as straw-plaiting, lace-making and woodland crafts. Daniel Defoe referred to the spread of straw-plaiting from Hertfordshire into Bedfordshire which corresponded to the fashion for straw hats which were made locally in Luton and Dunstable. Straw-plaiting was a home-based industry largely performed by women and children and went some way to alleviate the poverty that existed among poorly paid farmworkers. Arthur Young in 1804 wrote in *A General View of the Agriculture of Hertfordshire*, 'The farmers complain of it as doing mischief for it makes the poor saucy and no servants can be produced or any field work can be done where this manufacture establishes itself'.[15] Such industries tended to thrive in the earlier years of a national consumer market, but just as improved transport and international competition affected agriculture, so they all but destroyed these crafts in the late 19th century.

In landscape terms it was the spread of residential areas that came as part and parcel of the railway age which provided the greatest impact. Villages expanded into towns and encroached on the surrounding farmland. The Victorian phase produced its own distinctive architecture, especially the Rothschild life-sized dolls houses with red roofs and twirling chimneys, miniature versions of grander manor houses set in splendid parks (e.g. Tring park). Later the Chilterns became part of 'Metroland' with advertisements presenting a romantic image of a 'friendly green playground' away from the London grime. Metropolitan Railway literature of 1914 claims, 'The antique character of the medieval villages of the line—Chenies, Great Missenden, Wendover etc.—has always been carefully preserved and has remained unchanged during hundreds of years', whilst John Betjeman writes in *Summoned by Bells* that 'Metroland beckoned us out to lanes in beechy Bucks'.[16] Many of the towns along the railway lines such as Amersham and Beaconsfield can be clearly divided into the old, pre-railway town and a newer suburban post-railway town. The spread of Victorian and Edwardian villas was later followed by the growth of semi-detached suburbia.

The last half century has seen enormous changes both in our countryside and our towns and villages. The Chilterns are firmly part of the commuter belt with its dormitory villages and gradual infilling of open spaces. They do have some protection—they are in an Area of Outstanding Natural Beauty and incorporate part of the Green Belt and all is not lost. There is much to admire and discover for we write about an area steeped in history, a landscape that goes back for thousands of years. This book is very much a celebration of the richness of the Chilterns countryside. Before we can judge what needs conservation and where future growth and development are reasonable, we need to understand the history behind the present landscape. That is our story in the rest of this book.

Chapter Two

Early Landscapes

The Earliest Human Landscapes

A search for the earliest human landscapes in the Chilterns takes us, not to a picturesque hilltop on the scarp or into a secluded and winding valley, but to the site of Caddington clay pits, south of Luton. Brick-clay was dug here in the Victorian era, to supply the great brickworks of the Luton area, and it was this locality that drew the freelance illustrator and eminent amateur archaeologist Worthington G. Smith (Plate 7). In the 1890s Smith found evidence in these pits

7. Worthington G. Smith in Caddington clay pits. The Victorian archaeologist points out his remarkable discovery of a layer of paleolithic deposits containing the earliest evidence of human occupation in the Chilterns.

of some of the earliest human activity in Britain. He discovered a flint-working site buried beneath later brick-earth deposits, and preserved as a distinct layer or 'horizon' of flints. The sites dates from the Lower Palaeolithic, from before the last glacial period (though Smith himself did not realise it was quite so old), and it remains one of the most notable finds in Britain. Smith later found parallel sites at Gaddesden Row and Round Green near Luton. Subsequent in-filling has obscured Smith's pits, but a re-investigation by archaeologists in the 1970s located them and took some samples from nearby sites. Bones from the Palaeolithic layer showed deer, together with elephant and rhinoceros, species that only returned to the locality with Whipsnade Zoo in the 1930s. Pollen grains preserved in the clay layers suggest the occupation took place around a pond or shallow lake in rough grassland surrounded by dense woodland of oak, elm and ash. From re-examination of Smith's finds the 1970s' team were even able to distinguish different Neanderthal flint-knappers, with experienced and beginners' styles and mistakes being apparent.[1]

This evidence of the earliest hunter-gatherers in the Chilterns has been dated to the last interglacial, between about 125,000 and 70,000 BC. Other very early sites come at the southern tip of the Chilterns, as at Highlands Farm Pit near Harpsden, on an old loop of the former Thames from Caversham to Henley, and on the terraces at Burnham and Farnham Royal.[2] These must be put in perspective, however, with the earliest European man who was discovered in Tautavel (southern France) and has been dated to 450,000 BC, more than 300,000 years earlier than our first "Chilterns' Man". These small groups can have had only very limited impact on their environment, and such impact was swept away in the environmental changes of the last glacial and post-glacial period. We must not imagine man entering a fixed stage, newly minted by Nature and unchanging. The landscape and environment of the Chilterns have formed in partnership with human activity from its earliest beginnings. The natural environment fluctuates—as we recognise in these decades of 'global warming'—and the human role has gradually increased from these first primitive clearings so that man and landscape become integrated in their historical development.

The most recent phases of geological history overlap with human prehistory. These periods with the Ice Ages, the glacials, interglacial periods and postglacial, are central to the appearance and character of the Chilterns. The underlying chalk skeleton of the Hills long predates man's existence (even Caddington man), but much of the Hills is covered with superficial deposits of 'clay-with-flints' and 'plateau drift'. These deposits are very variable, and may be only a few feet deep. A very thick deposit at Ibstone showed 13½ ft. of clay-with-flints, with 5½ ft. of Plateau Drift above that. These layers owe much of their origin to the glacial and inter-glacial periods. Ice-sheets as such probably reached the northern edge of the Hills, but for considerable periods the Chilterns experienced 'periglacial' or tundra conditions: frozen ground, freeze-thaw, and blowing sand or 'loess'. The deposits originate from the weathering of the chalk and former layers above it, such as the sandy-pebbly Reading Beds that now only exist as a few rumps above the chalk. These layers were churned, broken up and moved by the tundra processes. Where the major source is the chalk layer there is the heavy, impermeable clay-with-flints; where the origin is the Reading Beds or wind blown sands, there is a more permeable, loamy cover.[3] Much of these deposits was formed before the last glacial, but it was the last stages that covered over the flint-sites at Caddington, sealing them until they were unearthed by the Victorian brick-workers.

Other aspects of the topography of the Chilterns come from these glacial periods that drove man out of the British Isles again. The frozen subsoil meant that the chalk was then impermeable, so running summer water could rapidly erode valleys, and gushing springs could sap into coombes along the scarp face to give us the dry Incombe and Coombe Holes near

8. The Pednor Valley near Chesham. A typical Chilterns dry valley: old enclosed fields, fragrant lanes and beech hangers clinging to the hilltops.

9. The village at Aldbury. A picturesque scarp-foot village clustered around the pond and village green.

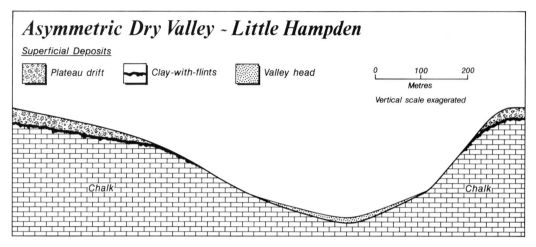

10. Cross section of asymmetric dry valley. (Based on Ollier and Thomasson, 1957, and Avery, 1964.)

Ivinghoe and the boxwood-covered Happy Valley at Kimble. The deeply-dissected valleys and 'bottoms' of the Chilterns dip-slope owe much of their form to these times. As the writer J. H. B. Peel commented of the ridges and valleys between Prestwood and Naphill: 'the Bottoms are so steep, and the valleys so narrow, that the bed is hidden—as the ditch of a ha-ha is hidden—until you come upon it'.[4] Many of these valleys are also asymmetrical, with steeper, more eroded west- and south-facing slopes, probably the result of the more effective afternoon sun warming the frozen, icy slopes.[5] As Ollier and Thomasson have shown, these steeper slopes usually bear the wooded 'hangers' of today (Plate 11).

This legacy of old, weathered deposits churned by frost and freeze-thaw gives to the Chilterns much of their uniqueness. In the archaeologist J. G. Evans' words: 'it has given to these hills a character, environment and history very much their own.'[6] The former course of the River Thames, then to the north of its present valley, also gave rise to many sandy and gravelly deposits which are difficult to distinguish from those of glacial origin. The region became a patchwork or chequerboard of 'bottom' and ridge, with dry, chalky or sandy soils alternating with blocks of heavy impermeable clays. These clays are thin, but heavy enough to retain water in local ponds on the plateau summit, as at Russell's Water or Northend, though such ponds have been maintained by man (Plate 19).

After the Last Ice: the Mesolithic
It was with the last ice retreat and the gradual warming of the British climate after *c*.10,000 BC that the permanent human occupation began. As the ice and tundra shrank northwards, a succession of tree-species colonised the landscape of lowland Britain. First came birch-clumps, then pine, and later the mixed, broad-leaved woodland of oak, elm and lime. Beech was a much later arrival. The rising sea-level finally severed Britain from continental Europe around 6600 BC. By 7000 BC new hunter-gatherers who used flint axes, tools and spear-tips arrived into this woodland environment. These Mesolithic groups undoubtedly used the Chiltern valleys and woods for collecting nuts and fruit, and chasing and trapping wild game. Here they acquired the flints for their axes and 'microliths', small flints which generally had cutting edges and were either mounted several together or used individually for arrowheads. Finds of Mesolithic axes and microliths are multiplying across the Chilterns, from Kimble Farm at

Stonor and Bolter End in the west to Chesham and Gerrards Cross in the east. Michael Farley, the Buckinghamshire County Archaeologist, has suggested that the plateau as well as the valleys 'may have been quite heavily exploited'.[7] A particularly interesting site has emerged from beneath a 17th-century cottage in Chesham: below two feet of later hillwash deposits a rich layer of Mesolithic flints was discovered, clearly a local flint-working or occupation site.[8] Animal bones were also present, showing that red deer, wild boar, and the auroch, *Bos primigenus* (forerunner of the domestic cow and probably like the Chillingham wild cattle), were successfully hunted. Radiocarbon dating of the auroch bones gave a date of 3940 BC.

It is difficult to say what impact such groups had on the Chiltern landscape. Their total numbers at any time were probably quite small, and any effect was less significant than the natural climatic and vegetation change. But their woodland clearances, by axe or fire, to create the right conditions for trapping and managing game, and their selective use of woodland species, probably influenced the composition and development of the woodland. They were already beginning to give the landscape a more open appearance. However any such impact paled before the changes that were about to take place.

Settling the Landscape: The Neolithic and Bronze Periods
The whole degree and pattern of landscape impact changes with the beginning of farming in the Neolithic period (between 3500 and 4000 BC) when permanent settlement and cultivation first emerged. In this and the succeeding Bronze Age the hunter-gatherers were replaced by

11. Air photograph of asymmetric dry valley at Radnage, looking south-east from near Radnage church. The steeper side of the valley is clear on the left-hand side of the photograph, and woods occupy the shoulders of the valley.

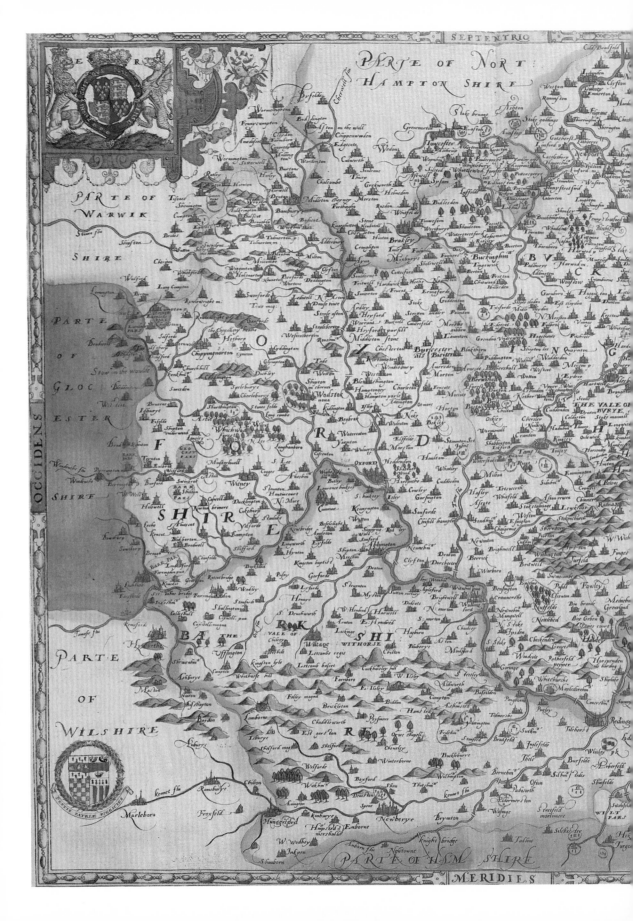

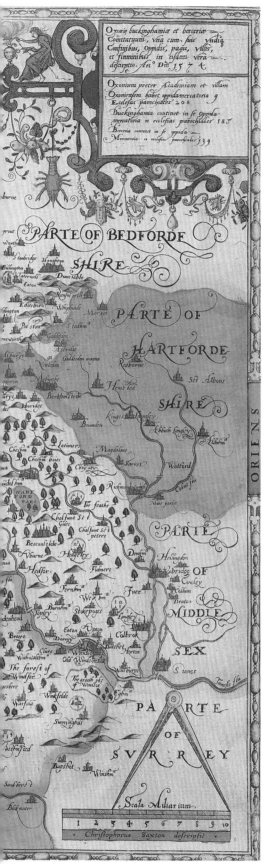

farmers who created and tilled arable fields and tended domesticated animals. They permanently cleared large areas of natural woodland, and left behind them remains of dwellings, settlements, burial mounds and ceremonial monuments. They also began to make, and more importantly break, pottery for cooking, eating and storage, to leave behind the identifiable broken pieces or 'sherds' so vital to archaeologists for the dating and study of all later groups.

These Neolithic and Bronze-Age farmers appear to have settled and exploited only limited but distinctive parts of the Chilterns region. The word 'appear' is important because our understanding is based on the map of archaeological sites, and this depends on the pattern of survival and discovery. Neolithic and Bronze Age remains have survived best as 'fossilized landscapes' in marginal areas where later human and environmental change has been least active. We shall need to look at these issues more closely when the landscape revolution of the late Iron Age and Roman times is examined. For the present, let us use the evidence available, but use it with caution.

Early agriculturalists preferred lighter, well-drained, easily-tilled soils, and the chalk downlands of southern England and the gravel terraces of rivers such as the Thames were exploited early. The Wessex and Wiltshire downlands, with great monumental sites at Stonehenge and Avebury, became important cultural heartlands. The Chilterns, much more heavily drift-covered than the chalk hills further south and west, were less attractive, as many generations of archaeologists have recognised. However, certain localities in the region did attract settlement, and we must also view the region within a wider geographical context. The Chiltern escarpment-edge played a particularly important role.[9] Here the chalk reaches the surface, woodland is less dense and more easily cleared, and the spring-line provides a good supply of water. As a consequence there are pockets of settlement along the scarp itself. The scarp-line was also used as an important routeway between major cultural 'cores' in Wessex and East Anglia. This

12. Saxton's map of the Chilterns, 1574. This map of Oxfordshire, Buckinghamshire and Berkshire, which appeared in Saxton's *Atlas* of 1579, is one of the few that show the Chilterns as a whole.

'Icknield Way' ran the full length of the Hills from Goring on the Thames to Hitchin and beyond into East Anglia. The historic route was not, of course, a road as such, but a band of tracks following the scarp just above the springline for most of its length. It is marked today reasonably closely by the bridleways and paths of the Upper Icknield Way. This corridor, sandwiched between the wooded clays of the Chiltern plateau and those of the clay Vale, meant Chiltern scarp settlements were in touch with cultural influences across southern England, rather than being just remote, peripheral upland sites. In addition to this corridor role, the Hills were also linked into the economies of the adjacent lowland zones, a linkage that has continued throughout the later history of the region. At this period, for instance, the southern Chilterns, especially the area around Nettlebed and Rotherfield, provided an upland source of flints for the lowland settlements of the Thames gravels.

Within the Chilterns, three localities of Neolithic and Bronze-Age occupation stand out. Here we are inevitably telescoping together vast periods of time, probably 3,000 years from c.4000 BC to c.1000 BC, but we do not think this does any great injustice to the patterns. The first zone is along the southern edges where the Thames gravels are wide enough for exploitation, as in the Taplow-Hitcham areas, and up river near Wallingford and North Stoke. The second is in the northern Chilterns around Dunstable and Luton, where the rounded hills have more of a downland feel to them and gradually roll into the chalklands of East Anglia north of Hitchin. There are important sites at Totternhoe, Ivinghoe and Dunstable. Thirdly there is the Bledlow-Risborough gap, where the Chiltern scarp opens up and a broad lowland area leads via the Saunderton-Bradenham valley through to the Wye and thence to the Thames. The Buckinghamshire archaeologist J. F. Head argued forcefully that this Bledlow-Wye-Thames line was an important early routeway through the Hills, attracting groups of settlements, but the idea of early communication routes is still very difficult to prove.[10]

These localities provide some fine Neolithic and Bronze-Age sites. At Maiden Bower near Totternhoe, on a ledge extending outwards from the Chilterns near Dunstable into the Vale, there is a Neolithic causewayed enclosure beneath a later Iron Age encampment. The site has not been fully excavated, but it lies on the edge of the great Totternhoe quarries and details are exposed in the quarry edge. Moreover this area, and the nearby Puddlehill site at Dunstable, has been the focus of excavation and field survey by the notable Manshead Society, a group of amateur archaeologists led by the late C. L. Matthews, who for over 40 years have added so much to our knowledge of the prehistory of the Chilterns.[11]

The causewayed camp is an enclosure interrupted by ditches with 'causeways' in between. These were major centres, 'foci' of the local Neolithic population with some occupied and others having major ritual and burial functions. Along the quarry edge the post-holes of the later Iron-Age hillfort dug into the fill of the Neolithic ditches could be seen until quite recently. On nearby Puddlehill the Manshead group found Neolithic storage and waste pits dug into the chalk, containing late Neolithic pottery sherds, flint tools and animal bones. These bones show both domesticated species (sheep and domestic pigs) and wild species (wild pigs and aurochs), suggesting that the settlement was close to considerable woodland. At Waulud's Bank by the source of the River Lea in Luton there is a very different site: a ditched and banked Neolithic enclosure that may have been a religious site at the river's source. It is probably from this Neolithic period that we can date the flint-mines to be found on the face of Pitstone Hill above the line of the Icknield Way, although they have never been excavated.[12] The hollows left by the shafts and adits of the workers seeking clean, sharp flints are still prominent today. Hawthorn bushes thrive in the greater depth of soil that has accumulated within them, and the shelter they provide (Plate 20).

Much of our more detailed knowledge of these very early cultures comes from peering into their graves: for many of the people were buried along with a variety of possessions some of which have withstood the ravages of time and previous raiders to allow us to make inferences about their lifestyles. The shape of the various burial mounds gives us clues as to their date for there were fashions for barrow shapes which can be linked to their chronology. Thus long barrows were the earliest Neolithic barrows and these later gave way to various types of round barrows in the Bronze Age.

The Neolithic period in the Bledlow-Risborough area is marked by a long barrow high on the scarpline just south of the chalk Whiteleaf Cross. This barrow, in fact kidney-shaped, is today overgrown with bushes and trees, but is still readily traceable on the ground. It was excavated in the 1930s by Sir Lindsay Scott who found a wooden burial chamber containing part of a skeleton.[13] He also found a high density of broken pottery in the soil over the barrow. These sherds came from about 57 pots, and their freshly-broken edges suggest deliberate smashing in some sort of ceremony before completing the barrow. We do not know, however, whether this barrow reflects a population living locally on the scarp or whether the barrow, set on the skyline, was built by a group residing well away in the Vale below.

The number of Bronze-Age round barrows suggests growing occupation both in the Bledlow-Risborough gap and in the north Chilterns, where Five Knolls near Dunstable provides a very visible example (Plate 17). The smaller round barrows of the Chilterns, as elsewhere, have been extensively ploughed out by modern farming, and we only know of the existence of many through survival as 'crop marks' on air photographs (indicating variations

13. View from the Neolithic barrow at Whiteleaf, standing near the top of the chalk cross with a panoramic view over Bledlow Cop, Risborough and the Vale.

14. Chiltern scarp near Whipsnade. The junction between late-enclosed open-field landscape on the Icknield belt and the downland on the scarp. The lion was an early 1930s addition to advertise Whipsnade Zoo.

15. Ivinghoe Beacon. A most familiar skyline near Ivinghoe with the Beacon on the left, site of an early Iron-Age hillfort.

16. A woodland path from Parslow's Hillock towards Windsor Hill. The path follows the line of the 'Black Hedge' and the Anglo-Saxon boundary charter.

in soil depth and fertility) or through the records of earlier antiquarians. The Bledlow gap locality provides some good examples (Plate 18). Round barrows of the Bronze Age have been excavated at The Cop (Bledlow) and Lodge Hill, and there are several other barrows visible.[14] In addition over half a dozen more can be identified in the gap on air photographs. To the south, on the higher ground of the Oxfordshire-Buckinghamshire border at Stokenchurch, former evidence—now destroyed—is mentioned in the manuscript history of Stokenchurch

17. Five Knolls and the scarp looking south from Dunstable. A group of Bronze-Age round barrows can be seen in the foreground.

written by the local schoolmaster the Rev. Thomas Delafield in 1747 and preserved in the Bodleian Library: 'on the left-hand side of this Colliers Lane ... are two hillocks or tumuli of a moderate size and height, in a field called Banky Burrowfield'.[15]

Both this evidence, and equivalent evidence for the northern Chilterns from Dunstable to Hitchin and beyond, points to a growing, if localised, density of occupation. What sort of an environment surrounded these sites? A standard scientific method for reconstructing past vegetation and environments is to study the pollen grains preserved in waterlogged, acidic soils such as peats and muds, and to examine the changing proportions of species in the different layers. This was the method used at Caddington brick-pits, but for much of the Chilterns, as for the chalklands in general, there are few suitable sites because pollen grains do not survive in the dry alkaline soils. National 'pollen profile' maps have a blank over the Chilterns region, and one has an ellipse with 'No Data' inserted in the manner that medieval cartographers filled gaps with 'Here be dragons!' Thus archaeologists were forced to seek an alternative dating procedure and they turned to the local fauna rather than flora, and examined the tiny broken shells of long-deceased snails. The pioneering work on such snail remains has been largely developed by John Evans in the Chilterns, and centres on the use of preserved fragments of snail's shells in the various soil layers—examining the proportions of different types of snails.[16] There are many species of small snail, each with its own ecological niche in arable, short or long grassland, or wooded country, and they have proved an excellent indicator of past environments and vegetation cover in chalkland regions.

Beneath the Neolithic barrow on Whiteleaf the surviving snail remains suggest a woodland environment, presumably cleared shortly before the barrow was constructed. In contrast the Bronze-Age barrow at Bledlow has beneath it snail remains characteristic of more open grassland. Undoubtedly by the late Bronze Age substantial areas of woodland around these settlement localities must have been cleared and converted to grassland and arable. At Pitstone a buried soil-profile, revealed in the chalk-quarrying, has been studied by Evans and Valentine.[17] Buried soils, or palaeosols as they are technically known, are ancient soil-profiles that have been covered over, and so preserved, beneath later sediments. They commonly occur at the base of slopes, beneath later accumulations of soil and sediment that have been washed off the slopes after the area has been cleared and the surface exposed to rain and weathering. The buried soil at Pitstone has snail remains that show a sequence of woodland, woodland clearance and tillage. Fragments of carbon, possibly resulting from the vegetation burnt after

18. Air photograph of round barrows in the Bledlow gap. Aerial photography of this area began with Major George Allen in the 1930s, and it is steadily adding to the number of prehistoric sites, which show up as shadows and crop-marks.

17. The hilltop pond at Northend. One of the hilltop ponds on the impermeable plateau clays—an important source of water in these otherwise dry hills. This one is particularly attractive with a pink bloom of pond weed for part of the year.

18. Earthworks on the summit of Pitstone Hill. These hollows may be evidence of early flint mines in a locality with many prehistoric ditches and banks. The hawthorns have taken advantage of the deeper soils and shelter provided by the old shafts.

21. Holloway above The Hale. This deep holloway runs along the parish boundary between Wendover and Halton.

clearance, gave a radiocarbon date of 1960 BC, dating this to the late Neolithic or early Bronze Age and showing that certainly by the Bronze Age this was a 'controlled' landscape.

The Last Millennium BC

The last 1,000 years BC sees the emergence of a new prestige metal and technology—by 500 BC iron technology was common and gave its name to the Iron Age.[18] The central characteristic of the Iron-Age Chilterns in the period 900 BC-100 BC (and we shall see it is very important to separate the last century BC) is evidence of growing intensification of occupation of the scarp region, and of social tension and increased territoriality. It is from this Iron-Age period that we can date, with reasonable certainty, the most prominent and visible prehistoric remains—the hillforts and the major ditch sequences collectively known as 'Grim's Ditch'. However there is no correlation—or perhaps a negative one—between the physical prominence of an archaeological feature and our ability to date and explain it. It is often the buried site, obscure before and after the excavation, that yields the best archaeological evidence.

The Iron Age in southern Britain is a period of accelerating population growth, a curve that rises steeply towards the end of the millennium. It was also an era of climatic deterioration, with colder, wetter summers. Christopher Saunders' survey found permanent settlement along the length of the Chiltern scarp from Hitchin south to Lewknor, and along the Thames.[19] Although there are hillforts on some of the interior ridges, Saunders could assert that 'settlement on the dip-slope itself is very rare and is apparently unknown on the valley-floors'. This was written 20 years ago, but the additional evidence available today does not seriously alter this picture.

Occupation sites at Puddlehill and Chinnor can be used to illustrate the period. At Puddlehill the Manshead Society have excavated a series of Iron-Age settlement phases, showing a sequence of separate occupations. Whether these arose from a policy of periodic movement and rebuilding, or because marginal land was abandoned

22. Reconstruction of an Iron-Age round house from the Chiltern Open Air Museum. The reconstruction is based on evidence from the Puddlehill excavations.

and later reoccupied we do not know. The enclosures there contain storage pits, hearths and houses. From the pattern of surviving post-holes the form of these Iron-Age houses can be reconstructed, and a replica has been built at the Chiltern Open Air Museum (Plate 22). The density of settlements along the scarp seems to have been sufficient to encourage local 'culture' to emerge at this time. For example, in their 1951 excavations on the hill above Chinnor, Richardson and Young found distinctive and sophisticated pottery bowls with flaring rims and shoulders, decorated with strong geometric patterns. This 'Chinnor ware' is also found on the sites at nearby Lewknor, Ellesborough and Bledlow, and is probably the work of a specialist local potter or group of potters.[20]

The study of buried soils from the scarp-foot suggests that this was a period of considerable woodland clearance and agricultural expansion. Studies at Chinnor, Risborough and Pitstone show woodland species at the base of the buried soil, then a clearance phase followed by open country. At each of these sites Evans found Iron-Age pottery sherds in the ploughwash, indicating erosion in the Iron Age or, in some specific localities, in the late Bronze Age.[21] Such plough- and hill-wash can be quite deep: up to 10 ft. in scarp coombes and two ft. in dip-slope valleys, as at Chesham. The streams below the Chilterns scarp flow into the Thame and so into the Thames, and the cumulative impact of woodland clearance and slope erosion around the whole Upper Thames basin was to build up sediment in the river and increase the severity of seasonal flooding in low-lying parts.

Field Systems

Little evidence survives of the so-called 'Celtic' fields tilled by Bronze- and Iron-Age groups in the Chilterns. These were squarish in shape and roughly 64 metres square, the amount that could be ploughed in a day. They are marked by lynchet banks on slopes: positive lynchets where the soil builds up at the bottom of the boundary, and negative lynchets where it erodes at the top. Most have been obscured and destroyed by later intensive agriculture in medieval and modern times. The Bledlow-Risborough gap, for example, has great activity in all subsequent periods. Only where later ploughing has been negligible do they survive today, as on parts of the Wessex Downs, but in 1940 C. F. C. Hawkes found possible late Bronze-Age lynchets on the north-east side of Totternhoe ridge.[22] The best Chilterns example is hardly visible at all on the ground but appears in air photographs (Plate 25). This is on Pitstone Hill where the square Celtic fields, probably Iron Age, can be seen, along with the more strip-like lynchets associated with medieval farming here.[23]

The Hillforts

In addition to the undefended communities like Chinnor and Puddlehill, there are the numerous hillforts that stretch the full length of the Hills from Ravensburgh on the north-facing scarp west of Hitchin to Bozedown at Whitchurch near the Thames. Many of the sites, such as those at Boddington Hill above Wendover or at Pulpit Hill, are not as visible as they used to be, because the scarp-edge has become more wooded in the last 100 years. They are well worth exploring. Most are largely unexcavated and in these days when financial resources are limited to 'rescue archaeology' they are likely to remain so. Each fort dominated an area along the scarp and each represented the focus of increasingly large groups, even tribes. In the early Iron Age they were symbols of power but some were also centres of redistribution, storage and local crafts. It is difficult to assert that they are all defensive and it would be wrong to assume they all co-existed simultaneously. Some are very early—that on Ivinghoe Beacon is one of the earliest hillforts in Britain—whereas others only came into use hundreds of years later (Plate 26).

The low ditches of Ivinghoe hillfort stand out to the walker or the air photograph because the hilltop remains grassland and unwooded. Through the finance of Sir Alan Barlow it was extensively excavated in the 1960s, revealing a site on the Bronze-Iron transition: an early hillfort, made of ditch and a box-like wooden rampart, but with bronzework finds rather than ironwork. In date it is probably 800-700 BC. One characteristic, shared by other excavated hillforts, is the evidence for a limited period of occupation: 'after little more than a generation the settlement was abandoned, no doubt in favour of a less-exposed locality somewhere below.

23. The 'Black Hedge' near Brimmer's Farm above Risborough in early summer. The line of the hedge stretches the length of the plate between Risborough Kop and Windsor Hill.

24. A closer view of the 'Black Hedge' in autumn. This picture gives a better impression of the variety of species in this ancient hedge which is at least 1,000 years old.

25. Celtic field systems on Pitstone Hill. This vertical air photograph shows the outlines of prehistoric rectangular fields beneath the modern field pattern. At the base of the picture tracks and holloways leading up to Pitstone Hill can be seen.

Thereafter, the rampart was rapidly weathered away by the elements and the ditch in time almost obliterated'.[24] We do not know whether the occupiers were invaders, establishing their control, or local groups responding to a period of threat and uncertainty, but such hillforts characterise the landscape of large areas of Iron-Age southern England. Later sites than Ivinghoe have different construction, with a ditch and dyke being made into one formidable feature, with ramparts on the dyke, or later multiple ditches.

The great majority of the hillforts are along the scarp, looking onto the Icknield Way, but a few penetrate the interior ridges of the Chilterns. Above the Wye valley there is a hillfort at West Wycombe, where the hilltop church of St Lawrence lies within the hillfort. Other forts can be seen at Cholesbury, Whelpley Hill and Gerrards Cross. Cholesbury is a particularly fine site to visit, situated by the village green, and again with the local church (also a St Lawrence) inside the Iron-Age enclosure. Such locations suggest an expansion of settlement deeper into the Chilterns, but the excavation evidence is very limited. At Bulstrode it was highly inconclusive, and at Cholesbury a very late (1st-century BC) date was suggested. At present we do not know if such enclosures were short-term, ill-fated 'adventures' into new territory or whether they were surrounded by cluster of as-yet-invisible farms and settlement sites.

The Chiltern Grim's Ditches
Across the Chilterns there are several sets of linear earthworks that have become collectively known as 'Grim's Ditch or Ditches'. The first mention of the name in the Chilterns is a grant

26. Hillfort on Ivinghoe Beacon. The outline of the ditch and ramparts of this early Iron-Age hillfort is much better defined on the air photograph than on the ground.

of 1170-79 in the Missenden Cartulary referring to 'Grimesdic'.[25] Earthworks or ditches with this name occur in several parts of England, and it should not be assumed that different sections have a common origin or purpose.[26] They are, however, notable landscape features, running for several miles across country. In the southern Chilterns the Mongewell section runs in a virtually straight line for three-and-a-half miles from near the Thames at Mongewell up onto the plateau at Nuffield. Further north there are sequences running in great arcs from Lacey Green to Hampden (six miles with a right-angled bend), from The Lee to Cholesbury and Wigginton, and a third section from Pitstone to Ivinghoe.

Some sections, like the Mongewell ditch, survive as bridleways and parish boundaries. A 10th-century Anglo-Saxon boundary charter for the Mongewell area includes the phrase *and be than Ealden Wege* (and by the Old Way), referring to a stretch of Grim's Ditch there. The Lacey-Hampden section provides some interesting walking, but other parts, as near The Hale, are very overgrown, and best traced in winter when the vegetation is low. As well as being long, the ditches are sizeable: at Hastoe the ditch is 3½m. wide and 2m. deep, with a bank of similar height and an overall spread of 13½m. When fresh and new, the ditches must have been major features, and their construction involved massive amounts of labour, which leads us to speculate why they were built.

For hundreds of years there has been much debate on their origin, with suggestions of Anglo-Saxon or prehistoric date. In the 1670s the Oxford scholar Robert Plot tried to trace the upland sections of the Mongewell ditch: 'From Tuffield [Nuffield], I was told, it held on its course through thick Woods ... but the Woods scarce admitting a foot passage, much less for a Horse, I could not conveniently trace it any further'.[27]

The ditches are not defensive, as is shown by the way the earth from the ditch has been thrown up to build the dyke on the easier, downslope side, rather than on the upslope side for more formidable defence. There have been limited excavations of most sections, and Iron-Age pottery sherds have been recovered, suggesting the likely date is during the denser occupation of the Chiltern hilltops in the Iron Age.

This still does not settle the issue of purpose. In fact it is very likely that at least two different sorts of features have been mistakenly grouped, for the Mongewell section does not fit with the others. The other three sections run in arcs on the Chiltern uplands, whereas the Mongewell ditch runs from lowland up to the Chiltern plateau. It fits as a transverse boundary, designed to delimit territory and control north-south movement along the southern Icknield Way. It is therefore similar to the Dray's Ditches north of Luton, now almost obliterated but clearly observed by Leland in 1540: 'in the hye way I saw hard on eche syde 3 longe trenches, as they had been for Men of Warre'. Excavation and field survey by James Dyer have shown that these Dray's ditches were a boundary for Iron-Age territories, controlling movement of cattle and carts, and are part of a set of Iron-Age boundaries probably linked to the territories of the hillforts.[28]

The other three sections of Grim's Ditch are different, and there is no really convincing explanation. They do not seem to demarcate hillfort territories (though one section may be related to Cholesbury hillfort), but to delimit upland zones of clay-plateau when viewed from the Vale. Perhaps the most satisfactory explanation is that of Jean Davis and John Evans, who suggest that Grim's Ditch demarcates an upland 'common grazing' zone from the parcelled-out land of the scarp, defining an area for cattle and pig grazing.[29] It still seems a massive endeavour, and possibly dates from a projected but not necessarily successful scheme of land-planning and colonisation. Whatever the original aim, it is unlikely to have been cut through dense woodland, as several long, straight sections must have been 'sighted', so either the countryside was open, or it was linked to woodland clearance.

Chapter Three

The Roman Chilterns

Introduction

In the two centuries spanned by the years 100 BC and AD 100 a landscape and cultural revolution was to sweep away the simple home-spun Iron-Age lifestyle and replace it with a civilisation. To an elderly citizen born a few years BC the changes must have paralleled those of our present-day octogenarians who watched in their youth the first papery aircraft sputter across the Channel and who can now marvel at spacecraft shooting between planets.

The less substantial Iron-Age houses sank back into the mud as new generations of solid villas with tiles and terraces, heating and drains rose to dominate the principal valleys, effecting great shifts in the pattern of settlement and landholding in the Chilterns. The economic and political changes which traversed the whole of southern England were a response to increasing contacts with Gaul and the expanding Roman Empire; Julius Caesar made his temporary incursions in 55 and 54 BC and permanent Roman occupation followed after AD 43.

The region adopted Romanisation early and rapidly—not merely because it was expedient or desirable but also because the infrastructure was in place after the changes that began in the late pre-Roman Iron Age. The period is remarkable and formative and deserves detailed examination.

The Late Pre-Roman Iron Age

During the first century BC the great cultural changes occurring in south-east England were undoubtedly related to contacts with Gaul. Coinage began to circulate, wheel-thrown pottery was introduced, and new forms of settlement and burial practice emerged. New tribal group-ings and political organisations were established. These changes used to be explained by 'Belgic invasions' from Gaul, but it is now recognised that these invasions were more limited, and that some if not all of the changes were indigenous. Opinions still differ widely, and this leaves us with a question of how to refer to the 'Belgic period'. Some, like Professor Barry Cunliffe, write of 'Aylesford-Swarling culture', after two Kentish cemeteries where 'Belgic' wares were found; others prefer the unpronounceable acronym LPRIA (for 'Late Pre-Roman Iron Age') suggested by Martin Millett, whilst the recent English Heritage excavation report on the King Harry Lane site at St Albans just refers to 'Late Iron Age'.[1] For simplicity we shall follow those who continue to refer to 'Belgic' but place it firmly in inverted commas.

Whatever name we choose to employ, the 'Belgic' period saw the growth of a tribal core region focused on the lower ground of the eastern Chilterns in present-day Hertfordshire. 'Belgic' pottery and settlement sites are found in the valleys east of the Ver, rich princely burials (known as 'Welwyn-type burials') are located there,[2] and new settlement foci, known to the Romans as *oppida*, are found. These, as at Wheathampstead, are vast enclosures of 30-50 hectares and probably served semi-urban, central-place functions, as well as containing houses and cattle-enclosures. Unlike the earlier hillforts these lowland *oppida* had limited, linear defences, designed to give extensive defence of a wide area against chariot attacks.

Here we are on the edge of 'proto-history', for the archaeology begins to link up with written documents, in this case with our old friend or tormentor of schooldays, Julius Caesar's *De Bello Gallico*. Caesar invaded Britain in 55 and 54 BC, and north of the Thames encountered resistance from groups headed by Cassivellaunus. Pursued to his *oppidum*, 'a place of great natural strength and fortified', Cassivellaunus was eventually defeated by Caesar, as some readers may recall translating:

> Caesar learnt that he was not far from Cassivellaunus' oppidum, which was protected by woods and marshes, and had been filled with a large number of men and cattle ... After a short time the enemy proved unable to resist the violent attack of the legions, and rushed out of the fortress on another side (*De Bello Gallico*, V).

Sir Mortimer Wheeler thought this *oppidum* may have been Wheathampstead, though there is no definite proof that it existed as early as 55 BC. The exact location may be unidentified, but Caesar was certainly in the east Chilterns at this time.[3]

27. Dyke in Prae Wood near St Albans. The many earthworks in Prae Wood were part of the 'Belgic' settlement of the pre-Roman period. This photograph was taken during the Sir Mortimer Wheeler excavations in the 1930s.

Exactly how far the new 'Belgic' period had developed by 55 BC is uncertain, but undoubtedly the development between then and the Claudian occupation in AD 43 was profound. A tribal and political grouping known as the Catuvellauni emerged as controlling the whole Chilterns region and also extending eastwards into Essex. Wheathampstead was certainly the major *oppidum* in the latter first century BC, and its dykes can still be seen today, as can the associated frontier marked by the formidable line of Beech Bottom Dyke on the outskirts of St Albans. This deep gully, partly natural but greatly accentuated by digging, is 100 ft. wide from lip to lip and 30 ft. deep even today after much filling-up with earth. Coins found in the layers of the fill firmly date it to the pre-Roman period, and it probably marked the boundary in an early phase of conquest between the more open and occupied countryside to the south, between the Ver and Lea rivers, and the heavier, more wooded lands to the north.

Close to the turn of the millennium, Wheathampstead seems to have given way to a new less-defensive *oppidum* at Prae Wood and Verulamium, west of modern St Albans. Within Prae Wood many earthworks are preserved beneath the trees (Plate 27), but much of this sprawling *oppidum* extended over at least 1,250 acres west of, and down to, the river Ver.[4] The original name *Verlamion* may mean 'The great pool' or marshy river Ver, fordable at this point and so an obvious site for an administrative and commercial settlement. The centre may lie beneath the forum of the later Roman city: coin mint moulds have been found around there, and traces of houses somewhat more elaborate than the basic circular living-huts of the farmsteads. The north-west boundary of the *oppidum* was probably at Devil's Dyke, a 50-ft. wide ditch running across a tract of open chalky soil, still to be seen today.

As the Catuvellaunian state developed, the political centre moved to Camulodunum (Colchester in Essex), but the Verulamium *oppidum* remained an important urban centre.[5] In these decades before the Roman occupation, control seems to have extended far afield, as evidenced by coin and pottery finds. For example, a rich 'Belgic' burial has been found at Watlington below the Chiltern scarp. It is dateable to AD 10-40, and the woman was buried with a service of fine table-ware, suggesting a Catuvellaunian aristocracy acquiring lands in these western areas.[6]

The Question of Land Colonisation

These changes seem to have shifted the whole centre of gravity of the human geography of the Chilterns. The new focus is the Verulamium (St Albans) area, with settlement in the valleys of the Chilterns rather than along the scarp. We must ask ourselves to what extent this shift represents a genuinely new pattern of settlement and colonisation, and to what extent it is a mirage produced by variations in the pattern of archaeological survival and discovery. The few available archaeological finds suggest that 'Belgic' settlement in the Hertfordshire region was largely new, with little sign of earlier occupation of the valleys.[7] Thus at Gorhambury, just to the north-west of Verulamium, excavation of the 'Belgic' and Roman site produced no signs of earlier Iron-Age occupation, though there was evidence of a Neolithic hut with oak charcoal giving a radiocarbon date of c.3800 BC.[8] West of the river Ver, in the main Chiltern valleys, the evidence points even further. In Keith Branigan's words, it suggests 'something rather different and potentially more interesting': land colonisation in Roman times after AD 43.[9]

Despite current convictions about this being newly settled territory, we must maintain a hint of scepticism. Accounts of the Chilterns used to suggest that much of the area was only settled and exploited in the Anglo-Saxon or even medieval periods. Now we suggest the 'Belgic' and Roman period. Is it not likely this should be pushed back further, into the Bronze and early Iron Ages? Landscape historians such as Christopher Taylor suggest that most archaeological distributions are misleading, and that growing evidence shows most regions of

28. Section of Roman town wall at Verulamium (St Albans). This close-up shows the layers of flint set in mortar alternating with layers of the distinctive thin Roman bricks.

Britain were occupied before 100 BC.[10] There are indeed good reasons why such evidence might be hard to find in the Chilterns. The wooded cover hides sites from the aerial photographer, and the sloping valley-sides encourage lateral soil movement and the burying of sites, together with their destruction by continuous agriculture. In the dry valleys of the Sussex Downs the archaeologist Martin Bell excavated systematic cross-sections through the sediments, revealing much greater amounts of prehistoric (and later) activity than appears from the normal excavation sites, and it would be fascinating to repeat such a research study in the Chiltern valleys.[11] So although we believe for the present that the 'Belgae' and Romans were the first to colonise these valleys on any substantial scale, we remain circumspect and acknowledge that deep beneath the surface remains of earlier occupants may be awaiting discovery.

Early Romanisation
The Claudian invasion in AD 43 led to the Roman occupation of the whole of southern Britain, an occupation that lasted over 350 years until final withdrawal *c.*410. The Roman takeover defeated the Catuvellaunian state, yet Verulamium and the surrounding region quickly became strongly Romanised, and Verulamium became a capital for the area.

A Roman fort at Verulamium was replaced around AD 49 by a new and deliberately planned town with *municipium* or chartered status. From this very early date the layout of Verulamium was organised on a rectilinear grid divided into 'insulae' or building islands.[12] The earliest buildings were mainly of timber-framed construction, and the town was severely burnt in AD 61 during the revolt by Boudicca, queen of the Iceni. However by AD 80 the forum and basilica were being built, and the town thrived and expanded, with rows of shops and workshops, elegant town houses and public buildings. In the second century a theatre was added and, as the town population grew, new city walls and defences were built. Although worked stone, including Barnack rag-stone, was brought in for some major buildings, most construction in Verulamium and the Chiltern region used a combination of flints set in mortar together with tiles and the distinctive thin Roman bricks (Plate 28). Throughout the 350 years of Roman Britain, Verulamium was one of the leading towns of the Province and an important regional capital and commercial centre.

The remains of the Roman city were extensively plundered in later times, with the bricks, flints and worked stone being robbed for new buildings. The great tower and nave of St Alban's Abbey are built with Roman bricks and flints. After St Alban's Council acquired part of the site in 1929 for playing-fields, an excavation was run by Sir Mortimer Wheeler in the 1930s. This was one of the major urban Roman excavations in Britain, but still only 11 out of 200 acres were excavated. More recently Professor Sheppard Frere has led a series of digs. These were very much 'rescue archaeology', a mere 100-ft. strip each side of a new road, but they generated major discoveries. Yet most of the Verulamium site still lies unexcavated, buried beneath the farmland, playing-fields and the buildings of the St Michael's area.

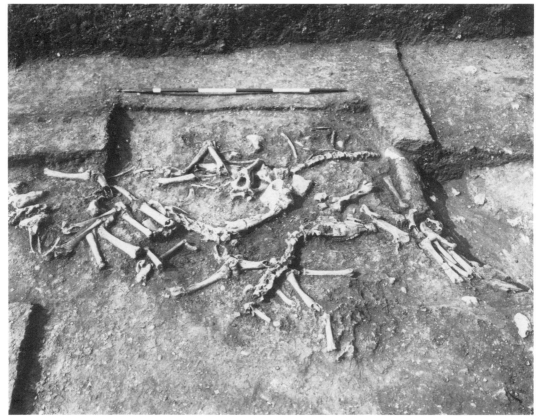

29. Dismembered horse bones photographed during Sir Mortimer Wheeler's Verulamium excavations. Wheeler thought that the style of butchery might suggest that here was the site of a Roman horse-sausage factory.

30. The Roman theatre at Verulamium.

31. Reconstruction of Roman buildings Insula XXVIII, 1 & 2. These buildings were a major part of Frere's excavations. The foundations we can see today near the theatre are of the buildings on the right. The remainder have been totally destroyed by the building of a new road.

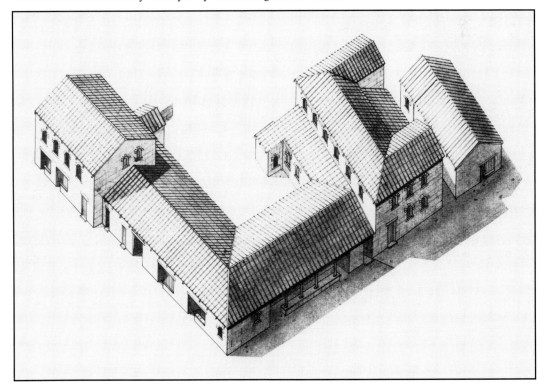

32. A restored panel of wall-plaster recovered from Insula XXVIII, Building 3. This timber-framed building was destroyed by fire AD c.155. As the timbers burnt at the base, large sections of wall fell over in one piece, and were preserved by the debris falling on top.

Almost all of the excavated areas are now back under the grass of the football fields, or destroyed by the new road, but a few portions can be seen: parts of the 3rd-century city wall, showing its brick and flint construction; a restored bath-suite and hypocaust (central-heating system) of a house; the remains of the Roman theatre (Plate 30). Many of the best finds, and excellent reconstructions, can be seen in Verulamium Museum. What comes across vividly is the quality of the decorations and objects. There were houses with bath-suites and central heating provided by warm air conducted through under-floor ducts. The rooms had beautiful floor-mosaics and elegant painted wall plasters. Many of these plasters have been recovered from collapsed walls and reconstructed by techniques first developed on the Verulamium site by Norman Davey. The many household objects included lamps, decorated pottery, jewellery and brooches, craftsmen's tools and medical implements, toys and gaming boards, all testifying to the civilised quality of life in the Roman town.

Close to the remains of the theatre, but probably overlooked by most visitors, are the preserved foundations of 'Insula XXVIII, Building 1' (Plate 31). There is nothing very grand to see, but we find it fascinating and evocative, part of the Roman town *in situ*, something tangible to relate to the detail in Frere's massive excavation reports. Frere excavated here in 1958-59, and much of the building was destroyed by the new road. The brick and flint foundations we see today were part of a complex built AD c.200, some fifty years after a major fire had razed earlier timber-framed houses. It is from this earlier house that some of Verulamium's best wall-plasters and a Dolphin mosaic were recovered (Plates 32 and 33). Today we see part of an underground shrine, probably later used as a storage cellar, and the plan of several heated rooms with an unusual 'union jack' shape of central-heating channels (Plate 34).

This Roman town of Verulamium was no 'city in the wilderness'. It was the political capital and economic centre for a whole region that also strongly felt the Roman impact. In the countryside around Verulamium, Romanised farms or 'villas' were also established soon after the conquest. Some were on the sites of 'Belgic' farms, as at Gorhambury, Park Street and Lockleys, but others were on apparently new sites, as in the Gade and Bulbourne valleys to the west of Verulamium. These villas, even in their earliest timber-built forms, show strong Romanisation and the same features found in the Verulamium town houses: verandahs, internal divisions, bath-houses, painted wall-plaster. Indeed, until the mid-2nd century most of these villas were more impressive in their architecture and furnishings than the town houses. The floor-mosaics are amongst the earliest in the whole Roman province of Britain, and in these comfortable farmhouses one is in a different world from the Iron-Age dwellings of less than 200 years before. In many ways it was a modern world with the trappings we recognise as civilisation.

Why was Romanisation so early and so profound in the east Chilterns? It probably reflects the fact that Catuvellaunian society was strongly hierarchical and centralised: the upper aristocracy accepted and embraced Roman control and Roman ways after AD 43 and had the wealth and landholdings to make the most of it. By contrast, other centralised groups who opposed Roman authority, like Boudicca's Iceni from Norfolk, had their social system and centres destroyed. In addition, the Verulamium area was in a pivotal geographical position on the new road system built by the Romans, with Akeman Street striking west up the Bulbourne valley and Watling Street as the major route to the north west.

33. Dolphin mosaic recovered from Insula XXVIII, Building 3. Here the mosaic is *in situ* as it was uncovered from the debris of the fire and later buildings.

34. Insula XXVIII, Building 1 today. Here in room 18 we can see today the remains of the unusual channelled hypocausts in the form of a Union Jack, radiating from a central distribution box.

These roads are amongst the most enduring legacies of the Roman period. Designed and engineered roads do not pre-date the Roman era and, after the Romans, were not to reappear until the turnpike roads of the 18th century. For much of their routes these ancient highways are followed and overlain by modern highways—Watling Street by the A5 and Akeman Street by the A41. But in some stretches the older line has not been followed, and sometimes the work of the Roman highway engineer can be detected in the Chilterns landscape today in terms of alignments of raised banks, the ridge or 'agger' of the Roman road, and the laid foundations of stones and sand beneath. One such stretch can be faintly traced beside the A41 north of Berkhamsted by Cow Roast.

A number of other Roman roads undoubtedly existed, to link Verulamium with its hinterland and other regional centres, and I. D. Margary and a group calling themselves the 'Viatores' tried to locate them in the Chilterns region.[13] Using maps, field survey and limited excavation of aggers, they traced the possible alignments of several routes. In particular the Viatores identified several stretches of a possible road running through the Chalfonts towards Wycombe and the Thames at Hedsor, but major sections of this road seem completely lost.

The Lower Icknield Way, weaving along the low ground below the Chiltern escarpment, is also likely be of Roman origin. It runs parallel to but below the prehistoric or Upper Icknield Way. The many villas along its route suggest it must have been in existence by the early 2nd century. There are signs in many places of a definite agger to the Roman road, and it runs very straight, being followed by the B4009 for long stretches, but also becoming a lane and footpath in some sections. An interesting stretch to walk is that south-west from Chinnor through lanes and fields to Lewknor. Although now used as a post-enclosure boundary line, it can be clearly seen and named on pre-enclosure maps, such as that for Lewknor in 1598 (Plate 98).

Villas in the Chiltern Valleys

A substantial number of Roman villas have been discovered in the heart of the Chilterns, in the valleys west of Verulamium.[14] They line the valleys of the Bulbourne, Chess, Misbourne and Wye, running along the rich band of soils at the foot of the Chiltern escarpment, with sites at Totternhoe, Terrick, Little Kimble, Saunderton and Bledlow. By the Thames there were villas at Marlow and Hambleden. The existence of some of these villas has been known about for a long time, and some had rather crude Victorian excavations. Others have only been discovered quite recently, like the villa at Northchurch on the Bulbourne, uncovered during housing development, or the Saunderton Lee villa located by air photography in the 1960s (Plate 36).[15]

Professor Keith Branigan, the leading authority on the Roman Chilterns, has argued that many of these Chiltern valley villas were established as farms in the last decades of the first

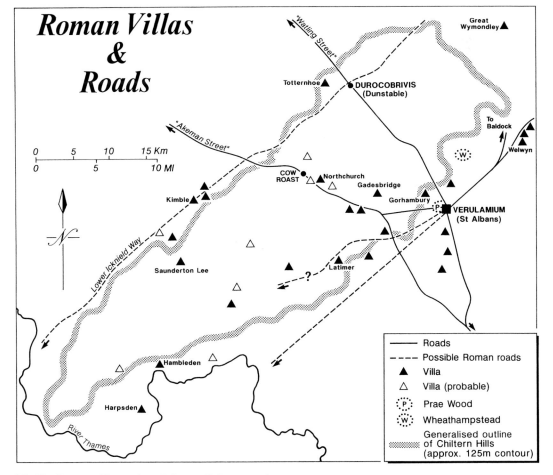

35. The Roman villas and roads in the Chilterns. This map portrays a very 'conservative' picture, and there are many other 'possible' and even 'likely' sites (see Branigan, 1985).

36. Aerial view of the Roman villa at Saunderton Lee. This villa, as yet unexcavated, was discovered by Professor J. K. St. Joseph in July 1962 during an aerial reconnaissance. It lies two miles south of the well-known villa by Saunderton church, and shows a substantial villa of basilican plan.

century AD. Some were initially 'native' farms of 'Belgic'-type, but with the pottery finds suggesting that their occupation took place after the conquest of AD 43, and they were later transformed into flint and brick villas (as at Latimer and Sarratt). Indeed Branigan argues that the first phase may have been in anticipation of a road-building programme that did not in fact materialise until the 2nd century. He further argues that the regularity of spacing of the villas along the Bulbourne, Chess and Misbourne valleys suggests 'a deliberate and controlled settlement policy there'.[16] A look at the Ordnance Survey map will confirm just how evenly apart these villas are. Along the valleys each would have had an estate of 450-500 acres, with meadow, arable, pasture and woodland. Branigan led a major excavation at the Latimer villa in the Chess valley.[17] Here the date of the villa establishment seems to coincide with the desertion of the hilltop settlement at Cholesbury (where there was 'Belgic'-type occupation), and Branigan suggests there may have been an organised movement of labour from the ridge and into the valley. There may be a similar connection between the desertion of the 'Belgic' village on Lodge Hill and the new villa estates at Saunderton and Saunderton Lee.

The Roman settlement pattern in the Chiltern valleys is almost completely dominated by the villas, and this is a distinctive and interesting feature. Throughout Roman Britain, the continued growth of population led to much settlement expansion, but frequently in the form of isolated or dispersed 'native' farmsteads such as scatter the Nene and Ouse river basins and the Vale of Aylesbury. In southern Britain most Roman landscapes are a mixture of villas and scattered native farmsteads. But in the Chilterns there are very few such native sites. Some may be obscured by woodland and slope sediments, but even given the problems of detection by air photography in these valleys, Branigan believes 'we are looking at two different patterns of land-holding and settlement'.[18] It may be, in fact, that the 'virgin' nature of the Chiltern valleys allowed such planned, villa-based colonisation. The Romanised colonisers could clear the woods and lay out the estates like beads along a string. There are a few non-villa sites, but they are industrial, such as the Fulmer and Hedgerley sites. In the 1970s a geophysical survey on the route of the A41 north of Berkhamsted revealed an important Roman industrial site at Cow Roast.[19] Excavation, especially of the debris found in a number of wells, suggests a metal-working and iron-smelting site, occupied over a long period and still active in the late 4th century. There was also certainly some iron-smelting and a great deal of smithing at the villa at Mantles Green Farm, Amersham.

There is very little visible to see on the ground at most of these villa sites today—they lie under grass, or have been destroyed by recent housing developments. Some of the excavated finds can be seen in the County Museums. At Little Kimble, however, on a site as yet little excavated, there is a substantial villa lying under the churchyard and the surrounding fields. Survey and surface remains show a large villa still awaiting excavation, and the site reveals Roman pottery from the late 1st to 4th centuries, together with blue tesserae from mosaics.[20] This location, between the Upper and Lower Icknield Ways, has occupation sites from prehistoric times to the present day, and it is a favourite spot, with the box-woods on the scarp behind and the medieval church on the Roman site.

The villa at Latimer can provide our example of a Chiltern valley site.[21] It lies on the south side of the river Chess, above a good area of river meadow. Keith Branigan's excavations revealed a 1st-century 'Belgic' farmstead that was later abandoned before the flint-and-brick villa was constructed in the 2nd century. Between the two periods there was time for a tree to grow within the site, with the tree-rings suggesting at least a 25-year gap. The 2nd-century villa was a simple structure, like many of the Chiltern villas, but from the very start it had a bath-suite with heating, a long corridor, mosaic and some painted wall-plaster (Plate 37). Later it was extended with four more rooms, further underfloor heating and a more elaborate bathhouse, together with further mosaics. During the 3rd century Latimer, like other villas, shared a series of economic and political hiccups, and may have been abandoned for a time. It then saw renewed prosperity in the early 4th century: there was extensive rebuilding, with new projecting wings, and the courtyard was enclosed by a wall with gatehouses.

It must have been a pleasant and comfortable farmhouse. The owners had glassware, a wide range of iron tools, kitchenware, keys, hooks, brooches and pins. Other objects include bronze tweezers and an ear spatula. The courtyard had bedding trenches for plants, and a small iron turf-cutter has been found. Evidence for the economy of the villa is rather limited, as it

37. A portion of mosaic floor at the Roman villa of Latimer, revealed during Keith Branigan's excavations in the late 1960s.

is for the other Chiltern villas, and it must be pieced together from scattered finds. This suggests a mixed economy, with a strong pasture element of sheep and cattle to judge by the finds of animal bones. The arable side of Latimer is more elusive. There are some signs of plough-marks from beneath the earliest buildings. The flints used for building are clean and weathered, and were probably collected from open, ploughed fields. Branigan estimates 22,000 cubic feet of flints were needed. However, there is no evidence of granary buildings or corn-drying kilns that would suggest strong arable dependence. In this Latimer is typical of the Chiltern valley villas, and contrasts with the scarp-foot villas, where quern stones, used for grinding corn, and granaries are found. The Hambleden villa by the Thames seems to have been exceptional, for it shows evidence of both large-scale grain and meat production, possibly for the military in London.

Branigan estimates the Latimer estate was some 550-600 acres, with meadow and cattle pasture by the river, arable on the lower slopes, and woodland on the upper slopes and hilltops. It is much the same size as a medieval estate, but the proportion of arable was probably considerably less in Roman times. The woodland was not just a nuisance to be cleared in the colonisation stage, but an important resource for building and for fuel—the central heating systems must have been very demanding—and the woods would have been managed carefully. The breaking in of the valley lands was assisted by improvements in farming methods, using heavier ploughs with iron coulters to cut the turf vertically. The Romanised farmers probably improved the heavier soils by marling, a method that has been a standby in the Chilterns ever since: it involves digging pits to extract underlying chalk and mixing it with the heavier clay soils. Pliny the Elder wrote c.AD 75: 'There is another method, discovered in the province of Britain and those of Gaul, the method of feeding the earth itself, and the kind of soil called marl ... the substance brings wealth to the provinces of Gaul and Britain'.

Latimer and the other villas are very impressive achievements, yet in some ways the Chiltern and Verulamium villas failed to live up to their early promise. Their fortunes fluctuated with regional and local economic and political shifts, ebbing in the 3rd century but showing some recovery in the 4th. But, for early villas with such early mosaics and Romanisation, they did not keep pace with the scale and substance found elsewhere in the 4th century—here the villas did not expand greatly in size and there are few later, grander mosaics.[22] The form of the villas remained simple, and few developed into courtyard villas with deep flanking wings, though this did occur at Latimer, Totternhoe and possibly at Kimble. It is hard to say why this early potential fizzled out. Perhaps it was because the modestly-sized estates found the growing burdens of taxation and inflation difficult to counteract. Here the original land-planning may have caused some of the problems: the initial spacing of the estates in the constricted Chiltern valleys gave them little scope for later geographical expansion, in contrast perhaps to the estates in the Icknield Belt and Vale, which were less hemmed-in. Some new villa developments did take place later: the Harpsden villa, south of Henley (in fact by one of the holes of the present Henley Golf Course) was a small winged-villa of the mid-3rd century, and there may have been another villa nearby at Bix.

The Later Roman Occupation

One wonders how secure the Roman way of life appeared to the villa owners as they managed their estates and visited town-houses in Verulamium. The 3rd-century setbacks must have damaged self-assurance, but the 4th century saw expansion and new building in many villas. At Gadebridge a major baths complex was built that may have been a private health spa—a 4th-century Roman Champneys. However, by the middle of the century definite signs of distress became apparent. Out of 10 excavated villas in the Chilterns, five or six were abandoned or drastically reduced by the 350s. High Wycombe and Harpsden seem abandoned after this date, and Park Street after *c*.370. Others were temporarily abandoned but later reoccupied in a new manner. Repairs to buildings and rooms were patchy, rooms were shut off by roughly-built walls, and mosaics were repaired with rubble or cleared away. During the second half of the century the Latimer villa saw each of these changes, and the baths were abandoned and later used for rubbish. What had been at its peak a villa of nearly twenty rooms and a large bath-suite was reduced to just two rooms and two sections of corridor. Similar reductions took place at Totternhoe and the other villas. This may suggest a change in the system of land management, with the owners staying in Verulamium and leaving local bailiffs or foremen to run the estates.

The causes of these changes may lie partly in local circumstances, but the ultimate source lies in the strains faced by the Roman Empire. The culture and wealth of Romanised areas like the Chilterns was closely bound up with the economy of the Empire. This economy centred on high taxation being recycled into state and military expenditure. To pay taxes landowners needed to generate market surpluses, and state expenditure led to strong demand for agricultural produce, with gold and silver coinage playing a key role in this revenue/payment cycle. In the later 4th century, under pressures from many parts of the Empire, this system began to collapse from within. Commitment to Britain declined, and eventually in the early years of the 5th century, *c*.410, Rome formally withdrew, leaving local groups to manage as best they could.

The collapse was immensely disruptive to both society and the economy, especially in those most Romanised parts of the country, those most integrated into the monetary economy of taxation and state expenditure. Little new coinage entered Britain after 400 and had prob-

38. A late Roman 5th-century water-supply pipe-trench cut through an earlier floor in Insula XXVII, Building 2, at Verulamium, evidence of Romanised culture and techniques in the town well after AD 410.

ably ceased all circulation by 425. The Verulamium area must have been hard hit. Yet the city continued some form of urban life for longer than most towns in Britain. In 429 Bishops Germanus of Auxerre and Lupus of Troyes visited the shrine of St Alban (martyred at Verulamium c.209), and met a delegation in the town. Frere's excavations in Insula XXVII have uncovered a remarkable late construction. Here a building erected c.380 was later replaced by a barn-like structure, and this in turn was demolished and a trench made for a wooden water-main, with some of the iron collars used to join the pipes found *in situ* (Plate 39). All dating after the cessation of coin-supply is difficult, but Frere believes the water-main must be after 450, possibly as late as 475, and must have been linked to a functioning aqueduct. As Frere says

> the need for a perpetual flow of clean water ... shows that civilised habits had not yet died away; there is surely significance in the fact that the last glimpse we have of ancient Verulamium should so clearly illustrate its continued commitment to the classical tradition which it had fostered over four centuries.[23]

This building was the sole exception and not the rule. It is the only one out of 13 excavated buildings to suggest such late development. After 420-30 there is no evidence of other inhabited buildings in this core area of old Verulamium, and we cannot tell to what extent it shows that urban life survived in the locality. Frere has, however, commented that the late buildings have been extensively damaged and even destroyed by later ploughing, so what we have of 5th-century Verulamium is minimal and its rarity may give a false impression.[24]

Away from Verulamium itself, what remained of a Romanised way of life in the villas must have collapsed rapidly. The most Romanised parts of the countryside, the regions of villas rather than Romano-British scattered farmsteads, would have suffered most. The Chiltern villas had already been scaled down and during the 5th century they disappear from view. At Latimer a post-villa timber building takes occupation to c.450. The animal bones from these last phases at Latimer suggest an emphasis on cattle and on hunted deer. But the collapse of Roman Britain was so total that it is difficult to trace this post-Roman or 'British' occupation. Society did not return to a pre-Roman cultural level. As A. S. Esmonde Cleary has recently written, 'Instead of the graph of the observable material culture dropping back to such a level and steadying, there was instead a vertiginous drop practically to zero'.[25] Not only coinage vanishes, but all artefacts, even the art of the potter's wheel. In Sir Mortimer Wheeler's words, 'the culture of sub-Roman Britain was as nearly negative as any culture in these islands has ever been'.[26]

These post-Roman Britons may be invisible to us, but they were there. There is general evidence, not for the Chilterns as such, of a population decline in the post-Roman centuries to accompany the economic collapse, but where they went, how many were involved and whether they really disappeared are among the tantalising and unanswered questions which remain for this period. The Chiltern valleys, opened up during the Roman period, would not have been deserted. Some of the farming estates would continue, for even without the sophisticated exchange economy of long-distance trade some of those who remained must surely have continued to farm and make a living. Did others return to a subsistence economy, perhaps with hunting and gathering? The frontier of agricultural exploitation probably retreated, with bushes and trees growing on some former fields. Nearly four centuries of Romanised civilisation in the Chilterns had been swept away. One is reminded of John Buchan's words: 'You may think that a wall as solid as the earth separates civilisation from barbarism. I tell you the division is a thread, a pane of glass. A touch here, a push there, and you bring back the reign of Saturn'.[27]

Chapter Four

The Anglo-Saxon Chilterns

Introduction

Six hundred and fifty years separate the end of the Roman Chilterns (around AD 410) from William the Conqueror and the Normans. At the start of these centuries we have a British population which retained a Roman superstructure for a generation, with a literate Christian culture. Then the local leaders, threatened by Picts and Irish, hired Germanic mercenaries, whose numbers increased until they revolted and shattered the fragile economy. Over much of what was to become England they came at first to plunder rather than to settle, but with the collapse of communications and market towns and villas the British population reverted to subsistence agriculture at a low material and cultural level. The later years of the 5th century and the first half of the 6th are the darkest period in our history, but during those years the Britons retained their identity and independence in the Chiltern region longer than in other parts of south-east England.

The Anglo-Saxon migrants and their descendants gradually gained control and imposed a new language and culture on the region. At the end of the period William's great Domesday Survey of 1086 records much of the Chiltern pattern we still see today—the villages, the isolated farmsteads, the manors and parishes, the woodland, the extensive arable. Much of our present network of county and parish boundaries and winding lanes and bridleways was then in existence. Most of the region's place-names are Anglo-Saxon in origin, and, although there were to be great changes in the medieval period, the basic landscape pattern was well established by 1066.

The story of this long formative period is a fascinating one to trace, to find out how the Chiltern Britons gave way to the new Anglo-Saxon order, and to consider what was inherited and survived from that earlier legacy, and what was new and revolutionary. Yet this great formative period is also 'The Dark Ages', in comparison with the rich and datable Roman culture and the detailed legal documentation of Norman England. Our sources for discovering what happened in these centuries are limited, fragmentary and sometimes contradictory. The post-Roman Britons are almost invisible: they left behind virtually no archaeological remains, no identifiable pots, or burial goods. They had no coinage. The invading and migrant Anglo-Saxons are slightly more visible, with pottery, brooches and identifiable burial customs. But their wooden buildings, surviving only as foundations and post-holes, are a poor substitute for the flint-and-brick villas and structures of the Roman period. It is only after conversion of the English to Christianity in the 7th century that we see such building materials reappear.

There is some documentary evidence, mainly from the Anglo-Saxon side, but it is late in date and takes the form of royal charters granting privileged estates, wills of magnates and records of their disputes, rather than being routine, administrative records like those of Norman England. Even such exceptional documents had little chance of survival unless they came into

51

monastic hands. There were monastic histories and biographers of great merit but they wrote from a special point of view. Place-names can be interpreted by specialists to trace how language use developed and thence to try to date the chronology of settlement. But such information can be difficult and uncertain, as the earliest mentions of the name 'Chiltern' reveal. The earliest sure naming is in the tribal name *Ciltern saete* ('dwellers in or by the Chilterns'), listed in the Tribal Hidage discussed later, but an almost contemporary passage in Eddius Stephanus' *Life of St Wilfrid* for the year 686 says, 'a certain exile of noble descent called Ceadwalla came from the desert places of Chiltern and the Weald', in Latin, *de desertis Ciltine et Ondred*. This may be an early Chiltern reference, and *desertis* (wastes) has been used, and misused, to imply impenetrable wildwood. Yet some experts think that this may all be based on a misidentification, and *Ciltine* may refer to the district of Chiltington in Sussex and not to the Chilterns at all.[1]

The picture we can build from such limited sources is inevitably patchy and depends a great deal on how we fit the pieces into a wider national framework. There is scope for considerable variety of interpretation. Yet, like an impressionist picture, although the detailed dots and spots may individually be imprecise and sometimes wrong, we can be reasonably confident of the overall theme. Where there is greatest uncertainty is in trying to connect— to touch finger-tips even—the post-Roman legacy with the new settlers. Here, as we shall see, much depends on how dramatically we view the post-Roman collapse, and here, in truth, we remain very ignorant.

Early Anglo-Saxon Settlements

The earliest Anglo-Saxon settlers in the Chilterns region appear not to have been 'invaders', but groups of mercenaries, or *foederati*, and their families. They were brought in by the Romano-British authorities to help guard the surviving state centred on Verulamium (St Albans) in the early 5th century, and by other authorities in the neighbouring regions. These appear to have been strategically positioned in sites encircling the region rather than within it. Settlement and cemetery sites have been found and excavated to the south west at Dorchester-on-Thames, to the north at Sandy and Kempston in Bedfordshire, and below the escarpment at Aylesbury (to guard Akeman Street) and near Luton (to guard Watling Street). The Aylesbury site at Walton has been excavated to reveal several sunken-floor houses and some early Saxon pottery sherds. At least two of the houses probably date from the 5th century. A late Roman buckle was found, but it may be a casual acquisition, and continuity cannot be assumed. Since archaelogists cannot distinguish 'ethnic Saxons' from Britons adopting Saxon artefacts, the excavation could not resolve any major historical questions about the transition.[2]

The most intriguing aspect is just how little expansion of Anglo-Saxon groups there seems to have been from these initial centres. Only around Luton and Dunstable is there any real growth, and this probably took place after 500, at locations near Puddlehill and further out into the Vale at Leighton Buzzard and Toddington. At Totternhoe there is evidence of Saxon occupation of the old Roman villa site at this time. However, serious expansion seems to be delayed another hundred years, until shortly before 600. Settlement sites and cemeteries then began to multiply around Aylesbury and Luton. The site at Puddlehill, on the chalk scarp at Dunstable, reveals basic sunken-floored houses with wooden posts and roofs detectable by the surviving post-holes.[3] Pagan cemeteries and inhumations have been dated to this period for sites along the Icknield Way at Ellesborough, Little Kimble and Bledlow. In the Thames valley there is the rich burial of a very important leader at Taplow (the name is probably *Tappa's hlaew* or burial mound) which is datable to *c*.600. Since this is the next richest grave to the ship burial at Sutton Hoo, he may have been a royal reeve of very high status, possibly even a member of the Kentish royal kindred.[4] Why he was at Taplow, and what substantial territory he controlled, remains as yet a mystery. The rich finds from this burial are still on display in the British Museum, showing that his whole panoply of goods is Kentish, including big drinking horns that must have been ancient heirlooms dating back to the earlier 6th century (Plate 39). Along the Thames other pagan sites were uncovered at Hitcham and at High Wycombe.

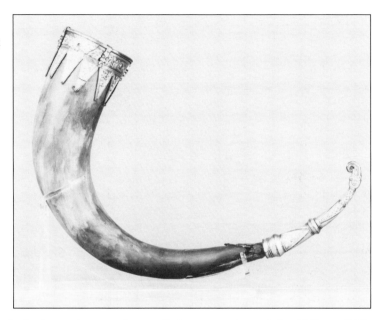

39. The drinking horn from Taplow. The large burial mound within the churchyard at Taplow was excavated in 1882. The rich finds suggest that a very high ranking noble was buried here. They include decorated drinking horns, a 12-in. Coptic bronze bowl, elaborate gold buckles, and several shields and spears.

The overall archaeological picture is one of very little penetration of the Chiltern Hills before the end of the pagan period (c.650), but of a notable expansion around the perimeter of the Hills two generations earlier. At Puddlehill and at sites near Aylesbury the grave goods include West Saxon saucer brooches, evidence perhaps of a West Saxon élite brought in to control the new area. This occupation was clearly not entirely peaceful: Puddlehill contains the grave of a Saxon warrior complete with shield and fatal blow to the skull (Plate 40).[5]

This archaeological evidence can be looked at in relation to the historical record. An entry in the *Anglo-Saxon Chronicle* under the year 571 records that the Anglo-Saxon leader Cuthwulf 'fought against the Britons at Biedcanford [unidentified], and captured four towns, Limbury [now part of Luton], Aylesbury, Bensington [Benson] and Eynsham; and in the same year he died'. Much ink has been spilt debating this entry. As Sir Frank Stenton wrote, 'no annal in the early section of the Chronicle is more important than this, and there is none of which the interpretation is more difficult'.[6] It may record a Saxon victory over the Britons, giving the Saxons access to all the Vale and Icknield Belt. But is the date even approximately reliable, is the annal genuine at all or is it a retrospective entry made to bolster a later Wessex claim to the royal vill at Benson? Whatever the truth, such a victory is consistent with the other evidence of expansion and important shifts in the balance of power late in the 6th century as the emerging Anglo-Saxon kingdoms asserted wider authority. The Oxford archaeologist Sonia Chadwick Hawkes writes: 'leaving Eynsham aside, the other towns captured seem to mark West Saxon expansion into the Chiltern-foot zone, which, from the fifth century, had remained British apart from the original federate colonies of Saxons'.[7]

40. Saxon warrior from Puddlehill. This burial of an early Saxon warrior with his shield and spear was uncovered on the very edge of a quarry. He died from a fatal blow to the head.

How does the evidence of place-names support or contradict this picture of settlement? In many ways the last generation of research has muddied the waters. The traditional 'received wisdom' was that place-name elements based on social or group habitation (village or farm of Fred or the people of Fred, with forms in -*ing*, -*ham* and -*ingham*) were of great diagnostic value for the historian. They were used by early settlers, and changing fashions in name could be used to date (or at least put into sequence) the progress of settlement. In contrast topo-. graphical or 'nature' names (such as -*well*, -*dun* [hill] or -*denu* [valley]) were thought to be late in date, so of little interest historically. Since the Chilterns almost totally lack the significant early habitation names, but are overwhelmingly topographical names, this gave place-name support to the picture of late Anglo-Saxon settlement.

More recently these supposed sequences of early names have been exploded by new generations of scholars. In some ways the revisions do not affect the Chilterns very much at all. The region has so few habitative names that revised distinctions about their dating in the period 400-650 are irrelevant. For example, -*ham* (homestead) names are now thought to be an early layer, but the local examples confirm the existing picture: they encircle the Hills in the areas of pagan burials—Puttenham, Hitcham, Cippenham, Burnham, Farnham, and the interesting Studham near Dunstable, which Cox speculates might have been a stud-farm connected to the military population around Dunstable.[8]

However, we can no longer be so confident that some topographical names are not 'early'. They are quite widespread in pre-730 written sources, and were generally in use for a very long time. Margaret Gelling has worked on place-names just across the Thames in

Berkshire, and she argues that some of the nature names are very early and also points out that habitation names were absent from areas of known early settlement.[9] The same is most likely to be true in parts of the Chilterns, possibly around the early settlements at Benson and Ewelme. Such revisions, like the discovery of new archaeological evidence, blur our picture at the edges, suggesting that there could have been more nibbling into the Chilterns before 650, but so far no one has suggested any need for a major reinterpretation. Recent work on place-names does provoke new interest in topographical names and settlement structure. Overall, despite re-evaluation and new evidence, scholars are agreed that there was little penetration into the Chilterns before 600. The post-571 expansion did, however, finally cut off the remaining Britons of the Chilterns from groups further west, creating an enclave within the Anglo-Saxon zone. In S. S. Frere's words, 'the Chilterns did form a British reserve until the renewal of Saxon conquest in this area in 571'.[10]

The British Enclave

This British enclave does leave us wondering why the Anglo-Saxons were so reluctant to settle the Chilterns until so late. Earlier generations of historians could see it simply as a result of regional unattractiveness: the Chilterns were wild, wooded hills and wastes, largely virgin and unexploited, sheltering a small and probably hostile British remnant. But in the light of all the recent discoveries about the quite intensive Roman occupation of the region, we need a fuller explanation. It seems unlikely that the formerly-farmed valleys and managed woodland were completely abandoned and their potential simply overlooked by the Anglo-Saxons.

Kenneth Rutherford Davis has argued that the Chilterns enclave or 'reserve' survived because there was a continuing British political organisation based on the old Roman centre of Verulamium.[11] Only such an organised state, he argues, could have resisted the outside pressures. It was only after 571 that this state, now isolated from other British groups to the west, finally collapsed, so allowing the Anglo-Saxons to enter and settle the Chiltern hills and valleys. Davis' view has considerable appeal: a British zone in the heartland of south-east England associated with the longest-surviving Roman *civitas*. But his case is perhaps over-stated and it has met with much criticism. It depends on a continuing survival of urban and political organisation in Verulamium not just to 500, but to 571 or 600, and this goes against the views of Verulamium's recent excavator, Sheppard Frere, who has commented as recently as 1987: 'our verdict must be against organized survival much later than 500'.[12] Davis' argument assumes more than just a flickering urban life in Verulamium; it also requires a state capable of projecting power and asserting authority throughout the whole Chilterns region, and this is even less likely.

If we are to provide an alternative interpretation that pieces together the little strands of information that we have, then we must look again at the way the Anglo-Saxons settled. The view of surging military and migration waves restricted only by countervailing power (in our case a rush of angry Britons from the woods) has to be revised. Instead, apart from Kent and East Anglia, this wave is increasingly seen as a smaller-scale movement. The Anglo-Saxons gradually infiltrated new regions and the existing British population became assimilated within them. After all, there was not any great pressure on land after the population decline with the economic collapse of Roman south-east England. Therefore only patchy Anglo-Saxon settlement developed, leaving vast areas of wooded hilly country to the more aggressive local chieftains who would have led pockets of local resistance, but in a less structured way than Rutherford Davis' Chiltern state.

In the Anglo-Saxon settled regions local Britons, without any strong surviving culture of their own, became 'anglicised' or 'saxonised' at the lowest social level. They gradually acquired Anglo-Saxon goods, so that we cannot assume all Saxon graves were of 'ethnic Saxons', and adopted the English language as larger political groupings and new states emerged. The Chilterns are then absorbed and settled after the states of Wessex and Mercia and the Middle Saxons began to gain firmer political control over wide areas, and especially those surrounding the Chilterns, after 571-600.

Settlement of the Chilterns, 600-750

The political changes of the late 6th century did not lead to any sudden surge of settlement and colonisation of the Hills. Burials from the pagan period—which takes us beyond 650—remain around the outer edge, with some expansion from the Thames into the Wye valley, for there is a burial of this date at Castle Hill, High Wycombe. Rather it was a slow, tidal spread over a century or more. Some insight comes from a late 7th-century document, the Tribal Hidage (Plate 41), listing kingdoms adjacent and possibly subservient to Mercia.[13] This document gives us our first certain use of the term Chiltern: 'Cilternsaetna landes is feowere thusend hyda' [the land of the Chiltern dwellers is 4000 hides].

41. Extract from the *Tribal Hidage*. This document gives us the first definite use of the term 'Chiltern', and dates from the late 6th century. The phrase *Cilternsaetna landes*, 'land of the Chiltern dwellers', can be read quite clearly on line 13. [BL: Harley 3271, 6v.]

Cilternsaete or 'people of Chiltern' is a delightful term, from which we could have obtained a county name of 'Chilterset' on the same principles as the names of Somerset or Dorset. These 'people of Chiltern' probably lived mainly in the Vale, focused on the royal centres around Aylesbury. By 650-700 they were taking control of the hill area for woodland and grazing, and for permanent settlement, locking the Chiltern countryside into land-units that survive in our present parishes. Their colonisation spread into the headwaters of the south-east flowing Chiltern streams, especially the Chess and the Misbourne. Missenden ('Myrsa's valley') was settled from the Vale, and nearby Hampden may be an unusual and early *ham-denu* or 'homestead-valley' place-name. Arnold Baines has suggested that we may see some signs of this pagan period in the area: Aylesbury may be named after Aegil the sun-archer demi-god, and his mythological brother, Weland the Smith, may have been honoured at Weland's Stock, a prominent hilltop between Risborough and Hampden.[14] The bounds of a 10th-century charter record a 'King's street' running from Weland's Stock towards Aylesbury, crossing the Upper Icknield Way at a 'heathen burial place'. Baines suggests the ruling house of the *Cilternsaete* may have claimed descent from one or the other of these demigods.

The slow absorption of the Chilterns came from all sides, with the different small states eating in towards the centre. For the northern Chilterns the Tribal Hidage records the *Hicca* with only 300 hides, usually taken to be in the Hitchin region. In the east an Anglian group called the *Waeclingas* held the St Albans area in the 7th century, and East Saxons expanded into the Hemel Hempstead area, where the *pagus* or region of Haemele occurs in a 704 charter. The unusual Latin term may indicate a post-Roman territorial unit annexed by Saxons.[15] In the south the longer-established Thamesside Middle Saxons colonised the Wye and lower Misbourne and Chess valleys, pushing the furthest into the Hills from the outer perimeter. A separate expansion in the upper Thames focused around Benson colonised what became the Oxfordshire Chilterns. Eventually the colonising groups met each other, and parts of that frontier are marked on the map today: where the *Cilternsaete* met the Middle Saxons from the Thames is marked by the line between the Three Hundreds of Aylesbury and the Chiltern Hundreds, a line still followed by many parish boundaries today.[16] The old border in the Chilterns between Oxfordshire and Buckinghamshire, before later Victorian transfers of Stokenchurch to Buckinghamshire, also probably marks such a frontier.

The British Chiltern population must have been absorbed by this colonisation and dominated by it. Only a few British place-names survive, but the form of Wendover ('clear streams') passed into English with the correct plural form, suggesting a bilingual population there. The name

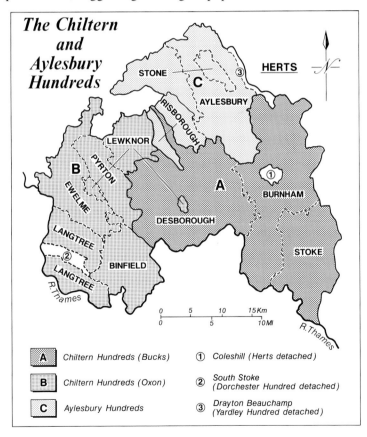

42. The Chiltern and Aylesbury Hundreds.

identifies a clear stream from the chalk—its corresponding English name would be Shirburn which occurs further down the scarp-foot in Oxfordshire—and can be contrasted with the river Thame in the Vale, denoting a dark stream full of sediment. We know virtually nothing about the estates and homes of these surviving Britons. In places they must have continued to farm lands occupied by Roman villas and then either become 'Saxonized' or lost the lands to new colonisers. Since we know so little of the territories of Romano-British estates it would be difficult to recognise continuity. One classic example is that of Wymondley, near Hitchin, where Seebohm thought that the open-field layout mapped onto a regular Roman grid of fields.[17] There is a Roman site next to the church, and continuity is very plausible, but the eye of faith is needed when looking at the field pattern and we may regard the case unproven.

Baines has suggested that such survival of estates as functioning land-units was most likely in the rich Icknield Belt, and that the inner Chilterns at this time 'were reverting to scrubwood on its way back to high forest'. He also suggests that the Middle Saxons in their expansion 'could secure ready-made estates, with slaves to cultivate them until a new peasantry could move in; thereafter the Britons would still be needed on the demesne and as swineherds in the woods'. This may be the origin of the great estate of Chesham.[18] Definite signs of this transition are almost impossible to find, but John Chenevix Trench has pointed to the high percentage of slaves or serfs (*servi*) in these Chiltern districts in Domesday Book, possibly marking the last refuge, and ultimate fate, of the independent Britons.[19]

The desire to go further and see stronger signs of Roman to Anglo-Saxon continuity and British survival is a powerful one. Some have even claimed to see Celtic (British) characteristics in the recent population. Beddoe marked the Chilterns as a 'Celtic island' on his 1885 map of the races of Britain, and Anthony Collett wrote in the 1930s:

> In all the Chiltern country, right away from Hitchin, on the North Road, to Henley-on-Thames, a large proportion of the people are small-bodied, with small, dark faces and dark hair and eyes. The type is very distinct, and is probably due to a strong strain of British blood left from times when the steep hills and tangled thickets of the Chilterns were avoided by the Saxon invaders.[20]

Such ideas ignore the history of ethnic mixing, but the reader is left to make his or her own assessment of friends, neighbours and 'natives'! Part of the impulse may be religious—to try to see Christian continuity at Verulamium and elsewhere in the Chilterns. This comes out clearly in Father R. J. Stonor's engaging history of the Stonor family. At Stonor in the Oxfordshire Chilterns there has certainly been continuity of Catholic worship since medieval times, and in the district since Anglo-Saxon times. St Birinus engaged in early missionary work in the region in the 630s, and Father Stonor tries to link this to Romano-British survival: 'in these hills, so all the fragmentary evidence seemed to show, British Christians had dwelt continuously since the days of the Romans', and so:

> it is quite possible... that the chain of Masses stretches back, celebrated by Celtic priests, long before the coming of St.Birinus, until we come to the martyrdom of Saint Alban on the other side of the Chilterns and the mission of Pope Eleutherius, when each morning's Mass was separated by less than a hundred and fifty years from the Upper Room in Jerusalem.[21]

It is indeed just possible, but it defies reason to turn such speculations into facts or even probabilities. There remains an unbridgeable gap between Roman society and Anglo-Saxon culture in the Chilterns.

Place-Names and the Landscape

It is well worth looking more closely at the mass of Anglo-Saxon 'nature' names in the Chilterns. They can help reveal how the settlers and farmers saw the landscape and what sort of environment it presented. The various names for hill and valley are not merely synonyms: just as the Eskimos have different names for the many types of snow, so the Chiltern settlers labelled the landforms and features in considerable detail. Ann Cole has already explored these forms in the Chilterns by mapping place-names and relating them to the appropriate landforms on the Ordnance Survey maps and on the ground.[22]

Several words are used to name types of valleys and hills. A clear contrast emerges between -*denu* (den) valleys and -*cumb* (coombe or combe) valleys: -*denu* describes a long, often winding valley, usually on the dip-slope of the Chilterns, such as the Assenden valley north of Henley, or Hambleden, Hughenden and Hampden. Harpsden, west of Henley, winds deeply for several miles. Thirty-three such forms have been identified in the Hills, with 29 of them on the dip-slope. However, -*cumb* is used for the heads of bowl- or trough-shaped valleys with steep sides, more usually found on the scarp edges. It is a British loan word, taken up by the Anglo-Saxons, possibly because they had little experience of such forms on the continent and so had had less need for a distinct word of their own. Examples are Swyncombe, Coombe below Chequers, and the old site of Watcombe now called the Howe. Two -*cumbs* behind the scarp are Coombe Farm near Hughenden and Warmscombe, a lost village in the Assenden valley marking a scallop in the valley-side.

Hill and -ridge are common distinctions, but we can also distinguish -*hoh*, -*dun* and -*ora*. The -*hohs* are projecting ridges or shoulders, often jutting out from the scarp—as at Ivinghoe, Sharpenhoe and, as ridges out into the Vale, Totternhoe and Segenhoe (later called Ridgmont). Such topography is commonest in the north Chilterns. -*duns* are rounded hills like upturned bowls, and are commonest in the little hills that occur in the Vale (as with Long Crendon). Both -*dun* and -*hoh* contrast with the -*ora* landform, which can be identified as an elongated hill like an upturned canoe or punt, with a large flattish top and rounded shoulders at one or both ends; -*oras* cluster in the south-west Chilterns around Chinnor, Stonor, Clare (clay -*ora*), and Golder (golden -*ora*). Such -*ora* names refer to the hills and not to the present village sites, which in some cases like Lewknor have moved off the scarp side. A few -*ora* sites occur further north, at Pednor, Honor End near Hampden, and at Aldbury Nowers. The appropriateness of the names depends very much on the angle of view: when approached along the ancient Knightsbridge Lane from the Oxford or Vale side, the *ora* which has Clare and Golder at opposite ends is an obvious feature, but from the Chiltern side it seems insignificant.

Water, its availability and its shortage, is central to settlement siting, vegetation and farming in the Chilterns. The chalk rock is permeable and springs and surface-flow only break out when the percolating water meets an impermeable rock-layer or the water-table reaches the surface (Plate 43). Within the chalk the underground water-table rises and falls with the seasons, so that dip-slope streams only flow in their upper reaches in winter ('winterbournes') or intermittently. Large-scale permanent settlement was either along the scarp spring-line (with names like Ewelme, 'strongly-flowing springs', Sewell or Crowell), or below the spring points in the dip-slope valleys. Such upper reaches are marked by names like Mobwell at the source of the Misbourne and Dudswell near the source of the Bulbourne. The Chiltern water-table has risen and fallen with climatic changes through history, and recent years have seen significant drops with water extraction for the big towns. In Anglo-Saxon times many streams probably reached further up into the hills than today. Names ending in -*well* usually denote springs rather than actual wells, which are a more recent, but still very old, feature. However on the Chiltern plateau the very variable patches of clay-with-flints allow some surface water to be retained in small ponds, and such water has been vital to the dispersed hamlets and farms of the hills. We can detect these in place-names in -*mere*, as at Homer Farm, Uxmore and other sites in the dry country near Checkendon, Parmore above Hambleden, and Hazlemere and

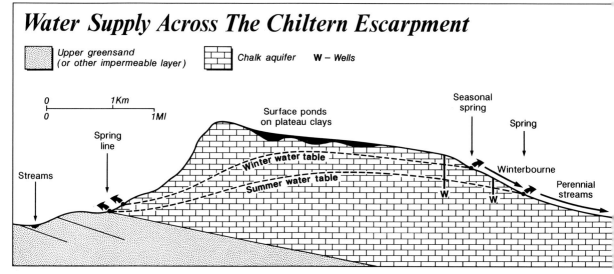

43. Water supply across the Chiltern escarpment. An idealised section through the Chilterns to show the main features of water supply in this chalk region.

Holmer Green above Wycombe. In addition, the use of -*burna* for spring-fed clear streams is found in the Chilterns at Bourne End and Redbourn.

The Anglo-Saxon place-names also indicate patterns of vegetation and, as one would expect, -*wood* and -*ley* (wood, or 'clearing in wood') names are very widespread, though they are hard to date and some may be medieval rather than Anglo-Saxon. The -*feld* names form an interesting group. The term was used to denote tracts of open country, often employed for upland common pasture before farming intensified, but contrasted with adjacent woodland: the *Ormulum* (*c.*1200) listed contrasts of country: 'wude and feld and dale and dun'. In the Chilterns feld names particularly pick out parts of the plateau with thin coverings of pebbly sands and gravels, country that was dry and once cleared of wood the infertile soils would not encourage regeneration, unlike the clay-with-flints patches. There is a grouping in the extreme south: Nuffield, Greenfield, Rotherfield ('open land grazed by cattle'), and Binfield. A short distance to the north lies Turville—*thyrre feld* or dry open-country, a name, as Baines has noted, that well describes the land of open common, heath and bracken between Northend, Turville Heath and Southend, but not the present village location in the valley on the edge of the parish. North east of Turville is a large plateau area, formerly known as Abbefeld, between Stokenchurch and Cadmore End. Abba's feld is certainly pre-9th century in origin, forming dry and wide commons in upper Lewknor Hundred.[23]

Anglo-Saxon Estates and Land Structure

We can see something of how the Anglo-Saxons organised their Chiltern estates and territories, and of how these estates then evolved into the manors and parishes of Domesday Book and medieval England. By piecing together diverse later sources on administrative, church and tax linkages between places, and by the evidence preserved as a sort of 'archaeological layer' in our long-surviving local boundary units, we can rediscover some of the ancient territorial units. This is a risky business, but the results parallel those found in other hill-vale areas in Berkshire, Surrey and the West Midlands, so we are on reasonably firm foundations, especially for the scarp region and southern Chilterns.[24] In the north and east the later Danish overlay has lost us much of the earlier detail.

The essential administrative and economic units of the early Anglo-Saxon kingdoms were the royal -tunas or villae regales, royal vills with substantial dependent territories to support mobile royal and noble groups.[25] The four -tunas mentioned in the Annal for 571— Benson, Aylesbury, Limbury and Eynsham—were all named as royal vills in a later chronicle by Aethelward, and the first three were in royal hands at the time of Domesday Book. Other possible royal vills include Hitchin, Thame, Risborough and Houghton Regis. Closely associated with the royal vills were the minster-churches, established as missionary and pastoral centres with teams of priests serving wide rural areas. Such minsters were often founded close to, but distinct from, the royal vills.[26] The see of Dorchester-on-Thames, only four miles away from Benson, was founded in 635 on the site of a Roman and early Anglo-Saxon settlement. Bede later wrote that King Cynegils gave to Bishop Birinus 'the civitas called Dorcic to make his episcopal seat there'. At Aylesbury the minster associated with St Osyth was established, close to the royal palace at nearby Quarrendon.

The network of estates dependant on these royal vills has sometimes been preserved in the groups of 'Hundreds' of later times. Though the formal use of the term 'Hundred' as an administrative and military area of nominally 100 hides dates from the 9th and 10th centuries, it has been shown that many have their origins in earlier Anglo-Saxon land-units. Evidence of the groupings is sometimes shown in entries in Domesday Book. In the Oxfordshire Chilterns the '4½ Chiltern Hundreds' of Lewknor, Pyrton, Binfield, Langtree and Ewelme (the half-Hundred) were all linked to the royal manor of Benson : 'the jurisdiction of four and a half Hundreds belongs to this manor'. Helen Cam, the leading historian of the Hundreds, suggests that these 4½ Hundreds are the 'Bynsington-land' of a 996 charter.[27] For Aylesbury it is the minster holding in Domesday Book that reveals the old dependent areas:

> From the eight Hundreds which lie around Aylesbury each sokeman having one hide or more renders one load of grain to this church. Besides this also one acre of grain or four pence used to be contributed by each sokeman to the church, but after the coming of King William this payment was not made.

These Aylesbury Hundreds include those of Risborough, Stone and Aylesbury itself, stretching deep into the Chilterns. The eight, 'viii' in the manuscript, may in fact be a mistake for three, 'iii', referring to this three grouping which has remained known as the Three Hundreds of Aylesbury.

In medieval and later records, the Hundreds are often seen as groupings of parishes and manors, but in many areas the real order is probably the reverse: the parish and manorial estate units grew out of the fragmentation of these larger and older land-units. This fragmentation is one aspect of a major land revolution that seems to have taken place in 8th-9th century England, stemming from political and economic changes. Land ownership—in the sense that land could be inherited, exchanged and kept as personal property—only gradually emerged as the mobile, 'tribal' states became established. Grants of land were made to endow the Church and its minsters, and to sustain the expanding minor territorial nobility. A Chilterns illustration is provided by a charter of 887: Aethelred of Mercia gave 14 hides of land in Brightwell and Watlington (including some outlying woodland) to the Bishopric of Worcester to support a minster church at Readenoran (later Pyrton).[28] The grant also included stock and ploughing equipment, and six men 'who formerly belonged to the royal vill at Bensington', and named as Almund, Tidulf, Tidheh, Lull, Lull and Gadwulf. As such land-grants to the church and laymen acquired a permanence and became inheritable, they led to fragmentation of the old multiple estates into smaller, manorial estates.

The results of this fragmentation are best preserved in the map of church parishes. The splitting of territorial units was followed later by the creation of the parish system, with local manorial lords often taking a lead in establishing churches on their estates. The parish geography probably emerged well after the original estate-splitting, but it mirrored it closely. The manorial geography later became more complicated, through further splitting, groupings and Norman rearrangements, until the pattern was frozen by the statute *Quia Emptores* in 1290. But, once formed, the parish geography has had enormous longevity and its boundary lines fossilise for us the structure of late Anglo-Saxon land-units.

In the Chilterns this geography of Hundreds and parishes reflects both the history of the Anglo-Saxon settlement, with its colonisation into the Hills from the surrounding lowlands, and also the logic of resource use. The Hundreds are large, with their initial foci of settlement, vills and minsters in the lowlands of the Vale or Thames valley. But they extend their claims up into the Hills, with the Aylesbury and Oxfordshire Hundreds extending well over the scarp itself. These hill and wood regions were not intensively settled in the mid-Anglo-Saxon period, but they provided areas of transhumance (where summer pasture for sheeps, pigs and cattle was found) and vital supplies of wood.

The slicing up of these larger units produced interesting results. To maintain shares of resources—vital economic resources in a time of expanding population—the new estates and parishes became long strips, some wafer-thin but each sharing in the cross-section of countrysides and resources, and running at right-angles to the scarp and the Thames (Plate 44). As a pattern of exploitation it must be very old indeed, and the Roman villa estates must have had similar outlines, but the pattern we see today can be traced back to this Anglo-Saxon shift. Along the scarp south of Wendover the splitting can be seen very clearly: Kimble splitting into Great and Little Kimbles, with Ellesborough as a probable third element. Similarly neighbouring Risborough also split into West and East Risborough (with a boundary charter described later). The legacy we see today is a line of five scarp-foot churches in fewer miles between Risborough to Ellesborough.

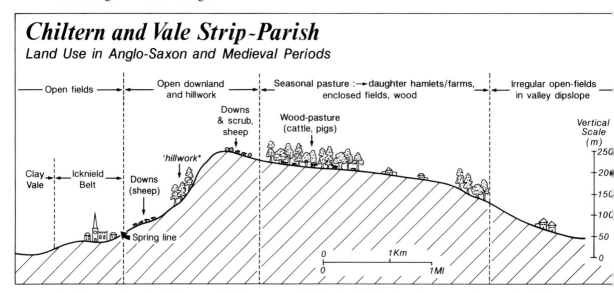

44. Cross section of a Chiltern and Vale scarp-parish. On this idealised section we see the way in which a long strip-parish had a share of a variety of land uses on different parts of the scarp and slope.

This territorial reorganisation seems to have been associated with other changes in settlement and agriculture. As the larger units split up, the newer manorial units were thrown back on their own local resources—hence the strip structure to give all a share in different soils and relief. Settlements, especially in lowland areas like the Vale, seem to have been relocated and nucleated into villages at this time. This may be the time when the Puddlehill settlement site, high on the scarp, was abandoned and life moved down to Houghton Regis in the Vale below. The new name may also be significant: -ton names only became common after c.730 and may reflect settlement reorganisation.[29] Such names are common in the Vale, but absent within the Hills, where there was probably much less reorganisation and farms remained dispersed. This mid-Saxon transformation may also have seen the formation of communal open-field agriculture with strip fields (discussed in the medieval chapter). Evidence for this landscape change is very scattered, but scholars are increasingly convinced that it occurred over large areas of Midland England, including the Vale. The result was to increase the contrast between the Vale and Hill landscapes, a contrast that has lasted to the present day.

Throughout the Hills the length of many of the strip-parishes is quite remarkable. Some are six or eight miles long but incredibly narrow: parishes like Pitstone, Drayton Beauchamp, or Newnham Murren in the extreme south. Many have subsequently lost their upland tails, as the seasonal huts grew into fully-fledged daughter settlements, and some broke off into separate parishes: Cholesbury in the middle ages, Lewknor Uphill (Cadmore End) in Victorian times, and Stoke Row as late as the 1950s. Even in their original form many units did not have all their upland pasture and woodland as a contiguous part of the parish. Detached areas, some a considerable way from the parent settlement, were commonplace. A notable feature is that such detached portions were nearly always within their group of Hundreds, and then mainly within the same Hundred, supporting our views on the antiquity of the Hundreds. In John Blair's words, 'as a territory was split up into manors, so too were its woods and commons fragmented into complex, interlocking archipelagos of individual pastures'.[30] Thus Watlington and Pyrton both had detached areas, at Warmscombe and Stonor, but they lay within the same Pyrton Hundred. Those parts of the Hundreds located in the woodless Vale often had their detached Chiltern pasture and woodland. Weston Turville had the Lee (beyond Wendover), Marsworth had Hawridge, and Stoke Mandeville parts of the Hampdens. The latter linkage was one that survived into the 17th century in the ancient tax of 'ship money' and was the occasion for John Hampden's stand against King Charles I. In the Buckinghamshire Chiltern Hundreds there were several such detached areas, like Penn which belonged to Taplow.

There were some interesting exceptions to this pattern of allocation within the groups of Hundreds. The line between the Aylesbury Hundreds, colonised from the Vale, and the Buckinghamshire Chiltern Hundreds was very enduring. Despite this, the infertile Wycombe Heath, which straddled this line, was intercommoned by 13 parishes from all sides. Clearly there was little pressure for formal subdivision of this waste. A detached portion of Lewknor, known as Ackhamstead and located at Moor End, was within Buckinghamshire, whilst Coleshill (north of Beaconsfield) was attached to Tring and so became part of Hertfordshire. It remained so until 1844 and we can still see 'Little Hertfordshire House' in Coleshill today. This county anomaly was very useful in later times to Quaker dissenters like Thomas Ellwood, who could reside there and avoid the local Buckinghamshire magistrates. John Chenevix Trench has intensively studied Coleshill's history and shown that the anomaly arises from the very early settlement of Coleshill.[31] He suggests that it was originally upland pasture colonised across the frontier-line by the *Cilternsaete* in Aylesbury Vale, and became associated with Tring, which had no readily available upland region close to it. Coleshill lies a good ten miles from Tring. Tring later fell under Danish control and it eventually became part of Dacorum Hundred, the

Hundred of the Danes. Coleshill became attached too and so followed the same subsequent history into Hertfordshire. Chenevix Trench suggests Coleshill may contain the Danish name 'Kolr' or 'Koli' and was permanently settled by Danes. It is interesting to note that Danish settlement is also found in and close to the uplands of Abbefeld and Ackhamstead, in names like Skirmett and Fingest and in personal names like Tovi. It may be that vacant spaces still remained in these two detached upland areas for small groups of Danish settlers in the 10th century.

Lewknor Hundred, which is one of the Oxfordshire Hundreds related to Benson, provides an example of all these various patterns and changes in the Chilterns (Plate 45). It is by no means a 'textbook' case, but it is an area we will return to later in the book. Settlement in this Vale-Hill area has a very long history, and the archaeological research generated when the M40 motorway sliced through the escarpment here has shown Iron-Age, Romano-British and Anglo-Saxon evidence. Trevor Rowley has suggested that it is 'a likely candidate for continuous occupation from prehistoric times to the present day'.[32] The Hundred boundaries undoubtedly show later adjustments, but the core unit probably has great antiquity. Mary Lobel in the *Victoria County History* wrote of Lewknor and the group of Chiltern Hundreds: 'this system was itself descended from a far older system, antedating the formation of hundreds and shires, by which royal estates were the centre of a wide territory supplying them with food rents'.[33]

Lewknor Hundred, in common with all the Hundreds dependent on Benson, has a topographical name, like the ancient land-units Margaret Gelling identified in neighbouring Berkshire. Below the Chiltern scarp, Lewknor Hundred has a Vale landscape littered with nucleated -*ton* and -*cote* villages, where classic open-field farming developed. There are Aston (East-ton), Henton and Kingston (King's-ton), and nearby, but outside the Hundred, are Weston and Pyrton (which earlier had the topographical name of Radenora). Above the chalk scarp hamlets and dispersed farms developed, some not until the medieval period, though the name Abbefeld suggests early occupation for at least pasture. Fragmentation into strip parishes did not in fact proceed as far here as in some localities: Aston and Kingston remained one parish, but developed separate manorial and open-field systems. Access to Chiltern upland resources involved detached portions as common pasture and woodland became divided: Aston held the Wormsley valley on the dip-slope, whilst Lewknor held a detached portion of Abbefeld beyond Aston's pasturelands. Later medieval records show disputes over this pasture: in 1206 Alan fitz Roger was summonsed for burning the Abbot's pasture in Abbefeld and in 1240 in a woodland

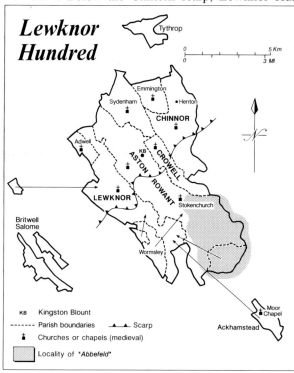

Lewknor Hundred

Tythrop

0   5 Km
0   3 MI

Emmington
Sydenham
Henton
CHINNOR
Adwell
KB
ASTON
CROWELL
ROWANT
LEWKNOR
Stokenchurch
Britwell Salome
Wormsley
Moor Chapel
Ackhamstead

KB   Kingston Blount
------- Parish boundaries   ▲▲ Scarp
✝   Churches or chapels (medieval)
[ ] Locality of *Abbefeld*

45. Lewknor Hundred. This map shows the interlocking parishes of the Hundred and their detached portions, often some distance away.

dispute a jury testified to the intercommoning of 'Eustwode' (Eastwood is still on the map) between the Aston and Lewknor portions.[34]

Boundary Charters

Amongst the Anglo-Saxon charters for the Chiltern region are a small number that include boundary descriptions—written outlines of the landmarks and routeways that define the estates. Some of these boundaries can be re-traced on the Chilterns landscape today. Because our parishes have been so unchanging, the Anglo-Saxon charters often define the same land-units that were first mapped in detail by the Ordnance survey in the early 19th century, with more than 1,000 years between. Where the parish map can serve as a historical 'template', careful study and fieldwork can help identify the locations described in the charters.

The most useful Chilterns boundary charters are for sections of the Oxford and Buckinghamshire scarp region, and we have nothing comparable for the northern and eastern Chilterns. The various charters are all preserved in the Cotton, Harley and Stowe manuscript collections in the British Library. These parchments—some worn and difficult to decipher, others clear and legible—are older than Domesday Book and some are over 1,000 years old.

46. The boundary Charter for Monks Risborough. This is a late 10th-century copy of a charter of *c*.903. The illustration shows the reverse side, giving the bounds and a list of witnesses. [BL: Stowe Charters 22, 1v.] The translation by Dr. Arnold Baines reads:

'These are the land-boundaries. First, from the gore along in the black hedge. From that hedge downwards along in the foul brook. From the foul brook to the west of the ash-tree on the bank, thence into the old ditch to the west of the herdsman's buildings. From that ditch so as to come on to the ridge of wood on Eadric's boundary. Along Eadric's boundary so as to come on to Icknield. Along Icknield as far as the heathen burial-place. Thence on the king's street. Up along (that) street to Weland's stock. From that stock downwards beside the roe-deer fence. Then to the hay glade. From that glade downwards so as to come back to the gore.'

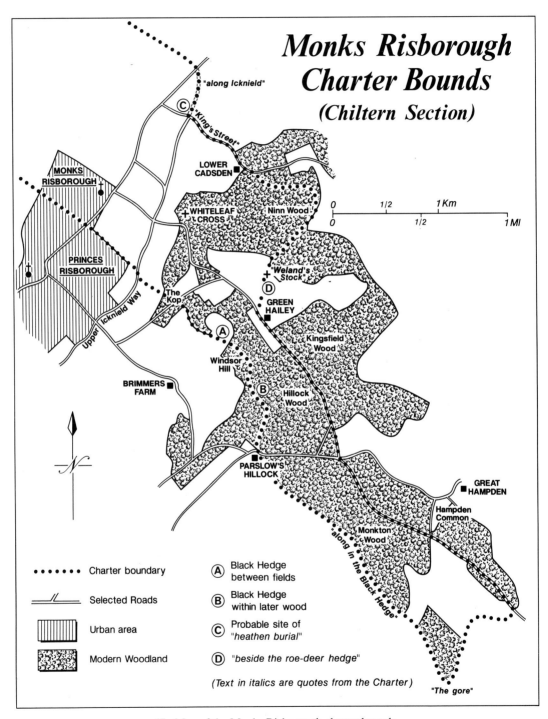

47. Map of the Monks Risborough charter bounds.

48. Air photograph of Monks Risborough. With a combination of map and air photography the way in which the Anglo-Saxon boundary relates to the present landscape can be traced quite clearly. The section of the Black Hedge running between two fields ('A' on the map) is visible in the centre of the photograph.

There is a magic in seeing and reading them in the British Library Manuscripts Room and then returning to the Ordnance Survey map and walking the boundaries today.

A charter for 966 gives the bounds of Newnham Murren, a strip-parish running from the Thames near Wallingford into the heart of the southern Chilterns. It undoubtedly defines the same outline as the 1825 parish map, but research and fieldwork have so far only identified some of the charter names. But it mentions *Graegan Hane* (grey stone) and Greyhone Wood is still on the map today, as is *Hearp Dene* or the Harpsden valley. By contrast a 996 charter for two hides in Benson or 'Bynsington land' cannot be related to later parish boundaries, nor can the detached portion of woodland, where the section begins: *This sind thaes wudes gemaere the to tham lande gebryriath* (These are the bounds of the wood that belongs to the land).[35]

Arnold Baines has traced the bounds of two Chiltern charters in great detail. The first, for Pyrton and Stonor, had puzzled and tantalised experts for a long time, until Margaret Gelling and Arnold Baines showed that it described not one outline but two: the old parish of Pyrton, together with its detached portion of Stonor, separated from each other by a narrow neck of Watlington land.[36] The second is for Monks Risborough in Buckinghamshire, and we shall examine this in more detail.

The Monks Risborough Boundary

The Risborough charter is a late 10th-century copy of an official Mercian document of 903, which authorised Aethelfrith to reproduce his lost landbooks from memory (Plate 46). The attached bounds outline the parish of East (now Monks) Risborough, and the landmarks have been traced in detail by Arnold Baines and Michael Reed.[37]

We can follow here the details for the Chiltern section. The survey begins at the furthest point in the Hills: 'first, from the gore along in the Black Hedge (*blacan hegcean*)'. The gore or spear of land is where Risborough parish just reaches into North Dean. From this point the bounds are beaten sunwise (clockwise), the usual Anglo-Saxon procedure. The boundary runs along the edge of Monkton Wood, and the estate line is traceable by wood-banks and ditches to Lily Bottom and Parslow's Hillock. Here it runs into the remarkable surviving Black Hedge, which runs partly through the Hillock. This section is now wooded, but was more open ground until the 1800s. The boundary then emerges as a clear hedge across open ground from the northern foot of Windsor Hill. It is aligned on the summit of Risborough Cop, until it swerves to the right to cross the scarp at a col. Long stretches of the thick hedge and its ditch survive, with the blackthorn from which it gets its name still very evident. Whitethorn or hawthorn, however, is also very common along major sections (Plates 23 and 24).

Species counts of shrubs in the hedge suggest it is indeed 1,000 years old, though such techniques are of rather limited accuracy. From the Cop the charter bounds go 'from that hedge downwards into the *fulan broc* or "foul brook" ', a tributary of the Thame. They can then be traced out to Waldridge in Vale country, but let us pick them up again as they re-enter the Hills: 'along that boundary so as to come onto Icknield'. This is the northern boundary between the ancient estates of Risborough and Kimble. The bounds follow a short section of the Icknield Way, now a bridle-track, for 500 yards to the junction with Cadsden Road and then run up this road (referred to as the King's Street) to Weland's Stock on the hilltop. The charter and parish boundary then runs 'beside the roe-deer hedge' and to the 'hay clearing' (the farm of Hailey is still on the map here), and back to the starting point at the gore.

Conclusions: 'An Old Country'

By the end of the Anglo-Saxon period in the 11th century, the settlement pattern of the Chilterns was well established. Many areas of woodland and waste, both large tracts and small pockets, remained, but the broad patchwork of arable and woodland is recognisable. The Domesday Survey of 1086 records this landscape, what R. Lennard called 'an old country'.[38] This survey forms the foundation for the study of the medieval period, but let us summarise the Anglo-Saxon impact in a few examples.

The network of parish boundaries was well established, as must have been the lanes and routes running up from the Vale and lowlands up into the Hills. Some are now steep, narrow roads, as at Monks Risborough or Buckland, where Dancers End Lane leads up to the Hobbit-like atmosphere of the wooded, twisting Crong. Others have remained as unmade tracks and bridleways, as at Kimble, Crowell and Lewknor. Some are actually still called 'Woodway', as at Aston Rowant and Princes Risborough. The old boundary lane between the Lee and uphill Aston Clinton is called Arrewig Lane, retaining the old Anglo-Saxon form *-weg* for 'way'. Above The Hale, the triple junction of the parishes of Wendover, Halton and Aston Clinton is marked by a splendid set of hollow-ways (Plate 21).

The Anglo-Saxon impact was marked even in parts of the Chilterns that have remained remote and secluded to this day. In the Oxfordshire Chilterns, to the north of Henley, much of Bix parish is still only accessible by single-track roads with passing-places. Yet by 1086 there were two manors at Bix, later to become known as Bix Gibwyn and Bix Brand, with considerable arable land:

> [Walter Giffard] holds 2 1/2 hides in Bix. Land for 7 ploughs. Now in lordship 2. 6 villeins have 2 ploughs. Meadow 3 acres, woodland 12 acres
> [Hervey] also holds 2 1/2 hides in Bix. Land for 7 ploughs. Now in lordship 1 plough with 1 serf. 8 villeins with 2 cottars had 5 ploughs. Meadow 3 acres, woodland 12 acres.

Even in the upland pastures above Lewknor permanent settlement had been established. Under the 1 hide held by Peter de Wheatfield in 'Levecanole' (Lewknor), but identifiable as Abbefeld, there was: 'Land for 1 plough, with 2 serfs, and 2 villeins have half a plough [i.e. 4 oxen]. There are 6 acres of meadow'.

The Anglo-Saxon achievement was remarkable. The records only give us the skeleton, showing settlement patterns, boundaries and estates. We must await the medieval records to put flesh on the bones and see the landscape and society in day-to-day functioning form.

Chapter Five

The Medieval Chilterns

The Domesday Link

We enter the medieval period with William the Conqueror in 1066. He came to the Chilterns at Berkhamsted to take over Harold's lands there. Subsequently he was to shake up the English countryside with a series of fundamental and measured reforms that stratified society and regulated the landholdings, giving him the control to float off the cream of a wealthy nation as he watched it settle after the Conquest. Not that the Anglo-Saxon society which the Normans inherited was in any way homogenous: from King Alfred's time the King and the lords of the manor had established power and created a widening gap between landowners and peasantry. But it is at this point that we can see the transition to the medieval system because William was to bequeath to us the unique treasure that recorded the countryside of England and its peoples as he found them—the document known to us as Domesday Book. Through its immaculately scribed pages we can conjure up a picture of the post-Anglo-Saxon landscape in a detail that is not available for the Anglo-Saxon period itself. Its compilation involved the King's Commissioners asking a group of jurors from each manor or estate over twenty questions about that manor, and also asking for valuations for three separate dates: pre-Conquest, for 1066-67 and for 1086. Thus we can see the Norman takeover of landholdings, especially of large estates, and we can record changes in value which may show areas wasted by the Conquest itself or conversely areas which have increased in value because they were expanded and ploughed in the space of 20 years. If we look at the Domesday entry for Berkhamsted we can see one such case of the former where Robert, Count of Mortain, was granted the borough, displacing a thane called Edmer:

> The Count of Mortain holds Berkhamsted. It answers for 13 hides. Land for 26 ploughs. In lordship 6 hides; 3 ploughs there; another 3 possible. A priest with 14 villeins and 15 bordars have 12 ploughs; a further 8 possible. 6 serfs. A dyke builder has half a hide and Ranulf, a servant of the Count, 1 virgate. In the borough of this town, 52 burgesses, who pay £4 from the tolls, half half a hide. 2 mills at 20s; 2 arpents of vines; meadow for 8 ploughs; pasture for the village livestock; woodland, 1000 swine and 5s too. Total value £16; when acquired £20; before 1066 £24, Edmer, a thane of King Harold's, held this manor.

Robert, Count of Mortain, was in fact the king's half-brother, acquiring lands in 20 different counties, and he can be seen in a section of the Bayeux tapestry in discussion with William and Bishop Odo. He was also granted the smaller Bledlow Manor where the following entry in Domesday Book occurs: 'The land of the Count of Mortain in Riseberg Hundred: The count himself holds Bledelai'.

By combining the entries for all the manors, like Berkhamsted and Bledlow, which make up the hundreds that include the Chilterns, we can gain our first overall picture of the human landscape. Previously the only reliable written evidence came from charters which gave spotlights on tiny areas but did not enable us to visualise any general pattern. What is unique about this Domesday record is that it does cover so much ground, providing us with a base map onto which we can add detailed overlays. The late Sir Clifford Darby and his associates spent decades mapping and reconstructing the geography of the Domesday Book record.[1] For the Chilterns and the surrounding counties, their maps reveal the two important features. First, the Chilterns stand out as a region of lower population density. There were fewer plough-teams

49. Ploughing. Illustration for the month of January in an 11th-century English calendar. [BL Cotton MS. Tiberius B V f3.]

(the major indicator of arable lands), and wealth per head was lower than in the Vale and surrounding lowlands. There was much woodland and very little meadow. The water-mills recorded by Domesday lie at the scarp-foot or in the lower parts of the valleys, and the water-short uplands stand out starkly. But there is a second, contrasting aspect to the Domesday record: if the Hills were underdeveloped in relation to other areas, they were still being exploited quite extensively. Population and plough-teams were inevitably lower in the Hills—this was largely dictated by topography—but they were substantial. There was much potential for expansion, but all the valleys already had their villages, hamlets and farmlands. The Chilterns were a mixture of arable and woodland by the time of Domesday Book, which gives us this first freeze-frame picture. To understand it and follow the dynamic changes of the medieval period, we need to examine the other documentary sources available and describe the elements of feudal agriculture, before looking at the detail of the medieval Chilterns.

The Medieval Documents

Beginning with the great Domesday Book survey, the medieval period provides us with a wonderful wealth of documents that chart the fortunes of local communities and reveal the lives of individuals. The written records of the Norman legal and administrative system highlight individual manors and villages, even the most obscure places and humblest people, and in medieval times we can see the life of communities in action. This wealth of documents underlies any knowledge of the medieval Chilterns, and we shall use (and illustrate) many types of record.

The first group, preserved mainly in the Public Record Office, consists of the many royal and state records of taxation, legal cases and major surveys. Taxes and subsidies such as those in 1334 and 1341, and the poll tax of 1377, demanded returns by local communities, and many of these records survive. A projected national survey of holdings and tenures in 1279, now referred to as the *Hundred Rolls*, was planned on an even larger scale than Domesday Book, and gives information about individual tenures and duties. Records survive for only a few counties, but these include the Oxfordshire Chilterns. *Inquisitiones Post Mortem* were surveys of the estates of deceased tenants-in-chief of the Crown, and they show holdings and detailed valuations of the estates (Plate 50).

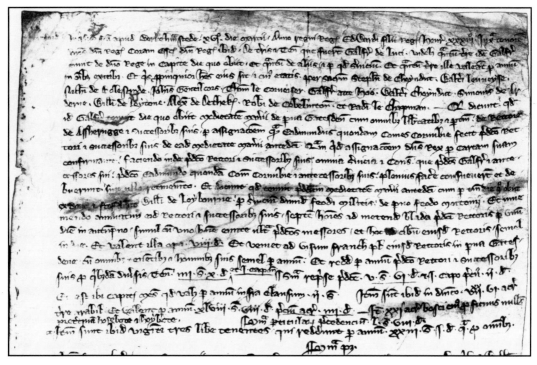

50. Extract from an *Inquisition Post Mortem* for Little Gaddesden, 16 March 1306. The estate was in Edward I's hands because the heir, a Geoffrey de Lucy, was under age. The *IPM* gives details of a portion of the manor held from the Rector of Ashridge. As well as rental and supplying labourers for the Rector, the estate also paid '4s 10d and a capon', which can be read near the bottom of the extract (underlined, four lines from bottom). [PRO: C/133/18/17.]

The second group comprises the estate records, charters and court rolls kept by landowners. The ones that have survived the centuries best are those of the church, its major bishoprics and abbeys, and of institutions such as Oxford colleges that have themselves continued to the present day. Many ecclesiastical bodies held estates in the Chilterns, and they include Canterbury, Winchester, and St Paul's, as well as the more locally-based abbeys at Dunstable, Missenden and St Albans. Several Oxford colleges (notably Christ Church, All Souls and Merton) were also Chiltern landholders, and some remain so to this day: All Souls has gradually built up the holdings in Lewknor which it first acquired in the medieval period. The best detailed year-by-year accounts are for the Bishopric of Winchester's estates (which included West Wycombe and Ivinghoe), and these reveal agricultural practices and yields. Manor court rolls and court books show land transactions, farming, local regulation and infringements; surveys, rental and extents list holdings, tenants and duties. Charters and grants record both major and minor land transactions.

Whilst undeniably excellent, this medieval record is also unquestionably biased. The written record is the product of the feudal system and administrative structure of the time. It was written by an élite, largely ecclesiastical, operating in a largely illiterate society. It is a view from the rich and powerful, both lay and church. The peasants, their activities and holdings do appear, but not in their own right, only when they interact with authority. In the Chilterns this biases our picture towards communal life and farming, rather than the more individual activities in isolated farmsteads and hamlets. But, if we recognise this bias, a great deal can still be winkled out of oblique and passing references.

Elements of the Medieval Scene

If we are to understand the distinctive nature of the medieval Chilterns we have first to identify the central elements of the feudal system of land tenure that William the Conqueror imposed. The pattern of land holdings was already very complicated by the time Domesday Book was commissioned, with many manors already in existence before the Conquest. What changed was the distribution of land and wealth and what emerged was a rigidly stratified society— summed up very neatly by W. C. Sellar and R. J. Yeatman in *1066 And All That!*:'William next invented a system according to which everybody had to belong to somebody else, and everybody else to the King'.[2] Thus the King proclaimed himself as the legal owner of all the land. Beneath him was a hierarchy of people and institutions to whom he granted land which they 'held' in return for obligations or services—military services by higher ranks, tilling the lord's lands by the lowly. We see in Domesday Book that many of the existing manors and lands were re-granted to William's followers to become great estates in the hands of either ecclesiastical institutions or lay aristocrats, who were known as his tenants-in-chief. The lord of an estate, however large or small, could either draw his income by running it himself, or he could lease it out to a sub-tenant who took over both the running of the estate and the rights over the peasantry.

The lowest unit of estate administration was the manor, and it is worth breaking it down into its separate components before venturing into the bewildering array of variations and alternatives that exist in the literature for our region and its surrounds. Much of the semantics of medieval history is very specific and needs clarification at the outset if we are to avoid being hopelessly confused when systems become complicated—as they will. The landscape of most manors comprised some or all of the following parts: the demesne, the open or common fields, the closes, the woodland, and the waste. The demesne was the lord's home farm and was usually a series of scattered strips in the large open fields surrounding the manor house. These strips were worked by the obligatory labour of his tenants, who in return for their labours and dues also held strips in the fields. These villeins (together with cottars, borders and serfs) were only semi-free: they could not leave the manor, or marry without permission, and they only had their land by the lord's favour and the custom of the manor. The open fields were cultivated on a communal basis with everyone working the same rotation so that one of the fields was always fallow and allocated for grazing. It was in this communal sense that they were 'open' and it allowed for cooperation in pasturing and ploughing. Sometimes the demesne strips were grouped into blocks, and sometimes separated completely from the tenants' strips.

The closes were very different. These were parcels of land, usually fringing the open fields, and were not under manorial control. They were normally held by a more independent group of peasants, the freeholders (*liber tenentes*), who held land solely for money rents and occasional, less servile duties. These freeholder closes were referred to as 'in severalty' (outside the communal control) and were hereditary or for life. A close by definition was land that was 'enclosed'—it was fenced and usually hedged and could come in all shapes and sizes.

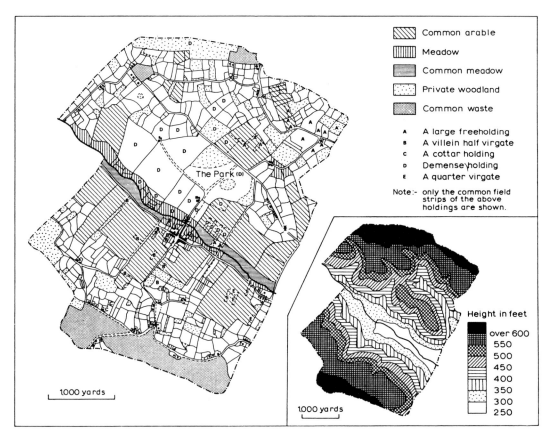

Common arable

Meadow

Common meadow

Private woodland

Common waste

A   A large freeholding
B   A villein half virgate
C   A cottar holding
D   Demense holding
E   A quarter virgate

Note:- only the common field
        strips of the above
        holdings are shown.

The Park (D)

1,000 yards

1,000 yards

Height in feet

over 600
550
500
450
400
350
300
250

51. Idealised medieval manor. This hypothetical manor illustrates the different elements in the medieval farming community in a Chiltern valley [from Roden, 1973].

The woods and the waste were the uncultivated part of the manor but they were not unimportant. The woods were such a significant part of the medieval Chilterns landscape that we devote an entire chapter to them. The waste provided additional grazing and foraging, albeit not good quality, but it also provided the opportunity to increase productivity with individuals and groups hacking away at its fringes and bringing more land under the plough.

English Medieval Landscapes
The different elements we have described could be blended in various combinations to give very different local landscapes. Across lowland England several types can be recognised. In a broad belt across the Midlands running from Yorkshire to Dorset, the medieval landscape was dominated by nucleated villages with the farming organised into communal open-field systems. Most of the parishes in this 'Midland system' had little remaining woodland or waste. There were few closes available for independent farming, and the life of the peasants revolved around the two or three common fields with their scattered strips. The landscape was open over wide expanses, with few hedges or trees to break up the scene. A very contrasting landscape could be found in much of south-east England, and to the west of the 'Midland system'. This landscape was more diverse, with many hamlets and isolated farms, dominated by hedged closes, winding lanes and patches of woodland. Where there were open-fields they were

'irregular' in comparison with their Midland neighbours—individually smaller, but more numerous, and not organised into such rigid, communal patterns. In later years, during the 16th century, writers were to describe the two types of landscape as 'champion' or open-field and 'woodland', the latter after the 'bosky' appearance given by the hedges, hedgerow trees and small woods rather than by any necessary presence of substantial woodland.

The historical origins and reasons behind these two types of medieval countryside have been much debated, and the debate goes on. Early writers such as F. Seebohm and H. L. Gray sought the origins in ethnic and racial differences.[3] Seebohm in fact used Hitchin and Wymondley in the north-east Chilterns as one of his classic examples of open-fields, but it lies right on the edge of the 'champion' countryside. We now know that the Midland system and its nucleated villages developed after the Anglo-Saxon settlement, probably in the 8th to 11th centuries, and grew out of an earlier more dispersed pattern found in Romano-British and early Anglo-Saxon times. How and why this happened is much more contentious.[4] There is little in the way of contemporary sources, and we have to read back from medieval documents that describe the system already formed.

Two factors seem to stand out. The first was the expanding population in later Anglo-Saxon times, which put pressure on the remaining waste available to pasture the animals. A solution was to allocate part of the fields for pasture and part for arable, and then to rotate the parts, giving each field a chance to rest whilst being fertilised by the animals. Each individual would have had very few animals, and there were economies of scale in managing flocks and herds, making a communal system seem sensible. Rotation of the arable and fallow meant, however, that each peasant had to have a share in the different fields, and this generated a pattern of scattered strips. In turn this scattering of strips made a central village more logical than dispersed farmsteads and cottages. In some villages a two-field system of arable and fallow was practised, in others a three-field system of two arable and one fallow (which generated higher food output if the soil was fertile enough).

The second factor combined political and tenurial changes. In late Anglo-Saxon times the multiple estates were being broken up into smaller, more discrete blocks as land was granted as semi-permanent property to individual lords and the church. This threw the new estates onto their own resources, often leaving them with less available pasture. At the same time the growing control of local lords and the manorial system reduced the independence of the peasantry, who had to meet increased dues and taxes. Strong local lordship seems to have allowed reorganisation of settlement into more nucleated villages and the allocation of strips in the large common fields. Very rarely can we see such reorganisation in action, but one, rather late example comes from near to the Chilterns. It is for Segenhoe, now called Ridgmont, near Woburn, but a hilly locality with many Chiltern characteristics.[5] There had been recent colonisation of the woods and waste, and the records of Dunstable Priory note that, around 1160, there was a re-allocation:

> At the court of each lord and by the knowledge of six old men—knights, freemen and others...
> surrendered their land under the supervision of the old men and by the measure of the perch,
> to be divided as if they were newly-won land, assigning to each a reasonable share.

Why did such a regular system not develop in south-east England? In some parts population pressure on waste and woods was less intensive, but this is not true of much of East Anglia. In some parts the power of the manorial system and local lords was less successful, and a higher percentage of independent-minded freeholders survived, but this is not true of most areas. There is no fully-accepted explanation, but Tom Williamson has argued that the difference does go back to the roots of settlement and that Anglo-Saxon settlement was more intense and more disruptive to the existing order in areas such as the Midlands.[6] Greater continuity from pre-Anglo-Saxon times in south-east England meant the region was less susceptible to major social reorganisation, and such reorganisation only occurred where *both* manorial control became strong *and* waste became in very short supply.

The Chiltern Variations

We can now return to our Chilterns region and examine how it fits in to these regional landscapes of champion and woodland. Domesday Book records the amounts of woodland for each of the villages and manors across the region. It shows that the Chilterns were one of the two great areas of woodland in south-east England. The hilly terrain and the many hamlets and isolated farms gave the Chilterns many of the characteristics of wooded or 'ancient' landscape. The line of the scarp between the Vale of Aylesbury, with its Midland-system, and the Chiltern Hills is often seen as one of the great cleavage lines between the two types of countryside, as clear a dividing line as one can find anywhere in England. This division becomes clear when we compare two of the estates granted by Walter de Merton in 1270 to the college that he had founded in Oxford, those of Cuxham and Ibstone. Cuxham, in the Oxfordshire Vale, is a classic three-field village, made renowned by Paul Harvey's detailed study using the Merton College records.[7] Virtually all the land was included in the three common fields. Ibstone is only five miles away, but up in the Chiltern Hills. Here virtually all the land was in closes, individually controlled by the manor, tenants or freeholders.[8] One farming landscape had given way to another as the scarp was crossed.

Yet this apparently vivid contrast can be a little deceptive. The difference between the two landscape types became more marked in post-medieval times, and along the scarp itself the Vale-Chiltern contrast was probably sharpest in the 18th or early 19th century. In medieval times many parts of the 'ancient countryside' of south-east England had open-fields—irregular but open-fields nonetheless—and the Chilterns were no exception to this. For if Domesday Book records very substantial woodland in the 12th-century Chilterns, it just as surely records very substantial arable farming in the returns of plough-teams and arable hides. For all its merits as a great survey, Domesday Book does not tells us how the land was farmed, or what the field-systems were like, or where within the manors the arable fields and woods were located. So much is concealed, but it does show us that the land was principally under crops in all the main manors and settlements. This fact is worth emphasising: in 1086, as in the centuries after, the Chilterns were an arable farming region.

How does this arable character fit with also being one of the two great woodland regions in south-east England? The answer is that the Hills are so dissected by the valleys and bottoms that the woodland was not in a solid, upland block with a character and economy of its own, but split up into many pieces on the steeper valley-sides and ridges. The extensive woodland has, however, sometimes lured historians into seeing the Chilterns as a 'wood-pasture region'. Even that doyen of landscape historians, Maurice Beresford, was led to write of the Buckinghamshire Chilterns: 'The medieval villagers were able to maintain themselves in these areas by exploiting the resources of a forest economy. The arable played a subordinate part in their lives ...'.[9] In fact, the relationship in the Chilterns was rather the reverse. Whilst wood-pasture and wood-products (especially fuelwood) were significant aspects of medieval Chilterns society and economy, the Chilterns were never a wood-pasture region in the sense that the major economic base was pastoral and woodland activities. This distinguishes the Chilterns from some other regions that might initially seem very comparable in settlement history—like the Weald, Arden, or the Forest of Dean—and it has implications for some later developments.[10]

Although the medieval Chilterns were arable, they did not conform to the classic Midland system with its huge open fields and minimal waste. They were heavily wooded, but they did not fall within the classic mould of pasture-woodland. Nor did they fit entirely the pattern of other ancient countryside and dispersed settlement. What we have is far more interesting: a landscape in which we can see the different elements coming together within quite small distances and within individual parishes. The balance between Midland-style and ancient woodland countryside tips one way and another in different parts of the Chilterns, giving considerable internal variety. The distinctive character of the Chiltern farming systems lies in the local combination of diversity, a combination that is ultimately deeply rooted in the local diversity of relief and soils. Howard Gray recognised something of this character in his *English Field Systems* (1915): 'The Chiltern area should, therefore, be looked upon as a boundary region so influenced in its field system by its topography that its original affiliations cannot readily be discovered'.[11] Gray inevitably wrote without detailed knowledge of the mass of medieval Chilterns documents that lead us into the complexities of the field systems. Any investigation of these today follows in the footsteps of David Roden, who has done more than any other scholar to trace the medieval landscape of the Chilterns.[12]

The medieval documents that describe Chiltern field systems date in the main from the 13th century, and especially the later 13th century. The period from 1086 to 1300 was one of rapid economic and population growth throughout England. Estimates vary greatly but current views suggest around two million people lived in England in 1086, rising to five or six million by 1300.[13] This growth was only possible because of a big increase in agricultural production, and this was partly achieved through colonisation of woods, heaths and marshes, creating new farms and fields. The Chilterns shared in this population expansion and were one of the areas of colonisation. Population within the Hills rose two or three times (the national norm) in most settlements if we compare Domesday figures for 1086 with later estimates for the 13th century, such as those based on the 1279 *Hundred Rolls*. Some grew much faster: Kensworth south of Dunstable may have increased six-fold from 1086 to 1222, and the Gaddesdens fourfold in 200 years. Outside the Hills, growth was slower; by the Thames, Marlow hardly grew at all between 1086 and 1279.[14] Since the information on farming systems dates largely from after this expansion, it will be useful to look at the colonisation before moving on to the intricacies of the Chiltern field systems.

Colonisation

The colonisation of the Chiltern woods and wastes is a long saga, reaching back long before the Conquest. If Domesday Book records a single-frame from this sequence, the medieval documents give us parts of the final reel of the film. Much of the medieval burst of expansion eludes us, happening before the records develop, or occurring as invisible peasant activity. Yet the results of all this activity can be seen, and sometimes the breaking-in of the ground, 'assarting' as it was known, is itself recorded.

The initial creation and expansion of many upland 'daughter-settlements' certainly took place before records become more available after 1150. These hamlets, originally huts for seasonal grazing, are rarely mentioned in the Domesday Book entries for their parent manors and vills, and they only emerge from nameless obscurity in late 12th- and 13th-century documents. Yet this does not mean they did not exist in 1086. Most probably did, but their final (and in many cases, substantial) expansion, filling out the agrarian landscape, took place in the 11th and 12th centuries. In some cases growth may have predated Domesday, but the population expansion from 1086 to 1300 suggests most took place later. Hamlets and villages emerge, such as Penn (a daughter hamlet of Taplow), Beaconsfield (of Burnham), and Seer

Green (of Farnham). In the hills between Chesham and Tring, the hamlets of St Leonards, Cholesbury, and Hawridge appear, off-spring in the upland portions of the Vale parishes of Aston Clinton, Drayton Beauchamp and Marsworth. In the Oxfordshire Chilterns, places like Stokenchurch, on the scarp above Aston Rowant, and Woodcote uphill from South Stoke are revealed. By 1200 most had little dependent chapelries, some of which still survive today, with pieces of Norman architecture to be seen. At Ackhamstead, the detached portion of Lewknor on the plateau near present Moor End, there was the little 'St Mary de More' chapel, where diocesan records note that Mass was said every Sunday in the 13th century. The foundations of this chapel can still be traced at Moor End.[15]

It is the latter stages of such colonisation that the records pick up. The Domesday woodlands and wastes show there were considerable reserves throughout the length of the Chilterns, though not all had agricultural potential. Assarting can be seen along their whole length, mainly in small-scale nibbling away with each valley and existing settlement. We can look at a series of examples from different parts of the Hills.

The northern Chilterns, with their rolling valleys and loamy-brickearths, were already more treeless and open in appearance than the southern parts, and medieval colonisation was to complete the process. For instance, a substantial area of upland wood-pasture existed on the borders of Bedfordshire, Hertfordshire and Buckinghamshire, in the locality of Whipsnade, Gaddesden and Kensworth. Many communities drew on this common area, and, as parochial claims led to division, it became a complicated mosaic of narrow necks, interlocking parishes and detached woodland. These woods were largely assarted in the 12th and 13th centuries. At Kensworth the 1222 *Domesday of St Paul's* describes 330 acres as an assart, and several female religious houses were founded in the local woods and assarts.[16] The Priory of St Giles-in-the-Wood was founded for 13 nuns in a woodland clearing 'with all the great assart' in Flamstead. In neighbouring Markyate the Priory of the Holy Trinity *de Bosco* (in the wood) was created, with 'The lady Christina of the wood' as the first prioress. Christina had spent years as a woodland recluse at Markyate, and a fascinating medieval biography of her survives.[17] In Nettleden, on a narrow neck between Little and Great Gaddesden which belonged to Ivinghoe parish in the Vale, a nunnery of St Margaret's de Bosco was established *c*.1160, and the grant confirming this by Thomas à Becket the famous Archbishop of Canterbury still survives in the Bodleian Library (Plate 52). St Margaret's is also still there on the map. All this medieval assarting was located cheek-by-jowl with older settlements: Markyate and Flamstead are both on Watling Street. Gaddesden is on the River Gade; it is mentioned in Anglo-Saxon charters and is only three miles upstream of the Roman villa of Gadebridge.

Many assarts were simply added to existing farm-holdings, but from this period probably date many new small hamlets and individual farms, some still bearing their medieval names. Cheverell's Green, just south of Flamstead, is probably named from the 12th-century John de Cheveron, and there are many others. At Kings Walden land was still being reclaimed in the mid-13th century, and we can see a good illustration of a new assart lying next to an earlier clearing in a grant *c*.1250 (Plate 53) in which Robert de Astholt gave Robert de Hurne land including:

> the two acres which lie in my large croft in the old assart between my demesne land on both sides; one end extends onto my new assart and the other end extends onto the land which was Matthew's; excepting the pit with water which remains with me.

With water at a premium in this region, Robert shrewdly kept his pit for himself! The Chilterns landscape is littered with 'ends' and 'greens' that mark these last stages of expansion. As assarting came to a close and the woodland diminished in the north Chilterns, so houses

52. Charter from Thomas à Becket to Ivinghoe Priory. This letter (*c*.1166) from Thomas à Becket, the famous Archbishop of Canterbury, confirms the rights of the priory in the woods of Ivinghoe (lines 3 to 4: *de bosco de Ivingehou*) and gives them protection. [Bodleian: MS Charters Bucks a.4 73.]

53. Charter from Robert de Astholt of Kings Walden. A grant *c*.1250 in which Robert gives Robert de Herne land in Kings Walden, except for his 'pit' with water. The quotation in the text is taken from lines 2 to 4. The term 'assart' appears twice in line 3, and *puteo cum aqua*, 'pit with water' in line 4. [BL: Add. Charter 35614.]

accumulated around the remaining commons, which gradually lost their remaining wood. Breachwood Green in King's Walden was wooded in 1300, but tree felling, authorised by charter in 1333, reduced it to a green before 1400.[18] In parts of these north Chilterns the clearance and assarting left very little woodland between the fields and closes of neighbouring hamlets. In some places, as at King's Walden, the field-systems of the hamlets were joined together into a larger, rather complicated system.

In the central Chilterns an Augustinian Abbey was founded at Missenden in 1133. This received many gifts and grants of land from local landowners in the 12th and 13th centuries. A 14th-century Cartulary or copy of many of the original charters is in the British Library, and Eleanor Vollans has used it to trace colonisation in the region.[19] In 1190-1200 Ingelram of The Lee granted to the Abbey *totum essartum de Pedenora* (all the assart of Pednor). We learn no more of this assart, but Peter Casselden has recently examined all the hedgerows of the Pednor ridge and valley west of Chesham.[20] Early woodland clearance can sometimes be detected by botanical techniques, recognising the relict woodland hedges by their botanical richness including slow-colonising species such as dog's mercury, bluebell and wood anemone. Casselden has mapped a number of hedges that may be relics of the medieval assart, and they are clearly differentiated from later hedgerows. Plate 73 shows one such old wood-edge near Little Pednor Farm.

The biggest area of Abbey colonisation lay on the uplands between Missenden and Wycombe, in the lands of Peterley and Kingshill and the significantly named Prestwood. Here grant after grant refers to 'land with wood' of 'land lying between woods'. The Abbey established a grange (or outlying farm) at Honor, with at least three fields. Alexander de Culewurthe gave the monks a virgate of his own lands in Hampden, and reached an agreement about common pasture (Plate 54). At Peterley, a grant of c.1170 by Faramus gave all of the land 'which the canons have surrounded with ditches and hedges, and which previously lay waste and uncultivated'.[21] To the south at Kingshill was 'Ininge Canonicorum' or 'inning' (a piece of land taken in or enclosed) of the canons, mentioned in several charters, and probably the origin of Grange Farm and Ninneywood.

The Oxfordshire Chilterns have remained the most wooded part of the Hills. There was colonisation and assarting here, but it took place earlier than that around Missenden. Most expansion probably straddles the two sides of the Norman Conquest of 1066. The surviving records reveal the results of assarting, rather than the process itself. For these areas we have a remarkable source in the *Hundred Rolls* of 1279, which paint a picture of the settlement, recording tenure and obligations at the individual level, giving much more detail than Domesday Book (Plate 55). These data have been used by two Russian historians, E. A. Kosminsky and J. R. Ulyanov, interested from a Marxist viewpoint in the transition from feudalism to capitalism.[22] Kosminsky drew attention to the high percentage of freeholders in most of the Oxfordshire Chilterns, and argued that 'perhaps the farming conditions of the wooded Chilterns were not favourable to the development of servile labour dues and villeinage'.[23] Some of these 'peculiar characteristics' (as Kosminsky terms them) date back to Domesday Book: Oxfordshire as a whole records only 23 freemen, of whom 19 were in the Chiltern parishes of Aston Rowant and Pyrton. By 1279 the distinctiveness was even more marked, and much of this must be attributed to colonisation. The Rolls need more research, but examination of the names and entries shows time and again the high percentage of freeholders in the Hill parts of these strip-parishes, with colonisers establishing their freeholding in the Hills. Ackhamstead, for instance, has nine free tenants and no villeins noted; Stokenchurch records nearly 30 freeholders, and the same is true of most identifiable hamlets.

54. Extract from the Missenden Cartulary. This extract is a grant of land at Hampden from Alexander de Culewurthe to the Abbey, c1170-79. The land was at honor (*Hanora*), between Great Hampden and Prestwood. The boundary of the land is to be marked by a ditch through 'Waltringden', with one boundary stone (*signia lapidum*) in Waltringden and the other 'beyond Hoacmer above Grim's Ditch (*ultra Hoacmer' super Grimesdic*). A hedge was to be planted on top of the ditch (*super crestam fossati*). The grant also gives the Abbey common pasture rights in the wood and field for 10 sheep, 10 oxen, 10 cows and their young, and 40 pigs. Also, when the Abbey's third field (the nearest from Grim's ditch and Alexander's land) is not sown, then Alexander and his men shall have right of common pasture on it. [BL: Harley 3688, 50 and 50v.].

This list of names gives us direct contact with the individual medieval peasants. For example, at Ipsden in 1279 they include a customary tenant, Andrew ate Wode, who held half a virgate and an assart of three acres, and a freeholder, Philipp Coleman, who held one virgate and three acres of assart, for which he paid five shillings. At nearby Wyfold there had probably been much assarting: the monks of Thame had established a grange there, and the 1279 returns

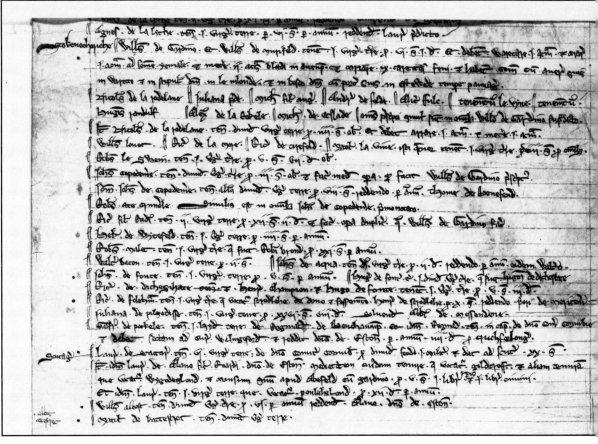

55. 1279 *Hundred Roll* entry for Stokenchurch. It gives the long list of free tenants, their holdings and their dues, beginning with William de Gardino and William de Murfeld. One of their entitlements was to feed their pigs in the wood of Eastwood 'at the time of pannage'. [Full transcription given in *Rotuli Hundredorum* (1818), II, 785-786.] [PRO: SC5 Oxford/Tower/7.]

record the tenant holding in an unusual fashion. Instead of virgates, they are recorded for ten different tenants as 'crofts' with groves or woods attached; so Peter Hok held three crofts and one grove for three shillings and two days autumn work.

Chiltern Field Systems

The descriptions of Chiltern field arrangements that we find in the 13th-century documents often show a bewildering complexity, and it should be remembered that we have no maps to help us interpret what the charters and manorial extents say until the late 16th century or even much later for most places! What is clear, however, is that open-fields, with scattered strips and communal organisation of a sort, were very widespread through the Hills. Only in the most isolated spots did they not exist at all. But the field arrangements were much more complicated than the prairie-like two- and three-field systems of the Midlands: the fields were numerous, sometimes as many as twenty or thirty, and often quite small. The closest appearance to Midland-type fields were in the largest valleys, at places like Amersham or Wycombe, and around the lowland edges of the Hills by the Thames or along the scarp-foot. Nearly every-where there were also numerous small closes, held by both villeins and freeholders, and managed separately from the common fields. One characteristic of most Chilterns' manors was that the demesne lands were mostly held in separate closes by the 13th century, rather than being themselves scattered strips in the common fields.

In these complicated Chiltern field systems, most farming still followed a standard three-course rotation: autumn-sown corn, a spring-sown corn, and fallow. Manors and communities achieved this by allocating each common field to one of the three groupings. If there were 12 common fields, then fields 1, 3, 5, 7 and 12 might be put in group A; 2, 4, 10 and 11 in group B; and 6, 8 and 9 in group C. All group A fields then sowed an autumn corn, group B a spring-corn, and group C left fallow. Such groupings could be flexible and changed periodically. Since most peasants (and the manorial demesne) did not have their holdings randomly scattered across all the common fields, but tended to have them concentrated in a few of the fields closest to their homes, the overall rotation system could create imbalances in what a peasant's strips produced: all his strips might be in fields allocated to barley and fallow-use, and so give the peasant no wheat at all! But this could be counterbalanced precisely because most peasants also held and managed their own closes. These closes could then grow the missing wheat to balance things up. The combination of closes and multiple common fields allowed great flexibility.

Such was the operational pattern of farming in the medieval Chilterns around 1300. Perhaps the most striking feature is not that the common fields were complicated and only part of the picture, but just how widespread they were. For at rock bottom the common field system was, in Harold Fox's words, 'an agricultural system founded upon a shortage of pasture'.[24] Here was a region of extensive woods, commons and scarp-crest sheepwalks still apparently short of pasture! If it was in short supply here, no wonder the Midlands were in dire straits. Yet this was the case. The quantity of common waste pasture was declining—as common woods and wastes were colonised and woods passed into severalty—and the remaining quality was low. Certainly there were areas (like the Dunstable Downs) where many sheep grazed, and then transferred the nutrients onto the fallow fields by night folding, but these areas were limited. Each parish was locked into its own territorial boundaries, literally its own 'space-capsule' and had a diminishing amount of waste grazing. Fallow and stubble grazing was essential, and growing more so. Time and again, even in hilly regions, there are references to pasture shortage.

Even so, the arable-oriented Chilterns still seem to have had bigger sheep flocks than in Vale Buckinghamshire. Demesne flocks, pastured on both downland and the fields, were anything between 200 and 900 on estates like West Wycombe and Berkhamsted. Numbers fluctuated a lot from year to year, depending on how many were kept over the winter for breeding and on the prevalence of disease. Peasant sheep flocks could also be significant. At Swyncombe in the south Chilterns, where we find 'Swyncombe Downs' today, the 1279 *Hundred Roll* notes 10 peasants, each with a smallholding of eight acres but each also freely entitled to graze 50 sheep on the common pastures. A 1332 Tax Return reveals a ratio of 20.7 sheep per taxpayer in four Chiltern Hundreds townships, contrasting with a mere 3.2-6.8 in the other Buckinghamshire Hundreds.[25] In Ellesborough at the scarp-foot, Walter Cosin had '20 rams 30s, 20 hoggets 25s, 12 ewes 14s, 10 lambs 8s 4d, fodder 17d'. Recent research has shown that several manorial demesnes in and around the Hills included specialised dairying.[26]

As the waste margins were pushed back, and population pressure increased, the Chilterns displayed many 'Midland-system' features. Yet other factors clearly slowed this trajectory and diverted it. Our knowledge of these dynamics is really quite limited, but two factors do stand out. The first is quite simply the topography: the valleys, slopes and varied soils inevitably lead to more small and irregular fields, whether these are common or enclosed.

The second is the timing of colonisation and population growth. As Christopher Dyer has written of England in general: 'Assarting as a concept and an institution was an innovation of the 12th century. Before that date new lands were incorporated into the field system and tenures of the village without being given a special status'.[27] There is a particular relevance in this statement for the Chilterns. The colonisation of many of the plateau uplands, probably in the 10th-12th centuries, led to new small open-field systems, as at Woodcote (in South Stoke parish), above Watlington village and at Stokenchurch. Small clearances were added to existing village open-fields, as with the many 'brache' (breaking in), ridding, ley and grove names found in the furlongs, like those in the charters for scarp-foot Kimble. The later, recorded assarts of the period after 1150 virtually always became closes in severalty. Where they became divided into strips with different tenants, it was as a private side-arrangement, *not* as part of the common fields. Thus David Roden has used the Court Book of Codicote to trace the history of one five-acre Crawley Croft next to the heath in Codicote.[28] Over a 50-year period between 1282 and 1336 it performed a cycle from one piece to miniature strip-field and back as portions were leased out. There are apparent exceptions: at Coleshill in 1272 Henry Sampson gave Missenden Abbey a rent charge on a plot in the *cultura* or furlong called 'Sampsonsbreche'. This was probably an assart made by an earlier Sampson, but seems to have become part of the large common field called Coleslett Field. The interpretation can be argued, but the site of Sampsonsbreche can still be seen today. The soil is still stony and flinty, and the field still abuts against the wooded boundary path of Maldemareputh as the 1272 charter says.[29]

Let us take this one stage further, even though it must be speculative and controversial. The heyday of major creation of Midland-type common field systems seems to have been the 9th-11th centuries, also an age of growing and harsh peasant obligations. Later it became more difficult to impose or agree such communal landscape revolutions. Where arable communities ran out of pasture resources in the earlier phase, the economic rationale of open-fields was imposed or agreed. Where such pressure only occurred later, and built up more slowly, more individualistic and hamlet-based patterns persisted and were expanded, with both old and new enclosures side by side. This seems to be true of the Chilterns, and we wonder whether places like Kings Walden—where several hamlet-based field systems came to rub up against each other—would have been taken by the scruff, nucleated and replanned if the waste had run out four centuries earlier? Whatever the speculations about origins, the Chiltern systems of the 13th century worked through a combination of closes and common fields. The balance varied across the region, but within each parish there was usually a local mixture of elements, best illustrated by looking at three contrasting examples.

Watlington

Watlington is a classic strip-parish in the Oxfordshire Chilterns, with a mixture of common fields, upland colonisation and isolated farms. Below the scarp is a large area of good soils where Watlington village (and later market-town) grew up. The parish then extends up the steep hillside to the flat plateau, and a thin neck leads deeper into the Chilterns.

At Domesday Book there was land here for 21½ ploughs, but only 18 or 19 were working so land use was not at capacity. Conversions of medieval measures to acres are hazardous, but the Russian historian J. R. Ulyanov made a special study of Watlington using Domesday Book, the *Hundred Rolls* and *Inquisitiones Post Mortem*.[30] He calculated that the total arable increased by some 50 per cent in the 200 years after Domesday. A charter of 1217 mentions ten assarts, but most colonisation predates such records.

The medieval farming pattern shows a common field system around the village. A mid-12th-century grant suggests a two-field system by referring to 20 acres of demesne, 10 acres in one field and 10 in another (*in uno campo...in alio campo*), but by 1272 there was a three-course rotation.[31] This may hint at a two- to three-field conversion, but equally Watlington may always have had the multiple fields it had in post-medieval times. Outside the village there

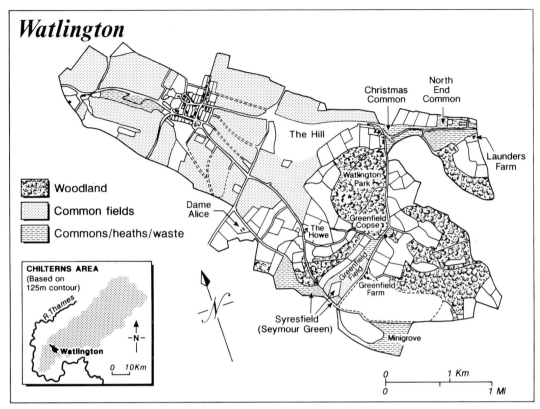

56. Watlington Parish, c.1800 before parliamentary enclosure. [Based on Lobel (1964) and the inclosure award and map in Oxfordshire Record Office.]

were hamlets in scarp coombes at Watcombe (now The Howe) and on the plateau at Greenfield and Syresfield (later Seymour Green). These seem to have had a mixture of closes and small open-fields. The 1279 *Hundred Roll* shows a very substantial freehold population (more than twice the number of villeins) and many substantial freeholders are associated with these Chiltern hamlets, such as Richard and John de Syresfield, William de Hattecomb (Watcombe) and possibly Richard de la Feld. Beyond the plateau commons (Christmas Common today) lay the isolated farm of Launders, still there today. In c.1216 the freeholder Henry de Lavenora (Launders) granted a wood 'which is between my stony croft and Pyrton wood', and in 1279 the freeholder Simon de Lavenore held one virgate for a rental of ten shillings.

Codicote

Codicote lies in the north-east Chilterns, rising from the floodplain of the little river Rhee, and its medieval field system typified this part of the Chilterns. By the 13th century there was some remaining heathland, but very little woodland, and assarting had reached its limits. The parish contained the substantial village of Codicote, with its weekly market, and several isolated farms and hamlets around greens. The manor was held by the Abbey of St Albans and their Court Book preserves much fascinating detail.[32]

Most of the cultivated land was arable, with one-third in common fields and two-thirds in severalty. The closes varied greatly in size: most tenant closes were less than 10 acres, but

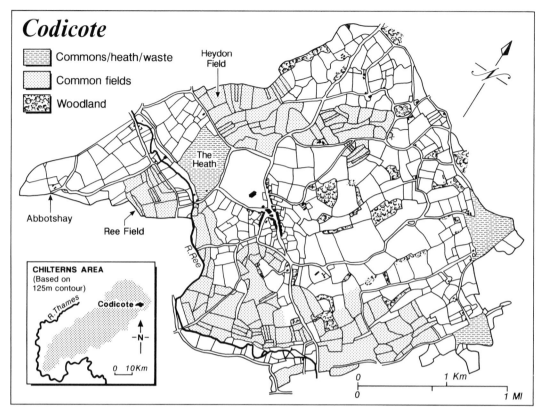

57. Codicote, showing common and enclosed fields *c*.1600 (with detail of field-boundaries from map *c*.1800). [Based on Roden, 1965 and 1973.]

some demesne closes were large, with one of 60 acres. Pasture was very limited and carefully stinted; in 1332 'each acre of Codicote is extended at four sheep at the time of fallow'. The common fields numbered at least 20, including names such as Heydon Field, Marcolf Field, Ree Field and Thurboldescroft. Tenants held very varying proportions of common strips and closes: in 1291 all of Aldith Colesmith's 10 acres was enclosed, whilst all of Edward de Bromeshale's five acres were common strips. But most held a mixture, like Margaret Carpenter in 1300 with two acres of close and three of common. Tenant strips were also strongly clustered in subsets of the fields, suggesting that holdings originated in earlier hamlet-based colonisation. Over this mosaic of common fields the Abbey superimposed a three-course rotation, probably in a very varied pattern. The inevitable imbalances were met by adjusting the sowing of the closes, as is shown by the demesne records for 1332: the first demesne cropping course comprised 82 acres in the common fields and 53 acres in enclosed fields; the second course was entirely on common arable in two fields; and the third was entirely on enclosed demesne lands.

Ibstone

Our third example is Ibstone, a hilltop parish on a ridge south-east of Stokenchurch, and includes the northern side of the dry Turville valley.[33] The land-unit is pre-Conquest in origin, and at Domesday (and long after) Ibstone lay half in Oxfordshire and half in Buckinghamshire. This strange anomaly that may be due to late pre-Conquest colonisation. Certainly at Domes-

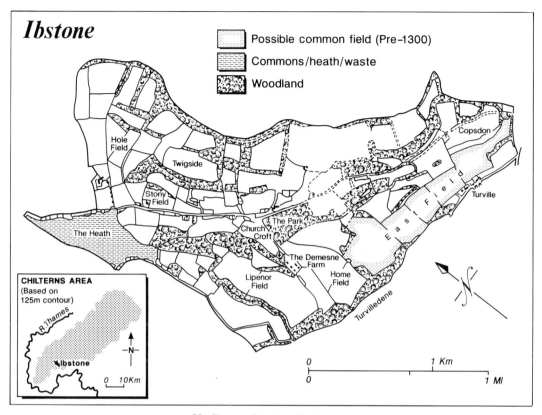

58. Ibstone [based on Roden, 1966].

day it was held by one 'Tovi', a Danish name (and probably the same man as 'Novitovi' who granted parts of Lewknor to Abingdon Abbey). Danish landowners may have helped carve out a frontier estate here in the 10th-11th centuries.

By the late 13th century, when Merton College acquired the estate, all assarting had ended, though two crofts were called 'Inning' and 'Saarte'. Nearly all the cultivated land was in closes. There may have been a residual open-field at 'Eastfield', abutting Turville village, but even this was on the way out, and demesne and tenant farming (for both freeholders and villeins) was organised around the closes, some of them very large (30-70 acres). The emphasis was on arable farming with a standard three-course rotation, with larger closes being temporarily subdivided into cropping units. The important sheep flocks were folded on the fallow, and it is noteworthy that pasture was scarce, despite the apparently large areas of wood and waste. Carts taking wood to Cuxham would return with hay. The folding seems to have been done close by close, not in common, and it was a very individualistic system, contrasting sharply with the common fields of Merton's Cuxham estate. Most of the wheat crop was sold, being taken to Henley or High Wycombe for the London market. Ibstone is a pointed illustration: of the role of arable and shortage of pasture even deep in the Hills; of the importance of individual farming at an early date; and of linkage to a wider commercial market.

Controlling the Community

To modern eyes one of the strangest and most alien features of the medieval Chilterns scene is just how communal and cooperative it had to be to work at all, both to survive and to prosper. The Chilterns farming allowed a lot more individuality than did real champion countryside, but there still had to be a large measure of community decision-making, control and enforcement. The manorial court rolls, Court Books and by-laws record this process. The feudal system enforced the obligations of the many to the few, and insisted on the rights of the lords. The documents record the villagers' duties of services and rents, and fines for failure. In addition to their feudal obligations, villagers also had to cooperate and obey by-laws on the farming system. Regulations for ploughing, harvesting and pasturing had to be agreed and enforced.

We have already seen that tenant and villein services varied enormously from manor to manor, and specific services varied with individual holdings and dues. Some records lay these duties out in detail. One example is from the Bec Custumal for the village of Bledlow, and it concerns a William Ketelburn.[34] William held half a hide of land for 9s. a year. In return he did not have any week-work (giving up time every week to work the lord's lands), but he had a long list of seasonal boon services. He had to plough and harrow in both the winter and Lent sowings, and again in the fallow in summer. He was obliged to hoe for a day, mow for six days and carry the hay to the carts. William also must reap the lord's corn in autumn for three boonworks—any more and the lord had to pay extra, pay pannage for pasturing his pigs on the beech-mast, and after that he could pasture his own sheep until Lady Day. In addition his daughter could not marry without the lord's permission, and on his death the lord was entitled to his best beast.

Many manors had much more onerous services than these, but gradually rent payments tended to replace direct duties, especially week-work, and the lords used more of their own hired labour. Whether it was rent or services, the landlords wanted their pound of flesh. The religious houses were amongst the most strict, and St Albans Abbey had periodic conflicts with tenants over duties and holdings. One widespread manorial right was that all corn should be ground at the lord's mill, the lord receiving a toll or 'multure' of the corn ground, and the Abbots of St Albans were firm on these rights. Peasants and townsmen alike often wanted to use their own hand-querns, and a serious conflict broke out in St Albans in 1331-32. The Abbey seized the hand-querns, and added insult to injury by setting them into the floor of the monks' parlour. The young Abbot at the time was the talented Richard of Wallingford (Plate 75). Having then asserted his authority in St Albans, Richard subsequently took a more relaxed view, and he was soon licensing hand-mills in Codicote, to Stephen le Bray and John Dolitel for 1d. and 2d. a year.[35]

Regulation in the fields was often set out in village by-laws, and they do not leave us with the impression of a placid, honest or well-behaved workforce.[36] The by-laws tried to prevent the locals from getting up to no good, and court rolls give examples of those caught. Controlling the day-to-day activities in the fields was primarily the responsibility of the Reeve. His was a very important post, looking after crops, rotations and productivity. The officer in charge of the lord's arable was the Hayward, and he was generally paid with a parcel of land. He sometimes received help from a group of 'Wardens of the Autumn (or Harvest)' who were elected officials. In this role they were village rather than manorial officials as they did not perform services for the lord, nor were they paid. In Halton near Wendover, their sworn duty was 'to see the observances of these ordinances [the by-laws], to attach wrongdoers if any are found, and to present wrongdoers [to the court]'.

The *Seneschaucy*, a book of advice to Stewards and officials, paints a marvellous picture of peasants disappearing with grain stuffed into every available garment: 'The Reeve should take care that threshers and winnowers do not take corn and carry it away in their dress, boots, shoes, and pockets or in sacks and bags hidden near the grange'.[37] The by-laws of Halton demonstrate the lengths to which it was necessary to go to prevent such removal in pockets

59. Harvesting in medieval times. The reeve overseeing the peasants reaping the harvest. From the Queen Mary Psalter, early 14th century. [BL: Royal MS 2 B VII, f.78v.]

and boots. 'No one shall cart by night but only between sunrise and sunset'; the cover of darkness was not allowed. Harvest hands should be paid their wages in sheaves at the barn door, not in the field, and 'No one shall pay anyone with sheaves in the field unless he reap for sheaves'. A Matilda Trystram was fined in Halton on Wednesday, 16 November 1379 because she stole four sheaves.[38]

There were similar sets of regulations in villages to control pasturing. In 1329 the Halton by-law stated that 'No one should enter stubble with their sheep before pastured by the beasts of the plough'. Straying animals were always a problem. The Halton Rolls record infractions when Roger Marewell and others 'let their sheep in the stubble in autumn time before the plough-beasts have depastured it and against the ordinance of autumn'.[39]

How many animals you could graze, and exactly where, was also controlled, tied into holdings and tenancies and often specified in grants and charters. In King's Walden in 1319 a grant by Isabella Passelewe and her son to John de Dokesworth specified pasturing rules for Ashcroft field. Rights of common pasture existed in the field, but numbers were stinted 'according to the measure of their lands'. Beasts and horses could be turned in only after Michaelmas, and sheep had to wait until after the Feast of All Saints. In Codicote there was a similar limit on the number of beasts allowed. In 1332 three tenants were presented to the court because they overstocked the common pasture (Plate 60). The jury responded that each acre of Codicote is extended at four sheep at the time of fallow. This is not many by present-day standards where we see fields of artificially-fertilised grass maintaining scores of sheep at a time. Grazing rights in the complicated Chiltern field-systems were usually confined to men holding land in the fields specified. At Caddington those without strips in Mill Field and North Field were not allowed to pasture there.

Improving the System

We must not see medieval farming as unchanging or static, though ultimately the system was

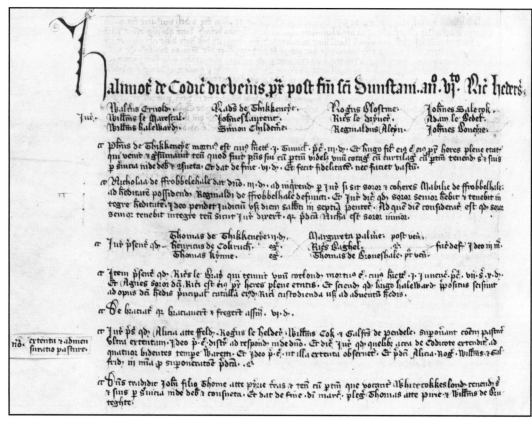

60. extract from, Codicote Court Book 1332. This records cases before the manorial court of Codicote of which St Albans Abbey was the Lord of the Manor. The marginal entry refers to *extenda at admensuratio pasture*, and here three tenants are being censured for overstocking the common pasture. The jury record that 'each acre of Codicote is extended at 4 sheep at time of fallow'. [BL: Stowe 849, 55v.]

unable to generate long-term and sustained growth. Medieval landlords and peasants were constantly trying to improve their lot, endeavouring to keep body and soul together as population grew and there was less land to go round. These struggles to grow more food and to add to family incomes sometimes brought landlord and peasant into conflict as their interests diverged.

In the Chilterns there were several ways of increasing food output, and we have already looked at colonisation or extending the land-margin. This was the first line of attack in the battle for more food and income. Another route was to intensify production, to get more productivity out of the existing land. In many parts of the country this meant increasing arable at the expense of pasture, with the risk of reducing soil fertility. Replacing animals with crops effectively shortened the food chain and reduced energy loss, and labour could be used to increase productivity (though poor labour productivity was probably more of a barrier to growth than poor land productivity in medieval times). Writers used to see transitions from two- to three-field open systems as an example of such intensification, reducing pasture from half the area to one third. Harold Fox's research has, however, largely quashed this notion; the choice of two- or three-field system was a question of basic soil conditions, not progressive change.[40] The natural fertility was the deciding factor, and few villages changed from two- to three-fields. One notable exception is in the extreme south Chilterns at South Stoke where, in

1240, a freeholder accused the Abbot of Eynsham of depriving him of his common pasture by dividing into three parts land which had previously been in two. In most of the Chilterns the irregular field systems sidestepped such issues, and reorganisation of the fields was more piecemeal and small-scale.

These piecemeal changes concerned the scattering of strips in the common fields. Explanations of the logic of common fields are weakest on this scattering, and it is not an essential feature. Some argue it spread risk; others that it was equitable when major changes took place (as at Segenhoe or South Stoke). From the lord's viewpoint, each strip had a price-tag in terms of labour services and scattering kept individual tenants politically weak and in line. Perhaps the most convincing argument is that of Carl Dahlman, who argues that scattering gave everyone a strong commitment to the efficient working of the system—they needed to cooperate and could not opt out if they felt like it.[41] In the medieval period it was certainly a source of tension. Landlords who held consolidated holdings themselves often resisted tenants who tried to do the same and make their holdings more compact and efficient, with less wasting of time.

When looking at the documents for individual estates and manors, one is immediately struck by the sheer volume of activity recorded. Pages and pages of immaculately listed transactions show parcels of land changing hands in a constant stream of swapping and selling. It is only when we sift through and look at the acquisitions and losses of an individual that we can observe the reasoning behind such an active land market. Peasants worked to build up holdings, and if possible group them into convenient lots, reducing the complicated jiggery pokery of scattered strips. Younger sons, inheriting little, could sometimes put together viable holdings. In the Chilterns both freeholders and villeins engaged in this. We have chosen one

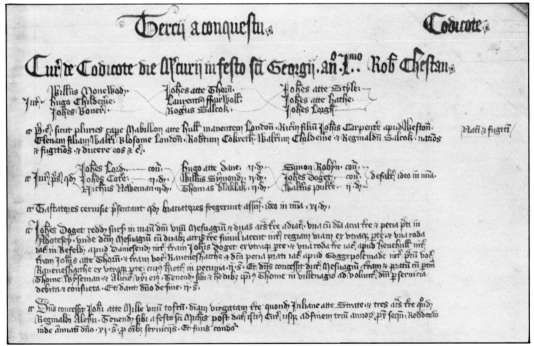

61. Holdings of John Doget recorded in Codicote Court Book. This extract (in the large paragraph) gives holdings of John Doget who, over a period of time, acquired several new pieces of land in Ree field adjacent to his existing pieces, only to surrender them 16 years later. His holdings included portions at 'Abotesey', today the farm of Abbotshay to the south of Ree field. [BL: Stowe 849 104.]

62. Abbot Robert de Norton. A very strict lord of the manor who clashed frequently with his tenants. [GESTA ST. ALBANI, BL Cotton Claudius Eiv (1) f113v.]

such villein (because his name has a familiar ring to it) to illustrate the point, from the Court Book of Codicote.[42] In 1362 John Doget obtained four pieces of land in Ree Field next to land he already held there (Plate 61). Ree Field is still there today—we photographed it in late summer newly ploughed, exaggerating the contrast between the brown soil of the arable of what was the large open field and the smaller green meadows near the river (Plate 80). John Doget did not enclose his pieces, but surrendered them 16 years later to another tenant.

In Berkhamsted an Adam Pusse was accumulating land in the common field of Lokslade, acquiring four parcels next to land he already held there in 1295-97. In King's Walden both demesne and tenants were active in such transactions. In 100 surviving charters that record land transfers between 1250 and 1330, at least 33 involved land next to existing holdings of the purchaser, and 23 of these were in common fields. John de Dokesworth was particularly active here, where he held one of the manors, and in all he acquired 22 different pieces next to land he already held, eventually amalgamating his enlarged holdings in Flexmore Field and Pyricroft.[43]

This very active peasant land market saw family and individual fortunes rise and fall. In Codicote the St Albans Abbot Robert de Norton tried in 1275 to restrain and control the market by a set of strict ordinances, stopping villeins and freeholders exchanging lands and insisting on registration through the manorial court. But locals transferred by charter instead, and the Cartulary for 1280 notes 24 charters recording transfers from local freeholders to villeins who lived in Codicote.[44] Despite the activity in the peasant land market, however, it was mainly manorial lords (some quite small scale) rather than peasants who benefited from consolidation.

Two further routes towards economic growth were improvements in technology, and commercialisation of the market.

Technology and Innovation

The Middle Ages was not a period of great innovation in agricultural technology, but compared with earlier periods there was a quickening in the tempo of invention. Experts have recently studied the introduction and diffusion of three significant innovations: the windmill, horse-ploughing, and the use of legumes such as the vetch. The patterns show the character of our Chilterns region, its peculiar identity and its role in innovation and agricultural change.

The mills recorded in Domesday Book were water-powered, and the first documented windmill is in 1185. The new invention spread rapidly across the country in the 13th century.[45] The Chilterns participated in this spread, for wind-power brought corn-grinding to dry and upland areas, whereas previously only hand-quern grinding was possible, or else one faced a long haul down to scarp-foot water-mills. Thus we see Merton College building a hilltop windmill at Ibstone in 1293-94. But the Chilterns were not distinctive in this spread. The windmill was too useful to be restricted by region, and it became a feature across most of lowland England. Along with other parts of the country, the medieval skyline of the Chilterns would have been punctuated by as many mill-sails as church towers. Across the Hills surviving mills, of post-medieval date, are a picturesque feature at Pitstone and Ibstone, and at Cholesbury, Coleshill and Lacey Green.

The two other innovations show a more regional pattern, and reveal the Chilterns as an area of early adoption. At Domesday nearly all ploughing was done by teams of oxen, and so it remained for much of the country. In the south and east, however, horses began to play a greater role—first for carrying and hauling wagons to market, and then for ploughing. Horses for hauling are recorded in many medieval accounts: a Penn manorial account for 1372 notes: 'and in food for horses hauling 'tallwoods' to the Thames ... 6 bushels'.[46] John Langdon has traced in great detail the spread of horse-use in ploughing on demesne farms, both as mixed horse-oxen teams and as all-horse teams. His maps show a slow diffusion (Plate 63), but early adoption in Norfolk, east Kent and along the Chilterns: 'Soils undoubtedly accounted for the presence of all-horse farms on or very close to the Chiltern Hills ... a string of demesnes from Wheathampstead and Kingsbourne in Hertfordshire to Checkendon in Oxfordshire'.[47] Horses coped much better with the thin and stony soils, on which oxen slipped, whilst oxen coped better with the heavier soils of the Midland Vales. Walter of Henley advocated the oxen rather than the horse-plough: 'if the lande be not stonye so that the oxe cannot helpe himselfe with his feete'.[48]

The adoption was not just a function of the stony, flinty Chiltern soils. Horse-ploughing was also much more flexible for smaller-scale operations than were oxen. The Chiltern land-scape was one where individual peasant landholdings covered the greater part of the cultivated area. The enclosed fields, dispersed smallholdings and small, irregular open-fields could be much better cultivated by the adaptable horse than by large-teams of oxen plodding slowly and laboriously and demanding enormous turning circles. Horses could plough small, awkwardly-shaped closes faster and straighter than oxen, and they could also be used for a range of non-ploughing activities. Against this, the ox was cheaper to feed, and had a use on retirement, as Walter of Henley notes:

> And when the horse is olde (and worn out) then hathe he nothing but his skynne. But when the oxe is olde with xd. [10d.] of grasse he wilbe made fatte to kylle or to sell for as muche as he coste youe.[49]

Adoption of horse-ploughing seems to have spread upwards from the peasant farmers to the demesnes. We can watch the replacement of oxen by horses on the Bishop of Winchester's West Wycombe estate by looking at the Pipe-rolls. The earliest rolls for 1217 show 31 oxen and nine work-horses or affers, but after 1320 there is a complete reversal to 18 horses and no oxen. The surviving 1332 Taxation records for Buckinghamshire show how the better-off peasantry (those within the scope of the Tax) also followed the demesne and smallholder pattern. At Medmenham and High Wycombe, the demesnes were all-horse, as were all the peasant plough-animals, whilst at Beaconsfield and Penn there was a mixture, but with horses predominating.[50]

This picture of the Chilterns as an innovative region is reinforced by study of 'the humble vetch'. Bruce Campbell has linked the increased use of legumes such as the vetch as fodder crops with the introduction of all-horse farms.[51] The growing of leguminous crops to replenish nitrogen in the soil and to provide feed for livestock was only slowly adopted in many regions, and there is a striking coincidence between the areas of early adoption and the map of horse-domination. Campbell notes the close association between vetch cultivation and the chalk and limestone uplands of south-east England, and 'in particular a band of demesnes can be identified scattered along the chalk belt, stretching north-eastwards from Berkshire, along the line of the Chiltern Hills ...' towards Norfolk. The pattern reflects localities with poor endowments of meadow rather than stony soils, but the other factors are the same: flexible field-systems and cropping, and peasant-led innovation spreading to demesnes, together with market-connections. What these innovations show is that the Chiltern Hills, although not endowed with the best soils or terrain—and so somewhat 'marginal' in physical terms—were not marginal in economic terms in the medieval period. Rather the opposite.

The Growth of Markets, Towns and Trade

The population expansion and agricultural growth of medieval England generated a corresponding increase in trade and commerce. New markets and fairs were created to attract local trade and exchange; new towns were 'planted' to stimulate commerce; markets and

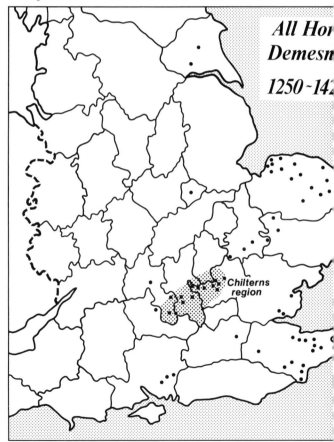

towns grew to deal with longer-distance trade in corn and other commodities. As the economy and population of the Chilterns grew between 1200 and 1350, the region shared in this increased commercial life. The area started from quite a low base, but offered landlords and traders good opportunities, both for local commerce and for supplying the rapidly-growing London market.

Domesday Book records few boroughs or markets in or around the Chilterns. Berkhamsted is noteworthy with its 52 burgesses, and further into Hertfordshire there was the much more significant centre of St Albans. Tolls, probably indicating markets, are mentioned for Aylesbury and Luton. The markets at Marlow, Wendover and Wycombe also seem to be early, established by custom rather than explicit charter. After c.1200 landlords sought charters to create markets and

63. The distribution of all-horse demesnes and vetch cultivation in medieval England. These maps of two medieval innovations illustrate the nature of the Chilterns as a progressive farming region. [Based on Langdon, 1986, and Campbell, 1988.]

fairs on their lands, hoping to benefit from the rents and commerce.[52] Some were just once-a-year fairs, some local weekly markets and others more ambitious. Not all succeeded, but all were trying to benefit from the economic expansion of the region.

Most were unpretentious gatherings with little capital outlay where a combination of agricultural produce (grain, vegetables, livestock), prepared foods (such as bread and ale), and craft products such as leather and cloth were sold. Alongside these were the 'imported' goods brought by travelling chapmen, who sold ironware, salt, fish and coal. We see just such a market in Codicote, where in 1268 the Abbot and monks of St Albans were granted the right to hold a weekly market on their manor. By the end of the century there was a flourishing small market centre, and the Court Books record cottages, shops, stalls and vacant plots with storehouses within and around the market place. At Watlington a grant in 1252 created a regular Wednesday market, followed by a Saturday market and yearly fair in 1302. Other markets included Amersham (1200), Beaconsfield (1255) and Chesham (1257). At Ivinghoe the Prioress and nuns of St Margaret de Bosco were granted an annual fair in 1227, held on the vigil and feast days of St Margaret and the five succeeding days. Much later, in 1318, the much more significant local landlord, the Bishopric of Winchester, obtained a grant for a Thursday market in Ivinghoe. The Pipe-rolls record that the Bishopric then spent 28s. 2d. on building a lath-and-plaster 'seld' or small market-hall 54-ft. long and 10-ft. wide. The market thrived, acquiring within 30 years inhabitants called Carpenter, Sawyer, Cooper, Smith, Threadman, Capper and Chapman.[53]

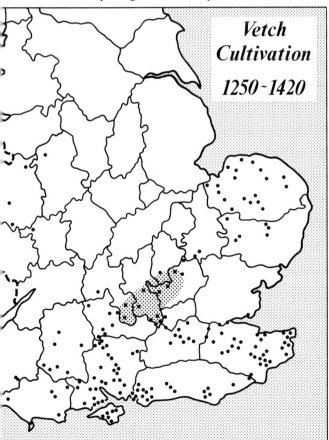

Vetch Cultivation 1250-1420

This expansion left the Chiltern counties well endowed with a dense network of small markets and fairs, more dense in the Vale and lowlands around the Hills than within the Hills themselves. Which markets then grew to become regional centres and boroughs depended on fortunate siting: location on major national routes or at key points in regional trade flows. Dunstable, Wycombe and Henley provide the best Chilterns examples.

Dunstable was a 'planted' town, one of the first such recorded in England.[54] Henry I created the town by charter around 1119, locating it right on the crossroads of the Icknield Way and Watling Street, the major road from London to the midlands and north-west. It proved to be a profitable location, and Matthew Paris (a St Albans monk) focused the centre of his schematic map of England on the spot. The charter granted that 'the men of Dunstable and their heirs shall have the liberties and quitances throughout his whole kingdom that the city of London or any borough of England has had from old'.

Twelve years later Dunstable Priory was founded, and granted the borough with four fields lying around the vill, the market and schools of the vill and common pasture in four surrounding parishes. This amounted to 450 acres taken out of Henry I's manor of Houghton Regis. Fairs were to be held at St Peter's Tide, together with a weekly market. The early management of the town was formalised in a set of Customs drawn up in 1221. They illustrate all too graphically just how unsavoury medieval urban life must have been:

:Shopkeepers must not have pigsties outside their doors
:Butchers must not cast blood and filth into the street
:A Burgess might have a dunghill so long as it did not obstruct the King's highways
:Market booths must be cleared away on the day of the market
:Victuals must not be sold before 1:00

This town at the crossroads thrived, and became an important centre for the wool trade, collecting not just from the Chiltern downlands but from a wide surrounding area. Dunstable wool merchants became rich and important in the 13th century. Sixteen were granted export licences in 1271-74. The Duraunts were particularly prominent.[55] John Duraunt's goods were valued at a massive £20 16s. 8d. in the 1297 assessment, and his house was later used by the royal retinue when they travelled to tournaments. By 1329 it needed repair to bring it to the required standard, and seven carpenters, six tilers and two plasterers worked for nine days using 1,000 tiles, 1,000 lathes and over 4,000 nails. When Thomas Duraunt gave a local feast, the Chronicler of Dunstable Priory notes 'our prior was present against all the rules of the house. But he must be excused, for we were in debt to the said Thomas for a great sum and therefore dared not offend him'.

Dunstable became wealthier than Bedford itself, and a taxation return for 1297 identifies goods and activities in the borough. As well as animals and cereals they include tiles and lime; skins; tanning stock; felt; meat; skinners' stocks; fish; grease and tallow; fruit; wood and charcoal; spices; iron; leather; cloth; poulterer's stock; malt; and the contents of a tannery.

Further south, High or Chipping (Market) Wycombe was also on an important route cutting through the Chilterns from London to the Midlands, Oxford and the royal palace of Woodstock. This highway is shown on the Gough map made around 1335. Wycombe grew as a regional centre and as a half-way point to break journeys between London and Oxford. The market developed in the 12th century, and as it grew the merchants or burgesses struggled to get the independence to run their own affairs.[56] The battle was protracted and complicated, as in many other towns. The right to become a free borough was a fundamental one; it meant the town was separated from the surrounding 'unfree' countryside. In Wycombe the prolonged legal battle ended in 1226, when the local lord Alan Basset granted them 'the whole borough of Wycombe, with its rents, markets and fairs and all other things to a free borough pertaining, without any reservation'. The market-place was large and early 13th-century grants by Adam Walder to Godstow Abbey refer to two 'seldes' or market-booths in Wycombe market-place, lying between the selde of Robert of Croinden and that of Robert Rut'. In 1226 the burgesses included Baldwin le Seler (saddler), Simon the Tanner, Ralph the Smith and Hugh the Smith. Other 13th-century names indicate the variety of trades in the borough and include Fuller, Potter, Mercer, Draper, Goldsmith, Baker, Bowyer, and Cornmonger. It was the corn trade that gave Wycombe, along with Henley, a wider regional significance, and it is the regional nature of that corn trade we must now look at.

Recent research has shown that medieval London was probably a city of 80-100,000 people in 1300, much larger than previously thought and possibly the second largest European city north of the Alps. The 'Feeding the City' project run by the Centre for Metropolitan History in London has been investigating the impact of this city on its hinterland.[57] Such a city

64. Bread making. Bread was the staple food in medieval times. Wycombe became the centre of a bread-making industry with royal patronage, using the high yields of wheat from the Winchester Estates. In 1241 Henry III ordered a hundred shillingsworth of good bread at four loaves a penny to be delivered for his festivities. [BL: Royal 10 E iv f145v.]

would have consumed more than a million bushels of grains and burnt over 100,000 tons of wood each year, and the project is uncovering a wide regional network of trade to supply this wood and grain. Much of south-east England became engaged in this supply, but especially areas close to navigable rivers or the sea, for transport by water was much cheaper than by road. It is becoming clear that the southern Chilterns, close to the Thames, were very active in this trade.

The early medieval grain trade was very much the preserve of large estates. Some of their records have also survived, as with the Bishopric of Winchester's accounts. Such estates engaged in 'internal' trade, moving goods between their manors to meet their own needs, often aided by 'carrying service' or *averagia* specified in the customary duties of their tenants and villeins.[58] These estate records sometimes show the transport of grain or wood to London, as to the Bishop of Winchester's estate at Southwark, and these must be distinguished from genuine market sales to London. By the late 12th and 13th centuries this trade was becoming more commercial and large-scale. In 1210-11 the Winchester estates of Brightwell, Harwell, Wargrave and West Wycombe hired boats to carry 1,130 quarters of grain by water to London at 2½d. or 3d. per quarter, but this transport cost was only six per cent of the final price when the grain was sold in Southwark market.[59] Soon, however, they ceased to do their own shipping, and middlemen and London merchants entered the trade. The Thames became a major grain route from the south Chilterns to the City. The 'Feeding the City' project has examined demesne accounts for sample years within the period 1288-1315 for eight manors in or around the Chilterns. They are Berkhamsted, Bledlow, Ibstone,

65. Medieval Carter. This carter is driving a four-wheeled cart, loaded with wrapped merchandise. He sits on the horse, probably safer if the roads are bumpy. [BL: Royal MS 10 E iv f41.]

Ivinghoe, Watlington, Wendover, Whitchurch and West Wycombe. All eight manors sold a substantial proportion of their wheat, ranging from 43 per cent to 95 per cent of 'net receipt', the amount of grain available after deductions of tithe and seedcorn.

Chipping Wycombe became an important collection point for wheat and barley from the Chilterns, most notably the Winchester estate at West Wycombe. Some was shipped from Marlow and Hedsor (where a medieval wharf was excavated earlier this century), whilst some may have travelled by road despite the poor quality of some medieval highways. In 1351 Walter Neel a London corn-dealer left a bequest in his will for the repair of the highway from Newgate to Wycombe.[60]

Henley in the south Oxfordshire Chilterns was, however, the main beneficiary of this London grain trade, becoming the major centre for grain from the south Chilterns and the entire Upper Thames region. How this came about is an interesting story, unearthed by the Oxford historian R.H.C.Davis.[61] Henley does not appear at all in historical records until 1179, when the king bought land there 'for making buildings'. By 1269 the town had a merchant guild, with 46 members in 1296. The principal reason why Henley grew to dominate the Upper Thames trade was the state of navigability of the River Thames itself. We know that at the very beginning of the medieval period it was navigable up to Wallingford, Abingdon and even Oxford. At this time Wallingford was the regional centre for south Oxfordshire and parts of Berkshire, and several manors (such as Harwell) named Wallingford in their feudal right to carrying-services. Davis showed that this trading pattern changed as the river became less navigable. As the number of mills increased vastly along its banks, so did the number of weirs associated with them. These made transport quite perilous as boats had to 'ride the flash', and they also decreased the volume of water and encouraged the silting up of certain sections. Navigation beyond Henley became extremely difficult, and by 1250-1300 the town was effectively the head of navigation. Now goods to and from Oxford, Abingdon and Wallingford would be trans-shipped at Henley, being taken west by pack-horse or cart. One such journey is that of a new millstone bought by Witney in 1304 for 40s. 3d. in London. It cost 13½d. to load it from wharf to ship, but only 2s. to sail it to Henley. It then cost 9d. to transfer it to a cart, 4d. in toll at Wallingford, and 18d. for the cost of two labourers and four horses taking it to Witney.[62]

The big suppliers owned or rented granaries in Henley, selling their grain to the corn-dealers or bladers. The Merton College archives show that the manor of Ibstone did this in the 1290s, and the Merton manor of Cuxham regularly sent grain across the south Chilterns to Henley. In 1279 the tenants of Cuxham swore they were not obliged to carry their lord's grain except to Henley, Ibstone or Wallingford. Wills show the involvement of London bladers. One such was Adam Wade (died 1310), who had two granaries in Henley, a stone house next to the bridge, as well as interests at the major London corn wharf Queenhithe.[63]

The 'Feeding the City' project is continuing, and it contains some interesting questions about medieval farming in the Chilterns. Detailed maps of average wheat prices c.1300 show that the prices fall away rapidly north and west of Henley and Wycombe, because of the different costs of river and road transport. The more northerly Chilterns were thus much more remote from London, and this must have influenced the farming strategy of manors differently.

The network of local markets and broader connections can be seen in the 15th-century letters and papers of the Stonor family, not typical or representative but showing nevertheless the market system in the south-west Chilterns. Items like shoes, candles and eggs came from Watlington, lime from Nettlebed, bricks from Marlow, ale from Reading fair, and cloth from the Wallingford tailor. Wine, salt fish, glass, clothes and wax came by barge from London.[64] The Chilterns were embedded within the metropolitan economy. This was not an isolated rural region, but one whose fortunes would continue to depend on markets and trade with the capital.

Chapter Six

The Late Medieval Chilterns

Introduction

The first two hundred years after Domesday witnessed a heady climb towards a fall. The rapid explosion in population, the expansion in the economy and the extensions to the cultivated area were all to be put into reverse over the next hundred years as a series of crises and calamities befell the nation. Historians are agreed that by 1300 the medieval economy was stretched and stressed almost to breaking point, though they are less unanimous about the factors behind this. Some emphasise the way population was outgrowing available resources, leading to falling living standards and the over-cultivation of marginal lands, overstretching the ecological limits and leading to falling yields. Others blame the inherent problems of feudalism, with its exploitation of one class by another, draining the peasantry of their economic surplus, and with landlords failing to reinvest in agricultural improvements. Certainly by 1300 both local and national tax exactions were crippling.

For both sets of causes, medieval society was increasingly vulnerable and fragile, and the series of external 'shocks' were to catapult it into dramatic changes. Against a background of already substantial price inflation, a series of disastrous harvests pushed corn prices beyond reach and a famine of major proportions ensued. This was exacerbated by a series of livestock epidemics which combined to produce seven or eight years of the worst agrarian crisis since the Normans invaded. And even worse was to come: the outbreak of the Hundred Years War with France in 1337, the Black Death in 1349, and then the upsurge of religious insurrection and peasant discontent culminating in the Peasants' Revolt. Each was to contribute to the pattern of decline, death and disorder which dominated the late medieval period. The English population fell by over 50 per cent, dropping from its peak of 5-6 million in 1300 to about 2-2½ million in the late 14th century, almost back to Domesday levels.[1] These changes did not, however, simply reverse and undo all the events of the previous 250 years, and the Chilterns provide an illuminating case study of the impact of this depressing catalogue on the social and landscape order of a region which had been stretched to the margins.

Agrarian Crises

The period of agricultural disasters that began in 1315 was a succession of individual tragedies piled upon each other and inflicted on a farming community that had few reserves and a poor recovery rate.[2] In an atmosphere of impending gloom with corn prices already escalating, the harvest of 1315 was a disaster. The blame was laid squarely on the appalling English weather, after a wretched summer with torrential rains that destroyed the corn and hay crops and some believe heralded a gradual climatic trend towards cooler and wetter weather in Western Europe as a whole. The price of wheat rose from 8s. a quarter in the autumn of 1315 to 28s. 8d. by the summer of 1316, which, after renewed storms, had an even worse harvest than the previous year. By now England was experiencing a serious famine accompanied by a virulent enteric epidemic (perhaps typhoid) which greatly increased mortalities. Just as the harvest started to recover in 1317 and more so in 1318, when there was a plentiful crop allowing prices to fall and the worst of the famine to dwindle, another devastating blow was struck with the arrival of an epidemic afflicting cattle and oxen (probably rinderpest) which led to wholesale destruction of herds on an unprecedented level. Sheep flocks had already dwindled as a consequence of a murrain which had been rampant throughout the famine years. It was this dreadful combination which hit both the arable and livestock simultaneously that caused such grievous damaged to the community, though landlords benefited from the high grain prices.

The crises affected much of lowland England, and we can trace local Chilterns effects through records of grain yields and through mortality and crisis transfers of land. The detailed year-on-year records of the Bishop of Winchester's many estates, which included important estates at West Wycombe and Ivinghoe, show that wheat, barley and oats yields fell here by half in the crisis years. But Professor Titow's extensive studies of the Winchester yields suggest that fertility and yields had already begun a long-term decline, and the crisis years merely accentuated the downward curve. He suggests a link between falling fertility and marginal colonisation: the greatest deterioration of yields in the early 14th century and before occurred on manors (including West Wycombe and Ivinghoe) known to have been colonising in the 13th century, and perhaps pushing the limits too far. The deterioration in yields was most evident in the barley and oats figures, and more recent agricultural experiments at Rothamsted in Hertfordshire have shown why: barley has a much greater dependence on surface soil than does wheat, and so shows signs of exhaustion earlier. Titow's analysis helps explain why the period of greatest expansion was followed by a period of low yields as the poorer soils quickly deteriorated, though some scholars would take issue with his interpretations.[3]

The flurry of transactions that accompanied landscape calamities left many of the most vulnerable landless, homeless and poverty stricken. This can be seen in the peasant land-market in Chiltern villages, as the number forced to sell or give up took a sudden leap during the crisis years. In Codicote nine holdings were surrendered in 1314, rising to 29 and 38 in the two following periods 1315-16 and 1317-18.[4] Most of these were tiny holdings surrendered to the lord in desperation. The example of Michael Gorman gives a poignant picture of a typical personal tragedy. He surrendered five parcels in all between 1315 and 1318. By 1321 he was dead; the Court Book simply states that there was 'no heriot because he had nothing' [heriot was a death duty]. Like so many victims of this period, his impoverished condition probably combined the shortage of seed corn, the weight of taxation and rent, and the falling fertility of his land.

Harvest yields continued to be unreliable, though the 1330s seem to have been rather better. However, the limited recovery can be vividly seen in the returns for a tax imposed by Edward III in 1342 to assist him in paying for his new French wars. This taxed one ninth of the value of corn, wool and lambs produced in the realm, and the returns are documented in the *Nonarum Inquisitiones*. The values were compared to a previous assessment compiled for taxation by Pope Nicholas IV in 1291 and discrepancies had to be accounted for.[5] The results give a graphic record of areas where arable had contracted, and the Chilterns and surrounding lowlands are one of only four regions which showed significant amounts of abandoned land. The others were North Yorkshire, Shropshire and Sussex. In Buckinghamshire more than half the parishes recorded uncultivated land, especially in the extreme north and in the Chilterns. Perhaps the most interesting were the 14 villages where soil poverty is explicitly mentioned as a factor in abandonment. Eight of them lie in a line below the Chiltern escarpment, and two in the Chilterns themselves. They include Pitstone, Ivinghoe, Buckland, Ellesborough, Great Missenden and Hughenden. The details for both Princes Risborough and Drayton Beauchamp note that the abandoned land was in the *Ciltr* or Chiltern parts of the parishes. The return for Little Kimble specifically states that one-third of the arable had been abandoned 'propter debilitatem terre' (because of the wearing-out of the soil) and that the untilled acres lay above 'Ekeneld' or the Icknield Way. The photograph illustrates history repeating itself, as the land above the Icknield Way in Great Kimble today has been 'set aside'. This has let the weeds take over in a field previously planted with oil-seed rape and created the paint box of scarlet and yellow we see in the picture (Plate 79).

The impoverishment of the soils was probably secondary to that of the tenants; there are many examples of land abandonment because the peasants could not afford to work the land. Thus at Ivinghoe over 400 acres lay neglected because 'the parishioners were impoverished, having neither animals for ploughing, nor seed for sowing'. Similar reasons are given for 200 acres at Great Missenden. Other records reveal decay and dereliction. In Studham 60 messuages (properties) were uninhabited, and at Codicote in 1332 there were five empty plots in the market-place. At Ibstone the mill built in 1293-94 was in bad repair. Smaller sheep-flocks were also notable despite the arable land that had tumbled to pasture. Harsh winters took their toll on a weakened flock—one entry for Toddington relates that 'almost all mother sheep before or in the process of giving birth died on account of the harshness of the winter'.[6]

The crises of the early 14th century had severely bruised the medieval economy and society of the Chilterns and surrounding regions, effects that clearly lingered into the 1340s. Whether the society would have recovered and limped along or gradually decayed is a 'might-have-been' of history. For it was pushed over the edge by a far greater catastrophe in 1348-49, the Black Death.

The Black Death

The Black Death is believed to have reached England with the arrival of an infected sailor on a ship from Gascony to Bristol on the feast of St John the Baptist in 1348. The lightning speed with which it spread to the rest of the country suggests it was a pneumonic infection passed on by coughing and sneezing. As in other parts, it raged throughout the Chiltern Hills. Early references to its passage appear in West Wycombe where 'decline of rents through pestilence' became a feature of the accounts from 1348 and only a small quantity of flour was produced because of plague and the death of the miller. In Codicote there were 59 deaths in the period between 1 November 1348 and 19 May 1349, and the Wymondley Court Roll for 1349 suggests that the total mortality there must have approached two hundred. The evidence suggests that the effects were perhaps greatest in the north-east Chilterns, where population was reduced by a half to two-thirds, but there appear to be very few places that escaped the grip of this terrifying epidemic altogether.[7]

The immediate impact of death on this scale was abandoned lands and holdings, decayed dwellings and cottages, and signs of commercial decline. Much of the land did not stay abandoned for long. For there were plenty of potential tenants ready to step into dead men's shoes and holdings. In Chalfont St Peter the admission of 12 new tenants in the autumn of 1349 may well have filled all the vacancies created by the Black Death.[8] There was a massive transfer of property. David Roden estimates that 600 acres of villein lands changed hands in Codicote and 900 in Abbots Langley.[9] The epidemic certainly reversed the pressure of population on the land and, for those who survived, basic living standards rose substantially.

The consequences of so much death and decline must have been obvious everywhere and traversed all social boundaries, as seen in the entries for Berkhamsted, where a special survey was commissioned because of the great changes in landholding following the epidemic. These describe tenant houses in 1351 to be very ruinous or greatly in need of repair; buildings on the demesne farm to be on the point of tumbling down, and even the castle was derelict, 'the greater part having fallen to the ground'.[10]

The drop in population created a new economic situation, a long period without real economic growth until the 16th century. Trade and markets declined; the population of London fell by up to half and its magnetism as a market centre declined even though the surviving people were richer and consumed more. The price of grain fell as there was lower demand. However, the economy did not shrink as much as the population, and wages and demand for labour rose. The whole relationship between landlord and peasant changed, bringing a succession of social changes. The acute labour shortage meant that peasants could try to escape the shackles of villeinage, customary services and manorial control, sometimes fleeing their lords to work for higher wages or rent land on better terms elsewhere. There is a lot of evidence for peasants indulging in their own kind of opportunism. In 1352 five villeins who had fled from Sharpenhoe were brought back by the lord. They had run off to take jobs in Caddington, Streatley, Luton and St Albans at high rates (John atte Well received 10s. a month at St Albans); all five came from one family.[11] In Chalfont St Peter three villeins were reported to have fled the manor in 1357 and Ralph Hatchet was fined 6d. 'on account of his rebellion' before he obviously cut and ran again, as the next entry reads: 'one curtilege formerly Ralph Hatchet's which used to pay 12d. a year and 3 days' work at Harvest is in the lord's hand for lack of a tenant'.[12]

Some landlords tried to enforce their rights and keep their tenants on the old terms, but others were only too keen to get new tenants. Woodcote in the south Chilterns lost a quarter of its men in the Black Death, and a 1366 rental shows the changes. There were 32 properties in the hamlet, of which seven were vacant and eight had changed ownership. Walter atte Welle had acquired four holdings in the villages, but all at money rents without any customary services, liability to heriot etc. that other tenants had. He seems to have been a businessman making his own terms. One of his holdings was a field in Woodcote called Oldland, held for 4d., and there is still a field called 'Old Lands' in the Exlade Street part of Woodcote today.[13]

In localities where landlords did not recognise and adjust to the new circumstances, there was great underlying social discontent. This discontent ran deepest on the estates of

66. Abbot Thomas de la Mare of St Albans, who employed great severity towards tenants in the 1370s. [GESTA ST ALBANI, BL: Cotton Claudius E iv (2) f232.]

the great abbeys and monasteries, which tried to keep the tightest stranglehold on their peasants. In Hertfordshire there was a long history of conflict between St Albans Abbey and the town and rural tenants. Although week-work duties had been largely abandoned, harvest duties were stiff. The Abbey kept strict records of land transactions, enforcing entry fines and rules. The Steward of St Albans was under very specific instructions not to grant adjacent holdings to one man (so restricting consolidation) and to insist on the unfree nature of the tenures. In the 1370s the new abbot, Thomas de la Mare, tried to reinforce these rights, and employed 'implacable severity' towards his tenants (Plate 66). On one occasion after a quarrel with a John Chilterne the Abbot seized 15 beasts from his herd and let them die of hunger. It is therefore no surprise to find St Albans peasants and burgesses active in the Peasants' Revolt of 1381. This revolt was sparked off by three new government poll taxes, but also contained demands against the church and for an end to villeinage. In St Albans Abbey buildings were sacked, and court rolls and records were burnt. The burgesses also hacked up the floor of the monks' parlour, which had been paved with seized mill-stones after the dispute of 1331, and distributed the shattered fragments as trophies of their victory. The Peasants' Revolt was tricked into defeat, but the tide was turning against the landlords and it marked the beginning of the end of feudalism.[14]

The Late Medieval Landscape

Many of the effects of the Black Death and the subsequent population and economic changes we have described were widespread, affecting much of England, and certainly the Chilterns and surrounding counties. It is in the longer-term working out of the chain of effects that we see regional differences clearly emerging. Then we can see the distinctive character of the Chilterns laid bare. This is perhaps most apparent when we look at the geography of 'deserted villages' and the factors behind it.

One long-term consequence of the post-1348 decline was to make sheep farming increasingly profitable, especially in regions distant from the diminished London market. This gave landlords the incentive to turn over the demesne and village fields from corn-growing to sheep-grazing.[15] Small and reduced villages which had lost a lot of their population were the most vulnerable. Landlords could evict the remaining villagers and grass over the fields. Only the foundations of the houses were left as mounds and outlines in the turf. The Midland counties have many such deserted villages, with both Oxfordshire and Buckinghamshire having high percentages. The process was long and drawn out, mainly occurring in the 15th and early 16th centuries, picking off small communities as they faltered. It was very selective, shaking out the weakest and most vulnerable, and local factors were very important. The stronger open-field communities that survived in these areas were subsequently long-lived, and were only enclosed in the 18th or 19th centuries by Parliamentary enclosure.

One very clear feature stands out on the county maps. In Beresford's words: 'in the Chiltern counties the lost villages cease when the scarp slope is passed and the woodlands of the dip slope are reached'.[16] Around the very edges of the Hills there were desertions: at Mongewell and Newnham Murren by the Thames near Wallingford; at Golder and other Vale hamlets in Pyrton Hundred; and at Pendley in the Tring Gap Sir Robert Whittingham destroyed the village in the 1440s. But the Chilterns themselves were almost immune to this phenomenon. Why? After all, the medieval Chilterns had combined sheep with arable farming to a greater extent than many of the regions where deserted village are common. We can identify several reasons, many of which add up to greater adaptability and resilience in the Chilterns economy. Much of the region was close enough to London to still sell to the reduced market. The mixture of open and enclosed holdings allowed landlord and peasant to be flexible, and so kept communities viable. The many small fields and enclosures, and the hills and bottoms, were not ideal for the large-scale sheep grazier. The social structure was also important. In Hertfordshire desertions cluster in the north east, and Paul Glennie has argued that it was these areas with high villeinage and uncommuted week work that collapsed as population gradually migrated to more attractive locales.[17] Villages were most vulnerable where landlords had tried to keep tenants on the old, oppressive terms.

This is not to argue that the Chilterns escaped completely unscathed in terms of settlement. The desertion of whole villages is much easier to detect in tax records than the fate of the scattered farms and individual hamlets which are more typical of Chiltern settlement. Some hamlets did disappear, but they are very few compared with what happened in the Vale and midlands. In King's Walden the hamlet of Flexmore had vanished by the 16th century, and in Codicote Oxwik hamlet, which was three cottages and a farmstead in 1290, had disappeared by 1359.[18] There are also several genuine 'lost' hamlets: names that occur in medieval documents, but which no longer appear on the map. There was Fastnidge somewhere near Wendover (and possibly another Fastnidge near West Wycombe), and Pirenore, which is frequently mentioned with Peterley in the Missenden charters. But these may possibly be changes of name rather than desertions, and Pirenore may be modern Little Kingshill.[19] In one case we have the archaeological remains of a deserted farmstead, found on the scarp above Lewknor during work on the M40 route. Here the foundations are substantial, possibly made of limestone brought from the Wheatley quarries east of Oxford, and the pottery suggests occupation from c.1250-c.1350.[20] It may have been a grange of Abingdon Abbey, which owned much of Lewknor, and was deserted after 1350.

There are one or two examples of depopulation to create late medieval parks, at both Great Hampden and King's Walden. In Watlington parish the scarp hamlets of Ingham and Watcombe, together with the detached portion of Warmscombe hamlet in the Stonor valley, have vanished.[21] Warmscombe is still remembered in field and bridlepath names. These all became part of the Stonor estate in the late Middle Ages, and may have fallen to the Stonor's interest in sheep-farming. Similarly, at Chalfont St Peter the Brudenell family were converting land to pasture in the period 1488-1515, failing to repair farm houses and buildings, displacing some tenants, and being reported to the Commission on Inclosures.[22] On the whole these were of limited extent and significance compared with the changes elsewhere. There was local adjustment and realignment, but the Chilterns emerge much more resilient than many surrounding regions.

The changes within the Hills were more subtle. There was very little winnowing out of settlements, or transfer from arable to pasture. Instead it was the smaller tenants and landholders who fell through the sieve. The appearance of the landscape may not have changed greatly, but holdings were concentrated in fewer hands, and 'the once large class of small land-holders had virtually disappeared by 1500'.[23] In most cases these acquisitions did not lead to enclosure, but consolidation did create larger working strips. In Berkhamsted and King's Walden many open-field parcels grew to 5-20 acres, rather than the one acre or smaller parcels of earlier centuries. Actual enclosure was uncommon, and mainly by the manor rather than by sub-tenants. Common fields acquired piecemeal by the manor in both Codicote and King's Walden were enclosed in the 14th and 15th centuries but, with the large number of common fields, such changes did not disrupt the system.

We know very little of the late medieval population history of the Chilterns. Little research has been done, and it is an important topic for the future. Julian Cornwall has made the hazardous comparison of the 1377 Poll Tax Returns (Plate 67) and the 1522 Muster Rolls.[24] He has suggested that Buckinghamshire's population remained almost static around 37,000, but this county figure hides a major regional difference between Chiltern and Vale. The

67. 1377 poll tax receipt for Beaconsfield. The tax collector Richard Gregorye gives a receipt to the villagers for the tax they have paid. In this case the sum was £3 4s. 8d. paid by each of 194 villagers over 14 years of age, at a flat rate of 4d. each. The receipt was indented across the top, and the seals of the tax collectors are still attached to the little cutaway strip of parchment. See Fenwick (1983) for other returns. [PRO E 179/77/22 Item 6.]

Wealth in Buckinghamshire towns, 1334-1552					
Town	**£ 1327**	**rank**	**£ 1524**	**rank**	**% growth**
Beaconsfield	50	13	511	4	922
Amersham	78	8	765	3	851
High Wycombe	180	2	1181	1	556
Great Marlow	73	11	407	7	458
Aylesbury	190	1	1005	2	429
Stony Stratford	166	3	(356)	9	396
Buckingham	87	6	419	6	382
Princes Risborough	75	9	317	10	320
Winslow	53	12	200	12	277
Olney	135	4	504	5	273
Ivinghoe	75	9	259	11	245
Wendover	95	5	261	13	175
Newport Pagnell	80	7	389	8	116
County	10077		32581		223

[Based on Cornwall, 1988.]

surviving returns for the Chiltern Hundreds of Buckinghamshire suggest a 17 per cent increase to around 9,800, so there must have been a balancing decrease in north Buckinghamshire. This contrast fits well into the national map of change. The areas of relative gain in population and wealth were those close to London, regions of irregular and enclosed fields, and 'woodland regions' offering opportunities for green- or commons-side cottages and employments in the woods. The Chilterns may in fact have grown by migration from the Vales to the north. Cornwall's comparison of how towns in Buckinghamshire fared between the taxes of 1334 and 1525 brings out the contrast well: the Chiltern boroughs like High Wycombe, Amersham and Beaconsfield have prospered much more than those in the Vale and beyond. All these are tantalising glimpses, but much more research is needed for this period. What does become clear is that the long, late medieval retrenchment did not just reverse the earlier medieval expansion. The Chilterns survived the collapse better, and changed less dramatically than many regions. As a result it was better prepared for rapid modernisation as national growth restarted in the 16th century.

The Legacy of Medieval Buildings

The medieval period has left its legacy on the Chilterns in many forms—in the patterns of fields, settlements and woods, in the names and layout of streets in boroughs such as Berkhamsted and Henley, in place-names, and in a variety of earthworks. One very visible legacy is the surviving medieval buildings. This is worth touching on here because the medieval Chilterns are the earliest period from which substantial buildings and structures still survive in the modern landscape. Earlier periods have left remains and foundations, but not working buildings.

The survival of buildings is very selective, and it depends on the durability of the original materials and the history of repair and maintenance. Stone structures built and maintained by families and institutions that have themselves weathered the centuries are the most likely survivors. The Chiltern churches are the finest example of this. From the late Saxon period, churches began to be constructed of stone, rather than wood. In the Chilterns there is no good local hard building stone suitable for exteriors. Instead the ubiquitous flints were used to great effect. The solid, rather squat flint churches with square towers and tiled roofs are as integral a part of the local scenery as the beech hangers and the sunken lanes. Flints, if well knapped and protected from the weather, last indefinitely as some of the beautiful and very ancient churches will testify. Part of lovely St Mary's Northchurch is pre-Conquest; the delightful little church of St Botolph tucked away at Swyncombe is very early Norman; and the magnificent and unusual saddleback of St Bartholomew at Fingest has a 12th-century tower built wider than the knave, as in pre-Conquest churches. Although many are now renovated and have lost much of their medieval character, there remain some perfect treasures with original wall paintings, tiles or windows. The parish churches of Bledlow, Little Missenden, Monks Risborough and Little Kimble instantly spring to mind, but the Chiltern valleys have many hidden gems, such as the little church at Radnage. The interiors of many Chiltern churches were lined with the hardest stone that the region can provide—a local chalk mined at Totternhoe in Bedfordshire and referred to as 'clunch'.[25] It was easy to carve, but it weathers very badly outside and is nowhere near as hard-wearing as the flints.

Castles are the other types of building that often endure through the centuries. The Chiltern specimens are not very impressive, and are mainly low mounds and earthworks today. The early Norman motte-and-bailey castles were built from earth and wood, and only those that were kept in use were rebuilt in stone or flints. Norman authority was established quickly in the Chilterns, and castles such as Totternhoe and Luton became redundant. Luton Castle, in the heart of the town, was deliberately dismantled after the accession of Henry II in 1154,

68. Chiltern churches:*(from top left, clockwise)* Swincombe; Stonor Park; Little Missenden; Great Wymondley. Despite their individuality, these Chiltern churches from the early Norman church of St Botolph's, Swincombe to the later medieval chapel at Stonor and the little parish churches of Great Wymondley and Little Missenden, all show a common theme of flint walls and tiled roofs.

and its memory is preserved only in the name Castle Street. Totternhoe remains as earthworks on top of the hill, and must have dramatically dominated the local countryside in the few decades when it was operational. Some castles were rebuilt with flints, but lack of maintenance through the centuries has left them decayed. Berkhamsted castle remains merely as a set of stumps like broken gappy teeth set inside some impressive earthworks. Wallingford in the south west was once one of the strongest and most important castles in the country guarding the route across the Thames; now it is just shadows beneath the turf of motte, bailey and moat. Like Berkhamsted it gradually fell into disrepair after the death of Edward the Black Prince when it became less and less used. Both of these castles were robbed of their building materials, and this quickened their destruction. Part of Wallingford was re-cycled into Windsor castle and St Peter's Church in Berkhamsted contains much of the old castle walls.

There is one interesting exception to the history of castles in the Chilterns. This castle is Shirburn, below the scarp to the north of Watlington, and the home of the Earls of Macclesfield since the 18th century (Plate 69). Here we see a whole and surviving castle, using a different building material. It is built of brick, and is the earliest datable example of brickwork in the

69. Shirburn Castle. A 14th-century quadrangular, moated castle built in brick by Warin de Lisle by licence of 1377. It is the earliest datable brick building in the region. Later renovated and extended, it has been the home of the Earls of Macclesfield since the 18th century.

region, receiving a licence in 1377. Shirburn is a quadrangular moated castle, and has been kept in good repair through the centuries, standing today in the private parkland of the Macclesfield estate.

Brick and tile-making became a specialist industry in the south Chilterns around Nettlebed, using the local clays and fuelling the kilns with beechwood. In 1365 Nettlebed produced 35,000 tiles for Wallingford Castle, and the earliest use of the term 'brick' is in 1416-17, when

Thomas Stonor paid Michael Warwick £40 for making 200,000 'brykes' and a further £15 for carriage from the kiln site at Crocker End to Stonor. Thomas also employed 'lez Flemyngges', who were likely to be immigrant brick-workers. Part of this consignment of bricks probably went into the medieval chapel at Stonor that we can see today, and Stonor House has been described as a 'positive museum of brickwork'. The Nettlebed industry continued right through to the 20th century. In contrast the tile industry in Penn, which specialised in decorated tiles for interiors in the 15th century, seems to have had only a limited life.[26]

Most medieval houses were never built of flint, brick or stone, but were timber-constructions, filled with wattle-and-daub. The cottages and dwellings of the peasants have gone, and with them many of the grander manor houses. The fashion for moated houses (which could only be built in the clay Vale or on the clay plateau) has left a few examples, as at Moor Court in Lewknor and Dundridge near Cholesbury. The earthworks of others, and their fishponds, are sometimes visible from the air, as at Aston Clinton (Plate 70). Some are visible on the ground, like those of Little Kimble where there are mounds associated with a moated manor house behind the little church.

70. Aston Clinton moated manor house. All that remains of a medieval moated manor are the earthworks of the moat and fishponds. On the left more modern rectangular hedged enclosures overlie older ridge and furrow which is common in the Vale, as here, but rare in the Hills.

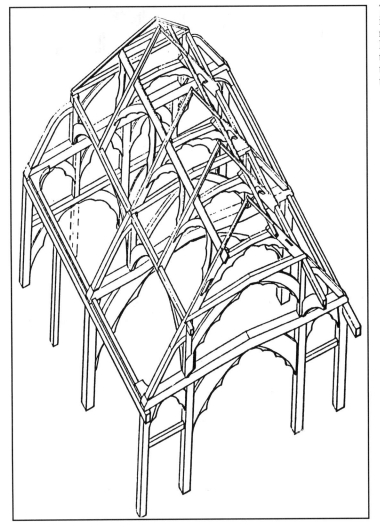

71. Lewknor Barn. This isometric drawing of the medieval hallhouse at Church Farm, Lewknor was made by the National Monuments record to show the structure of the timbers.

Yet research and accidental discoveries during the last 30 years have unveiled a substantial number of medieval timber-structures in the Chilterns. A fascinating medieval building that evaded discovery until 1969 is to be found at Church Farm in Lewknor.[27] Now it is a lofty barn full of tractors and farm machinery but the three tiers of cusped timberwork and huge 29-ft. wide tie beam are thought to be part of an uncompleted project designed as a grand hall and probably commissioned by John de Lewknor before 1349 (Plate 71). It was probably interrupted by the Black Death so that it never fulfilled its original function. It is all the more intriguing because the present farmyard exterior with breeze block and corrugated iron 'additions' totally belies the interior and the surprise on entering is all the more dramatic. In the hamlet of Sewell, near Dunstable in Bedfordshire, a near complete medieval hall house is part of the much extended manor (Plate 72). This hall has finely carved and beautifully proportioned timbers which are tiered and cusped and rise to a high apex, similar to those in the Lewknor Barn. We do not know exactly when the hall was built but it is a fine example, and

72. Sewell Manor. Another medieval hallhouse whose timbers show a striking resemblance to those of the Lewknor example.

the chief tenants who lived in Sewell either in this hall or its predecessor are documented as early as 1288.

More modest medieval manor-houses and farmhouses are also being discovered. These usually date from the 15th century. The medieval timber-frames are often hidden and well-disguised behind more modern façades of brick and later extensions. Many have only come to light during modernisation, or even demolition. The architectural feature often sought in dating early buildings in this region is a cruck construction with huge arched-timbers tapering to an apex and supporting cross or tie beams between them.[28] An example is Grange Farm, at Widmer End north of High Wycombe. Although the house is timber-framed, not much framing can be seen from the outside, because the walls were reconstructed in red brick during major alterations in the 17th century. The original house, however, combines both cruck-construction and the box-frame style. Grange Farm is typical of the Chiltern survivals in that it was a medieval manor-house (in this case of the 'lost hamlet' of Pirenore) which was rebuilt in brick in the great revival after 1550. These medieval buildings have survived because they were owned and adapted by the yeomen and farmers who prospered as the Chilterns recovered from the late medieval decline.[29]

Chapter Seven

The Medieval Woodlands

Woodland resources played a very significant role in the life of the medieval Chilterns country-side. To appreciate their significance we must forget our modern notions of amenity woods for leisure walks and picnics, forget also the Forestry Commission plantation directed solely at the production of tall timber, and see the medieval woods as the biggest natural resource of the Chilterns region. Wood provided construction material for the houses, barns, carts, fences, as well as all the fuel and heating for the medieval peasant and his lord. This vital resource was managed, and managed as a renewable resource. Woods at that time were not felled, cleared and replanted—planting is a much more modern concept. The medieval wood was based on natural regrowth after cutting and pruning.

This chapter examines both the nature and management of different types of woodlands in the Chilterns, at a time when they were a vital part of the medieval economy. It was during this phase of their history that the management practices—and the wooded landscapes that embodied them—became established and persisted until the late 18th or even 19th century. There is a further reason for devoting time to the medieval woodland: it was very different from the high beech forest with its dominance by enormous standard trees that we associate today with the 'beechy Chilterns'. A later transformation created that dominance around 1800, and to understand it we need to see what went before. As so often in the ancient countryside of the Chilterns, what went before is not entirely 'a world we have lost'. In the landscape today we can look behind more modern contributions and still see aspects of the medieval woods.

Domesday Woods
The Domesday survey of 1086, 20 years after the Norman Conquest, provided an inventory of the woodland then existing in England, though the measurements can be hard to interpret. The returns for Bedfordshire, Buckinghamshire and Hertfordshire use a 'pannage' assessment—tame pigs were turned out into the woods in autumn to feed on the acorns and beechmast before the winter slaughter and salting, and Domesday assessed 'wood for so-many swine'. The nut crop is very variable year-to-year, so with the best will in the world the figures are uncertain, but they do reveal the major woods throughout the Chilterns. Wendover had 'wood for 2,000 swine', Amersham 1,250, Berkhamsted 1,000, Chesham 1,650, Luton 2,000 and Tring 1,000. In Oxfordshire an alternative type of return was used, recording the size of the woods in leagues and furlongs, so that Watlington had woods 'seven furlongs long and three furlongs wide' and Pyrton woods were '18 furlongs long and half a league wide'. The *Domesday Geography of England* comments, 'the exact significance of these linear measurements is far from clear, and we cannot hope to convert them into modern acreages', though Oliver Rackham has argued that they are reasonably precise dimensions.[1]

Even if Domesday Book does not give us precise acreages and extents, we can see that the Chiltern Hills stand out as a heavily wooded region on the national map. The contrast is

73. Hedgerow near Pednor. This old hedgerow was a former wood boundary, now showing a rich variety of species including the slow-colonising bluebell.

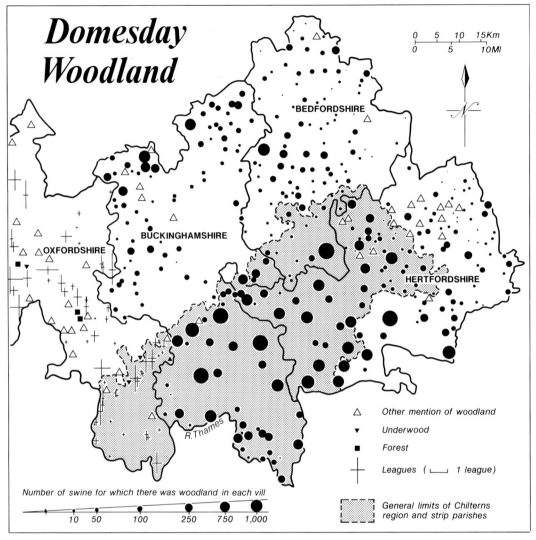

Domesday Woodland

BEDFORDSHIRE

BUCKINGHAMSHIRE

OXFORDSHIRE

HERTFORDSHIRE

R.Thames

0   5   10   15Km
0   5   10MI

N

△   Other mention of woodland

▼   Underwood

■   Forest

✝   Leagues (⌐⌐ 1 league)

Number of swine for which there was woodland in each vill

10   50   100   250   750   1,000

▓▓▓ General limits of Chilterns
▓▓▓ region and strip parishes

74. The Domesday woodland of the Chilterns and surrounding regions. [Based on the maps of H. C. Darby and others.]

not quite as dramatic as it later became, because wooded areas in south-west Oxfordshire and north Buckinghamshire (Bernwood especially) still survived at this time. In 1086, in Oliver Rackham's words, 'one of the largest wooded areas in England extended from the Chiltern escarpment down the dip-slope almost to the gates of London'.[2] (The other great woodland in south-east England was the Weald of Kent and Sussex.) The Chronicles of St Albans tell us that Leofstan, Abbot just before the Conquest, 'to provide safer roads, [Leofstan] cut back the dark woods which extend from the margin of Chiltern (*a limbo Ciltriae*) almost to London ... for at that time there abounded through the whole of Chiltern extensive, thick and abundant woods'.[3]

Within the Chilterns the map shows the woodedness of the central and southern parts. Because of the parish organisation much of the wood is recorded against manors on the edge of the Hills (seen most clearly in the line of Icknield Belt settlements in the Oxfordshire returns), but the woods themselves were in the upland and escarpment portions of the parishes. There was also substantial woodland in the northern part, as at Dunstable and Luton (presumably the large woods then existing at Kensworth and Caddington). Beyond Luton the open character of the north-east fringes is apparent.

Earlier chapters have shown that the woodland margin has fluctuated, and the medieval woodland recorded in Domesday Book was partly secondary succession and regeneration. Even where it was not succession over once settled and farmed areas, it was not wildwood. Men had penetrated and used the woodland since before Neolithic times and so selectively altered its ecology. Reports by medieval chroniclers like Fitzstephen (*c*.1180) that the Chilterns were 'the lairs of wild beasts, harts, does, and boars' were rather exaggerated, and the picturesque gravestone at Radnage supposed to be that of the man who killed the last wild bear in England is local myth, not real fact.[4]

Nor was the woodland a free frontier. Woodland was property—owned, inherited, sold or granted. Some was individually owned and some the common property of a group or community, who had specified and limited rights. Woodland resources were balanced and weighed against other possible uses of the land, and the woodland was managed in a variety of ways. But before we look at these ways, we need to know what the medieval woods really looked like.

The Nature of the Woods

Sources such as Domesday Book are largely silent on the actual nature and appearance of the Chilterns woodland, but scattered references in other medieval documents are more revealing. They show a more diverse picture than the great canopies of high beech forest today associated with the 'traditional' Chilterns wood, a picture more varied both in types of tree species and the size and appearance of the trees.

Beech was then, as now, the most common large tree. In the northern Chilterns at Caddington near Luton a survey of lands owned by St Paul's Cathedral in 1222 noted a great common wood of beeches 300 acres in size, together with two small oakwoods. The large common wood at Berkhamsted Frith was also mainly beech, whilst at Bledlow Wood there was an order to cut down 3,000 beeches in 1310. Further south down the escarpment at Watlington Sir William Stonor sold 500 beeches to John Mershe 'to be taken within all the grounde of Saunders and a grounde called Herryes landes at Greenfield' (15th century).[5]

Whilst beech was the prevalent large tree it was not as all-dominant as it later became. Oak, and to a lesser extent ash, were also important. At Ibstone, high on a ridge between two dry valleys in the south-west Chilterns, many detailed medieval records have survived because the manor was the property of Merton College, Oxford.[6] The College archives show that in the larger woods beech and oak were dominant (so that when gales flattened vast swathes of trees in Turville Dean in 1363-64 there were more than 100 beeches and 400 oaks toppled, suggesting perhaps more oak than beech here). In the smaller patches of woodland oak and ash were more important. Later references, all pre-dating the era of planting, also portray this species composition. A lease of Kilridge Wood (adjacent to Stonor park) in 1525 mentions 'beeches, ashes, withes, maples, appssis [aspen] and whitebemys'.[7] This pattern continued until much later. At the end of the 17th century the estate records for both Hampden and West Wycombe show that about one-third of the timber trees in the 'beechwoods' were in fact oak. As well as this greater variety of species, the woods and trees also had a different character. There were some tall, dense woods—at Stonor in 1365 a wood had 'nothing else because of the shade of the trees', and there are similar reports on woods at Amersham, Chenies and Medmenham.

75. Richard of Wallingford. Born in 1291-92, Richard became a distinguished mathematician and astronomer, as well as a leading churchman. He was a great clock-designer, and a replica of his astronomical clock is in St Albans Abbey. He became Abbot of St Albans in 1328. He developed a skin disease labelled as a 'leprosy' (and shown in the illustration) and died in 1336. [BL: Cotton Claudius E iv (2) f201.] (see biography by J. D. North, 1976.)

76. Sheep grazing at Ellesborough. Today's enriched and fertilised grass is much more uniform than medieval pasture and can stock many more sheep per hectare. This is one of the few scarp-edges south of Wendover still kept treeless by grazing.

77. Pitstone Windmill. This National Trust monument bears the date 1627 and is thought to be the oldest in the country.

But these woods of dense, high trees with little underwood were not the general pattern, nor were they the most useful or valuable. Many, probably most, woods were more open, with trees of different sizes and ages, and this was a reflection of medieval woodland management, seeking to grow wood of the right types and sizes for a wide range of different uses. Tall standard trees of oak or beech were only one element. Wood management was not based on clear felling and replanting, such as we associate with modern forestry. Instead it relied on cutting and felling and natural regrowth. Below the standards were the coppice trees, cut on a regular or irregular cycle to a stump close to the ground, from which new shoots or 'spring' rapidly grew. Such coppice trees might be cut every six to eight years to give smaller poles and wood. In some areas coppiced trees would be replaced by pollarded trees, where the cutting back was not to a ground stump but to a 'boll' of eight to 12 ft. high, so generating new shoots above the grazing height of animals. Between these were the bushes, low under-growth and fallen branches—all important elements in the medieval woodland.

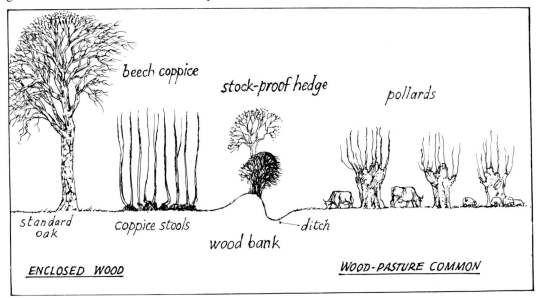

78. The main elements of the medieval woodland.

Uses of Wood and Woods

Each of these different elements corresponds to a great variety of specific uses in the Middle Ages. We must distinguish between the *timber* from the tall standard trees and the *wood* (or underwood) from the coppice stools or smaller growths. Timber was the large trunks, used for beams, posts, planks and gateposts. Wood from smaller trees, and coppiced or pollard trees pro-vided the poles for all smaller constructions such as sheep and cattle hurdles or pens, fencing, domestic articles and wattle-and-daub filling struts. Smaller wood was tied into 'faggots' or chopped into 'billets' for firewood, or made into charcoal for later domestic or industrial use in brick or tile kilns. These wood uses pervaded every aspect of medieval life, and the appearance of the Chiltern woods reflected those diverse demands. Once again we can take the case of Ibstone to see some of these uses in local detail. Wood and wood products were used in the village but also sold outside for cash. Some were taken to other Merton College estates in the Vale (as at Cuxham and Cheddington), where few woodland resources remained, others to Oxford itself.

Park, 100 spokes for cart-wheels and 28 quarters of charcoal. Other sales reported include sheep hurdles made from wattles cut in the manor (362 sold at Thame market in 1342-43 and 17 made and sent to Cuxham for sheep-fold in 1344-45).

Firewood and charcoal were major wood uses everywhere, using the underwood and fallen branches. In the Chilterns they were also an important use of larger wood, and especially of beechwood, and the smoke (and stench) of charcoal burning would have been common in the woods. Beech is not an ideal wood for structural and external work, in contrast to the more durable oak. Even in the beech-rich Chilterns oak is the consistent choice of timber to be found in the cruck farmhouses and the medieval houses of towns like Wendover, Chesham and West Wycombe. Beech is suitable for internal planks and boards but less desirable than oak, so that much beech coppice-wood and branches was sold for fuel or made into charcoal. Such sales were mainly to villages in and around the edges of the Chilterns, and especially in the Vale, but in the southern Chilterns access to the Thames provided an additional market in London. Thus just one example was firewood from the West Wycombe estate sent from Marlow by boat to Southwark, with a load of 14,000 bundles in 1218.[8] In later years, as London's demand grew, this trade became very important and was a major reason why woodland remained a more profitable land-use in the south Chilterns than elsewhere.

A document describing wood-sales on the Stonor estate in 1482 gives a good picture of the range of uses.[9] Wood was sold 'to my master's nailer', to a shoemaker (probably beech to make his lasts), and firewood to the tile kilns. 'Water wode' was sent to London 'for the household', and 'pale tymber' was given to the woodward Saunders for the park. 'Exule and plowyere' (axle and plough ware) were sent to Henley, and tenants were allowed coppice wood: 'Herry Parvin toke 11 load coppice in Bonell Hill to his fyre'. Thirty quarters of 'cole' (charcoal) were also sold.

The different uses and availability of wood in the Chilterns led to some interesting transactions, with local beech being sold for fuel and the proceeds used to buy oak, as at Berkhamsted Park (see below) and at Ibstone. Ibstone windmill was built on the ridge above Turville Dean in 1293-94 and the ridge is still dominated today by a very fine mill with a magnificent view (and very steep descent!) down onto Turville village (Plate 85). Some local timber was used for the 1293 mill, but 400 trees from Westgrove were cut to help cover construction costs. These included the big oak standard needed for the central post of the mill. One of the right size was clearly not available locally, and 'the carpenter had to search for a timber-tree for three days in the woods around Wokingham'.[10]

These direct uses of different types of wood for construction and fuel by no means exhaust the nature of woodland resources in the medieval Chilterns. The Chiltern uplands and woods had long been used for various types of pasture. In woodland the more open glades, grassland and rides provided good grazing at various times of the year, and the trees provided shade. Then the seasonal falls of acorns and beechmast provided food for the pigs—the pannage assessment of Domesday Book—whilst the lower bushes, shoots and holly provided winter fodder.

Pressures on the Woodlands

With so many pressures in a limited space, the woodlands were a zone of conflict. All these different uses of woodland resources were not easily compatible, especially if different groups of users claimed rights to the same woodland. Excessive cutting of brushwood and young coppice-wood for fuel could lead to a declining stock of larger coppice. More intensive grazing of woods meant young shoots were eaten and seedlings failed to regenerate, so gradually slowing reproduction of the woodland and degrading it into open pasture land. Coppicing and

79. Poppies at Kimble. This field of poppies is the result of a year's 'set aside', land taken out of cultivation in much the same location as land was abandoned in medieval times.

80. Ree Field, Codicote. This huge field was the open field in medieval times and today captures some of the scale, and contrasts with the smaller meadows and enclosures which are on the other side of the River Ree.

1. The parish church of Fingest. The church of St Bartholomew, Fingest, is an unusual saddleback design with the tower ider than the nave, as in pre-conquest churches.

2. The parish church of Bledlow. The church of Holy Trinity dates from *c*.1200, and has several early 14th-century windows the chancel.

pasturage do not go together very easily. The population growth of the early Middle Ages, up to around 1300, and the consequent expansion of villages and fields, not only reduced the area of Chilterns woodland but put more pressure on the remaining, still substantial areas. We must remember though that the Buckinghamshire Chilterns would still have had more woods in relation to population in 1348 than most of England in 1086. The pressure of the growing population accentuated the conflicts between uses and between different groups and communities. These conflicts in resource use could be resolved—or fought over—in a whole spectrum of ways. The sharpest conflict was between pasturage and young wood growth, and this was tackled either by attempting to exclude animals from the woods, or by managing the balance through regulation, legal rights and ownership. To understand the medieval Chilterns' woods we need to look at three forms: private or enclosed wood, common woods and wood-pasture commons, and medieval parks or private wood-pasture.

Enclosed Woodland

Private ownership of woodland was the most direct way of eliminating conflicts—other users were excluded and the owner could manage and balance his own use of the wood's resources. To be effective, however, such woodland had to be surrounded by a boundary, both to delimit land ownership and to exclude other users and wandering animals. These wood boundaries were substantial but necessary investments. They usually comprised a wood-bank and ditch, with a strong hedge or a line of trees a little way down the outer face of the bank to give a thick barrier. Hornbeam was often used on such wood-banks in the Chilterns (Plate 105). In the medieval Chilterns the largest private woods were owned by manorial lords as demesne woodland or private parkland. However each holding in the dispersed hamlets and farms of the uplands usually had its own small woods and groves too. As the individual land-market developed (and David Roden has shown it was very active by the 13th century) so parcels of woodland were sold and exchanged in the same way as fields. The charters of Missenden Abbey record many such transactions in the mid-Chilterns, and sometimes explicitly refer to the boundaries and hedges dividing the parcels. For instance when Hugh de Plessis granted woodland to the Abbey in 1277-79 the wood was delimited 'from there directly to the boundary post in the 'le Scires hegge' which divides my woodland from the demesne woodland of Henry Huse'. Similarly in Pyrton parish in the Oxfordshire Chilterns a 1387 agreement involved the whole wood called 'Harlyngruggewode' (in the vicinity of modern Hollandridge farm) 'with the hedges and hays there, and of all the woods, groves, hays and hedges of that parish'.[11]

Many such woods and groves were created out of woodland with common rights, and involved negotiation and conflict. Once again the Missenden charters provide an illustration. On 16 June 1284 the Abbey and Robert Mantel reached agreement over pasturage rights on their lands: the Abbey gave up rights of common pasture on Robert's lands in Little Missenden whilst he surrendered his rights on their land and allowed the Abbey to construct a ditch between the two properties, build a hedge along it, and enclose the 'Hydegrove Wood'.[12] In the countryside to the north of Little Missenden today there is still a Mantle's Farm, Hyde Farm and Hyde Heath.

The ditches and hedges kept out unwanted animals, but the wood owner could still lease pannage and pasture as he saw fit, keeping grazing intensity low and restricting it to specified months of the year or to years of heavy beech mast whilst earning additional income. Thus at Stonor in 1421 the woodward's receipts include pannage fees of £2 10s. 8d., the sale of acorns for 13s. 4d., and underwood sales for 23s.

The real justification of the enclosed wood was, of course, the growth of trees, both standard timbers and, more importantly, smaller coppiced trees. Valuations of demesne woods were usually based on the underwood, whilst medieval documents tend to record spectacular, but infrequent, large-scale fellings of timber trees. Much of the enclosed woodland was clearly more open than high beech-forest because the canopy cannot have been too thick to prevent regeneration and growth. How these woods were managed varied both through time and across the Chilterns. Where the wood was scarce (in the north-east Chilterns) careful management practices and 'coppice cycles' developed early, whereas some of these practices diffused more slowly to the heavily-wooded south-west Chilterns. Coppicing as a way of managing wood growth is very old, and the medieval documents are recording a long-standing practice.

Where woodland was plentiful in relation to demand, timber was simply drawn out as required. It was regarded as a capital resource and heavy felling and sales occurred at times of financial need, when crop income was low or when building bigger structures such as a windmill as at Ibstone. Sometimes storms and gales akin to those of early 1990 provided fellings: after the great storms of 1362 there were big sales from Ibstone, Berkhamsted and Princes Risborough. Neither the large trees nor the coppice were necessarily cut at regular intervals, but there was still careful woodmanship. The *Stonor Letters* record a sale of 1482 where the buyer of the 'Laned Wode', a William Fullard of Watlington, agreed he would cut no tree 'but yf he be above xx [20] ynche at brest heyth of man', and to ensure that 'the vode shalle be ryd at and draute [cut and drawn out] so the young copyse be not hurt'.[13] A sale of wood from Fawley, Hambledon and Turville in 1480 specified 'appultrez, peretrez, crabtrez and all wode of assise of x [10] inche'.[14] By the end of our period the Lewknor estate map of 1598 records: 'They do not fell the wood together but at every fall do glean and draw out only that which is about the growth of 21 years'.

In these reports one can see the gradual adoption of the more regular cropping established earlier in the north-east Chilterns, where coppicing was done in cycles, cutting different areas of wood at steady intervals. Regular coppicing was clearly the practice at King's Walden

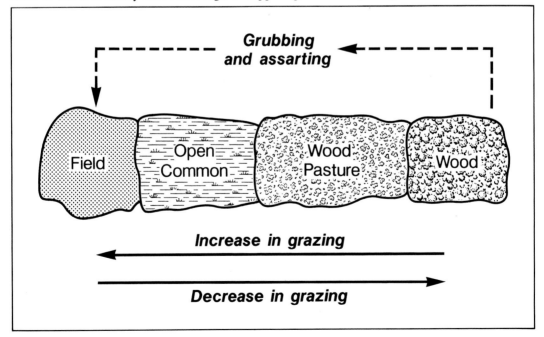

83. The relationship between woodland, pasture and assarting.

in 1388 when a wood is recorded as 'seven acres of wood which can be cut every tenth year and are then worth about 40d the acre, three acres having been cut within the last three years, and four acres within the last five years'. By 1405 the cycle had been reduced from ten years to seven. There are many parallel cases in the northern parts, and the Cartulary of Dunstable Priory contains a very worn entry, undated but from the 15th century, that records very detailed management at Shortgrave in Totternhoe parish: a 93-acre woodland was managed as seven

84. *(facing page)* The St Albans Book of Donors. This illuminated manuscript recorded gifts to St Albans Abbey beginning with the foundation of the Abbey by King Offa of Mercia in AD 793. The two donors with pictures of their tiled medieval houses are Will's de Langeleye and Agnes de Langeforde. [BL: Cotton Nero D vii f3v and f102v.]

85. *(below)* Ibstone windmill from Turville village, high on the hill with a commanding view over the valley of Turville Dean. There has been a windmill here since 1293.

blocks, each of 13 acres and cut in successive order every seven years.[15] By the 16th and 17th centuries, and probably earlier, these practices were common throughout the Chilterns— roughly regular cycles of coppice cutting and less regular felling of large trees. Most of the large trees were still quite young by broadleaf standards and nothing like the enormous oaks or beeches we see today.

Wood-Pasture Commons

Many of the largest wooded regions of the medieval Chilterns were common woods or wood-pasture commons—the two forms grade into one another (Plate 84). The most extensive was probably the 700 acres of Berkhamsted Frith and this adjoined other common woods to make an enormous block. There were some 600 acres of wood on Holmer Heath north of Wycombe, and many large common woods in the central and south Chilterns.

These common woods and wood-pasture commons attempted to combine multiple uses of woods more directly than the enclosed coppice-with-standards woods. Community rights to woodland were deeply embedded in the early medieval social system, and the move towards individual wood property can be seen as part of the broader growth of economic individualism. 'Common rights' did not, however, mean a complete free-for-all. Rights were regulated and restricted by tradition, charter and social position. This regulation could be difficult, especially where several different communities had rights to the same woodland. Seven different parishes all had common rights on Holmer Heath—Penn, Great and Little Missenden, Hughenden, Wycombe, Amersham and Wendover. No less than 11 parishes had claims on Berkhamsted Frith. As Oliver Rackham has noted, 'wood-pastures are less stable ecologically and socially than coppices'.[16]

The knife-edge on which common woods and wood-pasture exist is the balance between wood-growing and grazing intensity. It is a fine equilibrium easily tipped one way or the other: increase the pasturage (and the extraction of wood) too much and the wood degrades to open common or heath, a process widespread in the 13th-, 16th- and 17th-century Chilterns. Reduce the grazing of open commons or wood-pasture and the sequence of recolonisation begins, returning either directly or through stages to proper woodland, a process widespread on Chilterns commons since the late 19th century. The see-saw has tilted both ways in the Chilterns history.

Medieval communities attempted to keep the balance by regulation of rights. Rights to fell timber trees were usually restricted to the manorial lord himself, but tenants normally had rights ('bote') to cut and collect wood for fuel and their houses—'firebote' and 'housebote'— together with other rights such as cartbote, fencebote and hedgebote. Such rights are frequently mentioned in the Missenden charters, and one grant to Geoffrey of Kingshill and his men, dating before 1196, notes:

> *habebunt in bosco de Kingeshulle stipites et clausuram ad eorum sepes sine uisu forestarii et meremium ad emendacionem domorum per uisum forestarii.*
>
> (They are to have stakes and fencing wood in Kingshill Wood for their fences without the woodward's supervision, and timber-wood for the repair of their houses, under the woodward's supervision)[17]

To prevent over-exploitation of the woods, rights were often limited to certain times of the year. At Shirburn there was one week specified for the collection of firewood from the common wood. Sometimes the number of cartloads allowed was restricted (as at Studham near Whipsnade). In the Buckinghamshire Record Office there survives a medieval Wood Book for Pitstone, a strip parish with commons and woods on the escarpment near Ashridge. In Latin and dating from the late 14th century, it gives lists of names and entitlements to cartloads of wood: 'Sir Bernard Brocas for two virgates of land, four loads'.[18] Early 17th-century surveys often reveal these regulations better than the fragmentary medieval records. The 1604 Court Rolls for Lewknor record that the customary tenants had rights to the 'topping and lopping' of trees on their lands and lesser claims in Lewknor's common woods: one and a half loads of bushes yearly from Cowleaze Wood (which still survives) for firewood, and the underwood called ploughbote, cartbote and stakebote which they required for their work.[19] Housebote, for the repair or rebuilding of their houses, was given to them as the lord of the manor might direct—as in 12th-century Kingshill close supervision was still being kept over access to the larger timbers! The right to feed pigs in the woods, especially at mast time, was also controlled and tenants often had to pay pannage fees (frequently the only source of manorial cash income from the common woods). Other sorts of pasture, of cattle and sheep, were usually freely available to all the tenants, together with the right to collect undergrowth for winter fodder.

A particularly interesting case of common wood use was in the Chiltern escarpment parishes, which we have seen were focused in the Vale but extended as long fingers up the escarpment and into the high Chilterns to share in upland resources. Rights to wood from the common woods on or close to the escarpment edge were known as 'hillwork'. An *Inquisition Post Mortem* of 1293 for Princes Risborough records:

> Two foreign woods wherein all the men of four townships have free common, and all the free tenants of the manor have their pigs quit of pannage ... and all the tenants hold a wood called 'Le Hellewrk' in common [the term foreign comes from *forinsecus*, a word used to denote woods outside the manorial park or enclosed woods][20]

'Le Helewerk' also occurs in Chinnor in 1388 and later references, clearly reporting medieval practices, show how widespread it was. At Chinnor in 1579 a tenant was allowed 'a loade of wood in ye common of hylwarks when it is felled', and similar rights occur for Aston Rowant, Kingston Blount and other Icknield parishes.[21] These 'hillwork' woods were on the escarpment so that wood could be transported downhill to the Vale villages, whilst the further dip-slope sections of the parishes were used mainly for pasture and pannage.

The attempt to combine pasture and wood-growth, even when it succeeded reasonably well, altered the nature of the woodland, in particular the underwood. A 1335 report says the underwood of Buckland Wood, on the plateau above Wendover, had been cut down and devastated. A 1360 valuation of Pyrton said that the underwood of the beech common wood was worth nothing 'because the wood was held in common'. As pasture use intensified the existing standards would continue to grow but new shoots and coppice spring would be eaten. The solution was twofold: thorny thickets to protect new tree growth, and pollarding as an alternative to coppicing. By lopping the trees on wood-pasture commons at a height of eight to twelve feet the strong new growth is above the grazing height of animals. Like coppice stumps the boles or bollings of pollards can live for a very long time—many centuries—and continue to flourish and generate new shoots. The distinctive and distorted shapes of old pollards is one of the ways to identify old wood-pasture commons in the Chilterns. Pat Preece, who has made a particular study of the woods in the Oxfordshire Chilterns, has found little evidence of pollarding as a practice there, in contrast to the Buckinghamshire Chilterns.[22] Instead, coppices were enclosed for around seven years (by which time the new growth would be well established), and then limited grazing permitted. With ample woodland to rotate, the pressures of grazing could be accommodated by such a system.

Another distinctive feature lies in the shape or outline of the commons. Enclosed woods tend to be convex in shape, whereas commons funnelled out along tracks and roads, giving a fluted, concave outline. These shapes persist today both on surviving commons such as

86. Old pollarded oaks at Burnham Beeches.

87. Pollarded beeches at Frithsden, north of Berkhamsted. These old pollards clearly show where they were topped, probably in the 18th century, at eight to ten feet above the ground, out of the reach of grazing animals.

Naphill or Cholesbury and in the little village greens which may be their last remnants, as at Holmer Green.

Medieval Parks

The medieval park was a way the more wealthy landowners could successfully combine wood and wood-pasture use by zoning substantial areas for their own exclusive use. The parks were deer parks, an expensive status symbol that provided the luxury food of venison. The deer park usually contained areas of woodland, some of them divided off, and grassland 'launds' or lawns. Since these areas of wooded or semi-wooded landscape were often quite substantial, they were less common in regions of good farming land, but attractive to manorial lords in regions like the Chilterns.

Such parks were expensive to construct because deer require more effective enclosure than sheep or cattle. They required an outer fence or pale consisting of a strong palisade of cleft-oak stakes over six feet high. Some also had a ditch but, in contrast to wood boundary banks, they were inside the fence or hedge, and were designed to keep animals in rather than out. Studies by Hugh Prince have identified more than seventy such parks in the overall Chilterns region by the end of the 16th century.[23] Many are represented on the early county maps of Christopher Saxton and John Norden. They included Ashridge, Berkhamsted, King's Langley and Knebworth in the north Chilterns, Hampden and Chequers in the central part, and Stonor, Nuffield, Fawley Court and Watlington in the south west.

Like the creation of private woodland, parks often involved negotiation and dispute over contested rights. On the scarp above Watlington, Richard, Earl of Cornwall created a park before 1272 and this restricted the local commons. In 1276 it was maintained that the freemen of the area used to have free hunting there, and that some had enjoyed free common. This park was fenced, with 207 perches of fence made in 1296-97. Like other parks the wood-pasture could be leased, regulating the amount in different parts to reduce conflicts: in 1272 the pasture was valued at 5s. a year 'if the animals [deer] did not have it' and the park section was leased for 8s. 5d. in 1278. A later survey in the early 17th century (c.1616) described this park then as 'for the most part mountainous and barraine soyle', but with small timber trees, bushes and some underwood. The adjacent Greenfield Copse had pollarded beeches, young hazel and 'sellable oaks', but was said to be 'much abused by the browse of cattell and unfavourable felling'.[24] Amongst *The Stonor Letters* is preserved a note written by Elizabeth Stonor in London just before Christmas 1476 to her husband William at Stonor: 'as ye wryte that ye will sende me of a wylde bore and other venson ayenst Sonday, truly I thanke yow'.[25] The wild boar was very much a beast of the grandest parks.

Richard, Earl of Cornwall also held the park at Princes Risborough in the late 13th century. This park lay just to the west of the town, and the related buildings at 'The Mount' were excavated in the early 1950s. It was a stud farm as well as a deer park, and there was a running dispute with the Abbot of Notley who claimed rights of agistment or cattle-pasture in the park. In the 14th century the stud farm was developed further, for in 1324 it was recorded that there was no pasture revenue from the park because of the establishment of the King's stud there. Later in the century the manor and park came into the hands of Edward the Black Prince and detailed orders and accounts survive in his Register. After the great storm of 1362 the Risborough bailiffs were ordered to gather all the wood 'as is fit for timber, and also as much as is suitable for the paling of the park there, and keep the two lots safely and separately until the Prince has need of them, and to make "talwode" and "faget" of the remainder'.[26]

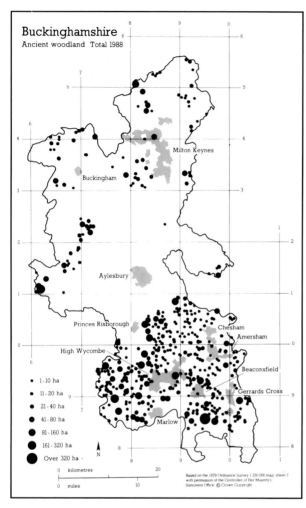

Buckinghamshire
Ancient woodland Total 1988

Milton Keynes
Buckingham
Aylesbury
Princes Risborough
Chesham
Amersham
High Wycombe
Beaconsfield
Gerrards Cross
Marlow

• 1-10 ha
• 11-20 ha
• 21-40 ha
● 41-80 ha
● 81-160 ha
● 161-320 ha
● Over 320 ha

N

0 kilometres   20

0   miles   10

Based on the 1979 Ordnance Survey 1 250 000 map sheet 7
with permission of the Controller of Her Majesty's
Stationery Office © Crown Copyright

88. Ancient woodland in Buckinghamshire. One of the county maps produced by the Nature Conservancy (English Nature) as part of their comprehensive inventory of ancient woodland. It brings out clearly the concentration of such woodland in the Chilterns.

Ancient Woodland Survival

The Chilterns remain to this day a heavily wooded region. In the ecologist G. F. Peterken's provisional national map of 'ancient woodland' the Chilterns stand out as a major area of old woodland, together with regions like the Weald, the New Forest and the Wye Valley.[27] Many other areas have lost most of their medieval woods to later clearance for farming. The Chiltern woods survive partly because the relief, slopes and soils were not so attractive, but more importantly because woodmanship and forestry remained more profitable here than it was elsewhere. The later story of the woods involved their transformation on a large scale. We must not expect the woods we see today to be like the medieval woods we have discussed. But strip away some of the later features, and the explorer can find ancient traces.

The large-scale transformation from coppice-with-standards to high beech forest, and the increasing monopoly of beech over the minority oak, altered the nature of the woods dramatically. Moreover the felling and planting associated with this change have led to big fluctuations in the woodland margins. Old woods have been expanded, then felled and replanted. Using a series of old maps of the Chilterns for various dates, and overlaying them, Anthony Mansfield has estimated that at least one-third of present woodland is on land used for farming at some time since the 17th century.[28] But these pulses—the expansions and contractions of woodland—have tended to be around the outsides of old cores of woodland. Through all the changes the identity of many old woods survives. Hailey Wood, on the escarpment above Lewknor and now sliced through by the M40 motorway, was 'Heyle Wood' in 1279. Bledlow Great Wood is still there, as is Venus Wood (above Chinnor), which was Fernor Wood in 1408 and Vernice Wood in 1840. This survival is not restricted to the south-west Chilterns: Frithsden Wood and Ashridge near Berkhamsted remain, Penn Wood is still there, and Lodge Wood, between Hampden and Great Missenden, is the last remnant (much altered) of the old 'Prestwood' and is called so on the 1st edition Ordnance Survey map.

Does anything more survive beyond the names? The answer is 'yes', and its detection owes much to the work of Oliver Rackham and other historical ecologists studying signs of ancient woodland. There are fossilised features directly surviving from the Middle Ages, and these are the archaeological traces of medieval woodland management. The woodbanks, ditches and earthworks were expensive to create and are also expensive to remove, so they often survive—banks somewhat eroded and ditches somewhat filled-in. Where the woodland has expanded they can be discovered within more modern woodland margins in many of the old wood areas of the Chilterns. One good example, actually marked on the 2½ inch (1:25000) Ordnance Survey map, is at Hampden in the central Chilterns. Here woodland margins have fluctuated dramatically: expanding across former open commons, being felled for arable land, then expanding again. Yet the old ditch and woodbank that divided Keepershill Wood and Hampden Coppice from Great Hampden Common can still be discovered and walked along, though the old Coppice is now high forest and the woodland edge has expanded onto the common, with the village pond now surrounded by colonising wood.

The trees themselves are sometimes living relics of the old wood. In the big beechwoods where clear-felling has not taken place, one can see old coppiced trees, long neglected and grown enormous with huge multiple leaders or trunks, but with the base and form revealing their origins. Such big beeches and oaks may be 150 to 250 years old, but the coppice stump will be much older still. Along former woodbanks one can also see outgrown coppice-trees with 'shoulders', the result of cutting to encourage sideways growth for a tree-barrier.

On former wood-pasture one can discover old pollards. Many of the medieval parks have gone, converted to arable fields and then built upon as at Princes Risborough and Berkhamsted, or dramatically remodelled into landscaped parks and gardens. Yet within the parkland of surviving parks such as Stonor, Watlington, Chequers, Hampden and Knebworth old pollarded trees can be seen along with the more classical beauty of 'natural' oak and beech park-trees. At Knebworth Great Park, on the north-east edge of the Chilterns, one can picnic under the twisted pollards whilst the children play in the Adventure Playground there or climb up the

89. Pollards in Knebworth Park. Old parkland dotted with very ancient gnarled pollards.

insides of the oldest specimens (Plate 89). The pollard bolls can live a very long time and some must be well over 300 years old.

The Chilterns were rich enough in large commons (and the competing pressures not too strong) for quite a number of these commons to survive. Many lost their trees under later intensive grazing, and then began to regain them when grazing declined and ceased, but there may be no direct continuity of woodland or trees. Thus some of the existing woods on the Chiltern escarpment today were open downland grazed by sheep up to the late 19th century, and ecological succession is rewooding them today. Most of the trees on commons in the Chilterns are less than 100 years old, but within some of these woods can be found old pollards—legacies from wood-pasture days, trees much older than the woods they now stand in. Such trees often provide the protection needed for new seedling and shoot growth, so that rewooding of the commons happens not as an advancing tide from the nearest woodland edge, but as little islands growing around the old pollards, then coalescing. Such expansion can be seen around the oak and beech pollards on the edge of Hampden Common and in many other places, but the finest examples are to be found at Naphill, Berkhamsted Beeches and Burnham. Naphill Common, north west of High Wycombe, is now a very extensive wood, but deep inside it, along its twisting paths, are some large and magnificent distorted pollards. Burnham Beeches, on the south-east fringe of the Chilterns, is the best known locality, purchased and preserved by the Corporation of London. La Sueur, an expert on Burnham Beeches, thought that the pollards originated on the heath around 1600 (although he does not give any direct evidence), though oak pollards such as Druid's Oak may be even older.[29] The beech pollards were certainly over 130 years and may have been much more ancient when the poet Thomas Gray wrote to Horace Walpole in 1737 of the 'most venerable beeches ... always dreaming out their old stories to the winds'.

In addition there is evidence of survival in the woodland ecology. Ancient woodlands tend to have distinctive and rich flora and microfauna which have had over a thousand years to colonise the woods and come to terms with traditional woodland management. Certain species of ground flora are only very slow colonisers, and some may be survivals from the original wildwood. Their persistence to the present day requires ecological continuity, stability of the woodland habitat to allow unbroken reproduction. The later conversion to high beech forest has restricted good light for undergrowth and ground flora so that some of the large beech woods are not as rich in flower species as many English ancient woods. Where the cover is more diverse, and around the more open edge, a richer ancient flora can be seen.

There are many 'indicator species' for ancient woodland—ground species that colonise only slowly. For the Chilterns there is no one single species as useful as the oxlip in East Anglia, but several together provide a good indicator. One of these is the bluebell, and its bright carpets in spring, with the sun glinting through the new tree foliage, is a sight to behold. It does colonise later woods and hedges (though it is also a good indicator of wood-relic hedges), but not in the great lawns of colour of ancient woodland like Ashridge and Frithsden. Other good indicators—and none is infallible taken singly—include lily-of-the-valley, wood anemone, wild service tree and dog's mercury.

Because of their grazing history wood-pasture commons have a much less interesting ground flora, but the old pollards, like old woodland trees, can provide a home and habitat continuity for distinctive lichen and insect populations. A number of the woods and parklands have been surveyed for their tree-bark lichens, and Francis Rose has found good indications of ancient woodland species at Stonor and Chequers Parks. H. J. M. Bowen has shown that several rare lichen species observed in the Chiltern woods by 19th-century botanists have now disappeared, probably due to increasing air pollution.[30]

The Woodlands of Berkhamsted

Many aspects of the medieval woodland can be illustrated and drawn together by looking at a one local landscape in detail. Several parts of the Chilterns would be suitable but let us choose Berkhamsted, partly because it is home ground but also because it is a good locality in terms of surviving documents and surviving fragments of landscape.[31]

The market town and commuter settlement of Berkhamsted nestles in the Bulbourne Valley of the Hertfordshire Chilterns. It was already an important borough at the time of Domesday Book and became more significant with the royal castle in the medieval period. By 1357 there were 114 shops and tenements in the town. The open fields ran along the lower ground south of the river and to the east of the town, while the demesne fields were on the north bank, west of the castle.

To the south old, steep hollow lanes rise to the plateau and a landscape of individual farms, closes and enclosed woods. 'La Magdeleine', now Marlin, is first mentioned in 1274. A charter of 1294 describes recently cleared land and wood in an enclosure 'Northrudyng' below the wood of 'la Maudelyne', whilst woods at Amberlains Hill (Hamberlins today) and Cock Grove (next to Marlin) are mentioned in later, pre-plantation documents. The major wooded regions were, however, north of the borough. The Park lay immediately north of the demesne fields and castle. Further north on the hillside and plateau was the enormous common wood of the Frith.

The manorial lord controlled not just his demesne wood but also the timber rights from his *boscus forinsecus* or 'foreign wood', the common wood of the Frith lying outside the park. The Frith occupied over 700 acres of the parish at the end of the 13th century but, as noted earlier, this was only part of the vast woodland spreading across several parishes. This would be the 'wood for 1000 swine' in Berkhamsted's Domesday Book entry. The timber, almost exclusively beech here, was reserved for the manorial lord and there are frequent references to it, especially for the mid-14th century when Edward the Black Prince held Berkhamsted as a royal manor.[32] In 1351 he made gifts to the parson of St Peter's of 'three beeches in the foreign wood for fuel'. He also gave his demesne farmer 'seven beeches yearly in the foreign wood for housebote and heybote', and in 1361 he ordered 600 beeches 'to be marked for future use'.

The men of Berkhamsted had rights of pasture in the Frith throughout the year, but they had to share them with other townships. When, however, they turned their pigs into the wood they had to pay pannage dues, despite the fact that the Rector of Ashridge and his tenants were exempt. This anomaly arose from a grant by Edward, Earl of Cornwall, in 1285 to the newly created monastery or college at Ashridge. This gave it lands 'and common of pasture in the wood of Bercamstede called 'le Fryth' for all their beasts; with leave to have their pigs in the said wood in the time of mast quit of pannage; with housebote and haybote and fencing of the said park of Esserugge in the said Fryth wood'. These multiple rights meant that gradually the common wood developed the character of wood-pasture, with pollarded beeches and oaks.

In 1353 the Prince acquired an extra 54 acres of land and 10 acres of wood to enlarge his Park and create a new 'lawn' there. He ordered his Constable to enclose the Park 'with a paling for the preservation thereof and of game there'. To do this he was to sell beeches from the Frith to £20 value and then use the money to buy oak timber for the rails and stanchions of the pale. 'All the beeches are to be cut down in different parts of the wood, as shall be most profitable to the Prince and least wasteful of the wood, and the stumps are to be marked with the axe appointed for the purpose.' As well as the Frith there were also substantial demesne and park woods, for, in 1300, 4,000 faggots were produced from the demesne wood, and in 1354 the Prince's baker was given sufficient beech from the Park or Frith for 'making three "gates" for his bakery, and the residue of the beeches for consumption in the ovens of the bakery'.

90. Woodbank at Frithsden Copse near Berkhamsted. The remnants of a medieval woodbank marking the boundary between the enclosed woodlands of the copse and pasture on Frithsden common.

What can we still detect of this medieval wooded landscape in the countryside around Berkhamsted today? The Park has gone, disparked and converted to fields in the 17th century, as was part of the Frith to create Coldharbour Farm in 1630. Yet many significant elements remain. One can drive or walk up the steep lanes such as Darr's, Durrant's or Hamberlin's to the Cock Grove or Hamberlin's Wood, ancient in much of its character and with old woodbanks that can still be seen. The remains of 'The Frith', in the form of Berkhamsted Common, were saved from enclosure in the 1860s and large areas are now owned and managed by the National Trust. They contain some fine trees known as Frithsden Beeches and Frithsden Copses, described by Dr. Oliver Rackham as 'a rare survival of the medieval Chilterns landscape'.[33] The Beeches are the remnant of old wood-pasture on the north of the Common (Plate 87). At their heart is a group of huge ancient pollarded beeches, with bases up to six and seven feet across. They are surrounded by old (but younger) beeches and then a fringe of oak and birch which has grown up after pasture ceased. Reportedly the beeches were last pollarded in the early 19th century but the bollings must go back to the 17th century.

A few hundred yards to the east are the Copses, given to the National Trust by the historian G. M. Trevelyan. They are old embanked coppice woods separated from the wood-pasture common. The Great Copse was replanted to mark the 1953 Coronation (much to the regret of wood conservationists), but the Little Copse is 'original'. The ditches and woodbanks around the Copse can easily be seen (Plate 90), together with the stumps and remnants of the old boundary hedge. The trees in the Copse are mixed, with much hornbeam and cherry together with standards of oak and the occasional beech. The hedgebank trees are hornbeam and beech and inside there are carpets of bluebells and anemones. Here one can see many elements of the ancient woods of the Chilterns struggling through to the present landscape.

Chapter Eight

Rural Change 1550-1800

Introduction

Sixteenth-century England saw a new vitality, a quickening in economy, society and national spirit. The Tudor monarchy brought a political stability and unity after the conflicts of previous centuries. England's population began to grow rapidly again, and economic growth flowed around a fast expanding London: from a population of about 55,000 in 1520, London grew to 200,000 by 1600 and 575,000 by 1700. The dissolution of the monasteries and abbeys in the 1530s and the rise of a new Protestant England meant that many lands changed hands, and 'new men' led a dynamism that gave the era of Elizabeth, Raleigh and Shakespeare what one writer called 'its spring-like air of expansiveness'.[1] This new progress faltered at times—there was a serious hiccup in the 1580s and '90s when the population grew faster than the food supply, and the next century saw the English civil war and periods of economic depression. But by economic and social change England avoided 'the medieval trap' of a limit to agricultural output.

The Chilterns participated fully in this era of improvement. They were close enough to attract London money and businessmen, and they were well-placed to help supply food and fuel to the growing City. Chiltern farming improved and prospered. The woodlands grew fuel for London. The Chiltern town and inns catered for the travellers and traders.

The Vanishing Open-Fields

Among the first signs of this new era in the Chilterns was the gradual disappearance of open-fields from the Hills and valleys by a process of piecemeal enclosure. This was not the depopulating enclosure for sheep farming, but a change from open arable to enclosed arable. Farmers saw opportunities for more efficiency and improvement if they controlled their own land and reaped all the benefits themselves. Progress could be individual rather than communal. Chiltern farmers knew this from their old enclosed fields, and Tudor writers like Thomas Tusser (brought up at Wallingford) argued the case:

> Good land that is several, crops may have three,
> in champion country it may not so be...

Tusser devoted a whole poem to *A Comparison between Champion Country and Several*,[2] including:

> The country enclosed I praise,
> The t'other delighteth not me!
> For nothing the wealth it doth raise,
> To such as inferior be...

The t'one is commended for grain,
Yet bread made of beans they do eat:
The t'other for one loaf hath twain,
Of meslin, of rye, or of wheat.
The champion liveth full bare;
When woodland full merry doth fare.

In woodland, the poor men that have,
Scarce fully two acres of land,
More merrily live, and do save,
Than t'other with twenty in hand.
Yet pay they as much fro the two,
As t'other for twenty must do.

The labourer coming from thence,
In woodland to work anywhere,
(I warrant you) goeth not hence,
To work any more again there...

The very flexibility of the medieval Chiltern field systems meant that they could be readily changed when the time was ripe. And ripe it was. Because there were so many fields and most farmers' holdings were in those closest to their dwellings, consolidation of strips and piecemeal enclosure could take place without challenging the whole communal system or getting everyone's agreement. Consolidation of strips had been taking place for a long time, and once the manorial court stopped enforcing common pasture of the arable, the enclosure of the fields was straightforward. At places like Codicote the Abbot and his monks had departed with the dissolution of the monasteries in the 1530s, and the new manorial lords were keen on improvement. A few decades brought a big change in attitudes. In 1524 at Little Gaddesden on the Hertfordshire-Buckinghamshire border, two tenants were brought before the manorial court for keeping land in severalty in the common fields after the harvest, but after 1550 there was much purchase, exchange and enclosure. Twenty-two exchanges of copyhold land are recorded between 1556 and 1583. Six involved land in Mill Field, and by 1579 a seven-acre piece there is described as 'now inclosed'. Strip by strip, field by field, the common fields contracted.[3] By 1600 at least three of Berkhamsted's common fields had gone, and the story is true across the Hills. Other large common fields were subdivided, as a prelude to further enclosure. For the most part we see only occasional transactions, surveys of holdings at particular dates, but the open-fields shrank and vanished like snow-patches in the landscape.

There were gainers and losers in all this. Those who accumulated in Tudor times were rarely the same families who consolidated in the 15th century, and large tenants and manorial lords gained over small tenants. Holdings became very unequal, and those with the smallest lost out to the new yeoman and tenant farmers as land tenures became more like modern freeholds and leaseholds. It was the little man (or woman, for holdings by females are not uncommon) who was left with strips in the residual common fields as his bigger neighbours agreed to enclose, and his ultimate fate was often as a hired labourer. A detailed survey of Great Hampden in 1653, which is preserved in the Buckinghamshire Record Office, illustrates the pattern.[4] The remaining open fields were only 244 acres in extent, and were clustered at the northern end of the manor below Little Hampden. The larger tenants, like John Lydall with 187 acres and Robert Morton with 179, had most of their land in closes, though they were also still the biggest holders in the remaining open fields. Smallholders like John Knight with his 3½ acres had all their land in the open strips.

This drawn-out process left its permanent imprint on the landscape. Sometimes fields have been amalgamated since, but many of the closes and their hedges are still there. In some places, as between Harpenden and Kings Walden, it is claimed the fields preserve the reverse-S shape of medieval ploughed furlongs.[5] The piecemeal enclosure proceeded fastest and furthest in the south-west Chilterns, where common fields had been fewer anyway, and more slowly in the north-east. Precisely because it was piecemeal, most localities retained a rump of open-field where agreement had not been reached. These were mainly historical hangovers, of less and less farming significance. In Codicote, for example, although most of the open fields disappeared, a few open pieces still remained in 1800, including a three-strip patch in the middle of Ree Field.

The real division was between the Chiltern Hills and the surrounding lowlands. In the Vale and along the Thamesside lowlands the open field systems were much more all-embracing, a strong oak hard to tamper with or pull down. Here piecemeal enclosure was impossible. As the open fields disappeared in the Hills but remained in the Vale, the contrast between 'Chiltern and Vale', 'champion and woodland' noted by Leland and others became more marked, and the Chiltern scarp became a great divide in the agrarian landscape.

A Tale of Two Maps

We can see this landscape contrast between the enclosed Chilterns and the open-field Vale first mapped out in Elizabethan times, and there are two lovely examples from the Oxfordshire Chilterns. In Elizabeth's reign map-making made great advances, both in general topographical maps and in detailed land-surveying. The first strand gave us the county maps of Christopher Saxton and others. The second has given us two late Elizabethan estate maps, beautifully drawn and coloured, for Lewknor and for Harpsden.

The Lewknor map is one of an extensive series of maps commissioned by Warden Hovenden of All Souls College in Oxford, recording the various estates belonging to the College (Plate 98). The Lewknor map was surveyed and drawn by Thomas Langdon in 1598,

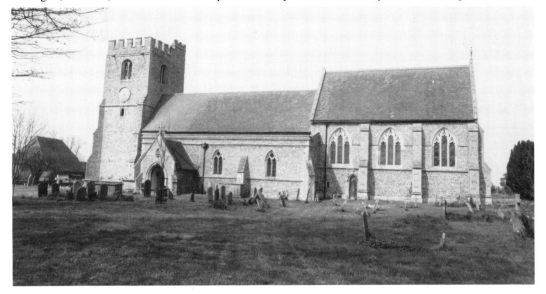

91. The parish church of St Margaret at Lewknor. From medieval times the living of the church was in the gift of All Souls College and the college remains the largest landowner in Lewknor today. On the left the roof of the medieval barn (Plate 71) can be seen.

and has not been reproduced before. All Souls had acquired rights to Lewknor church in 1442, and subsequently acquired further lands there, which they hold to this day. The map shows the open-fields of the village, picking out the strips belonging to the church (the glebe lands) and identifying their size and the landowners on either side. A court roll for 1594 notes that the strips were defined by stakes and merestones which were set down before the spring sowing at Candlemas.[6] The furlongs were made up of these half-acre strips. Many can be identified by name such as Filhole, Woodlande, Stonepitte and Preste Furlonges. In Preste Furlonge on the southern boundary (the right-hand side of the map) the strips of manor and glebe alternate, perhaps reflecting some reallocation. The old enclosures in the village centre stand out clearly, as do the church, and the manor house to the south. Weston Inclosure (in the centre of the map) can still be seen today. The map also shows 'the London waye' at the top (later to be the A40), and running diagonally through the fields is marked 'Hackeman waye' or the Lower Icknield Way. The grazing common of the Chiltern escarpment is marked, including 'Parte of the sheepe comon'. The text around the map records the tithes due from different land parcels, including those from Lewknor Uphill, above the escarpment and not shown on the map.

92. A Harpsden lane. This lane leads down from Upper House Farm to Hunts Green, still very much the same today as it was on the 1586 map.

Lewknor was to remain unenclosed for two more centuries, until 1815, and we will return to its story later.

The second map is a vivid contrast. Made by John Blagrave of Reading it shows the Harpsden valley just south-west of Henley in 1586 (Plate 100). Blagrave was a mathematician, author of *The Mathematical Jewel* (1585) and *The Art of Dyalling* (1609), and produced a small number of estate maps; his elaborate monument is in St Lawrence's church in Reading. His Harpsden map was drawn for Humphrey Forster of Harpsden Manor, and shows a totally enclosed landscape of hedged fields and woods. This landscape remains largely unchanged today with steep lanes and old trees around Hunt's Green (Plate 92). The list of the eight farms and their fields shows the land dominated by three farms of 520, 136 and 116 acres controlling three-quarters of the area, but with three smaller holdings around Hunt's Green. The colouring picks out the different land-uses: yellow/brown stripes for fields ploughed but left fallow; green stripes for the growing crop; light green for pasture and rough grazing; and a dark green for pasture by the river (off our map extract). As yet little is known of the earlier history of this manor, but the names of some of the closes suggest there were once open-fields that had been enclosed. Others have names like Stocking Croft and Upper Croft suggesting old enclosures. It looks like a classic medieval assarted landscape, but we should be cautious and remember that Harpsden Roman villa lay on the hillside just to the south and that *hearps denu* is mentioned in an Anglo-Saxon boundary charter. The wills of several of the 1586 farmers, like John Wydmore of Hunt's Green and William Pearman of Upper House Farm, are preserved in the Oxfordshire Record Office, and Ruth Gibson has studied the subsequent farming history of the valley in detail.[7] She has discovered that parts of the farmhouses shown on the 1586 map still survive, behind later additions and modifications. Bottom Farm (now 'The Old Place') includes a timbered portion with a mid-16th century style of spine beam, whilst the back of Hunt's Farm has a cruck construction that must predate 1586.

Farming Improvements

Throughout the 16th century the Chilterns continued to be dominated by the arable and by corn production. Wheat was the main commercial crop, with barley gradually becoming more important in some parts of the region. Much of the grain went to supply the London market, and was transported through a number of centres. The most notable were Henley in the south, High Wycombe for the central Chilterns, and a number of Hertfordshire towns for the northern parts.

Henley's waterborne links with London made it an excellent collection centre for the Upper Thames Valley, together with Reading and Wallingford. John Leland in the 1530s had written of 'plenty of wood and corne about Henlye'. London depended heavily on Henley's wheat in Elizabethan times: between 1568 and 1573 one-third of all English corn shipped down the Thames to London came from Henley.[8] The records of the London companies show the commercial links in more detail. After a scarcity of corn in London in 1586-87, the Privy Council ordered JPs to assess the quantities of grain in their locality, and, after deducting an allowance for family provision and seed, to require owners to bring the rest for sale 'in open markett'. The returns for the Oxford Chiltern Hundreds survive: for Ewelme the wheat in store was calculated at 943 quarters, and of this 310 quarters were thought to be surplus available for the market.[9]

Malting from barley also became an important trade, probably in the 17th century or even earlier. Richard Blome in his *Britannia* (1673) described the Henley market as 'very considerable for corn, especially barley, which is brought there for their great Mault-trade, there being oft-times sold in one day about 300 cartload of barley'.[10]

The Chilterns were well placed to meet this metropolitan demand, and farmers could make their own choices of crops and rotations on their enclosed farms. Rising demand gave good incomes to the yeoman farmers, which we can still see reflected in the Elizabethan and 17th-century timber-and-brick farmhouses and cottages of the south Chilterns, especially north of Henley. Real improvements in yield came more slowly, for the 'agricultural revolution' was a transformation over two centuries rather than a sudden change.

The continuing arable character of the whole Chilterns region finds confirmation in recent work on marriage seasons.[11] Ann Kussmaul has shown that in arable-dominated regions most people got married in autumn, after the harvest. In pastoral regions the weddings were in spring or early summer, after lambing and calving. There was no strong seasonality in non-agricultural or industrial regions. Although her Chilterns sample is not large, it is resolutely autumn-marriage.

Within this arable character, however, there was much local variation in what was grown and in what proportions. This sprang from that intense local variability of soils that characterises this region. As Thomas Delafield put it in his manuscript *History of Stokenchurch* (1744): 'I believe, a greater variety of soills, and more different forms of the scituation of lands, can hardly be found in any place than in these Chiltern Countrys; and by consequence greater occasions to exercise the Art and Capacity of the Farmer'.[12]

These regional characteristics were becoming recognised in the term 'Chiltern Country', used by many of the county and farming writers of the 17th and 18th centuries. Walter Blith, for example, in *The English Improver Improved* (1652) commented (in a general defence of enclosure): 'Consider the Chilterne countries, and you shall finde, that were it inclosed men would Plow little or no whit less than they doe, because nothing else nor no way else would yeeld the like Advance'.[13]

The pattern of Chiltern farming and its improvements are revealed through writers of the times. For greater detail historians and geographers have recently begun to make use of the mass of surviving probate inventories for 1550 onwards. These list domestic possessions, the crops stocked and sown, farm implements and other indications of wealth and farming practices. Pioneered by Michael Havinden for Oxfordshire, and recently applied on a large scale for Hertfordshire, these studies allow a more reliable picture to be constructed of just how many farmers did what, rather than recording the few innovators.[14] They show that, in Elizabethan and early 17th-century times, Chiltern farmers still followed three-course rotations. They grew wheat and barley, but also considerable amounts of oats and rye because of the acidity of the poorer soils. Sheep were important as an aid to arable production, rather than for their meat or wool. They grazed on the commons and wastes and were folded on the fallow. Pulses were grown as fodder, but in smaller quantities than in the Vale, where waste was scarce.

The inventories reveal that gradually this pattern changed, and grain yields increased, especially in the later 17th century. By 1700 they had increased by some 75 per cent and by 1800 by a further third.[15] The two major sources of this improvement were better preparation of the ground, fertilising the soil, and the use of different fodder crops and foreign grasses that could be used in new rotations.

Chiltern soils benefited enormously from treatment, especially marling, the adding of chalk or lime to the acid surface of clay-with-flints soil. It was an old technique, but now employed with a new vigour and on a large scale. Farmers dug pits in their fields through the clay layer, which might be 20-30 ft. at most, into the chalk. From the base of the bell-pit, shafts might be dug. The broken chalk, sometimes burnt in a kiln to make it into lime, was then spread on the fields. When the pit was exhausted, it would be boarded over and soil put on top; later rotting of the boards and their collapse has left the distinctive depressions in many a Chiltern field. Organic manures were also important, not just in the form of sheep-dung, but as human 'night-soil' brought from London to some parts of Hertfordshire. Shredded rags were also ploughed into the ground, to help lighter soils retain moisture. Throughout the 17th century probates show the increasing role of ground preparation, like that of Henry Tudder of Great Gaddesden, whose £200 include £10 for 'fallowing, stirring, dunging and dressing' the land.[16]

The second element, which probably contributed more after 1700, was the growth of fodder crops such as turnips and swedes and the sowing of new grasses such as clover and sainfoin. The new grasses enriched the soil and provided fodder for animals. Soil was improved, more animals could be kept (important where wastes were limited) and therefore manuring increased, so yields rose. Fodder crops and sown grasses could replace some bare fallowing, making more use of the land and generating complicated rotation patterns. At one time turnips were seen as the key to the agricultural revolution. This is no longer the view.

Although they were pioneered early, and may may have been grown in the Chilterns as early as 1670, they were slow to diffuse. Sown grasses probably had an earlier impact. Thus clovers are found in inventories from the 1670s in the Oxfordshire Chilterns.[17]

A single inventory can be used to capture many features of the late 17th-century Chilterns farming. It is for 'Rebekah Harding of Greenfield, widow in the parish of Watlington', dated 18 May 1685. Greenfield is one of the hamlets on the Chiltern escarpment above Watlington village, just south of Christmas Common. The inventory records her domestic goods, her bedsteads and sheets, pewter and brass, her table and cupboards; her 'four flitches of bacon'; her andirons for the fire, with tongs, bellows, spits and a warming pan. It lists 'for barrels and tubs and a salting trough in a room called the drink house', and then moves to the farming goods. These illustrate virtually all the aspects of Chiltern farming. Most of the crops are in closes ('for barley in a ground called Bakers Close £35'), but some are in the common fields of Watlington ('barley in Comonfield'). The crops include wheat, barley, oats and maslin (the mixture of wheat and rye). In Pond Close there was barley, peas, vetches and dills, and 'Clover gras and other gras' is listed. There were about 40 sheep, and 'two dungcarts on the wheels' (Plate 93).

During the 18th century rotations involving turnips and the range of sown grasses became the normal pattern in the Chilterns. This is documented in the County reports between 1794 and 1815, such as Arthur Young's *Oxfordshire*. He instances the Fane estate at Wormsley south of Stokenchurch, where a rotation of (1) turnips, (2) barley, (3) clover or trefoil or ray-grass, (4) wheat was followed. On drier land south of Nettlebed Mr. Dean of English Farm followed a similar sequence: turnips, barley or oats, clover, wheat, turnips, barley or oats, trefoil, wheat.[18] Bare fallowing was now very much the exception on these enclosed farms. Change in the open-field parishes of the Vale and other lowlands around the Hills was much slower. Some agreements for improved farming were successful, especially on the rich greensand loams of the Icknield Belt. As early as 1618 some arable strips in Aston Rowant were put down to pasture as temporary leys, and 'hitching' or fencing part of the bare fallow and sowing grasses was practised in some villages.[19] A lease of 1717, also for Aston, reports that the tenant was to have one ton of rags each year to put on the land, brought from London via Hambleden Wharf. At Lewknor in 1765 the 11 main farmers agreed to a three-year experiment of sowing clover in the spring field after it was cleared, and corn on the fallow land. However it expressly forbade any corn sowing on the hillsides of the sheep-walks. All these changes were, at best, partial tinkering, and in the Vale the full benefits of the new farming methods had to await Parliamentary Enclosure of the open-fields.

Ellis and Kalm

It is time to make the acquaintance of William Ellis of Little Gaddesden. Ellis (*c*.1690-1758) was a former London brewer who began farming in Chiltern Hertfordshire at Church Farm, where 'I occupy my own Farm and the Glebe-land of our Parish, containing in all twenty four inclosed Fields of several Sorts of Soils'.[20] He also became a prolific and influential farming writer, as well as selling advice, new implements like a four-wheel drill plough, and seeds. His books include *The Timber-Tree Improved* (1738), *The Practical Farmer or the Hertfordshire Husbandman* (1732), *The Country Housewife's Family Companion* (1750), and, in eight volumes, *The Modern Husbandman* (1750). For us, however, the most apposite is his *Chiltern and Vale Farming Explained* (1733). Ellis's writings are a real mixture: he is garrulous, he digresses, tells anecdotes and shouts his prejudices; but he is also a shrewd, detailed observer of landscapes and their farming potential, and a vigorous advocate of the new, improved husbandry.

93. Probate Inventory for Rebekah Harding of Watlington 1685. A very complete list of Rebekah's possessions including furniture, sheets and other household goods, farming equipment and the livestock and crops in the different fields and closes of Greenfield and Watlington.

In *Chiltern and Vale*, Ellis discussed the benefits of good and the 'sad effects' of bad management:

> The Chiltern, or Hilly Country especially, is more concerned in these Subjects, by reason it is mostly enclosed, and consists in diversity of Soils, of clays, Loams, Sands, Chalk, Stony Ground, Hurlucky and Gravelly Grounds, and several other Sorts, that bound more or less with Parts of these Earths. While the fertile Vale or low Country runs chiefly but in little other, than the black Loams or blewish Marly clays in open Fields, that are commonly under one and the same management of Culture; and is easier by far brought into a Tilth or Condition for corn, than this of ours, and with a great deal of less Charge and Trouble.

He recognises that the Vale clays and loams (especially the latter) are inherently more fertile than the Hill soils, but argues that Chiltern soils can give very good returns, if they receive investment, effort, and improvement: 'Not that I pretend to say a Chiltern Man can Farm as cheap as a Vale Man'. The ground needed extra treatment, more ploughing, and other bills were greater. Because of the stony flints, ''Tis therefore computed, that £5 will go as far in a Smith's Bill in the Vale, as 15 will in the Chiltern'.[21] Here Ellis is echoed by his contemporary, Thomas Delafield of Stokenchurch, who enthused:

> after a new plowing one would rather take the Ridges for Causeys Strewed with Stones to walk on, than for Lands to sow corn in: so very little of earth is to be seen among the stones that the Ploughshare in some places turns up. This makes hard service for the horse, and Expensive for the Master, but Profitable to the Smith that repairs the Irons. However these soills often rear plentiful crops of good wheat, often as good, and as much as in deeper Lands. To this the Flints are not a little contribution, by inbuing the nitre of the Air, and by their Proper Salt and Sulphur communicating its genial heat to the seed, by keeping the ground warm and hollow; by sheltering the new spring blade from the extremity of the winter.[22]

Ellis advocates all of the improvements we have seen in action, such as intensive dressings for the 'red clays' or clay-with-flints of the Hills, with both chalk and organic fertilisers: 'Twenty five or thirty Load will well chalk an Acre of Ground, which by discreet Ploughings will last twenty Years'.[23] For farmers within 30 miles of London (Little Gaddesden is 27 miles as the crow flies), he recommends soot purchased in the city:

> And that it may come cheaper home, we commonly carry up Chaff, Corn, Wood, Flour, or timber, and fetch, in Return, Soot in sacks, or loose, in a Cart or Waggon, which now is sold for Six-pence a Bushel, when in Winter, and at Spring, it is sold in London for ninepence. And in this Manner, you may bring down Coal-ashes, Ox or cow's Hoofs, Hog's or Ox's Hair, Trotters, Horn Shavings, Coney-clippings, Pidgeon's or Rabbit's Dung.[24]

He advocates rag dressing for chalky soils, and sheep dung for all soils in Chiltern and Vale. Ellis was also an enthusiast for fodder crops, and for 'resting the Ground chiefly by sowed Grasses' such as clover and lucerne, and not bare fallowing. One of the great gains Chiltern can have over Vale is 'the Enjoyment of the third Year (that with them lies Fallow)', and he admonishes conservative Chiltern farmers

> who are so byassed by their Ancestors Methods ... that many will justify (or at least endeavour it) the third Year's Ground laying Fallow, which indeed is putting the Enclosure almost on the same Footing of an open Vale Field, but this obstinate Absurdity brings them under less Profit, than those that husband their Ground otherways.[25]

Ellis and his writings are fascinating in themselves, but his encounter with Pehr Kalm is even more so.[26] Kalm was a Swedish-Finnish scientist who undertook a visit to England and North America in 1748-51, to look at agricultural practices. Once in England:

> I undertook at the cost and request of Herr Vice-President Baron Bjelke, a journey to see Mr.
> Ellis, who lived at Little Gaddesden in Hertfordshire. Mr. Ellis was a man who had made a great
> reputation for his Practice of Rural Economy, but still more for his many writings on the same
> Art, which latterly he had published yearly.

Arriving on 25 March, Kalm and his assistant Lars Ljungstrom spent three weeks at *The Robin
Hood* inn at Little Gaddesden (the inn still survives as a private house). His observations on
England were translated a century and a half later, and include over 150 pages on the Gaddesden
area. Kalm was a careful, scientific observer, and he beautifully records the contrasts between
Chiltern and Vale at that date. He walked the four miles to Ivinghoe in the Vale 'because Mr.
Ellis told us that the appearance of the country and the soil was entirely different from what
there was at Little Gaddesden'. Under a heading 'Evils of the common fields', Kalm wrote:

> Today we had manifold proofs of this, what harm and hindrance it is for a farmer to have all
> his property in common fields, with his neighbours, and on the other hand what an advantage
> to have an isolated farm and possessions all to himself, when he gets to manage and cultivate
> them according to his own discretion. Around Little Gaddesden and on all Chiltern-land every
> farmer more or less had his own severalties which he afterwards divided into small inclosures
> by hedges. There was one inclosure sown with wheat, another with barley, turnips, peas, oats,
> sainfoin, clover, trifolium, tares, potatoes, or whatever he wished.
>
> While the field were lying fallow, he could sow it with turnips, feed sheep on it, and afterwards
> plough down the remaining bitten turnips, and have thereby a much greater advantage than if
> he had left it fallow. In short, he could in a thousand ways improve his property and earn
> money. On the other hand, here about Ivinghoe, where the common fields are everywhere in
> use, no hedges are seen. Nor are there here any pease or kinds of grass sown as fodder for
> sheep, cows, horses and swine ...

Kalm recorded the plants, the trees and the chalk pits, the houses and the women (Kalm
was astonished they did no farmwork, but found them 'very handsome and lively in society').
But he was disappointed in his encounter with Ellis. He found Ellis rather wary and secretive,
and a demonstration of the new drill plough did not impress him. It kept breaking down: 'Now,
the seed would not run; now the mould stuck fast in the hole at the bottom of the funnel; now
the corn was not harrowed well down, so that there were here *frictiones frictionum*'s and less
than a pint of seed was sown in the afternoon. Looking round Little Gaddesden before he met
Ellis, Kalm was amazed to find that ill-cultivated fields belonged to Ellis: '"Mr.Ellis?" I asked
[the farmer], "you must have forgotten yourself, or is there more than one Mr.Ellis?"'

Unfortunately there was not, and Ellis's neighbours were not his most fervent admirers.
Pehr Kalm found a Mr.Williams very much the local model farmer.[27] Ellis himself quoted
Luke, iv, 24: 'No prophet is accepted in his own country', and Kalm certainly caught Ellis at
a period when writing took his energies—the booksellers are reputed to have required 40,000
words a month for the instalment publication of *The Modern Husbandman*. In his time, Ellis
was an influential proponent of improved farming and his reputation deserves some
rehabilitation.

Villages and Market Towns

The quickening tempo of farming life in the Chilterns after 1550 was reflected in much new
building and refurbishment in the villages and towns. Market towns were needed to trade the
produce and provide an ever-expanding range of back-up services. From 1600 the range of
urban crafts and services expanded rapidly, including not only the saddler, the shoemaker and
the blacksmith, but also clothing shops and the services of country physicians and lawyers for
the more prosperous. The inns were very important meeting-places for local business as well

94. Shardeloes, Amersham. The house was built in 1758-66 for William Drake, MP for Amersham, and designed by Stiff Leadbetter and Robert Adam. The house has a fine stone portico with Corinthian columns, facing northwards across the lake.

95. Humphry Repton drawing of West Wycombe Park. Taken from his 1803 book on landscape gardening, it illustrates the panorama after Repton had opened out the view of the lake.

as for travellers, and the towns were studded with an amazing number of them. Later the turnpike roads brought further trade to some of these towns, and along the Thames towns like Taplow, Marlow and Henley attracted wealthy Londoners, sometimes assisted by royal and aristocratic patronage.

This prosperity can be seen in the many buildings which survive from this period. At Watlington, Thomas Stonor, who was lord of the manor, erected the market and town hall in 1664-65, and in 1682 the Drakes of Shardeloes built Amersham town hall. The market hall in High Wycombe was first built in the 17th century too, but rebuilt by Robert Adam in 1761. The better-off tradesmen and landowners built elegant townhouses, though many are refacings of earlier dwellings, and much older structures are often to be found behind the layers. In the 17th century brick became the popular material. Good building stone has always been an expensive import to the Chilterns, and reserved for the grander public buildings and country houses. At first brick was employed to replace the wattle-and-daub fillings between timber structures, but in towns complete brick facings became fashionable. The result is best preserved in the old centres of Amersham, Beaconsfield and Marlow. Appearances can, however, be very deceptive: quite genuine old inns, dating to the 17th century, may have been faced several times, and the half-timbers may be modern mock-Tudor.

Some towns also acquired more specialist, semi-industrial activities. Malting (mainly to make beer) was carried on in a small way right across the region, but the London trade was

96. West Wycombe High Street. The High Street in West Wycombe retained much of its character, especially when this photograph captured it without any traffic at the turn of the century.

increasingly served by two groupings at either end of the Chilterns. Larger-scale malting became identified with particular towns. The Upper Thames barley was malted and traded at Henley and other towns beyond the Hills such as Reading, Wallingford and Abingdon. When John Grant, maltster of Henley, died in 1662 he left 60 quarters of malt in store worth £93, £120 in cash and credits for £180 for 'Maults at London'.[28] Breakspear's Brewery is the last survival of that trade. Wycombe was also an important supplier and a local maltster Thomas Oliffe sent as many as 1,500 sacks a year downriver from Taplow to Queenhithe in the 1730s.[29] In the northern Chilterns, Hertfordshire was a major supplier of London's malt. Tring, Berkhamsted, Hitchin (and Luton across the county line) all had their malthouses, but the industry became focused on towns to the east of the Chilterns, notably Ware which had river access to London via the Lea.

For a short period Henley had a glassmaking industry, though its history is still obscure.[30] In Charles II's reign, a London glassmaker, George Ravenscroft, was experimenting with fine crystalline glass. In 1674 he set up a glassworks in Henley,

97. Glass jug by George Ravenscroft, c.1676. This jug with mould-blown ribbing is an example of Ravenscroft's fine glass-making, and probably came from his Henley works.

probably attracted by local beech fuel and possibly by the Nettlebed sands and black flints mentioned by Robert Plot. It only lasted 20 years, but produced some fine specimens (Plate 97). Today the exact location of the glassworks has been lost.

Much more enduring were the activities of the water-mills. The Chilterns may lack surface water, but below the spring-line the streams can run swiftly and be good mill drivers. Most notable was the river Wye, with its many medieval corn (and cloth) mills near High Wycombe. They also began to be used for paper-making, and additional mills were constructed in the 18th century around Wycombe Marsh, Loudwater and downriver to Bourne End. The status of the industry was recognised by the award of a Royal Society of Arts gold medal to John Bates in 1787 for inventing a new high quality paper. The 1798 county occupation list (the *Posse Comitatus*) records 16 papermakers and three parchment-makers in Wycombe borough and 75 papermakers in Wycombe parish. These activities, together with the fledgling chairmaking industry, made the Wycombe area 'the nearest thing possible to an industrial valley without locally available coal and iron' (L. J. Ashford).[31]

Other valleys such as the Bulbourne below Berkhamsted also developed such industries, though most came after the canal in 1800, and there were other, more isolated semi-industrial sites. But they were the exceptions: the Chilterns remained predominantly a rural, farming community, and the towns were mainly market centres for that community.

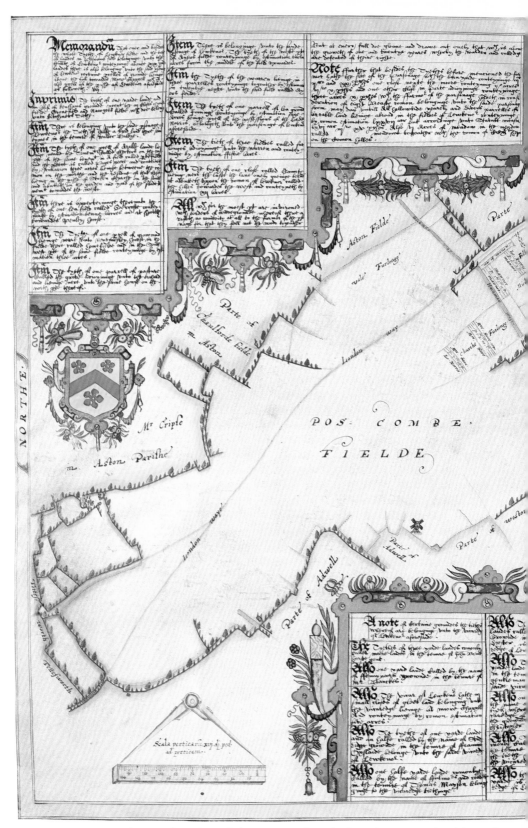

98. Thomas Langdon's map of Lewknor. This map, one of a series Langdon surveyed and drew of estates owned by All Souls College, Oxford, shows the open-field farming with individual strips and furlongs. The text records the tithes and entitlements owed to the college. [All Souls College, Oxford: Hovenden map IV:6.]

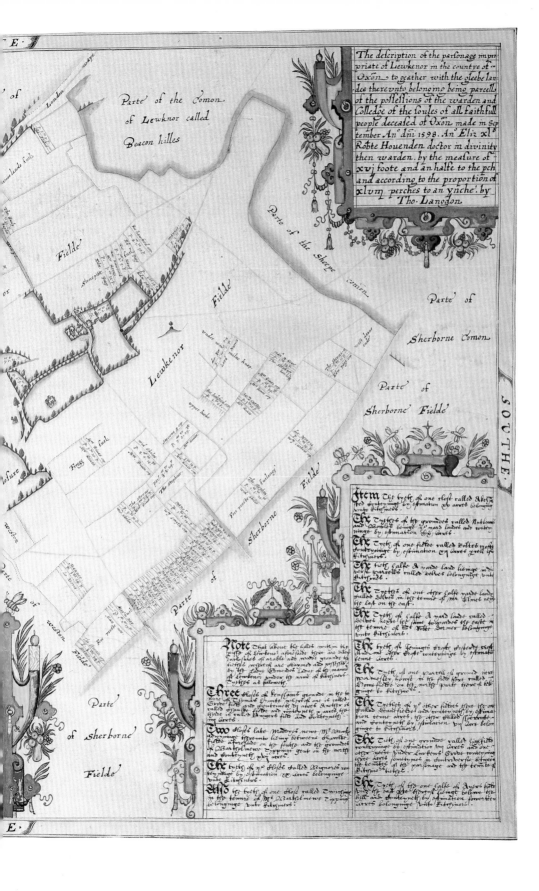

Parte of the Comon
of Lewknor called
Beacon hilles

The description of the parsonage impropriate of Lewkenor in the countye of Oxon together with the gleebe landes therevnto belonging being parcell of the possessions of the warden and Colledge of the soules of all faithfull people deceased of Oxon made in September Anᵒ dni 1598. Anᵒ Eliz xlᵗ Robte Houenden doctor in divinity then warden. by the measure of xvj foote and an halfe to the pch and according to the proportion of xlvm perches to an ynche. by Tho. Langdon

Parte of the Sheepe Comon

Fielde

Fielde

Parte of

Sherborne Comon

Lewkenor

Parte of

Sherborne Fielde

Frogs

Sherborne

Parte of weston

Fielde

of

Fielde

Parte of
of Sherborne
Fielde

Country Estates and Parks

The benefits to the upper classes of economic growth found expression in country houses and parks. The Chilterns attracted a lot of this conspicuous consumption, some originating from local farming wealth, but much also from 'outside money', earned in London trading and business, but spent on a country retreat reasonably close to the City. Hugh Prince has calculated that the Chilterns (including Burnham and Stoke Hundreds in south Buckinghamshire) had 250 parks of 10 acres of more in 1768, covering some 23,000 acres. By 1820 this had risen to a peak of around 600 parks covering 37,800 acres.[32] The Chilterns were attractive both because of their accessibility and also their areas of poorer-quality, cheaper land. Thus the sands and gravels around Burnham attracted numerous square, red-brick residences known as 'London Boxes'.

The Chilterns have country houses from every period and style from the 16th to late 19th centuries. As for the town buildings, stone was expensive here, and brick was the main building material. Warm brick is the most typical style, with some stone detail on the grander houses and flintwork on the lesser buildings. Many of the houses and parks are small-scale, often hidden away and unnoticed until one turns a corner and catches a glimpse through trees of a delightful Queen Anne or Georgian manor house set in its garden or park. After 1650 landscape design became fashionable and parks became more ornamental, rather than for the cultivation of deer. Much of the Chiltern landscape—with its bottoms and hills—was unsuitable for the 'grander design' of parks, but equally did not require it, for there were plenty of sites that gave superb vistas with only limited landscape engineering and planting. We think of the manor house at Dancer's End above Tring, with its view over the Bulbourne Gap, or the three country houses around Turville Heath, each with its own panorama in different directions from the ridge.

The Chilterns has, of course, its share of landscaped parks. Many of the more formal 17th-century gardens have been remodelled, but Edmund Waller's Hall Barn at Beaconsfield, built after 1651, retains much of its long straight walks and formal atmosphere. Later fashions encompassed both Gothic fantasy and classical severity. Both are combined in Sir Francis Dashwood at West Wycombe.

Dashwood is fascinating both as a character and because he put his stamp on so many landscape features still to be seen around West Wycombe.[33] Best remembered through distorted tales of Rabelaisian orgies at the 'Hell-fire Club' in Medmenham and West Wycombe, Sir Francis (1708-81) was a many-sided figure. An active politician who held high office, he was also a traveller who brought back styles and art-objects from Italy and the Mediterranean. At West Wycombe he transformed a plain brick house to Palladian style with stone colonnades and porticos, stuccoing the whole. He dammed the river Wye to create a lake in the shape of a swan, and embellished the grounds with statuary from Italy, temples, and a series of follies visible from the house. The mix of classical, gothic and English features made Benjamin Franklin call it 'a paradise'. Outside the grounds, Dashwood gave local employment by quarrying chalk from West Wycombe Hill and improving the road to High Wycombe. He took the opportunity to create a network of small caves there, still an attraction today. Rebuilding St Lawrence's church in 1763, he heightened the tower and topped it with a golden ball, made of copper. There are small seats in the ball, giving a magnificent view over the countryside. At the same time, with a legacy from a friend, he constructed the hexagonal flint mausoleum on the hill east of the church (Plate 99). The lurid tales of orgies and mock-religious ceremonies here and at Medmenham are hard to substantiate, and seem to originate in a political smear campaign by Wilkes and others. The reality of Dashwood's Wycombe remains an imposing but rather weird local landscape, one greatly restored by the present Sir Francis Dashwood.

Other Chiltern parks were created or remodelled by the great 18th-century professional landscape gardeners, Capability Brown and Humphry Repton. Brown's enthusiasm for wide vistas and water was not ideally suited to the Hills, but he worked at Moor Park (near Rickmansworth) for Admiral Anson, at Beechwood near Luton for Sir John Sebright, and at Latimer and Fawley Court.[34] His best local example is probably at Luton Hoo, where he worked in the 1760s for the Earl of Bute. Adding 900 acres of woods and fields to the park, Brown diverted the Luton to Wheathampstead road and created an ornamental lake nearly a quarter of a mile wide. Luton Hoo was typical of Brown's style, but his work for the Duke of Bridgewater on the waterless ridge of Ashridge is less so. Only part of his work remains, in the fine avenues and glades of the section known as Golden Valley.

99. West Wycombe: the church and mausoleum. This aerial view shows the hill dominated by Sir Francis Dashwood's reconstruction of the church and the hexagonal mausoleum he built immediately in front of it.

100. John Blagrave's map of Harpsden in 1586. In contrast to the open fields of Lewknor, this map is of a completely enclosed hedged landscape with each field numbered, its owner shown and each farm's holdings itemised. [ORO: Ms.C.17:49(129).]

Humphry Repton built on his predecessor's ideas, but his own style drew together more elements of both gardening and landscaping. He favoured banks of trees, rather than Brown's small clumps, and integrated the house and grounds more closely into the local landscape, in a deliberate political statement about the social role of the landowner. Repton worked at several Chiltern estates, including Bulstrode and Stoke Poges.[35] At Shardeloes outside Amersham, he remodelled the water and woodland for William Drake to give the present landscape of wide vistas across the valley from the elegant mansion. At the end of his life he worked on the garden at Ashridge, where his rosery and grotto survive. At West Wycombe in the 1790s he undid some of Francis Dashwood's work, removing some of the statuary and follies and clearing trees to reveal a view of the house. Repton's artistic skills were used in his *Red Books*, sets of watercolour drawings giving 'before and after' scenes that he used to sell his ideas and then presented to his clients. His books on landscape gardening also contain early flip-up illustrations to show his planned changes (Plate 95). Repton's comments on the Chiltern woods give an insight into both his tastes and the pre-1800 nature of the beechwoods:

> The beech woods in Buckinghamshire derive more beauty from the unequal and varied surface of the ground on which they are planted, than from the surface of the woods themselves; because they have generally more the appearance of copses, than of woods; and as few of the trees are suffered to arrive to great size, there is a deficiency of that venerable dignity which a grove always ought to possess.

> These woods are evidently considered rather as objects of profit than of picturesque beauty; and it is a circumstance to be regretted, that pecuniary advantage and ornament are seldom strictly compatible with each other.[36]

Most of these estates and parks have survived to the present day, though often in very different hands. Some are golf clubs (Moor Park), schools (Beechwood Park, Wycombe Abbey) or business colleges (Ashridge), and only a few remain with their original families. But Stonors are still at Stonor and Dashwoods at West Wycombe, though the present generation in both cases has had to fund the renovation and improvement from successful careers in the City and banking.

Chapter Nine

Turnpikes, Canals and Railways

Turnpike Roads

There was an astonishing gap between the end of the Roman period and the mid-1700s when roads with solid foundations were very rarely constructed. Many were simply rights of passage without any recognisable form or definition of purpose, hard and rutted in summer, wet and soggy in winter. The season of the year and the state of the weather became limiting factors in transport, and routeways zigzagged between drier sandy and gravelly soils to avoid the heavier clays, extending journeys and adding to discomforts and delays.

That the system functioned at all is remarkable, but it seems to have done so, until the expansion of business and trade placed it under unsustainable pressure. In 1555 the responsibility of parishes for the upkeep of their roads was formalised (and remained so for minor roads until the County Councils of the 1880s), but this did not work well for the major highways. At this time most goods were moved by pack-horses, singly or in convoys, and some of the old packhorse routes survive because they were bypassed by later improvements. Two such roads in the Chilterns seem to be Collier's Lane, between Stokenchurch and Radnage, and various routes between Henley and Wallingford, such as the 'Pack and Prime'. At Chazey Heath is the *Pack Horse* inn, but there is little documented history to support folk traditions about these roads.[1]

The 17th century saw a big increase in the movement of people and goods, and the old roads became increasingly inadequate. It was most especially the requirements for more wheeled transport—carts, coaches and carriages—which was both cause and effect in the clamour to improve the situation. Stage-coaches and Royal Mail coaches began to run between London and the provinces; coach services from Oxford to London via Stokenchurch and Wycombe began early in Charles II's reign.[2] When Parliament met in Oxford in 1681, the Earl of Shaftesbury noted: 'The road was so full of coaches that there were going down Stokenchurch Hill fourteen coaches and I believe thirty horse at one time'.[3]

Private carriages and wagons began to be used more, and their wheels rutted the surfaces and got bogged down in the mud. Ogilby's *Britannia* (1675), which gave the first detailed instructions on the routes and distances on the roads from London in the form of strip maps, is evidence of this expanding travel, and his technique was much copied in later years (Plate 103).

By 1700 it was clear that new sources of funding were needed for the major routes. The solution was an early form of privatisation, placing the financial burden of road upkeep onto a series of turnpike trusts who would become responsible for the good maintenance of the highways and were authorised by a Parliamentary Turnpike Act to collect tolls.[4] The trustees were no longer local villagers but county gentry often with vested interests in keeping the routes open. They could raise money to carry out improvements usually by mortgaging their future income from tolls.

The map of early turnpikes shows the importance of the capital: it was improving access to this rapidly expanding market that was the principal benefit of the whole system. The roads

101. Milepost at Stokenchurch. Well-hidden on the Beaconsfield-Stokenchurch-Oxford road, it is represented on Davis' 1797 map.

from London to Bristol and the west country (the Great West Road) and to York and Scotland (the Great North Road) outflanked the Chilterns to the south and east, but roads to Oxford, Birmingham and the North-West had to climb over the Hills. A section of Watling Street across the scarp from Dunstable to Hockliffe was turnpiked as early as 1711. Other sections came later, though it is noteworthy how 'patchy' the trusts were, and no single trust looked after the entire length of a major road. A major section of the London-Oxford road via Beaconsfield, Wycombe and Stokenchurch was turnpiked in 1719. The Henley-Oxford road via Bix, Nettlebed and Benson followed in 1736, and the Sparrows Herne trust, linking Aylesbury and Bushey on the present A41 route through Berkhamsted was set up in 1762. Some lesser and cross-country routes were also turnpiked later, such as the Great Marlow-Stokenchurch road

102. Bluebells in spring amongst the high beech trees of the ancient woodland at Ashridge.

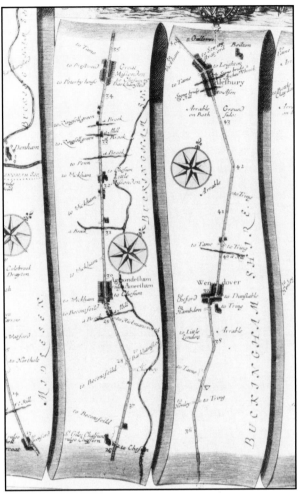

in 1791, and the Risborough trust in 1795 following the road from Ellesborough to West Wycombe.

The records of the turnpike trusts provide us with the kinds of task that had to be performed for the upkeep of these highways. The trusts employed 'responsible men' to act as surveyors but they were all amateurs, not the specialist road engineers like Telford and Macadam who were to come later. Their work varied tremendously in quality from place to place. Much of it involved repairing and surfacing the road. Local stones were the most commonly used roadbuilding material, and in the Chilterns this meant flint, which was not an ideal road metal. The flints were brittle and pulverised under the weight of the traffic, producing a thick layer of dust which had to be settled by 'watering' the roads. The Dunstable to Hockcliffe trust mixed the flints with sand because 'it had few stones except flints which ground to powder, but if mixed with sand they cement'.[5] Local travellers however complained that this mixture was loose and heavy. In many cases the flints were not broken down sufficiently beforehand, creating a very rough surface, which Arthur Young described on the Oxfordshire turnpikes as 'calculated for dislocation'.

103. Strip map by John Ogilby. Part of the London to Buckingham road giving details of the sections from Chalfont, through Amersham and Wendover to Aylesbury.

The turnpike trusts also undertook a programme of re-routing, straightening and widening the roads in order to speed up travel and cope with increased volume. The steep ascents and descents of the Chiltern scarp were difficult and hazardous for coaches and wagons, and needed constant attention. Aston Hill at Stokenchurch was the toughest, and even today the A40 here can be a hard climb. In winter wet, or after one of the intense summer thunderstorms that the Chiltern edge sets off, the road still streams with water, and these north-facing slopes are slow to dry out. The Minute Book of the trust on 2 April 1771 shows that trustees 'ordered that a fence of posts and rails be fixed at the foot of Stokenchurch Hill where the road turns to Aston to prevent accidents'. In 1824 this road was 'found inconvenient' and a new section constructed to be 'more commodious to the public'. The new section is the present A40 descent, whilst the old road survives as a pathway dropping through the tree-clad slopes on the north side (Plate 106).[6] The old *Drum and Plough* inn at the foot of the old road is now a much-rebuilt private house, and its successor, the *Lambert Arms*, stands further along the new road (Plate 107). This same stretch is remembered in a little notebook handwritten in

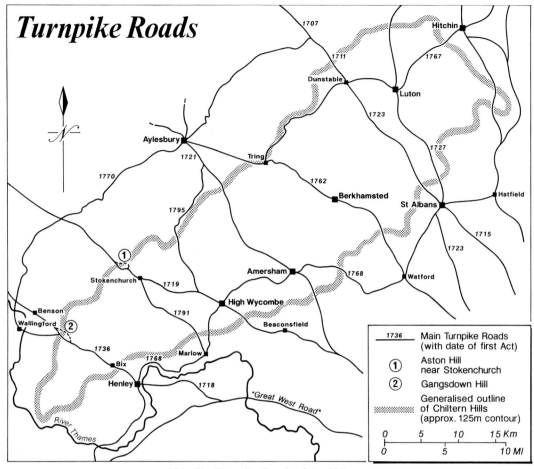

104. The Turnpike Roads of the Chilterns.

pencil by William Bayzard. He was guard on the Mazeppa coach in the 1820s and 1830s and later a janitor at the Radcliffe Camera in Oxford (the notebook is preserved in the Bodleian Library there). He wrote: 'on we go to West Wycombe when a blast to live from the horn and out came our jolly horse and long Jack to give us a pull up a tremendous steep pitch to Stokenchurch ... Change [horses,] put the skid on down Stokenchurch hill very long steep narrow and winding to the "Lambert Arms"—take the skid off and pull up for a glass of that excellent Marlow Beer to Postcombe and Tetworth 42½ miles.'[7]

The Henley-Oxford road also had its difficult stretches, notably the climb from Benson up Harcourt Hill and Gangsdown Hill to Nettlebed. An entry in the *Oxford Journal* for 29 March 1766 reads:

> a bargeman [from Henley?] was bewildered in snow near Harcourt Hill ... and dropped in quite over his head, but had the good fortune to get out again ... Having recovered the road, he found a postchaise which had been left stuck in the snow, and there took up his quarters for the night, which in all probability saved his life.[8]

This line was later rerouted, and again the old road survives as a minor lane and bridlepath. Other turnpikes realigned roads for convenience: the Risborough trust made a new

105. Hornbeam at Herbert's Hole, near Pednor. Hornbeam was frequently used as a hedgerow tree and on woodbanks in the region.

106. The Old Turnpike Roads on
Stokenchurch Hill. This path through the
woods from Stokenchurch to the bottom of the
hill was the turnpike road until 1824.

107. The *Lambert Arms* at Lewknor. This inn,
now heavily 'Tudorised', was built in the
early 1830s as the coaching inn to succeed the
old *Plough and Drum*.

108. Turnpike tollhouses. The top picture is the toll house at Bix on the Henley-Oxford road; below it is the High Wycombe tollhouse now rebuilt at the Chiltern Open Air Museum, with its table of tolls below it.

road on the northern side of Little Kimble churchyard to the church at Ellesborough—replacing the old road that followed the scarp-foot to Great Kimble.[9] The old road was closed but still has hedges visible today. Many turnpikes were straightened and widened and the trusts bought land on either side of the routes. This had to be fenced in or 'quicked' (hedged with hawthorn) in order to contain the route and it was an expensive business. The Sparrows Herne trust spent £134 on land for widening and £202 providing fencing along new sections between 1764 and 1769. The two largest payments (£92 and £72) were to contractors to maintain fencing for 10 years. It is interesting to watch the new replacement, the A41 bypass of Berkhamsted, being fenced before the diggers move in and to speculate on the costs of today's fences.

The initial setting-up of tollgates was sometimes unpopular with local country people who complained bitterly that they increased the cost of living because farmers had to pay to take produce to market. The distance between gates varied enormously: on the Bedfordshire stretch of Watling Street there were five tollgates each about two miles apart, but payment at one gate often freed the remaining trust gates. In contrast on the Sparrows Herne route there was no gate between the park in Watford and Newground in Tring, a distance of some 17 miles.[10] The tolls also varied: a score of cattle could travel for 10d. on the Sparrows Herne turnpike but were charged 1s. on Watling Street. Most tollhouses have fallen victim to modern road-widening schemes, but the Bix tollhouse stands little changed today on the Henley-Oxford road and the Chiltern Open Air Museum has preserved the tollhouse from High Wycombe (Plate 108).

In Acts from the early 1740s the trusts were required to measure and signpost their roads and this was made general after 1767. Quite a few of these turnpike mileposts remain hidden in hedgerows and roadside grass for sharp-eyed observers to seek out (Plate 101), and they are commonest in the south Chilterns. Their location is still marked on the 1:25 000 Ordnance Survey maps. Cecil Roberts who lived near Henley and wrote extensively about the local landscape tells the delightful tale of a perplexing milepost on the road from Henley to Marlow which declares that Hatfield is 42 miles away.[11] 'Why Hatfield?', he wondered. It refers to the 1768 cross-country turnpike of the Reading-Hatfield Trust, built to join a series of local markets (Henley, Marlow, Wycombe, Amersham) but also as a sort of '18th-century M25 or North Circular' to link the major turnpikes and avoid going into London. The trust was sponsored by two wealthy nobles, Lord Salisbury and his friend and neighbour Lord Essex. These two made yearly excursions to Bath to take the cure for their gout. Their new road led to Bath through Reading and avoided the jolting of the cobbles of London (though the switchback across the Chilterns cannot have been pleasant). Roberts' story is that it became known as the 'Gout Road'. Whatever the real truth, several milestones can be seen, together with the grander obelisk in Marlow Market Place which reads: 'Wycombe 5, Aylesbury 22, Oxford by Stokenchurch 25, Hatfield 36. Erected by the Trustees of the Reading and Hatfield Road. September 1822'.

The broader implications of the turnpike system are not, however, to be measured in terms of surviving artifacts or in the detail of the road pattern that was created for us to extend into the network of today. An enthusiastic pamphlet written by an Oxford rector Henry Homer was close to the truth when he forecast: 'that there is no one circumstance which will contribute to characterise the present age to posterity so much as the improvements which have been made in our publick roads'. The turnpikes heralded a new era of communication; people, goods and information services could travel throughout the year with, in Homer's words, 'Almost winged expedition between every town of consequence in the Kingdom and the Metropolis'.[12] The increased speed of traffic meant that a much wider range of places came within a day's journey of London. In the late 17th century a stage coach from Oxford to London took two days with an overnight stop in either Beaconsfield or High Wycombe. By 1800 the journey was regularly accomplished in a day. With new roads came advances in the numbers and types of service. Quick comfortable travel by flying wagons and postchaises was further improved when steel springs were adopted on stage coaches from about 1760 enabling them to carry more passengers with increased safety. The greater speed of journeys was also accomplished by reorganising the schedules; the mail coaches of the 1780s were now running all year and their speed and reliability increased from around 6mph in 1765 to 9mph in 1836 and an arrival that could be timed within minutes.

The transfer of goods travel from packhorse to wagon meant a dramatic increase in size of loads. Huge six-horse wagons could pull up to six tons compared to the one ton that six individual packhorses would have carried. It led to significant gains to agriculture, and changes which were to become more evident in the railway era stemmed from this time. As the roads improved to Wallingford for example, the production of malt in the town for shipment down the Thames to London more than doubled in five years (49,172 bushels in 1754 to 113,135 bushels in 1774). There were higher toll receipts on the Stokenchurch route from Oxford to London compared to the route via Henley, despite there being less coach traffic, because of the enormous numbers of wagons loaded with grain. Stage coaches took the Henley route to avoid them.[13]

The Stokenchurch Trustees complained bitterly about the onerous repair bills created by these large wagons: 'the wear of the said mileways has been greatly increased by the number of heavy carriages passing and repassing thereon since the establishment of the turnpike roads'. On 16 July 1770 they ordered that W. Newell write to Lord Willoughby de Brooke to acquaint his Lordship that he had incurred a forfeiture of £3 for his wagon carrying three hundred over weight on the turnpike road on 9 June last. However we note elsewhere that this trust had several years of inactivity pre-1770 when the road was leased out and not well managed. Individuals were frequently censured for milking and feeding hay to their cattle and digging up the surface and carting it away for their own use! The Minute Book ordered that 'Every person who shall take and carry away stones shall be prosecuted according to the law'.[14]

The settlements along the main routes expanded with the coaching trade. Dunstable almost doubled its population to 1,300 persons between 1760 and 1801 chiefly in response to the passage of travellers through the town. Similarly Berkhamsted grew on the main coaching route from London to Birmingham. Both were on drovers routes—Drovers Road in Dunstable now acts as a short cut through a housing estate to the A5, and *The Goat* and *The Swan* in Berkhamsted had closes for animals *en route* to market. The coaching inns were at the heart of this prosperity, and remain the most enduring legacy from the turnpike era. Coaching and posting inns became a necessity: a journey of fifty miles meant stopping for a meal; a journey of one hundred miles required an overnight stop. Old inns were enlarged and modernised and many new ones were established and they throve as never before along the turnpike roads. The trustees of the turnpike trusts held their meetings in these inns—the Sparrows Herne group met in the *King's Arms* in Berkhamsted. Regular stops like Beaconsfield, Amersham, Wycombe and Henley had many inns. (In contrast, market towns left off the main turnpike routes, like Watlington, did not prosper in these years.) Where later growth has been away from the old town, as in Old Amersham and Old Beaconsfield, the main streets and inns have kept some-

109. Amersham High Street, *c*.1900. The High Street early in this century with the traditional coaching inns, *The Kings Arms* and *The Crown*.

110. The *Magnet* coach in Great Missenden. This journey is obviously a later revival but the view is taken prior to 1913, and the street scene captures the atmosphere of earlier coaching days.

thing of their character. Many coaching inns are now picturesque public houses and restaurants with arched entrances to cobbled yards, converted for summer refreshments outdoors beneath colourful hanging baskets, as at the *King's Head* in Amersham.

The 1830s were the peak of this coaching trade. Pigot's *Directory* lists the services from Henley: in the London direction there was the *Defiance* from Oxford (leaving the *Catherine Wheel* inn at 12 noon daily), the *Rocket* from Shrewsbury (at the *White Hart*, 5.00 a.m.), the *Magnet* from Cheltenham (*White Hart*, 2.00 p.m.), and 12 others (Plate 110). There were also three carriers and five waggoners listed.[15]

The turnpikes had their share of problems. The trusts always struggled financially, especially in rural areas where the worst roads needing the most repair also collected the lowest tolls. Local people resented the increased costs, especially the heavier tolls levied on smaller narrow-wheeled carriages pulled by only one horse and usually owned by occupiers of smaller tracts of land. Homer was quick to notice that the encouragement given to broad wheels and heavy draughts necessarily threw the business of carriage into the hands of the wealthiest farmers. The great weighing engine at Stokenchurch was to record numerous overloads doing untold damage to the roads. Safety became a frequent issue as highwaymen plundered hapless passengers on remoter sections through commons and wastes such as Nettlebed Heath and Boxmoor Common where Snooks robbed, was caught and eventually was hanged amid great ceremony.

Yet despite these inbuilt weaknesses the turnpikes played a fundamental role in improving the road network to meet the demands of a rapidly industrialising nation. In this region, with the increasing numbers of mouths to feed in London, the turnpikes had to fulfil a double role because there were not the navigable waterways to move bulky goods until the hills were crossed and the Thames was reached.

Canals

One of the forefathers of canal building, the Duke of Bridgewater, stands perched on a column in the Chiltern woods at Ashridge above the village of Aldbury. His monument is very appropriately placed; it surveys the Bulbourne valley below, along which the Grand Union Canal slides as a permanent ribbon linking London to Birmingham. This canal was not built by the Duke but it is a testament to the new engineering skills that he and others financed and pioneered in the late 1700s. Canal building was to become a national mania in the 1790s with companies set up and permission sought in the House of Commons, following in the footsteps of the turnpikes. The early waterways were not subject to the 'rag, tag and bobtail' engineering of early roads; they heralded a new era of surveying and construction whose results have survived to wend their way through today's towns and countryside.

The canals were built as connections between provincial centres growing on the coal-fields in a newly industrialising nation. Along them barges, pulled by horses trudging along the towpaths, could carry enormous tonnages of bulky goods. The most important was coal, which fuelled the nation with steam power and eventually lit it with coal gas. The carrying ratios were discussed in the House of Commons and the *Journal* of 1768 notes: 'One horse will draw as much upon a navigable canal as one hundred will draw upon a turnpike road'. Only one canal was constructed across the Chiltern Hills, but this was the very important Grand Junction Canal (later part of the Grand Union system), which traversed through the Bulbourne valley to link the coalfields of the Midlands with the capital. The Oxford Canal, although it lay well beyond the Chilterns, was also of some significance for our region: opened in 1790 it linked the improved Upper Thames navigation to the Midlands, and allowed cheaper fuel and goods to reach the Oxford and Aylesbury Vales with effects on Chilterns markets.

The Grand Junction received Royal assent on 30 April 1793 and was opened to Tring summit in 1799, becoming for a while the largest joint stock company in the country with vast quantities of merchandise shuffling along its length in both directions.[16] The Grand Junction presented a major engineering challenge since the section through the Chilterns entailed climbing, via a series of locks, to a height of 430 ft. to the summit of the canal at Tring. The main difficulty came from the water supply, traditionally a nightmare in much of the region. The engineers were faced with a daunting prospect: to construct a watertight channel across a region of permeable rock, supplied by dubious and irregular springs that needed to maintain a permanent head of water on both sides of the summit. Two branches were constructed—the first was the Wendover arm which was designed as a feeder as it intercepted a series of springs and little streams coming off the Hills that could supplement the main canal. It was upgraded to become navigable at little extra cost and opened in 1797. The second was the Aylesbury Branch which was opened in 1815, a six-and-a-half mile long section with 16 locks falling from Marsworth to Aylesbury.

Unfortunately, almost as soon as the canal was opened across Tring summit it was clear that these water supplies were inadequate.[17] A system of reservoirs and pumps had to be constructed to assist. In 1802 the reservoir at Wilstone was built, along with a steam engine and pump of 30 locks capacity which was used to return stored water to the summit. Worse problems were to ensue as it became clear that the Wendover arm was leaking badly and actually draining water from the main canal. Major repairs of all sorts, including eventually lining the canal with asphalt instead of puddled clay, were all to no avail and in the end a dam had to be built at Little Tring Bridge to prevent any more water being lost. This was replaced with a permanent stop-lock in 1898, effectively closing the branch beyond Tringford. Subsequently, despite more pipelines, new and extended reservoirs and more pumps, it took a borehole at Cowroast eventually to save the day in the drought of 1902, and the borehole remains to this day.

Like the roads, the canals were affected by the seasons. They suffered under the threat of summer droughts when water levels were barely sustainable, and winter frosts which could close the canals for weeks. The winter of 1795 was one such year when bitterly cold weather froze the canals (notably the Oxford Canal) for 10 weeks and bulk transport had to be transferred back to land. It demonstrates clearly what a difference the canals were making to prices, for the *Oxford Journal* on 7 March 1795 talks of coals being brought by land costing 4s. 8d. per cwt. As soon as the waterway re-opened the price fell back to 1s. 6d. per cwt. This reduction in fuel price was the single most important benefit to the people who lived in the countryside. Broadly the price of fuel was cut by half, and this fall in coal prices was particularly important in parishes where timber was scarce. Many labourers and their families had been reduced to using the bakers oven once a week for their only hot meal, for this was a time of much distress in places where recent enclosure had resulted in loss of common rights. In the Chilterns, where wood was not in such short supply, the new fuel could still compete and was half the price of wood at the wharfside. Coal from Wednesbury in the West Midlands sold for 1s. 6d. per cwt. at Wendover wharf in 1810 and 1s. 7d. a cwt. at Oxford wharf in 1790.[18] The prices increased steeply away from the waterway such that at Chinnor wood chips from the chairmaking industry were still better value at 6d. a sack. However as roads improved they enabled better distribution from the wharves into the hinterland. The use of wood for fuel declined and was to alter the way in which the beechwoods had been managed since medieval times.

While an increase in the coal trade was the prime objective of the canal companies, there was a parallel increase in many other kinds of freight moved by water. Farmers could carry their corn to market more cheaply and the huge wagons of hay that were carried to London causing such damage to the turnpikes were now transferred to the canals. The barge 'Berkhamsted Castle' was used to carry hay down to London and return with coal. It was owned by William Butler, who ran the earliest boatyard in Berkhamsted from 1802. Everyone was to benefit from the cheaper merchandise that became available: iron ware from Birmingham and earthenware from the potteries were just two examples. The minute books of the canals paint a colourful picture of the unloading and loading of a great variety of goods which were increasingly sought as manufacturing flourished and people fled from the uncertainties of their agricultural livelihood to work in the towns. Along with coals and cokes, a Minute Book listed soaps, candles and other goods usually sold in shops, nails in bags or casks, iron tyres for wheels, gunstocks, iron arms, boxes for same, pig iron, all sorts of other iron, copper, zinc, saltpetre, lead, pavingstones, slates, cotton, Birmingham hardware and Irish linens.[19]

Once trade began operating on the canals receipts from tolls flowed in and the volume of goods increased rapidly. On the Grand Junction the value of trade increased from £17,176 in 1800 to £198,008 in 1836, the best year. The movement was in both directions. Most of the items in the list above were London bound, but other commodities such as grain and meal, potatoes and consumer goods were shipped up the Grand Junction and Thames-Oxford canals from London to the Midlands. The movement of grain was largely outwards from London because the city was still supplied by sea with corn from East Anglia, Lincolnshire and abroad. Flour mills grew up along the canals to grind the corn, like Meadsmill set up next to John Bushell's boatyard at Newmill on the Wendover arm near Tring. Grain came up the canal from Brentford to be turned into flour at a mill in Kings Langley, which dates back to Domesday and which was acquired by the Toovey family under whose name it operated until 1938.

In the earlier years of the life of the canal it was company policy to encourage trade by building wharfs, depots and warehouses which could be leased by independent carriers. One of the major carrying concerns was Matthew Pickford and Co. who operated day and night to strict timetables. This required relays of boat horses and they had a big stables at Dudswell Mill for 21 horses. It was positioned on the first night's stop for the fly-boat and other rapid services out of Brentford; each day up to forty boatmen would exchange horses there—today it has been converted to house people rather than horses and is still called mill although it never was.[20] There were numerous wharves along the canal designed to serve Chiltern towns and villages: in the short section from Tring through Berkhamsted there were wharves at Pendley to serve Tring, Newground serving Aldbury, wharves for Dudswell and Northchurch and several in Berkhamsted including Castle Wharf and Ravens Lane. Others were built to serve the new canal-side industries which flourished in the 19th century. Principal among these in the Chilterns were paper-making and timber merchants. In 1809 John Dickinson bought a converted corn mill at Apsley on the River Gade. He joined forces with George Longman and purchased Nash Mill, another ancient corn mill that had once belonged to St Albans Abbey. Once the canals opened the paper mills moved nearer to them. Both the raw materials for the paper (rags waste and wood shavings) and the coal to drive the new steam engine installed in the Apsley Mill in 1824, were ferried along the canal.[21] Timber merchants such as East & Son in Berkhamsted and Lavers at Cornerhall in Hemel Hempstead were wharfside industries and remain on the same sites today, despite railways and motorways having stolen freight haulage from the canals in the intervening period.

111. Dudswell Lock 1935. The canal with a horse-drawn pair of barges. Dudswell Mill stands in the background; it was never a mill, but a warehouse and stabling for the canal-horses.

The heyday of the canals was to last until the railways came, a span of some fifty years from their construction. They floated power, industry and increasing urbanisation into the corridors along which they travelled. By the late 1840s the canals were supplying coal to town gasworks manufacturing heat and light, drawing rural dwellers towards the towns. The countryside could supply markets in the north and midlands as well as the ever hungry London market, and in return consumers had a new level of variety and choice in manufactured products at more affordable prices. Away from the wharves, the sphere of influence depended heavily on the state of the roads and life probably did not change a great deal in the more inaccessible villages and hamlets in the heart of the Hills.

The Coming of the Railways

The arrival of the steam locomotive is recognised as the catalyst that forced the pace of change in many parts of the country in the 19th century. For almost immediately rail travel demonstrated its superiority as 'speeds raised from those of a carthorse to more than those of the fastest racehorse'. In contrast the canals appeared to be 'the embodiment of quiet, plodding, undisguised sluggishness'. In the years immediately following the first railway from Liverpool to Manchester, Britain's economic growth was at its maximum and there were investors with surplus funds. Railways fitted into the spirit of the times with their 'air of assumption and parade ... the very type of enterprise, energy and efficiency' that was to sweep the nation.[22]

As with the turnpike and canal building eras the Chilterns were early on the scene simply by default: they were in the way of the most important route between London and Birmingham with its links via the Grand Junction railway to Liverpool. The first proposals for this line were mooted in 1825 and presented to Parliament as a bill in 1830. The route, surveyed by Robert Stephenson, was to be through Uxbridge, Amersham and the Wendover Gap. The reaction was colossal and bitter and illustrates the constant battle between the protagonists and the opposers and the lack of order in the system. Jack Simmons in *The Railways of Britain* says:

> Since the State, therefore, had nothing to do with the planning and laying-out of the railways, they grew up haphazardly, not necessarily where there was most need of them, but where capital and leadership were most readily forthcoming, and—often quite as important—and where opposition was weak and negligible.[23]

In this case the Bill was rejected in the House of Lords after landowners (like the Drakes of Shardeloes), turnpike trusts, the Grand Junction and Oxford canal companies and coach and wagon proprietors had combined in a squall of indignant and antagonistic hot air. Indeed, 'the railway, with its tail of smoke curling across the country, blacking everything even to the fleeces of the wool on the sheep ... was to them everything that was disagreeable, vulgarising and mercenary'.

A new route was surveyed, east of the first line, using the Tring Gap and travelling via Ivinghoe and Bletchley to Birmingham. This line passed through the Ashridge estate, and the Countess of Bridgewater is reported to have told Stephenson: 'The land is already gashed by the Canal, and if you take that course you will have no severance to pay, it will disarm opposition, and the position of the locks will be some guide to you in your levels.'[24]

The last point contains not a little aristocratic condescension, but the route was eventually authorised in 1833 and finished by September 1838. It was part of 'the first great fit of railway speculation' in a 'feverish effort to extend railways in all directions' (Simmons).[25] Like the turnpikes, the routes directly north and west from London could skirt the edge of the Chilterns, but routes from London to the north-west had to encounter the Hills.

However, the fever was about to be abated during the period between 1838 and 1844, as a violent trade recession and poor harvest reduced credit and undermined confidence. The Chilterns did not see any new 'iron roads' until the great revival of promotional activity ushered in the 'railway mania' of the mid-1840s. The lack of any state planning meant that many provincial railway groups tried schemes to connect directly to London, and many of these involved crossing the Chilterns. The GWR line followed the Thames closely, and a branch from Didcot connected to Oxford, a circuitous path nicknamed 'The Great Way Round'. It was to be some time before the major part of the Chilterns between this line and the London-Birmingham line was crossed by a railway. In 1853 the West Midland group proposed a line from Oxford to London through Princes Risborough, Wycombe and Beaconsfield, but it was defeated.[26] A spur from the Great Western at Maidenhead to High Wycombe had been authorised in 1846 but its opening was delayed by financial hiccups until 1854 when it opened as a single, broad gauge and cheaply built track. In 1862 this line was extended right across the Chilterns via Saunderton and Princes Risborough to Thame, and the last 13 miles to Oxford were eventually completed by 24 October 1864.

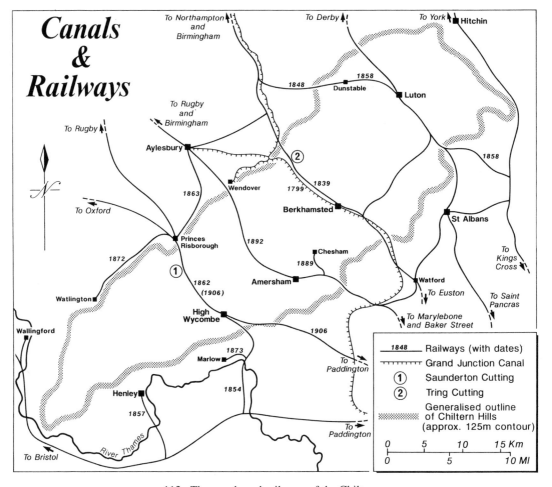

112. The canals and railways of the Chilterns.

113. Watlington station. This view was taken in August 1919. Note the various advertisements of the time.

By the 1860s and '70s branch lines were pushing the railways further into the countryside.[27] From the Great Western branch lines reached Henley (used to capacity in Regatta week), Marlow (a private line said to be built by the wealthy for the wealthy), and Wallingford. From the Wycombe-Oxford line, branches were built from Princes Risborough to both Aylesbury (1863) and Watlington (1872), and Risborough station became quite a country railway centre where the three lines converged. The Watlington branch was a delightful country line, with its little halts and stations used in later years as locations for period films (Plate 113). For many years the 7.10 Paddington to Birmingham express included a slip coach to Watlington for tired businessmen 'escaping to some of the loveliest and quietest countryside within easy distance of London', every night in summer, Fridays and Saturdays in winter.[28] However, tantalising gaps are left on the map of plans that never materialised, such as the link between Wallingford and Watlington, and the early, rather wild scheme to join Tring to Henley via Watlington with a major tunnel through to the Stonor valley.

In the northern Chilterns there was a similar story of gradual infilling of the network with the branch lines and country railways. The London and Birmingham sought a line to Luton and Dunstable and as early as 1845 a branch line was proposed from Leighton Buzzard. The inhabitants of Luton objected instantly to the loss of common pasture of Great Moor and under such pressure the line was forced to terminate at Dunstable, opening on 1 June 1848. The extension of the line to Luton and on to Welwyn took another 10 years despite 'Luton being the first town in the county as a place of business'. In fact, the census return for Luton in 1851 suggests that it was the largest town in the country that had neither railway or navigable river.

Hitchin, like Princes Risborough, was another small English town made into a junction. This time it was the aggressive and entrepreneurial Midland railway under 'King' Hudson which promoted a new line from Leicester to Hitchin with trains then transferring to the Great Northern rails from Hitchin to Kings Cross. The line opened in 1857, but there were enormous delays on the London-bound side and eventually the Midland route was extended into St Pancras in 1869. A branch line was also built from Hitchin to Royston and on to Cambridge giving the town an added connection to the east.

This network of Chiltern lines still left some very obvious holes even as late as 1870, and these remained until the late 1880s. The last new line to penetrate right through the very heart of the Chilterns was the Metropolitan railway from Baker street to Verney Junction via Aylesbury, giving stations to Amersham and Chesham. Ironically the line passed through the Wendover gap where the very first route through the Chilterns had been proposed and refused 69 years previously. The new line was to promote a whole new attitude to the countryside when the concept of Metro-land was born. Similarly, in 1899 the Great Central and Great Western formed an unlikely joint committee and improved the London-Wycombe-Risborough line to cope with the greater demands of local and express traffic. They rebuilt the stations at High Wycombe and Princes Risborough, but most importantly they constructed a whole new section from High Wycombe to London via Beaconsfield and Gerrards Cross. This section of line became a favourite for train enthusiasts; C. R. L. Coles describes it as 'one of the most exciting and memorable of the London suburban routes. From stopping trains made of ex-GC 4-6-2 tanks and a string of teak compartments one could glimpse GWR King class loco's thrashing through the middle road'.[29] This line had an impact like the Metropolitan and will be examined with it.

The construction of these railways meant overcoming technical difficulties arising from obstacles in the landscapes as well as obstacles placed in the way by powerful individuals. The most remarkable engineering achievements concerned reducing the gradients sufficiently to allow engines to climb over the highest points at Tring and Saunderton. In both, huge cuttings were excavated by armies of navvies using shovels, picks and wheelbarrows, with men precariously roped together on the steep sides. The earliest was the Tring cutting, its construction beautifully recorded amongst the lithographs of J. C. Bourne and often reproduced (Plate 114). One and a half million tons of soil were excavated along a two-and-a-half mile section to a depth of 60 ft. and then transferred to create an embankment six miles long. The Saunderton section was photographed in 1905 showing that methods had changed little. Engineers tackled the gradient problem to the summit by building up and down lines on different inclinations— the downline on the descent to Princes Risborough being visibly steeper. Tunnels such as that at White Horse farm between Beaconsfield and High Wycombe and the enormous mile-long tunnel at Watford were even more hazardous to construct. The Watford tunnel was necessitated by the refusal of the Earl of Essex to allow a railway near his mansion at Cassiobury and many lives were lost in the course of its construction.

The Impact of the Railways
The very first railways were concerned with the movement of freight. However, within a very short time it was obvious that the opening of the new railways had a more immediate effect on the pattern of passenger travel than it did on transporting goods. By the mid-1830s proposals to parliament for railway bills were assuming that twice as many people would travel by

114. Railway cuttings in the Chilterns. *Above:* The excavation of Tring railway cutting in 1837 as portrayed by J. C. Bourne in his lithograph. *Below:* Saunderton railway cutting. Excavation methods had not changed greatly when the High Wycombe to Princes Risborough line was upgraded and this cutting was made at Saunderton in 1905.

train than those who had previously travelled by coach or on foot. Those estimates were to prove very conservative because of a social revolution instigated by the railways. Robert Stephenson, who surveyed so much of the Chiltern track, told a select committee on railways on 2 July 1839 that there was 'a class of people who [had] not yet the advantage from the railways which they ought, that is the labouring classes'.[30] By 1844 provision of third-class accommodation at one penny a mile was part of Gladstone's Railway Act and 'people who had never strayed beyond the next town were liberated from the thrall of distance'. The reaction of the upper classes was less than enthusiastic to this new mobility of working men and women. In his novel *Sybil,* Disraeli, who lived in the Chilterns at Hughenden, portrayed the fears and inconsistencies of the members of his class: '... if we nobles do not make a stand against the levelling spirit of the age, I am at a loss to know who will fight the battle. You may depend on it these railways are very dangerous things'.[31] But there was much revenue to be gained and the numbers of third-class passengers increased sixfold between 1849 and 1870 (compared to a fourfold increase in first- and second-class passengers). The initial accommodation may have been spartan but it was infinitely better than sitting outdoors atop a bumpy carriage. It was to improve radically under the 'Apostle of competition', the Midland Railway, which abolished second class altogether in 1874 and then, to the horror of its competitors, upholstered all the seats in the following year. The excursion train gained popularity, especially from the summer of 1851 when the Great Exhibition in Paxton's Crystal Palace provided the opportunity for railways to promote trips for the masses.

The transport of freight by rail immediately challenged both the canal and turnpike trusts. The Grand Junction's main response was a vast reduction in tolls—in three years from 84½d. to 10d. a ton. The canals had their monopoly threatened and prices of fuel dropped as a consequence. The Grand Junction was prompted to improve various sections and it was more aggressive than most in protecting its trade. Similarly, the toll receipts from gates along the turnpikes were halved within a few years of direct competition from the railways. Trains enabled farm produce in particular to be moved for hundreds of miles as cheaply as carrying twenty to thirty miles previously by road. It was to mean the gradual disappearance of the traditional drovers' routes as livestock could now arrive in the market place at the same weight as it left the farm. The new trains were to create a greater demand for milk in the capital— the Aylesbury vale supplied vast quantities of milk especially during the years 1865-66 when cattle plague inflicted huge losses on the urban dairies. The milk vans, which later became known as 'Jersey Lilies', were generally attached to particular passenger trains and the milk was sold on arrival to the London wholesalers for distribution.[32]

The rise of the railway and decline of the turnpike greatly affected many Chiltern towns and villages. The long-distance carriers and coaches were no longer profitable, and the inn trade suffered. Towns on the new railways simply adjusted and grew, but those left off the network or at the end of a minor branch line were hard hit. The gaps in the Chiltern network meant that there were several of these. Henley was now an economic backwater, and its fortunes slumped until the growth of the regatta (which began in 1839) made it a leisure centre in later Victorian times. In the central Chilterns places like Beaconsfield and Amersham lost their long-distance trade, but the lack of a local railway did mean that local coaches and carriers were still needed. The country carrier performed as a vital intermediary between farmers and shopkeepers, and was the most usual means of dispatching bulky parcels and goods to the nearest town or railhead. The reduction in the number of coaches and carriers as a direct consequence of a railway station arriving in a town can be illustrated with a glimpse at the Kelly's *Directory* entries for Chesham. In 1847 there were 14 separate carrying services listed for local destinations and London; by 1891 after Chesham station was opened there were only four of whom G. Caitlin was the only surviving family name. The coach to carry people to and from Watford station before the Chesham line was built awaited the arrival of the 5.30 train from Euston, arriving at Chesham at 8 o'clock in the evening, a full two-and-a-half hours later.

The railways were also to provide opportunities for local employment at a time when the requirement for farm labourers was decreasing. The census return for Princes Risborough in 1881 gives an interesting list of eight railway employees and shows considerable mobility of the workforce: one railwayman came from Maidstone, a clerk came from Scotland, a signalman from Bishopstone and an engine driver from Essex. The other clerk, a platelayer, another signalman and a labourer were all local and almost all of them lived within two streets of the station. But the names of these railwaymen were extracted from long lists of people employed in a variety of occupations which owe very little to the coming of the railways, and the Chilterns did not acquire any major railway towns to rival Wolverton, unless one includes Slough on the GWR in the extreme south. Nowhere in the little towns along the line do we see evidence of an industrial revolution exploding in the Chilterns, with the exception perhaps of the paper mills at Apsley and Nash Mills. While the coalfields and the cities near them were sitting under a pall of factory smoke, the Chilterns remained refreshingly rural. The transport revolution had passed through: turnpikes, canals and railways strode the dominant valleys reducing journey times and costs. But away from these busy thoroughfares there must have been countless rural backwaters that the advances in transport seemed to have passed by. Of course they *had* been affected, but it was to take the 20th century and the motor-car (and bus) to significantly change their world.

115. Horse-drawn 'bus on the Berkhamsted to Chesham Road in the 1880s. This horse 'bus marks the end of an era—passengers from the railway station at Berkhamsted would have a long, slow journey back to Chesham, where the station had not yet opened, and the age of the motor 'bus had yet to arrive.

Chapter Ten

The Chiltern Beechwoods

Introduction

The high beechwoods are the crowning glory of the Chilterns. Captivated by their beauty, it is easy to think of the woods as a natural creation, free of human hand. We have already argued that this is not so. The survival of the Chiltern woodlands, their appearance and ecology, is the result of a long history of management. We have seen that the medieval woods were rather different in appearance to our beechwoods: they were more open and more diverse in species, made up of younger trees, and had much more coppice and underwood. They did not look like today's woods because they were not used in the same way, and it is changes in economic use that lie behind the transformation to today's high beech-forest. The most remarkable and fortunate aspect is that such vast stretches of woodland have survived at all. They may be depleted and altered, having weathered both the medieval onslaught and later changes, but they remain there to grow tall for us to enjoy today. The story of this survival and transformation is an intriguing tale that links the Chiltern woods to the rapid growth of London after 1550 and to the creation of a chair-making industry after this London fuelwood trade collapsed around 1800.

The Thames Wood Trade

The Chilterns wood trade, like the corn trade, was greatly stimulated by the rapid growth of London in the 16th and 17th centuries. Although London was buying vast quantities of the new 'sea-coal' from Newcastle, there was still a rapidly rising demand for wood as domestic and industrial fuel. The rising population also had rising expectations of comfort, and there was much chimney building. The real price of fuelwood rose by 75 per cent between 1540 and 1553.[1] There were sometimes crises of supply, and the City Council had to act. For 16 August 1559 the Patent Rolls note:

> Commission until Christmas next for Thomas Leigh, knight, mayor, and the aldermen of London to provide carriage by water at reasonable rates for 6000 loads of wood stored at Henley, Weybridge and elswhere against the winter, and to take further wood if necessary. The woodmongers restrict the supply to advance the price, and by their consent the said mayor has taken 6000 loads of their store for the use of the city; also the price of water carriage has been unreasonable advanced to more than half of what it was.[2]

Henley was the focus for the Chilterns trade, but did not dominate to the same extent as it did with the corn trade. The high costs of land movement of wood and timber meant that much was handled through many small wharves along the Thames, at Whitchurch and Mapledurham above Henley, and down river at Greenlanes, Mill End, Marlow and Hedsor. The accounts of Thomas West, a trader of Wallingford, for 1572-73 show his wood-sales from wharves between Wallingford and Henley.[3] He sold to the royal household (Queen Elizabeth did not like coal as a domestic fuel), and had difficulty getting payment:

I find that Master Browne and Master Shergent did cawes me to carry 20 loades of talle woode and 10 loades of billetes frome John Melsaides of Mapledorme [Mapledurham] unto the 3 Cranes [wharf] in London. It ys worth 2s 6d or 2s 8d, I trust you will pay 2s 6d. the woode was delivered at the Quene's House. Some ys: £3 15s.

We can get insights into the type and volume of traffic from deeds and probate inventories.[4] In 1677 John Taylor of Henley Park agreed to supply 1,000 loads of billet and stackwood to William Hawkins, a 'woodmonger' of St Margaret's, Westminster for £540, with delivery to the wharf at Greenlane on the Thames. The 1667 inventory for George Cranfield, a substantial timber merchant of Henley, reveals a diverse trade in billet, hoops and timber suitable for shipbuilding.

The Rawlinson Manuscripts in Oxford contain a volume of papers by the famous 17th-century diarist and Secretary to the Navy Board, Samuel Pepys. Amongst them is a page of *c.*1688, 'Notes about firewood taken at Henley'. We reproduce it here (Plate 116). He details the different sizes of wood available, and their prices, and adds

my enquiries thereon relate more p'ticularly to beach woode, which is said to burn sooner, clearer, freer from sparkle, and to make a better coale. yt will keep fire longer than those of oake, though oake last longer in ye burning then beach, the measure and price being (as I think they told me) ye same, or near it.

Some, like Robert Plot, thought that this London trade meant that the Chiltern woods did little to relieve the wood shortage of the Vale and lowland Oxfordshire.

The Thames trade was not purely a firewood trade, as George Cranfield's inventory testifies. Daniel Defoe, the author of Robinson Crusoe, recorded in his 1725 *Tour of Great Britain* that, at Great Marlow:

Here is also brought down a vast quantity of beech wood, which grows in the woods of Buckinghamshire more plentifully than in any other part of England. This is the most useful wood, for some uses, that grows, and without which, the city of London would be put to more difficulty, than for any thing of its kind in the nation.

1. For fellies [wooden wheel-rims] for the great carrs, as they are called, which ply in London streets for carrying of merchandizes, and for cole-carts, dust-carts, and such like sort of voiture, which are not, by the city laws, allowed to draw with shod wheels tyr'd with iron.

2. For billet wood for the king's palaces, and for the plate and flint glass houses, and other such nice purposes.

3. Beech quarters for divers uses, particularly chairmakers, and turnery wares. The quantity of this, brought from hence, is almost incredible, and yet so is the country overgrown with beech in those parts, that it is bought very reasonable, nor is there like to any scarcity of it for time to come.[5]

The Nature and Use of the Woods

The structure of the Chiltern woodlands at this period was little different from that of medieval times, though the management was probably more systematic. To meet the different demands for wood and timber, the woods were mainly 'coppice-with-standards', and the standards were both oak and beech. The different types of firewood—the billet, the stackwood and the faggots—required a range of tree-sizes. Robert Plot commented:

In the Chiltern Country they fell their Under-wood Copices commonly at eight or nine Years Growth, but their Tall-wood, or Copices of which they make tall Shids, Billet Etc. at no certain time; nor fell they these Woods all together, but draw them out as they call it, almost every Year some, according as their Wood comes to be fit Scantling for tall Shids or Billet, cutting every Shid of Tall-wood four Foot long besides at Kerf, and Billet three foot four inches.[6]

Notes abt Firewood, taken at Henly.

Fifty notches goe to a hundred, by wch stake it is meant a 100ᵗ wᵗ.

Five hundred goes to a Load.

The ordinary price for a Load is 4ˢ.

The price for a 100 Load (ye Quantity they comonly sell by to ye Woodmongers) is from 14 to 16ˢ.

Carriage by Water from thence down to London is from 15 to ꝰ ꝓ Load.

Two Loades is ordinarily stiled a 1000 off Billet.

Note that there is two or 3 degrees of goodnes of Billet, as by ye Sizes; some notches being larger cutt then other.   *Note*

116. Extract from the papers of Samuel Pepys. 'Notes about firewood taken at Henley' in Samuel Pepys' own hand from a manuscript in the Bodleian Library. [Bodleian: Ms Rawlinson A 171 f222v.]

(Shids and billets of tall-wood—from the Norman-French *boys de tailz*, coppice wood—were different sizes of firewood logs; the kerf was the oblique face produced by cross-cutting with an axe. Statutes of 1542-43 and later years laid down prescribed sizes.)

Various surviving estate accounts and valuations give us a clear picture of the woods at this time. Two valuations of the West Wycombe woods in the 1690s show us that about one-third of the standards (or timber trees) were oak, and that most woods had 10-25 standards per acre. This is in line with the 1543 Statute of Woods, which required 12 standards per acre in coppices, whereas a Victorian high beechwood might have well over 200 per acre. In 1692 the production from Cockshoots Wood (which is still there on the map) was 56 loads of beech timber, 36 of ash timber, 91 loads of 'towne billett', 49½ stacks of stackwood, 2,025 beech brush-faggots and 662 ash faggots.[7]

The Hampden wood-books provide the most detailed pictures of life in the woods.[8] For 1696-1705 they record the cutting and sales of both wood and timber, noting quantities for each woodland and who bought it. Of the 11 main woodlands on the estate half generated both wood and timber, whilst six only record timber sales, and may, therefore, have been higher forest. But in terms of production, twice as much underwood as timber was produced. Abel Taylor was the main woodman, and a man of the same name (a grandfather perhaps?) was a tenant in the 1653 Hampden Survey. Payments to him include:

April 16 1697
Hampden Coppice: for making 85 loads of country billet at 7d load: £2 9s 7d; stackwood 36.75 load and 2 quarters at 9d: £9 7s 8d; 16.5 loads of brush ffagots: 16s 6d.

The buyers of the firewood and other small wood came mainly from the woodless villages of the Vale of Aylesbury. The list includes Dinton (the biggest purchaser), Askett and Meadle, Hartwell, and Winchendon.

Valuations of the Upper and Lower Woods at Shirburn, on the Chiltern escarpment, in 1721 tell a similar story, and provide an interesting episode.[9] Walter Knight and Joseph Collier calculated:

Oaks in the Upper Wood	6563	£1699 13s
Ashes in ditto	3126	£218 13s
Beeches in ditto	22937	£1728
The stock left on the land under 1s a tree	1928	
Oaks in the Lower Wood	1337	£239 17s
Ashes in ditto	1792	£141 11s
Beeches in ditto	26443	£1786 16s
The stock left on the land under 1s a tree	1420	

Wood, Total: £8962 10s

Lord Parker, who was the potential buyer, called in a second opinion however, a local farmer John Toovey of The Howe farm. Toovey was very suspicious of Knight and Collier—'I find they are in ye Itrest of the Tranting Ffellows which Buy wood to destroy itt'—and his own method is worth setting out:

I have heare sett downe ye method I doe itt in. I have a man of sound Judgment in wood, and we have a gerle, which goes with us, for a sifer. She have I scraching Iron and maks marks on ye trees as shee goes, and my man goes about 2 poale ofe of her, and valews how many ffott of Beach their is betweene him and her, and as shee moves, he moves; and I goes ye same distance ffrom him and valews all ye beach wood by ye ffot to him; and soe wee goe over ye wood.

They then do the same for oak and ash. Toovey admits, 'we are not infalluable, but cann give As good a Gus to what is in A tree as any body Cann', and he is very sceptical of Knight's method, 'valews sume and Leaves sume to vallew by ye Aker; which I think be very nise to be done'. Toovey's valuation is interesting because it separates the oak into several categories: oak timber (worth £1,311 in Upper Wood), sapling oak under five feet (£46), oak bark for tanning (£254), top and lop for faggots (£60) and 'poor sapen oak with top and lop in' (£20). In contrast, all the beech is measured by the foot at 7d. a foot, top and lop in (£2,402), and was probably all seen as firewood of differing sizes.

Common Woods

The many common woods offered both opportunities and problems. The lord of the manor usually had all the timber rights, whilst various tenants had rights to grazing and small wood such as 'top and lop'. Exercise of the rights sometimes led to degradation to open scrub and common, and certainly limited the regeneration of the trees; existing standards and pollards were safe, but their successors had a hard time getting started. Landlords were keen to extinguish common rights to their woods, or at least to enclose temporarily whilst regeneration could take place.

The Upper Woods of Shirburn can again provide an illustration.[10] A century before Toovey and the 'Tranting Ffellows', the Chamberlains of Shirburn were enclosing woodland there in 1618, buying up the pasture rights of his tenants. The 60-acre Wergen Coppice, 'which had been cropped and spoiled about two years since by cattle' was enclosed and felled 'for better growth thereon again'. The common woods of different communities often abutted, however, and this was the case here. Sir Robert Scrope of Wormsley claimed that he and his tenants had pasture rights in parts of Shirburn woods, and drove 180 sheep, 11 beasts and two mares into this woodland. Villages well out into the Vale also had detached pieces of woodland up here on the scarp, legacies that probably dated back to Anglo-Saxon times. Wheatfield and Weston both had woods here, and both are still on the map today. Whitfield Wood was

> invironed on all or most parts with the woods of the manor of Sherburne, without any hedge or other mounde or fence to separate or dividie the same, but only some known marks upon trees & Baucks & such like meere, metes & boundaries to make known the boundes & lymitts thereof.

So claimed Sir George Tipping of Wheatfield in 1622, when accusing John Chamberlain of moving the boundary of Wergen Coppice into Wheatfield Wood, felling trees especially the 'pleashed' or marked boundary trees. Two Commissioners out of the Court of Chancery took evidence from the old men of the district, and got answers suggesting both parties had strayed. A Richard Seeley for Wheatfield, aged '80 and upwards', confirmed Tipping's claims, but others said that in the past Seeley himself had felled a marker tree which, if still there, 'would have made Whitfield Wood narrowere by an acre's breadth'. The final outcome of these disputes is unfortunately not preserved.

Common woods provide us with some of the very first evidence of planting of trees to regenerate the woodland. St John's Wood (later known as King's Wood) to the north of High Wycombe was Crown land, from which commoners had the rights of 'cutting and carrying away of willo, sallo, herge, maple, hazell and bushes'. Cutting young beech, however, was regarded as 'stealing'. A survey taken in 1649 includes a copy of the lease from James I to Sir Robert Johnson in 1611 (Plate 117). This noted that the wood had been 'wholly wasted and destroyed', and to return it to 'its ancient commodity and profit', James gave Johnson a 60-year lease 'to purge pull and dig up all old footes [roots]'. Sir Robert was to 'expand and

117. 1649 document concerning St John's Wood, High Wycombe. This Commonwealth Survey includes a copy of the terms of a 1611 lease of woodland by King James I. It gives instruction on the management of the wood, and is the first recorded evidence in the Chilterns of deliberate plantations to regenerate woodland. The wood was 'wholie wasted and destroyed' [line 3], but King James wished it to be 'restored to its ancient commoditie and profitt' [lines 4-5]. Sir Robert Johnson should 'purge, pull and digg up all ould rootes' [line 6], and then engage in 'the planting, manuring and inclosing the said woods and wood grounds' [lines 10-11]. The following paragraph records that he was not to 'cutt or fell down' [line 15] any of the wood or underwood for at least 10 years. [PRO: E 317/Bucks/10.]

lay out in and upon the plantings manuring and inclosing the said woods and wood grounds £200 of lawful money of England'. After planting no wood was to be cut until 'of the growth of 10 years or more', and at the end of the lease the wood had to be well stocked with standards. A reduced but substantial King's Wood still survives between the housing estates of Wycombe and Tylers Green.

Competition with Farmland

During this period the Chiltern woodlands were neither static nor unchallenged. Wood and timber production was profitable, although farming was often more profitable. The balance depended on price fluctuations and local circumstance, and woodland frequently lost out. Anthony Mansfield estimated that woodland in the southern Chilterns fell between 1600 and 1800 from half the area to one third.[11] Over much of the landscape, this meant both grubbing up of woodlands for farming on the one hand, and the planting of new woodland on former arable fields on the other (Plate 118). Thus a lease of Hollandridge Farm north of Stonor in 1693 referred to 'parcels of wood ground that was lately grubbed up and converted into tillage' and to Ballasdree Coppice which had also been grubbed up. But the lease also required the planting of trees of various species, listing oak, ash, beech and maple.[12]

One case is worth following in detail, for it concerns Upper Shirburn Wood again.[13] Here in 1747 three men (including a Ric Toovey of Watlington) who owned 52 acres of the wood were busy creating a new farm on the escarpment top. They covenanted with a Daniel West to grub up the wood and make four arable closes, which West would rent at 10s. an acre. The three agreed to build a thatched barn, a stable for four horses and add a room to the house

118. An extract from Bryant's map of Buckinghamshire, 1825. This shows the woods, commons and fields around Hampden, and demonstrates how the woodland edge has changed. High Wood, north of Speen, has become farmland, whilst much of Green Hailey Common and Risborough Hillock is now wooded.

which already existed. They agreed to complete 'fit for plowing, by Michaelmas 1750'. They were to plant a quick or living hedge around the 50 acres and three cross-hedges to divide the land into four fields. The new farm, named Portobello after a British naval victory of the time, has been there ever since (Plate 119). Further closes were added in 1776 and 1792, but the woodland fringe has later readvanced with 19th-century plantations like Bell's Plantation covering some of the fields.

During the later 18th century the woodland landscape was changing in several ways. The amount of oak in the woods was declining rapidly. By 1750 oak was only one-eighth of the timber sold from Hampden. In response to the Commissioners of Land Revenue enquiry into

119. Portobello Farm, on the plateau above Shirburn. This farm was created by Ric Toovey and others during very late woodland clearance in 1747-49. The brick and flint farmhouse still retains much of its original appearance as drawn on an estate map of *c.*1780.

Woods and Forests in 1791, Richard Davis of Lewknor wrote of the region: 'the quantity of oak timber is everywhere much decreased within Memory'.[14] Demand for oak timber was strong in these years, and drawings (fellings) probably exceeded natural regeneration. Beech grows faster than oak, and demand for beech coppice and the shading effect of the larger beech standards would have hampered the oak. William Ellis commented: 'it generally happens in our Chiltern that where a wood of oak has been felled a wood of beech has spontaneously succeeded; but when this once got dominion, it will always be sure to remain master'.[15]

The later 18th century also saw rises in the price of corn, and further incentives to extend the arable lands. Davis told the Land Revenue Commissioners: 'More Woods have been grubbed than Land planted since corn has borne so great a Price'. Thomas Langley in his *History of Desborough* (1797) claimed

> The quantity of beech woodland has diminished very considerably of late years, and many acres are now clearing for cultivation, so that no accurate statement of their extent can be given. If any survey had been taken last century, I have little doubt that we should have found that the number of acres were at least double to what they are at present.[16]

This may have been an overstatement, but the trend was clear to Langley. The war with Napoleon gave further impetus to arable cultivation. Woods at Stokenchurch and Wormsley had risen greatly in value, but this was because so much had been grubbed up. Arthur Young was able to give some firm figures in 1813:

Their profit now is considerable; but if there is a fair stock of trees, so is the temptation to grub: for a common offer is from £30 to £35 per acre, and to leave the land grubbed for the plough; thus the produce is sold at 30 or 35 years' purchase, and the land kept. If the money is invested at five per cent. the profit, in such cases of grubbing, is decided at the first blush. But some woods are on such steep declivities, that the land is good for little in any other application: the account, however, stands good, as cutting all does not necessarily imply grubbing: it may continue, wood demanding patience.[17]

Thus woodland in the Chilterns was rising in value, but at a slower rate than arable land, and so the area of woods was falling. The Chiltern wood-trade was also very dependent on the market for fuelwood, and this had started to decline. In London coal was increasing its dominance, and Pehr Kalm claimed in 1747 that it had almost entirely replaced the use of billet there. This severely curtailed the Thames trade, though coal remained very expensive in and around the Chilterns themselves. When coal was brought as a luxury to Hampden house in the 1760s, it had to come by sea from Tyneside to London, up river to Hedsor Wharf, then by cart over five miles of poor roads.[18] The market for beech billet and stackwood was, however, to contract in a major way. The ensuing changes were to alter the woodland landscape in a transformation that eventually produced the Chiltern beechwoods of today.

The Great Transformation
One of the explicit questions posed by the Crown Commissioners in 1791 was:

Question 10. Whether the Improvement of roads, and the Navigable Canals, have not introduced the Use of Coal in Parts of the country in which Wood was before generally used for Fuel? And whether, in such Parts, the Demand for Underwood, and the Value of it, has been increased or lessened?[19]

Respondents suggested that the demand for fuelwood had fallen. Supply had also been reduced through the extensive grubbing out of woods, making the net effect on price fairly small. Two years later W. James and J. Malcolm wrote that beech in Buckinghamshire was 'affording an abundance of fuel to that part of the Country where coals are scarce'.[20] This was just a brief respite, however. The new canals linked the Chilterns and Vale to the midlands and the north, and one of the effects was to allow coal to compete with beech billet. The London market had gone, and now more local markets were disappearing. Of course, the entire fuelwood market did not disappear: firewood continued (and continues today) to be consumed locally, but it was no longer an economic base, an 'export earner' for the Hills. This meant the woodlands were especially vulnerable: they had specialised very heavily in beech coppice, and the uses of such beech underwood were less adaptable than the coppice of many other regions. In these other regions underwood trades prospered in the 19th century, with a strong demand for hop-poles, basket wood and other products, which were made largely from ash and hazel coppice wood.[21] Beech, with its lack of flexibility, was not much good for these uses and the markets gave no support to the Chiltern beechwoods. For the Chilterns 'the fate of the woods hung in the balance'.[22] Away from Young's 'steep declivities', the woods might have been greatly grubbed up in subsequent decades.

The survival of the Chiltern woods has a certain irony to it. The economy and landscape of the Chilterns had always been focused on the needs of London. The death blow to the fuelwood trade came from the new industrialising regions of the north and midlands with their canals and coal. The salvation of the Chiltern woodlands was to lie in the growth of the chair-making and furniture industries. Those industries sold many of their products to the new consumer markets in the north and midlands.

120. Firewood being carted in the Oxfordshire Chilterns in the late 19th century. Firewood and fuelwood were still locally important in the wooded Chilterns despite growing competition from coal.

Chair-Making and the Bodgers

Although it drew on the local beechwoods and on traditional woodcraft skills, the Chilterns chair-making industry seems to have sprung from very humble beginnings to a substantial production within only a few decades after 1780. Earlier references are few. Defoe, as we have seen, referred to 'diverse uses, particularly chairmaking and turnery wares', but this applied to use in London, not in the Chilterns. In the 1760s the Hampden estate sold much beech timber to Isaac Eccles of Amersham for the making of 'coggs'. Towards the close of the century a series of writers reveals a changing picture. In 1794 James and Malcolm do not mention chairmaking in their survey of Buckinghamshire, but in 1797 Langley notes (of Desborough Hundred): 'The chief uses to which this [beech] wood is applied (besides fuel) are spokes, fellies, bedsteads, and chairs'. By 1810 St John Priest, in his updating of the James and Malcolm county agricultural survey, lists the uses in the order: the manufacture of chairs in Buckinghamshire and London; fuel; repairs to barn doors.[23]

The rapid advance of the wood-working trades is illustrated by the *Posse Comitatus* returns for Buckinghamshire in 1798. This was a census of all men aged 15-60, with their occupations, collected for possible military needs. It lists 76 chair-makers and 79 wood-turners (makers of a wide range of wooden ware, bowls and legs). The 76 chair-makers were strongly concentrated around Wycombe, with 18 in West Wycombe, 33 in High Wycombe Borough

121. Bodgers working Hampden Woods, *c*.1908. In the foreground are chopped wood lengths, ready for the boy to shave them into rough shape whilst the bodger himself operates the pole lathe, turning legs inside the hut. Stacks of finished legs are in the background.

and seven in the wider parish. The wood-turners were more scattered, with 31 in Chesham and 12 in Amersham.[24]

The Chilterns industry focused on making Windsor and cane-seated chairs. Chilterns chair-making was not a traditional rural craft, but a response to new market opportunities.[25] The raw materials were, however, of local origin: the legs, stretchers, spindles and 'sticks' (plainly-turned vertical back supports) were turned from local beech; the seats usually from elm; the Windsor bows from flexible woods like ash. The entrepreneurs were men like Samuel Treacher of High Wycombe, sworn a burgess in 1794 and described as 'Chairmaker'. Bailey's *British Directory* for 1784 records three chair-makers there, all three Treachers. By 1798 the List records far more chair-making families in the area: six Treachers, five Mulletts and two Wiggingtons, and three Harrises in West Wycombe.

The early organisation of chair-making had several elements. The turning of legs, backs and stretchers could be done direct from the round wood, and required very little capital. This work became the province of scattered individuals, often working directly in the woods, chopping up wood-lengths and turning the legs with a basic pole lathe. These woodland chair-leg turners later became known as 'bodgers', especially in writing which romanticised their craft. It should be remembered that firewood billet was quite substantial in size, and the chair-leg turners or bodgers could work with the same beech trees that had been used to supply fuelwood. Other parts of the chairs, and their assembly and polishing, required a workshop and a yard to store wood and chairs. This meant more capital. Public houses were often the interchange point, and chairyards and workshops grew at several, such as the *Bird in Hand* on the West Wycombe road, the Red Cow in Frogmoor (High Wycombe) and the *Hit or Miss* at Penn Street. The bodgers, and many of the other craftsmen, were outworkers, paid by the gross, often very badly. Good craftsmen could produce three or four gross a week. The stretchers—three to a chair— were 'included' in the production, so a gross actually meant 18 dozen pieces.

The market area for the chairs spread far afield. Benjamin North (born 1809) became an important manufacturer, and wrote a fascinating autobiography that captured much of the commercial scene of 19th-century Wycombe.[26] He recalls how 'the machine-work has destroyed every hope and probability of my getting employment as a papermaker', and turned to chair-making. He began as a traveller, taking his chair-van round the countryside until he had sold the load. After he began work for Thomas Harris of West Wycombe in 1837, his first tour took him through the East Midlands to the northern markets of Sheffield, Rotherham, Pontefract and Leeds. He later became a manufacturer in his own right, and part of his capital was put together by selling lace on his own account on return journeys with the empty chair-van. In the 1851 Census, North is a 'chair-maker's agent'; by 1862 his firm employed over 100 men, and by 1881 his son was running a firm of over two hundred employees.

North's success paralleled the rapid expansion of the industry. Sheahan, writing in 1862, reports that one Wycombe manufacturer made 8,000 chairs for the 1851 Great Exhibition at the Crystal Palace, and quotes *Knight's Almanack:*

> It is remarkable how suddenly manufactures are localised under favourable circumstances. Chairs were no doubt always made in this district ... But the Wycombe chairmaking trade was scarcely known as something remarkable twenty or thirty years ago. The demand for the chairs has grown with the enormous increase in the general population, the facilities for communication with the metropolis and the rapidly extending demand of our colonies.[27]

The colonial trade to Australia and New Zealand was partly met by sending crates containing several dozen 'packed flat' chairs for assembly at the other end.

As business expanded so did employment, and from the 1841 Census onwards we can follow it in detail. At West Wycombe, for example, numbers employed in chair-making rose from 95 in 1841 to 244 in 1851, 374 in 1861 and 431 in 1871. There were two aspects to this employment growth. One was the hand mass-production in the biggest centres at High and West Wycombe (including Downley, north of the West Wycombe road). These workshops and small factories, like Benjamin North's, had a growing division of labour: chair polishers and chair framers distinguished themselves from chair-makers and chair-turners. Chair-caning was mainly women's work, and North's wife is recorded in the 1871 as superintendent of 37 female caners.[28] The other aspect was the geographical spread of the industry, with a number of smaller factories and a whole network of bodgers across the Buckinghamshire and Oxfordshire Chilterns, affecting nearly every hamlet and village. In the southern Chilterns there were many bodgers in the woods and hamlets around Stoke Row and Checkendon, and in a line across the hills north of Wycombe from Penn Street to Naphill and Speen. To the west of Wycombe there was chair-making at Lane End and Wheeler End. Across the county boundary into Oxfordshire, Stokenchurch was an important centre, and below the escarpment Chinor had 43 chair-makers in 1851. A Factory Inspector described the Stokenchurch production in 1885:

> the male population is engaged one way or another in producing quantities of chair legs etc. there being only one manufacturer properly so called in the place, while steam sawmills are kept constantly employed in cutting up lengths of chair stuff which is turned by hand in the little workshops attached to the cottages and finds its way... in the form of 'spindles' 'stretches' etc. to the numerous manufacturers in Wycombe.[29]

During the latter part of the century production increased in scale and complexity. The turner or bodger became a smaller element in the final product, and their numbers dwindled. Eventually, towards the end of the 19th century, there was real industrialisation of chair and furniture production, with machine-tools replacing hand-crafting. Country-based bodgers, despite long hours for low returns, could not compete with the cost of machined, mass-produced legs. There was a 'de-skilling', and those who survived were driven to making tent-pegs and brush-backs.

At the turn of the century an even colder wind was blowing into the Chiltern woods: foreign timber could now compete in the market for mass production. In 1899 three-quarters of the timber used in Wycombe was from North America, and by 1905 Canadian birch was less than half the price of local beech. The Wycombe furniture manufacturers had developed the industrial impetus and adaptability to survive, but the Chiltern beechwoods were less and less part of their needs. In the southern Chilterns a few bodgers and craftsmen managed to continue their trades into the 1930s and 1940s: men like Samuel Rockall of Summer Heath (Plate 124), Jack Goodchild of Naphill. In Stoke Row, Silas Saunders of *The Crooked Billet* (Plates 122 and 123) and Albert Carter of *The Cherry Tree* both continued to work in their workshops.[30]

Whilst Wycombe and its hinterland became specialised furniture-makers, Chesham continued the more general turnery trade in which it had been prominent as early as 1798. The

122. Silas Saunders is seen stacking chairlegs near Stoke Row in the 1930s.

123. *The Crooked Billet*, Stoke Row. An old woodland pub up a winding lane north of Stoke Row. Here Silas Saunders had a chair-making workshop attached to the pub.

town became a little industrial centre in its own right, with a strong trade in bowls, brushes, and also the wooden spades that children used to use at the seaside.

Woodland Changes

These changes in the beech wood market after 1800 gradually began to transform the composition and ecology of the Chiltern woodlands. The rapid growth of the chair-making industry kept up the demand for beech after the decline of the large-scale fuelwood trade. Slowly during the 19th century this change began to be reflected in the appearance of the beechwoods. George Peterken suggests that 'perhaps the most interesting conversion from coppice to high forest in Britain occurred in the southern beechwoods'.[31] The village and town 'chair factories' demanded larger, timber trees; these were more economical to transport and were then be sawn up at the workshops. The local turners and woodland bodgers required smaller wood of the billet-type, so there was a complementary demand, met by what became known as the 'Chiltern selection system'. This meant drawing out scattered timber-trees from mixed size woods, whilst smaller wood was thinned and used by bodgers.

This was still a different pattern of demand from the pre-1800 woods. Coppice woods now had a very small market (except as an environment for sporting game), though one exception was the woods around Bix and Nettlebed where the coppice continued to be used to fuel the tile kilns.[32] The growing role of the chair-making factories increased demand for larger timber, and far more trees were left to grow tall and become 'high forest' woodland.

124. Samuel Rockall of Summer Heath. Samuel Rockall is putting the finishing touches to a turned leg on a wheel lathe. In the 1930s, Rockall was one of the last bodgers, and his tradition of craftsmanship was much extolled by H. J. Massingham in his writings of the 1940s.

There is much we still do not understand about the details of the transformation, and it would be interesting to discover a set of estate or business accounts linking the beechwoods with the chair industry. In the early 19th century the chairmaking industry gradually moulded the existing woodlands to its new needs. Where clear-felling and replanting took place, it was to create even-aged, high timber, and here there was a deliberate, and quite long-term investment in 'high-forest'. As the bodgers were squeezed out of business, the Chiltern selection system broke down and a lot of second- and third-rate wood was left to over-mature and degenerate, leaving a legacy of management problems that was apparent by the 1920s. Under the closed canopy of high beech, seedlings failed to regenerate and the ground flora became much more limited than in the traditional woods.

The history of these woodland changes can be read in the trees themselves. A great swathe of mature beechwood was clear-felled at Hailey Wood as the M40 motorway sliced through the Chiltern escarpment at Lewknor. George Peterken of the Nature Conservancy studied the age and ring-growth of the felled beeches.[33] What appeared even-aged in fact ranged over 100 years from 1760-1876 in date. The older trees had narrow growth rings up to about 1851, then spurted and later slowed in pace. For these and other details, Peterken suggests that before 1851 the wood had been repeatedly lightly thinned on the selection system, with regeneration in the gaps. A major thinning in 1851 led to a period of rapid growth, which ceased in about 1876 as the canopy closed and further seedlings failed to survive.

In the 1920s and 1930s the Cambridge ecologist A. S. Watt made a series of classic studies of the Chiltern beechwoods.[34] On the plateau he examined a whole group of woods around Hampden, and found that the approximate age of the high beech forming the canopy was 105-140 years, dating the bulk to 1794-1830. This was true both for the ancient woods named in the Hampden Wood Books like Hampden Coppice and Oaken Grove, and for the 'newer' woods such as Hillock's Wood, enclosed from scrubby 'hill-work' in the early 19th century. This evidence fits with our picture of the decay of fuel-wood coppicing, and woods like Hillocks must have been allowed to grow rapidly to high forest, though multiple leaders suggest some coppicing in the early years. Watt puzzled over whether this plateau beech could be regarded as the natural 'climax community', the natural and stable end of the process of ecological succession. On the thin, chalky soils of the escarpment edge this seemed possible, but he was dubious about the woods on clay-with-flints. There was too little oak, and high beech eventually degenerates the soil: 'the ultimate fate of the beechwoods would be retrogression to heath'. There was no evidence of the latter happening. It is hard, therefore, on ecological grounds to see plateau high beech as 'natural', but the ecological evidence fits very well with the economic and social history of the woodlands.

Chapter Eleven

The 19th-Century Chilterns

Parliamentary Enclosure

If we could have stood on the top of Coombe Hill near Wendover around the year 1800, we would have seen a landscape in transformation. The great canal from London to Birmingham had just been constructed across Tring summit, a branch to Wendover was being built, and the

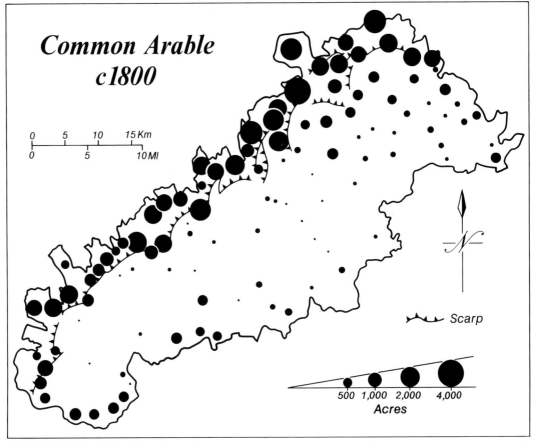

125. Common arable, *c.* 1800. The contrast between surviving common arable in the scarp-foot parishes and along parts of the Thames stands out clearly against the interior of the Hills where most common fields had disappeared much earlier. [Based on Roden, 1965. Note that Roden does not include south-east Buckinghamshire in his Chiltern region.]

land would still have seemed torn and scarred. In the Vale a process of enclosure by Parliamentary Acts was well under way, replacing the open-fields with a new planned landscape of enclosed and hedged fields. The fields of Wendover itself had been enclosed by Act in 1795. The very long-standing contrast of 'champion' and 'woodland' was to be softened by these changes as the new hedges began to green the bare browns of the Vale.

Across the plains and vales of midland England, piecemeal enclosure had made less headway than in the Hills. Enclosure of the big open-field systems had to be root-and-branch or nothing, and getting unanimous agreement of the landowners was virtually impossible. The solution was the process of Parliamentary Enclosure. This involved groups of landowners applying for an Act authorising enclosure, setting up Enclosure Commissioners to look into the details, adjudicate all the claims and make an Award.[1] The shared costs of the process could be high, and many a smallholder found himself with a tiny allocation of land and a bill to pay. Because the Acts were comprehensive they enclosed commons as well as common-fields, and the loss of such rights allegedly finished off many smaller farmers and cottagers. From 1740 onwards a wave of such Acts began to enclose midland England.

By the 1770s such Acts were lapping around the edges of the Chiltern Hills: Aylesbury in 1772 (the date of the Award), Waddesdon (1775), Wendover (1795), Tring (1804). Enclosure was slowest where a substantial group of prosperous landowners and smallholders shared in the open-fields. Getting sufficient support for an Act was difficult. Many of the Chiltern-foot parishes were of just this type, especially along the Icknield Belt all the way from Luton to South Stoke by the Thames. Enclosure came to the Kimbles and Ellesborough in 1805, Saunderton (1807), Marsworth (1811), Bledlow (1812), Aston Clinton (1816), Princes Risborough (1823), Ivinghoe (1825) and Monks Risborough (1839). In Oxfordshire, Watlington's fields were awarded in 1815, as were those of Lewknor. A similar process was also occurring on the other side of the Hills in south-east Buckinghamshire, with enclosure of the remaining open-fields at Iver (1804), Wooburn (1804), Upton (1819) and Farnham Royal (1831).

These Acts and their Awards redrew the landscape, with rectangular fields and new farms away from the village centres, what Oliver Rackham calls 'Planned Countryside'. At Lewknor today we can still see many of the hedged fields that were made (though some of the fields have since been re-amalgamated). The Award here allocated 1,800 acres, 1,550 former arable and meadow. Nine landholders received allocations, varying from 45 acres to over 400 for the lord of the manor and for All Souls College. As well as Church Farm, the College now held the new Field Farm (119 acres) on the Shirburn Road, and Hill Farm (also known as Linky Downs) on 260 acres of old sheep-walk and hill-land.[2] Parliamentary enclosure did not completely erase all signs of the previous system. From the escarpment slopes above Hill Farm one can look down on this 'new' rectangular layout of fields, and within it one can still trace survivals of the old open-fields. There is no neat ridge-and-furrow, for this was never very pronounced at Lewknor. Arthur Young wrote in 1813: 'In Aston and Lewknor fields ... the ridges broad, and very little arched; some nearly flat'.[3] But some old furlongs survive. Off the Weston road, just past the moated Moor Court, is a public footpath on the left. It is the old Lower Icknield Way, marked on the 1598 map, which takes you down to the Shirburn boundary. It is a dead-end, for beyond the boundary the old right of way has been extinguished, and this path will surely lapse in time. At the very end, to one's left, is a field running up the boundary to Field Farm and the B4009: this is the old 'Preste Furlonge' of alternating glebe and manor strips coloured on Langdon's map.

Some of the Chiltern-foot open-fields took an unconscionable time to die. They lingered on past the canal age and well into the railway age, and some are amongst the last Acts in the whole country. The Great Western Railway had cut through South Stoke village more than

126. Map of Stokenchurch and Lewknor, 1797. This extract from Richard Davis' very detailed map of Oxfordshire brings out the striking difference between the wooded and enclosed Chiltern country above the scarp, and the open, hedgeless Vale below. This contrast, probably at its most marked when Davis surveyed, was about to disappear. Lewknor was enclosed within 20 years in 1815. The accuracy of the Davis map is remarkable, but his hedged enclosures are somewhat 'conventional' in shape, and the reality was much less rectangular. Note also the commons and the turnpike milestones. [Bodleian: C.17:49.al.]

ten years before the 1,750 acres of open-fields, still made up of very scattered strips, were enclosed by an Award of 1853. At Crowell the little Watlington branch railway ran through the small open-fields there for 10 years before enclosure in 1882. In the north large open-fields lasted at Pitstone, Cheddington and Edlesborough into the 1850s and '60s, and at Totternhoe 1,717 acres were awarded as late as 1891. There the essentially medieval system is only a century away from us.

In one or two cases disputes and opposition to enclosure allow us to get a glimpse of the issues involved. In both Princes Risborough and Monks Risborough there were disputes that are well documented.[4] At Monks Risborough the Earl of Buckinghamshire (of Great Hampden House) was the leading landowner, and he applied for an Act of enclosure in 1830. The common waste on the Chiltern hillside proved the source of dispute—300 acres used for grazing and for fuel by the poor. A counter-petition came from four smallholders and another from the poor of the village. His lordship's agent argued that opposition was being led by those who abused their common rights, cutting wood not just for themselves, but to sell to commoners who lived too distant to collect their own. The Act was eventually passed, but with a unique clause appointing a special commissioner for the poor. The Earl was informed: 'Sir John Dashwood King is appointed Commissioner for the poor, it is a matter of no consequence he is a blundering blockhead and in fact will not trouble himself about the matter'. Sir John was, however, more active than anticipated, and it took until 1839 to get final agreement.[5]

In these Chiltern-and-Vale strip-parishes, such as Monks Risborough, the enclosure of open-fields affected lands at the scarp-foot in the Vale. The commons, wastes, and 'hill-works' allocated in the various Awards lay on the Chiltern scarp sides and summit. After the Awards some of these commons were enclosed and converted into farms and fields. Hill Farm in Lewknor is one example, and in Princes Risborough parts of Risborough Hillock near Lacey Green were enclosed into fields. Some land on the plateau top was fenced and converted to high forest, as at Hillock Wood in Monks Risborough. Some of the steepest or least desirable slopes were left open and somewhat neglected, to be reclaimed by scrub, juniper and expanding woodland. Reduced grazing pressure later in the century added to this last category, and parts of the scarp line put on a more wooded overcoat.

The parliamentary enclosure waves also ran over the residual open-fields that had hung on within the Chilterns themselves. In 1802, 500 acres in Kings Walden were Awarded. The largest was at Amersham in 1816, affecting over 900 acres, but most were much smaller scale, such as the 61 acres at Chalfont St Peter in 1847 that comprised Latchmore Field. At Little Gaddesden in 1836 it was the last 52 acres which were enclosed. The 19th-century tithe maps also revealed tiny blocks of common strips that had survived like dinosaurs of some former age, and which were extinguished by private agreement during the century. Within the Hills there was, however, an important category of late Parliamentary Enclosure. This was the commons and heaths, which deserve their own discussion.

The Chiltern Commons and Heaths

The piecemeal enclosure within the Hills after 1550 had not destroyed the major heaths and commons. They had been nibbled at and eroded in places, mostly small-scale but ranging up to the 300 acres taken from Berkhamsted Frith in 1616. Late 18th-century maps, like Davis' of Oxfordshire, demonstrate the sharp contrast of open Vale and enclosed Chiltern, but they also show the large areas of common surviving within the Hills (Plate 126). They included Wycombe and Holmer Heath, Naphill Common, Prestwood Common, Stokenchurch and Chequers Commons. In the Hertfordshire Chilterns there were commons at Berkhamsted, Wigginton and Cholesbury; in Oxfordshire there were heaths at Goring, Checkendon, Chazey and Ipsden, and such lists could be extended.

It is worth casting back in time to look at the role of these commons and heaths in the life and economy of the Chilterns. Many were on patches of the least fertile soils, such as outliers of Reading Beds and Plateau Gravels, with mixtures of sands, gravels and clays. Some had their own perched water tables. These commons provided rough grazing and fuel. Some were wooded, but others, especially in the north, had been so heavily used that they had very few trees or bushes left. Kalm described the furze only four inches high on Ivinghoe Common being cut by boys with scythes and bound into bundles for fuel. They also provided a safety-valve, a place where those without landholding could sometimes find a perch and scrape a livelihood. Here also industries like brick-making and tile and pottery kilns were located, making use of the local clays and sands, and wood fuel. Nettlebed Common provided quite

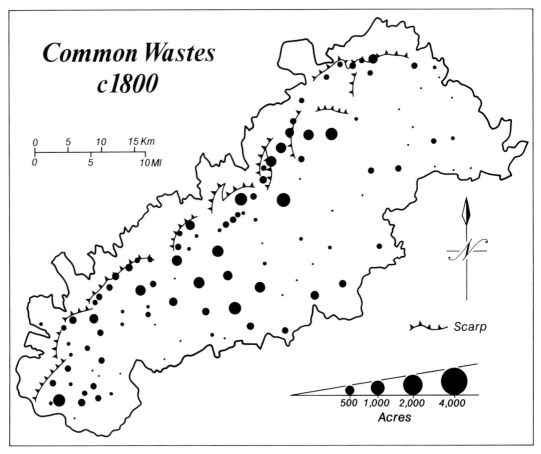

127. Common wastes, *c*.1800. Many commons and heaths survived within the Chilterns at this date, and waited until Parliamentary Acts enclosed them after 1845. Many have survived to this day. [Based on Roden, 1965.]

an industrial scene over many centuries, with claypits, waterpools, brickyards and tilekilns. In 1851 William Thompson of Nettlebed, brickmaker and potter, employed 30 men and 25 boys, and Thomas Hobbs employed 10 men and two boys there.[6] The last kilns closed in 1927, but tramways, pools, pits and a kiln can still be seen in Nettlebed (Plate 128). Russell's Water takes its present name from the Russell family of brick-makers, and Russell's kiln occurs in a Stonor rent account for 1695. The pool of the brick-works and an old kiln house of brick remain there today.

   The edges of such commons attracted cottages and 'encroachments'. Some individuals had legitimate rights, others squatted. Some were locals, others migrated from parishes where such havens did not exist at all. It may be an illusion produced by our random discovery of references, but cottage encroachments seem most active in the early 17th and 19th centuries, and the Chilterns may have attracted migrants from the less hospitable Vale country. Such encroachments were usually fined, but often allowed to remain, and later 'quit rents' some-times have their origin in such fines. The early 17th-century court rolls for Cholesbury contain several such entries, and several houses facing the Common today have their origin in these encroachments (Plate 129).[7]

By Queen Victoria's reign these commons were seen as targets by improving and profit-minded landowners. They were quick to catalogue abuses. In Hughenden in 1846 John Cartwright of Piggott's Farm was reporting to Edward Grubb, a London-based land entrepreneur: William Smith was 'cutting stone on Denner Hill Common'; Amos Tree was 'not filling all his stone holes up in Sprion Coppis'; and Cartwright asked, 'whether I should summon Morris Hearn son and daughter for cutting two beech trees in Sprion Coppis'.[8] In February 1852 the Rector of Radnage, a George Phillimore, was writing to the lord of the manor (in this case the Dean and Chapter of St George's, Windsor):

> Radnage common consists of 100 acres and upon this constant encroachments are made, frequently by parties who have no right of common whatever, who after a time, if not interfered with, have a legal right to the property to Inclose ... The same remark applies to other waste lands by the roadside, where houses have been built by parties not connected with this parish.[9]

128. The kiln at Nettlebed. This relic of 19th-century tile and pottery making in Nettlebed towers above a small cul-de-sac of modern housing.

The result was enclosure of many of the commons by the General Acts of 1845 onwards. Over 2,000 acres of Penn, Wycombe and Holmer Heath was awarded in 1855; 700 acres at Stokenchurch Common in 1861; 259 acres at Wigginton in 1854. Radnage and Andridge Commons were awarded in 1862, and Denner Hill (as part of Hughenden) in 1855. Some of this land was parcelled up and divided into fields, giving us patches of geometric field boundaries in the midst of the older Chiltern enclosures. Perhaps the two best examples are at Holmer Green, north of High Wycombe, and south of Wigginton. They stand out beautifully on the larger scale 2½ inch Ordnance Survey maps showing field boundaries, and at Wigginton a post-enclosure road across the former common runs in a straight line for two miles past the Champneys Health Resort. Not all the common land was actually enclosed. The ancient commons were often on poor soils, and even in the 19th century they were not worth farming. In several cases only the edges were fenced off and divided. At Naphill Common in Hughenden parish, sections on the north-east side were taken away, but most was left to revert to scrub and wood as grazing ceased, so that today we can discover pollards from the old common hidden amongst the later tall trees. Others found their fate as poor quality land available for later housing developments. The outline of modern, urban Prestwood fits almost perfectly into the old form of the common. Similarly the houses and estates of Hazlemere, Widmer End, Holmer Green and Great Kingshill follow closely the outlines of the 19th-century heath.

129. A 17th-century cottage on Cholesbury Common. This is one of the cottages mentioned in the 17th-century Court Rolls containing entries about building and encroachments on the common.

Many pieces of heath and common—even if not legally 'common'—have come down to us today.[10] That at Wheeler End, west of Wycombe and between the M40 and A40, is a good example of the sort of small common most Chiltern villages used to have. Larger pieces, like Naphill, have become overgrown, returning to scrub and woodland or to bracken and furze. Some were only preserved after dispute or public action. At Berkhamsted there were nearly 1,200 acres of common to the north of the town. In 1865 Lord Brownlow bought out the rights of many tenants and enclosed part of the area by five-foot iron railings. But he reckoned without Augustus Smith of Ashlyns, who had not sold his rights to the common: Smith brought in 120 men from London to pull down the three miles of railings, and eventually defeated Brownlow in the courts.[11] At Burnham Beeches in the south-east Chilterns the Corporation of the City of London bought the land in 1880 to preserve the old grazed common with its fine pollards as a public space.

Cottage industries: lace-making and straw-plaiting

Before mechanisation and the necessities of industrial discipline drove production into urban factories, much manufacturing was based in the countryside as rural crafts and cottage industries. Some, like the blacksmith and the carpenter, were found in almost every village as full-time occupations. Some were localised because they were tied to particular resources—like the brick and tile-making and the wood-bodging industries of the Chilterns. Others also grew up in a strongly regional pattern, but without the tie to natural resources. The agricultural historian Joan Thirsk has suggested that there was a strong association between wood-pasture regions and rural industries such as cloth-making.[12] Pastoral farming left men with time to take on secondary jobs such as weaving, whereas arable farming was more demanding the whole year round. As we have seen, the Chilterns were very much an arable rather than pastoral region, and they did not develop such cottage industries, although some writers have instinctively placed the woody Chilterns with such wood-pasture regions as the Weald and the Forest of Arden.

Yet the Chiltern counties did become centres for two cottage industries: lace-making and straw-plaiting. Starting slowly in the 17th century, they created a quiet revolution in employment, very different from the usual clatter of industry, and rose to a zenith in the 19th century when they employed tens of thousands across the counties and dominated many local communities. The employees were mostly women and children, many the wives and families of agricultural workers who were earning meagre incomes. In the Hills, at places like Stokenchurch, they were wives of chair-makers (Plate 130). It was rural poverty which the lace-making and straw-plaiting areas held in common: this transcended other boundaries of Chiltern and Vale, enclosures and open fields, arable and pasture.

To understand this rural employment, it is worth stepping back from the 19th century to examine their origins and growth. Both lace-making and straw-plaiting gave families the opportunity to supplement earnings. The opportunity arose from the extravagant tastes which had sprung from the Renaissance, and became popular in Elizabethan and 17th-century England.

130. Extract from the 1871 Census Enumerator's Return for Stokenchurch. These entries for houses on the village green show families of chair-makers and lace-makers, such as the Deans: James (46) and his son George (15) are chair-makers, whilst his wife Sarah (43) and daughter Clara (9) are lace-makers. [PRO: RG/10/14606/41b, 4.]

Contemporary fashions, most of which emanated from Italy, meant that lace edgings and later straw hats and bonnets were *de rigeur* and the women and children who made them were perhaps to give new meaning to the term 'slaves to fashion'. Rising incomes and population expanded the demand for such goods, and when both industries were at their height the women and children could earn much more than they would in either of the viable alternatives of agricultural work or domestic service. It also gained the women greater independence than was usual at that time. We see several instances of wives and families supporting unemployed husbands. The two industries had much in common, both in their geography and their organisation with cottage out-workers and 'schools', but each also had its own distinctive history.

Lace-making
English lace-making seems to have begun in the late 16th century, around the time when (in 1590) Sir Francis Bacon commented: 'Our English dames are much given to wearing costly laces', with most coming from Flanders, Italy and France. The location of English lace-making is traditionally ascribed to refugee Flemings and Huguenots settling in our region. This may have played a part, but there is little real evidence, and the early localities are quite scattered.[13] The earliest reference is for Eaton Socon (in north-east Bedfordshire) in 1596, when the authorities agreed to pay 'the woman that teacheth the pore chilren to worck bone lace ...'. The lace-making region came to span four local counties: Bedfordshire, Buckinghamshire, Oxfordshire and Northamptonshire. In Buckinghamshire centres became established at Olney, Aylesbury and High Wycombe where lace-makers are recorded to be in distress in 1623. In Marlow in 1625 Sir Henry Borlese established a school for 24 boys and 24 girls where the girls were taught lace-making. The industry expanded over the border into Oxfordshire, where it became particularly important around Chinnor, Stokenchurch and Henley.

The early references to 'Bone lace' were so called because it was first made using bone bobbins. It later became known as pillow lace because the lace-maker used a large stuffed cushion on her knees to support her work. She attached her pattern (pricked out on parchment) to the cushion, using pins through the small holes. The threads were looped around the pins with a bobbin on each end and the pattern was worked diagonally by twisting and crossing the threads using the bobbins in groups and adding new pins as each line grew. It was a skilled and laborious process not easily learnt or transferred. This helps to explain why it became so localised, and why lace-villages could co-exist with neighbouring communities where the skills were unknown.

The driving force in lace fashions was the tastes of the royal court and the wealthy. Changing and extravagant fashions in lace continued. The reigns of Charles II through to William and Mary showed lace cravats at the height of fashion, and the petticoats of the ladies of King Charles's court were noticed and recorded by Samuel Pepys, who writes in 1663 of a visit to White Hall Gardens: 'And in the privy garden saw the finest smocks and linnen petticoats of my Lady Castlemaine's, laced with rich lace at the bottom, that I ever saw; and it did me good to look at them'.[14] Fanciful lace fashions remained popular with the rich. The *Spectator* was soon deploring 'Childish Gewgaws, Ribbands and Bone Lace' and thought a woman wearing the latest lace gowns and high head-dresses with lace frills and flounces resembled 'a Friesland hen'. More important for the growth of the lace industry was the spread of lace-wearing to a much wider social range as part of the emergence of a consumer goods market. Daniel Defoe's Country Grocer's wife (1727) bought 'her Lace and Edgings from Stony Stratford the first and Great Marlow the last'.[15] The growing market was not, however, a very stable one, for the lace-maker had to keep up with the vagaries of fashion, constantly competing with continental designs. She also had to contend with very uncertain national policies on protection against foreign imports.

Just how many were employed at this time is difficult to assess; we only get reliable information much later with the 1851 Census. All we can say for certain is that the numbers were large and the impact on local communities quite substantial. Because women and children were the main workers, records tend to neglect the industry, and comments are sometimes patronising or slighting. Langley in his *History of the Hundred of Desborough* (1797) says, 'The lace manufactory, for which this county has long been celebrated, employs a great number of females. But from the general appearance of the peasantry, the trade does not induce the habits of neatness and industry which appear highly necessary to render an occupation beneficial to a county.'[16] Such stuffy and largely derisory remarks by middle- and upper-class gentlemen colour much of the literature and must be swallowed with the customary dose of salt!

Our best information records not the female and child lace-makers, but the lace-dealers and wholesalers who were normally men.[17] William Statham of Great Missenden died in 1685, leaving his household goods to his wife, 'excepting and other than my stock of lace silk thread and other things belonging to and concerning my trade and calling of lacebuyer'. One prominent local lace merchant was Ferdinando Shrimpton of Penn, who kept several hundred workers constantly employed, and was eight times Mayor of Chepping (High) Wycombe. He was one of many dealers and wholesalers who travelled to the London markets at Aldersgate, and was instrumental in gaining wholesaling status for the lace merchants so that they were not deemed hawkers or pedlars. The 1717 petition states that, 'The wholesalemen travel weekly to London, where they sell their lace and buy thread and silk which they bring home and deliver to their workwomen who by their directions work or weave it into several sorts of lace, as their respective masters direct, which when done, the workwomen deliver to their respective masters who can pay them what they earn'.

The lace-makers were wholly reliant on the buyers for their threads (which had to be imported from Holland and were expensive) and more importantly for their patterns. It was in this way that the merchants controlled their monopoly: all lace worked on a pattern supplied by a buyer must be sold back to him. The relationship allowed considerable exploitation of the workers, both in the selling of the threads and the prices paid for the finished lace. Translating designs into working patterns was the most difficult task and fashions for lace were constantly changing. From the late 1770s point ground lace with patterns copied from Lille or Mechlin were the staple pillow lace usually used for edgings, and large quantities were exported to the United States until the start of the American Civil War. The softer and lighter fabrics which were being worn in place of the stiff, heavy silks required simpler and less intricately woven lace and the local designs showed a light meshed background (the point) scattered with small sprigs. In the early 19th century Regency point lace was in vogue, and the frills and flounces of the wider skirts were trimmed in blond or black lace. Buckinghamshire black lace was renowned and highly esteemed. Local laces were displayed at the Great Exhibition in 1851, and this gave the industry a welcome boost by introducing Maltese guipure lace made of thread and silk. This style became very popular and it seriously undermined the older forms of Buckinghamshire lace.

Lace-makers tended to start learning their craft at a very tender age (five or six years old was quite normal) and to work for extremely long hours. The early apprenticeship was generally in a 'school' where they would work under the watchful eye of a formidable matron for anything up to 11 hours a day, and the children paid 2d. or 3d. to attend each week. Lace-making required considerable skill and instruction with the children bent over the bulky pillow

133. The lace-maker. An elderly lace-maker sitting at her cottage doorway in Princes Risborough, working on her lace with the parchment-pattern fixed to her lace-pillow.

for hours on end. Incentives came at the end of a big stick and special rhymes and tales were recited to reduce the tedium.[18]

Lace employment in the Chiltern counties probably peaked during the French wars, but there are no reliable figures before the 1851 Census. This records 17,991 for Bedfordshire, Buckinghamshire and Oxfordshire. The industry was threatened by machine-made lace, and prices and incomes fell. It proved difficult to maintain quality through the out-worker system. Lace-dealing was becoming concentrated in fewer hands and Thomas Gilbert of High Wycombe claimed to employ 3,000 in 1862, but this meant less frequent contact and supervision of pattern and quality. Old, worn patterns were used, innovation was less, and there was much 'pirating', with lace being sold by poor workers in short 'cut-offs' to meet immediate bills.

A few lace merchants tried to fight the decline. James Millward of Olney advocated copyright patents for designs, and Thomas Lester of Bedford argued that it was the lack of a school of designs which was effecting the decline of the industry. Lester successfully made the transition to Maltese lace, and his new designs helped to keep the Bedfordshire lace-workers employed for longer than otherwise.[19] Even he could not reverse the tide of machine production, and he only delayed the death of the cottage industry. By the 1870s even Maltese guipures were being produced by machine, and a commentator at the Chicago Exhibition in 1893 noted that the 'Coarser pillow laces from Buckinghamshire ... can never compete with the machine made lace, the resemblance being so close in all points except price'.

The problems in the industry were reflected in the Census: in 1881 only 9,520 lace-makers were recorded in the three counties. By 1891 it had dropped to a mere 2,672 and almost all of those were middle-aged or older. Long after the eleventh hour the government sent A. S. Cole to visit the region with a view to salvaging practical lace-making by concentrating on design. However, his conclusion was that 'Commercial influence is insufficient to foster the higher possibilities of lace making'.[20] He noted that in the appropriately named Chiltern village of Lacey Green, there were several very old, perfect and superior patterns in the hands of the village dealer, a Mrs. Forrester, which had never been worked because the purchasers 'will not wait to get a length' and the lace-makers were making quicker and simpler designs. It was left to the local nobility, distressed at the effect the decline was having on the poor in their neighbourhoods, to set up Lace Associations to collect and sell lace at a better price than they would get from the dealers. They collected patterns and revived interest in point ground lace but their efforts were to little avail and the industry shrank to almost nothing. However, a little vestige remained dormant until the 1950s, when an entirely new generation, with time to spare and the will to learn, started an enthusiastic craft pursuit. Today residential courses are held in Missenden Abbey, a far cry from the lace manufacturers of whom Cowper wrote:

> You cottager,who weaves at her own door,
> Pillow and bobbins all her little store;
> Content though mean, and cheerful if not gay,
> Shuffling her threads about the livelong day:
> Just earns a scanty pittance, and at night
> Lies down secure, her heart and pocket light.

Straw-plaiting

In the 17th and 18th centuries hats and bonnets were as essential a part of fashionable dress as lace-edged collars, cuffs and handkerchiefs. Straw-plaiting was already an industry around Dunstable in 1689 when a group of villages (including Edlesborough, Studham, Great Gaddesden and Flamstead) joined Dunstable and Luton to protest against proposed laws to enforce the wearing of woollen hats, claiming 'near a thousand families' depended on the straw-hat trade.[21] One of the reasons for the establishment of the straw-plaiting industry in this region may have been connected to the availability of a wheat straw that was 'best adapted in colour and texture'. It needed to be soft and pliable and the thin Chilterns' soils produced these easily worked straws in abundance. The fashion for straw-hats almost certainly spread from Italy where the Leghorn (Livorno) district produced very fine pale straw which was plaited and made into hats that were exported to England in ever increasing numbers. The numbers give an impression of the expanding consumer market: 17,117 imported in 1721, but 477,024 in 1760.

The straw-plaiting and lace-making regions overlapped, but the two were not coincident; by the early 19th century straw-plaiting extended further eastwards into Hertfordshire and Essex and did not drift northwards beyond the Ouse. The centre of the industry was first in Dunstable but later moved to Luton. It was very extensive with centres like those at Ivinghoe, Amersham and Tring and deep into traditional lace-making country at High Wycombe and Aylesbury where women switched crafts when demands for lace decreased and more money could be earned by plaiting straw and sewing bonnets. Gibbs in his *History of Aylesbury* (1885) confirms that: 'The fashion of wearing Dunstable straw hats had established itself, and many persons abandoned the working of pillow lace ... and betook themselves to straw plaiting, finishing and bleaching as a more profitable employment.'[22]

Straw-plaiting had a real boost while the French wars were being fought (1793-1815) and foreign plaits were not being imported. The quality of British manufacture was improved dramatically when a little device for splitting straws became widely available sometime around 1815, enabling much finer straw plait to be made. Numbers employed reached their peak in the 1871 Census when 45,179 female plaiters were counted. These Census figures are under-estimates because of part-time workers not declaring their occupations to the enumerators. The Children's Employment Commission of 1862 suggests higher numbers, varying between 50,000 and 100,000 depending on whether trade was good or bad. These figures exclude all those that were given employment besides those who plait and make hats and bonnets: 'bleachers, cutters, dyers, flatters, stringers, drawers etc', according to Gibbs. We do know that the craft all-pervaded some of the communities involved. Laszlo Grof has made a marvellously detailed

132. Hitchin plait market in the late 19th century, showing a hive of activity as women buy straw and sell finished plait.

study of Edlesborough, where over half the female population was employed in straw-plaiting in 1851: 459 out of 824.[23] At nearby Ivinghoe, the proportion was similar (275 out of 456 in 1871), and Pamela Horn has noted that these proportions are comparable to the figures for cotton employment in the industrial towns of Lancashire. Places like Ivinghoe were miniature 'industrial communities'.[24] James Greenwood in *On the Tramp* (1883) describes the scene in Hitchin (Plate 132) which was one of the larger plaiting centres and typical: 'Dozens and dozens of them, little girls, big girls, buxom matrons and dames bent and grey ... They moved among the men and lads laughing and larking, but never for a moment staying the movement of their nimble fingers'.[25]

How much they earned depended on how fast they could work and how complicated the pattern was. Like lace-making, there were a great many variations with each village having three or four patterns to which it became accustomed. We get a measure of the wealth of variety in the Stock Book of Henry Horn, a local dealer who carried 137 different kinds of plait in stock in the mid-1880s. His book, now in Luton Museum, shows how seasonal the work was, with the numbers of outworkers lowest after the harvest in August to October and then building up for the spring, when the ladies purchased their new Easter bonnets.[26] The adult plaiters in the 1870s could earn as much as 12s. a week doing 20 yards a day (though this was well above the average) and a child could add a further 6d. a day. Unlike the lace-makers,

133. Gray and Horn's stall on Luton plait market. This shows the variety of types of plait that were made.

whose mobility was restricted by their bulky pillow, the plaiters could work on the hoof almost continously, tucking their cut straw lengths under one arm, their semi-finished plait looped over it, and completing their one-woman band with a few split straws in their mouth being softened ready to work. The wages compared well with those of the average agricultural labourer who brought home around 13s. to 14s. a week.

There were inevitable consequences that stemmed from the long hours that women and children worked and also from the unusual degree of independence that straw-plaiting created in these starchy Victorian times. The bounds of respectability were stretched to breaking point and the women were reputed to be slovenly housewives, 'utterly ignorant of such common things as keeping their houses clean, minding their children's clothes and cooking their husband's dinners'. Worse still were the insinuations about their loose moral standards, some of which were said to be invited by their predilection for pretty clothes. The evidence does not substantiate what David Thorburn refers to as their 'supposed want of chastity and lascivious escapades' and he suggests that most were exaggerated stories.[27] Similarly Laszlo Grof fails to discover the untold numbers of unwed women and illegitimate children in Edlesborough that the diatribes of the Vicar of Toddington would have us believe were harboured in the straw-plaiting villages.[28] But observations as to the literacy, or lack of it, that the Vicar and others made about the women and children in these areas are borne out in parish registers, where few brides could sign their names and female literacy here lagged behind the rest of the country.

This was a consequence of the straw-plaiting schools, where children learned the craft but not their ABC. The plait schools were like those for lace, but often larger and in cramped conditions. We learn a great deal about these establishments from the evidence given to the Children's Employment Commission in 1864. Mrs. Wimbush's Straw-Plait School in Northchurch was typical—a room just over ten feet square with a low ceiling in which were squashed between forty and sixty children between the ages of four and fourteen. There was no fire in winter because it was essential to keep the work clean, so children brought their 'chaddy pots' filled with hot embers to keep their hands warm enough to plait, making the air close, heavy and smelly. At Mrs. Wimbush's, the Commission recorded: 'Sarah Wellin, age eight. Have been here since five years old. Did three score (yards) yesterday, 2½ of them at home after work at school. Do not know how much mother gets for my plait. Do not know A or B; go to Sunday school'.[29] Sixty yards is a huge amount for a little girl, and one suspects some exaggeration or miscounting here. The 1867 Workshops Regulation Act tried to ban all child labour under eight years, and only allowed 'half-time' for 8-13 year olds, whilst the 1870 Education Act was the first step in a long battle to ensure that children attended elementary school for at least 10 hours a week. Plait and lace children tended to become reluctant 'half-timers', but their attendance was often appalling and reflected their split loyalties. The Rev. A. Birch summed up the parents' dilemma: 'Plait means bread ... dearer than knowledge'. Improvements resulted less from the implementation of the Act than the collapse of the cottage industries in the last decades of the century.

The decline of straw-plaiting came quickly in the period after 1870. Change was largely brought about by cheap foreign competition from new and distant sources. The new Chinese plait sold at 7d. for 120 yards, compared with English plait which sold at 6¾d. for only 20 yards. Even the superior Italian plait was cheaper at 8d. for 50 yards. The result was that although the plait halls of Luton remained the 'Emporium for the World', by 1893 less than five per cent of the plait sold was English. The introduction of the sewing machine in 1874 meant that women could earn more by machining foreign plaits, their English equivalents being too short to machine. The price paid to the plaiters fell drastically, leaving the women 'plaiting eternally

134. Hat boxes at Luton station. These boxes are all filled with hats awaiting shipment by rail to the London market. The picture gives some idea of the scale of the hat industry in the early part of this century, and the industry is the source of the nickname for Luton Town football club, 'The Hatters'.

from morn till night, for a wage of about 1s 3d a week'. The manufacturers maintained that, just as with the lace industry: ' If the English plaiters would invent new designs and imitate new patterns for which there is a demand they could obtain good earnings'. But they could not or would not, and as a consequence many were forced to give up. The lucky ones who lived in the chair-making regions changed to chair-caning and some learned tambour beading. These remain within living memory: reminiscences in *A Pattern of Hundreds* include those of a resident of Stokenchurch who remembers women sitting at their front doors with a bundle of canes hanging from a nail, caning chairs for which they were paid 2d. a chair. In Lacey Green Mrs. Adams can remember sitting up all night with three others beading a dress for the theatre.[30]

Some workers found jobs in the factories in Luton where hat-making became an industrial occupation rather than a rural craft, and machinery replaced the hand craftsmanship of the home-worker. Other straw-plaiters returned to a pittance in the fields, or more often joined their families in the drift to the cities for new lives and new occupations. The era of the rural craft industry was waning and old ladies who could remember their patterns were all that remained of skills that had involved long hours for no great reward, but had brushed increased prosperity into so many households, before being swept away in the name of progress.

High Farming and Depression
The two decades after 1850 marked the high tide for traditional Chilterns arable farming. Corn was profitable, and farmers and landlords were doing well, even if their labourers remained badly paid. Most farmers followed the traditional four-course rotation, either by choice or because of restrictions on their leases. High output required much labour: farms in Watlington parish such as Lower Greenfield, Watcombe Manor and Dame Alice, all between 275 and 350 acres, employed 11 to 18 farmhands each.[31] There was investment in improving efficiency, and much chalk was dug out of pits in the fields to fertilise the clay topsoil. Many of the hollows or 'dell-holes' in Chiltern fields date from these years. Hedges were grubbed up to create larger fields, and in some Chiltern valleys more hedgerow destruction can be dated to these Victorians than to modern wheat-barons. Peter Casselden's detailed study of the Pednor district shows the loss of over 16,000 yards of hedgerow between 1843 and 1873, representing over 21 per cent of all the internal field-hedges.[32]

Water supply remained a persistent problem in many parts of the Hills, and these years saw many attempts at digging wells to provide upland farms and villages with a reliable and clean supply. For many homes the only sources were the local pond, and rainwater collected from the tiled roof into a tank. Stokenchurch was one village in this category. It suffered from persistent water-shortages in the summer months, when water had to be brought by horse-drawn wagons up Aston Hill from Lewknor. In 1870 the two leading landowners financed the digging of a well for the village. The water-table was not reached until a depth of 360 feet (110 metres).[33] Such depths were common on the Chiltern plateau: the Maharajah's Well at Stoke Row (Plate 135) reached water at 365 feet.

Many new houses and farm buildings date from this period, and the prosperity and confidence is marked by the many church 'restorations' such as Ellesborough, Great Kimble, and Turville. Some old medieval chapels were dismantled and rebuilt. The isolated St James in Bix was moved to the village (Plate 156), and the St Mary le More chapel at Moor End was rebuilt at Cadmore End.[34] At The Lee a Victorian church hides a tiny medieval chapel that still sits within the grounds.

The year 1879 probably saw the largest extent of ploughed arable land in the Hills at any date in history.[35] The following years saw the tide of rural prosperity turn and ebb. A succession of bad harvests hit yields, but the real damage was caused by foreign grain imports from new, cheaper sources in Europe and North America. English farmers found it hard to compete, and farming went into a depression that really lasted until 1940. Prices and incomes fell. Rents had to be reduced to keep tenant farmers, and the West Wycombe estate rentals fell by 19 per cent between 1876 and 1888. Fewer labourers were employed and, in Hugh Prince's phrase, 'the polish went out of cultivation'.[36]

The Chilterns suffered less than many areas, but the depression altered the face of much of the Chiltern landscape. Some marginal land was abandoned, and much went to weed and thistle. In the regular cropping cycle the temporary grasses or leys were extended from the usual one or two years to four or five years and many eventually became permanent pasture. Sheep had been kept mainly to fold on the arable, and their numbers were reduced as the arable contracted. This was to have major effects on the downlands along the scarp as scrub and bushes began to colonise. The number of cattle rose—'down corn, up horn' as the traditional expression has it—both as a by-product of the expansion of grass and to take advantage of new markets. The move towards dairy cattle was strongest in the south Chilterns, never the best arable land in the region. These areas were close enough to the GWR line to catch the milk-train or the 'Milky Way' as it was known, or to serve the Huntley & Palmer biscuit factory at Reading.[37] The improvements in well-digging and water-supply also helped the growth of dairying. Milk cows can drink 10 gallons or more of water each day and water shortage had been a major restriction on pastoral farming in the Hills. Full release from this constraint had to await piped water in the 1930s. This change to dairying can still be seen in the surviving farm buildings and equipment: large traditional barns from earlier centuries, together with late Victorian cow-stalls and feeding troughs. Richard, a farmworker at Newnham Hill near Stoke Row, was interviewed in his eighties in 1937 and recalled his youth: 'Then most of it was ploughed to grow corn and roots; now scores of acres have "fallen down" to grass, or grow nothing but weeds'.[38]

J. T. Coppock has traced the changes across the Chilterns, and we can use his figures for Great Missenden as an example of a 'middling parish' where change was marked but by no means extreme.[39] In the 1870s arable land made up 80 per cent of the farming area, but this fell to 70 per cent in 1900 and 50 per cent by 1915. Tillage (the land actually ploughed in any one year, so excluding temporary grass) dropped from 67 per cent to 50 per cent to 40 per cent, a significant 'greening' of the Chiltern scene. As well as growth in permanent pasture, there were other changes. Some former ploughland on hillsides was turned to woodland, and such plantations are often marked by

135. The Maharajah's Well, Stoke Row. A gift from the Maharajah of Benares in 1864-65. Edward Reade, a member of a prominent Ipsden family, was a District Commissioner in India. Hearing about the water-problems of this Chiltern hamlet, the Maharajah financed this well. It was dug to 365 ft. through the chalk before water was struck.

their straight boundaries and their names, such as Jubilee Plantations (at both Fawley Bottom and at Luxters). These woods, often of larch, are the beginning of conifer plantations in the Hills. Some areas closer to railway stations or to London turned to fruit-growing, such as the Holmer orchards. Parts of the Chilterns had a long tradition of cherry growing. William Ellis had lamented government interference in the trade (they were used in liquors and gins) as long ago as 1730.[40] Around Stoke Row, Checkendon and Highmoor cherry orchards became important, and parties of cherry-pickers came out from Reading, and later from London, at harvest-time (Plate 136).

The north-east Chilterns saw fewer changes in their farming traditions. The rolling loams had always given better wheat yields, and arable remained more profitable. The overall effect of the depression was to make the contrast between Chiltern and Vale more muted, and some of the unified character of the Chiltern scene began to be lost in these years.[41] As the Chiltern-

136. The cherry orchards at Checkendon. The southern Chilterns, especially the area around Stoke Row, was renowned for its cherry orchards. This photograph was taken in the 1920s before many had been removed.

Vale contrast lessened, so differences between the north-east and south-west Chilterns emerged more strongly. These internal differences were not to find full expression until more recently, but the divergence began in the 1880s.

This farming depression was part of a wider rural decline with crafts like lace, straw and wood-bodging also declining. Rural incomes fell, there was little investment, and people were migrating from the land. Many Chiltern parishes saw their populations fall in these years. Bledlow and Bledlow Ridge dropped from 1,070 in 1881 to 854 in 1901, and Radnage from 476 to 385. But population growth in the commuter towns and settlements along the railway lines offset much of the rural losses in the Chilterns themselves, and the region suffered nothing like the declines experienced in northern Buckinghamshire. The Chilterns' accessibility to London also continued to make them attractive as a location for a country home for the wealthy, like the London solicitor Sir Frank Crisp who built Friar Park outside Henley in 1889-90. The biggest impact of 'outside money' was felt around Tring and Aston Clinton, where the Rothschild family had a whole network of country houses. They spent a lot of money in these depression years rebuilding farmhouses and entire villages, all in the

137. Dancers End Waterworks. The Rothschilds built everything in their distinctive style, including this waterworks originally built to provide water to their estate villages.

distinctive Rothschild gothic-cum-Swiss style with tall, twisting chimneys. Everything was built to match, even the posh waterworks (at The Crong) to serve their estate (Plate 137).

The end of the century does indeed mark an important transition for the Chilterns. The traditional rural scene was in decay, setting in train changes in the landscape of woods and downs that only had their full impact over many decades. At the same time the area was becoming a dormitory region for London, a role that was to increase dramatically after the turn of the century. It was a new balance that had to be achieved between town and country.

Chapter Twelve

Metro-land

Metro-land is not strictly a place. It is an evocative name that christened an image: the metropolis on the move down shiny railway tracks with puffing steam trains pulling laden carriages of 'peaky' citizens out of the grime and into the countryside. The word 'Metro-land' was part of a very successful marketing ploy to promote the Metropolitan railway and it first appeared in 1915 as the title of their annual guide produced under their new commercial and publicity manager John Wardle.[1] The guide (which appeared each year from 1915 to 1932) claimed to be a 'comprehensive description of the country districts served by the Metropolitan railway' and was part of a growing mound of literature romanticising the countryside. The new *Metro-land* booklet (Plate 152), thanks to improved printing techniques, was enhanced by colour photographs, many of the more idyllic sun-dappled corners of the Chilterns and beyond. It marketed the villages and landscapes served by the line leading through Harrow-on-the-Hill to the Chalfonts, Chesham, Amersham and on to Missenden and Wendover. The descriptions of this 'rural arcadia', in varying hues of purple, painted their own scenes of the countryside—'Each lover of Metro-land may well have his favourite beech wood and coppice—all tremulous green loveliness in Spring and russet and gold in late October'. It also described the small towns and villages—'neat, prim little towns which keep their old-world aspect, like Amersham and Missenden and Wendover'.[2] Nostalgia was interrupted by tempting historical tit-bits and interspersed with allusions to the improved levels of personal well-being that were to be found in this milk and honey landscape: 'The good air of the Chilterns invites to health by day and to sleep by night'.

'The beautiful unknown country' was being laid open to a very wide market with the express intention of making it much less unknown. The inter-war period, despite the depression, saw a new attitude develop towards leisure and the railway companies were quick to catch on to its commercial possibilities. They encouraged a new wave of walkers and ramblers, many of them working-class Londoners who were exercising their fatter paypackets and longer weekends in the countryside. The Chilterns were a popular destination as visitors could step off the train and walk into the immediate surrounds through a series of public footpaths that weave in and out of valleys and hills, woods and fields. There were fewer problems of access and trespass than in many parts of England as so much ancient common and trackway had always maintained rights of passage in the Chilterns.[3] As early as 1905 the Metropolitan had started their *Country Walks* booklets, giving suggested walks along with little sketch maps enticing participants into the 'most charming and intimate rural recesses of Middlesex, Herts and Bucks'. This led some (including the poet Rupert Brooke) to explore the Hills before 1914, but the great enthusiasm for rambling came after the First World War. The Metropolitan advertised with slogans such as 'Go for a Ramble', and offered 'Cheap tickets to Metro-land' at about the single fare for the double journey on Thursdays, Saturdays and Sundays. Other railways later followed suit. The GWR produced its *Rambles in the Chiltern Country*, mapping

138. Metropolitan steam. One of Charles Jones' H-class engines starting a pull up a Chiltern gradient in the 1920s, taking Metro-land commuters home for the weekend.

an area completely separate from the Metro's Chilterns, but reaching up to Princes Risborough and Watlington.[4] After London Transport absorbed the Metropolitan in 1933, the Metro-land theme was dropped but they continued to promote the Chilterns. A 1936 press campaign featured various animals telling people, 'Good spot, the Chilterns' (Plate 139), whilst a second campaign used woodcuts and dialogue with Chilterns locals. No wonder the day-trippers poured out of the railway stations with their picnics of fish-paste sandwiches and lemonade, along with the serious hikers, in walking boots and with the latest Ordnance Survey maps (Plate 151), who could get special tickets to arrive and return using different stations. Behind them trooped the 'Week-enders' and the campers and golfers, all swayed by the growing national conviction that the fresh air would do them good.

Attracting tourists was only one part of the Metro-land publicity campaign. Most of all it was the new wave of house-hunters that the Metropolitan Railway sought to woo. In the annual *Metro-land* booklets, after the colour plates and seductive rural prose came the 'House Seekers Section'. The company was unique among its rivals at the time in holding a controlling interest in a property company ('The Metropolitan Railway Country Estates Ltd.') which was set up to build on land it had purchased during the construction of the line and never sold.[5] They started building on the first two estates at Chalk Hill in Wembley and the Cedars Estate at Rickmansworth in the early 1920s. Further estates were to follow at Rayners Lane and then deep into the Chilterns at Amersham. Eventually nine estates were opened, mostly with ready-

— though I know the place is my home,' said the Donkey, *'and I love my own juicy hedgerow there.   But, frankly, is there anywhere a view more glorious, more stirring, than from the top of Bacombe Hill and Coombe Hill on a clear Spring day? Is there?'*

'Good spot, the Chilterns –

Bacombe Hill begins near Wendover Station, on the Metropolitan Line, and rises gradually until it reaches Coombe Hill, the headland which, at 852 feet, is the highest point in the Chilterns. Cheap return tickets to the Chiltern country are issued, daily, from all stations on the Metropolitan and East London Lines. On Sundays and Bank Holidays by all trains. Mondays to Fridays between 10 and 4. Saturdays by all trains after 10. The return fare to Wendover Stn. is 4/3 from Baker Street (Metropolitan) or Marylebone (L.N.E.R.) Stations. AWAY BY METROPOLITAN

LONDON TRANSPORT

139. London Transport advertisement, 1936. This was one of a series of advertisements for the Chilterns which featured 'talking animals'.

built houses to buy, or as plots of land where purchasers could build individual architect-designed properties. The general manager of the Metropolitan line was intent on populating these estates with daily commuters (first class, please!) who could travel from the countryside to the city and back again. Sir John Betjeman captured it perfectly:

And woodsmoke mingled
with the sulphur fumes
And people now could catch
The early train
To London and be home
Just after tea.[6]

From 1910 the wealthier commuter could travel on one of two Pullman cars (the Mayflower and the Galatea) which marshalled individually in the centre of some express trains (Plate 140). For a sixpenny supplement over and above the first-class fare, these Pullmans offered spacious comfort, with armchairs, carpets and a bar where the weary traveller could refresh himself with a 'gin and splash'.

The Suburban Dream
The Metro-land Estates were the tip of a larger iceberg. The first encouragement of rail commuting goes back much further—as early as the 1850s the London and North Western Company were offering a free first-class season ticket to those building houses of an annual rented value of £50 or more at places as far out as King's Langley, Boxmoor and Tring. From late Victorian times well-appointed villas were being built around all the new stations on the Chilterns lines, especially the new Marylebone line out to High Wycombe and the Metropolitan line to Chesham and Amersham. The same was occurring on the main line routes of the GWR and LNWR at towns like Berkhamsted. However, it was after 1918 that the real

140. The Pullman Car. This is one of the Pullman carriages which enabled first-class passengers to travel home on the Metropolitan Line in the lap of luxury.

urban explosion took place. The period between the wars saw the urban area of England increase by 26 per cent, with housing as the largest single component: over four million dwellings were constructed in two decades as the suburban dream became a reality. Of course, in these years Metropolitan Country Estates only built the tiniest fraction of the new houses in the region, even in Metro-land villages. But *Metro-land* encapsulated and articulated a widespread suburban aspiration, and reflected the mood of the times. The Metro-land experience was contagious and it was caught by a broader society than the bank managers and company directors who lived in elegant Voysey-designed houses on the spacious Cedars Estate, or in Amersham and Chesham Bois.

There was a new breed of middle-class Londoners who, in Alan Jackson's words, 'Aiming at a new house in the suburbs were seeking to renew contact with the rural environment which their ancestors had deserted in the hope of attaining higher living standards in the metropolis'.[8] It was for this group that semi-detached suburbia marched into the Chilterns at places close to the railway line like Amersham, Chesham, Beaconsfield and Gerrards Cross, forming the first dormitory towns in the region. Jackson suggests that the semi-detached house was a popular and affordable compromise between the urban terrace with its lack of privacy, and the detached homes that were too greedy of land to come within the price range of the white-collars and artisans. Semi-detached homes were built at a density of ten or twelve per acre, allowing fair-sized gardens and an illusion of privacy with private access to back doors. Although the layouts were roughly similar, a measure of individuality was maintained by varying the style of the exterior elevations and the internal finishing. Many harked back to

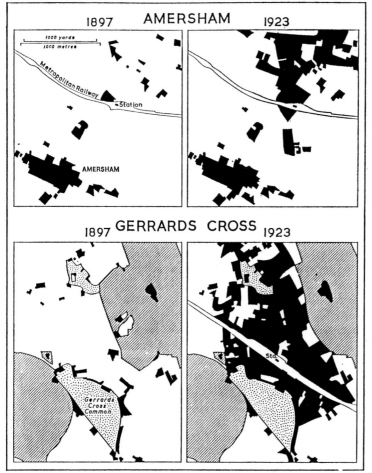

141. The growth of Amersham and Gerrards Cross. This map, from Coppick and Prince (1964), shows the growth of Metro-land commuter estates astride the railway.

'Tudor' styling with mock beams and leaded lights in the front door. The houses on some estates were matched by parades of shops, banks, public houses and even petrol stations, all with similar mock facades.

The influence of the railway on these early Metro-land estates in the Chilterns is unmistakable, because the railway line in many cases by-passed the old town, leaving the station on the outskirts. This created the opportunity for an entirely new dormitory town to spring up, near to the station and without interfering with the old town centre. Such was the case in Amersham with the new town situated on the hill, while the old broad High Street remained in the valley half a mile away. Prior to the opening of the station Amersham's population was falling, but it then grew rapidly as the suburban villa community of Amersham-on-the-Hill expanded. By 1931, when the Metropolitan acquired and developed the Weller estate there, the population had reached 29,000. Advertisements at the time showed, 'A few semi-detached and detached houses with built-in garages' available at £875 to £1,225 Freehold. A new straight row of mock-Tudor shops completed the scene, in sharp contrast to the old High Street with its broken skyline and pleasing cocktail of oddly-sized old buildings. In rather stark contrast to both mock-Tudor and genuine traditional styles, several concrete modernist houses, white with flat-roofs, were built on Amersham Hill (Plate 142).

142. Modernist architecture at Amersham-on-the-Hill. These were *avant garde* houses following Le Corbusier's ideas.

Beaconsfield, which had been something of a backwater between the end of the coaching era and the new railway station in 1906, was to grow in much the same way, with two distinct parts, although they now run into each other. The unmistakable dormitory complete with a heavily beamed Lloyds Bank sits astride the railway line (Plate 143). The building land was offered for auction by Verney and Sons, and the plans show the plots close to the railway at

143. Metro-land in Beaconsfield. These buildings typify the style of the period (*c*.1906-10), with mock-Tudor frontages on the road to the station. The bank is still there, now a Lloyds branch.

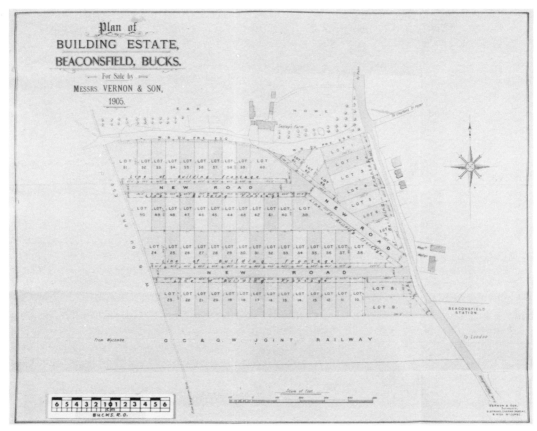

144. Plan of building plots offered for sale in Beaconsfield in 1905 by Vernon & Sons: 63 sites for 'villas and country cottage homes'. The location is immediately north of the railway line, and the 'new roads' are now Baring and Reynolds Roads. Lots 1-9 became shops, and a hotel built just north of the station has been pulled down to make way for the modern Waitrose supermarket.

low densities by today's standards (Plate 144). The development at Gerrards Cross, on the same line, went a stage further, transforming a tiny loose-knit hamlet scattered around the common into an entirely new dormitory that grew from a population of 552 to 2,942 in 30 years. The railway from Marylebone through High Wycombe opened in 1906, and along with it the rush for new houses. Farms and parkland were dug up to become the streets and gardens of over 400 houses, although the common remained intact. Neither Beaconsfield nor Gerrards Cross lies on the Metropolitan Line, but they display the quintessence of 'Metro-land' just as much as the Chalfonts or New Amersham. These leafy suburbs achieved much more of the Metro-land dream than did those closer to Baker Street. Pinner, Rayner's Lane and Harrow-on-the-Hill lost their rural context as development intensified, but here, further out in Chiltern country, more has survived and Metro-land seems less a case of advertising hyperbole.

Further west the town of High Wycombe was expanding, both from local jobs and commuting. Estates began to spring up on the hillsides north-east of the station. One of these was at Totteridge Farm, owned by a Charles Pettit. Together with Gilbert Lean, his architect and surveyor, he put together his own sales brochure in Metro-land fashion.[9] Called *High on the Chiltern Hills* and complete with photographs of local views, it asks:

The Question of Today

How can I find a real country home, in a healthy, elevated position, with unspoilt rural surroundings, and yet accessible by good main rail service to London?

The Answer

Take a contoured map of the country adjoining a main line, and, for choice, the newest (the G.W. and G.C. Railways joint line) as more likely to pass through unspoilt country. Ignoring suburbs and low-lying places, find a station within 30 miles where the ground rises to 500 feet above sea level within about a mile; and, if there is any choice, a station serving a large town. Select a spur on the station side of town, sloping southwards, and away from a main road. Go there, and you will discover the unique spot described in this booklet.

Another estate nearby was built on the fields of Bowerdean Farm. Here the transformation was captured by the local photographer Edward Sweetland, who photographed the rural scene in 1905 and again (with perfect repositioning) in 1938 when the houses were complete (Plate 146).

While it is not difficult to describe the growth associated with the inter-war period, it is perhaps more difficult to explain.[10] The changes that were taking place must be set against a background of a huge re-distribution of land holdings, with many of the big private estates being broken up and sold to farmers in much smaller units. The costs of running a big estate and especially the increases in duties and taxation meant that only very wealthy landowners could maintain the status quo. Added to this was the agricultural depression, with falling prices and contraction of the arable acreage especially in marginal areas. The last vestiges of rural craft were extinguished over this period leaving rural areas with a disintegrating economy. The opportunity to sell some of their land for development must have been a godsend to these new farming owner-occupiers who were struggling to make ends meet. And they were satisfying

145. Air photograph of Gerrards Cross. This tiny hamlet, built around the common, grew to become a sizeable town on either side of the railway. The common now remains as an island in the midst of a suburban sea.

146. Bowerdean Farm in High Wycombe, before and after development. This pair of photographs was taken by the local High Wycombe photographer, Edward Sweetland. Bowerdean Farm was on the hillside to the east of the railway station and old centre of High Wycombe.

a need; for although the population as a whole was not increasing, the south saw the migration tide of the previous century turn and people were moving away from the industrial heartlands of the north and the midlands and heading towards the Home counties. There was a new outlook among those seeking homes which sought to get away from the lack of space and privacy of urban housing, and the literature of the period created the image of the new estate as the place to live.

The improved life-style was not restricted to those who could purchase. There was an enormous increase in council rented accommodation and this was not confined to areas near to railway lines. It is hard to find a village or a town anywhere that does not have its rows of inter-war council houses fringing the older centres. The *Metro-land* issue for 1932 specifically mentions local councils who had built a number of estates in Chorley Wood and Chenies; in Chesham the 'Local Council have erected 150 houses and cottages, 50 more in course of construction, 200 more contemplated. Extensive private building is taking place on Lowndes Avenue, Shepherd's Farm, Charteridge lane and Chiltern Hills Estates'. The story was repeated over and again in almost every town and village in the region, with councils keen to replace former dilapidated farm dwellings (read 'picturesque cottage') and to house newcomers.

Preservation of the countryside
By the mid-1920s the threat to the countryside from unplanned mushroom growth was becoming increasingly apparent. It was not just the eruption of huge estates on the edges of existing towns, or the ribbon development creeping along the roads, but the fact that even the remotest spots were all succumbing to 'pepperpot development', where building was seen to be shaken at random and dabbed occasionally over the land. This growth could now be seen in a new perspective through the increased use of air photography and it was not going to be allowed to proceed totally unimpeded, or without protest. A growing body of people was moved to shout very loudly at what they saw as the wanton destruction of the countryside. It was apparent that the pace of housing development was way beyond the capacity of any statutory planning body to control or channel. Like a rash, building was breaking out all over the place, and no-one could forecast where it might appear next. The government produced a first effort at regulation in the Town and Country Bill in 1932, but it was not until after 1945 that planning gained really effective control.

It fell to the lot of voluntary bodies and individuals to protest about and protect the rural landscape. The National Trust had already demonstrated that Britain's heritage was not only its buildings, and G. M. Trevelyan had written forcefully on their behalf in a small book entitled *Must England's Beauty Perish?*[11] To Trevelyan, natural beauty was the highest common denominator of the spiritual life of contemporary Britain, and as a former Chilterns' resident he was particularly concerned about this region. So much so that he bought part of the Ashridge estate to prevent it falling under the auctioneer's hammer, and donated it to the Trust. Other preservation groups were set up during this period. The most influential among them was the CPRE (Council for the Preservation of Rural England), founded in 1926 under the enlightened eye of architect and planner Patrick Abercrombie. Beneath its umbrella, organisations and individuals concerned with rural preservation formed a crusade to reduce the scale of the 'personal and corporate thoughtlessness and selfishness of which the despoilation of the countryside was a symptom'. They attacked on a broad front and not necessarily with consensus: houses (especially bungalows), roads, petrol stations, electricity pylons and wirescapes, billboards and factories all came under fire.[12]

One of the most outspoken critics of the time was Clough Williams-Ellis who as a self-proclaimed angry young man published an impassioned plea against 'urban beastliness' in

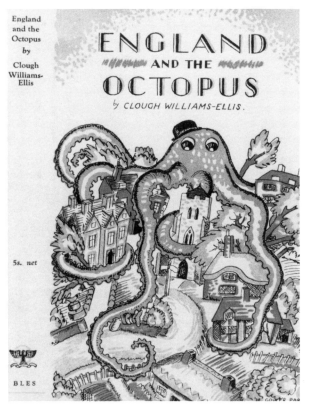

England
and the
Octopus
by
Clough
Williams-
Ellis

ENGLAND *~~~* AND THE *~~~*
OCTOPUS
by CLOUGH WILLIAMS-ELLIS.

5s. net

BLES

147. Dust cover for *England and the Octopus*, by Clough
William-Ellis. This was the most outspoken of the many
protests about the 'Octopus' of urban sprawl spoiling the
English countryside.

1928 in his book *England and the Octopus* (Plate 147). This was followed in 1937 by a series of 26 essays which he edited in *Britain and the Beast*.[13] The CPRE represented a very middle- and upper-class viewpoint, lamenting so many of the changes that were overrunning the countryside now that the big country landlords were no longer its guardian. They sent a travelling exhibition called 'Save the Countryside' with Saint George for Rural England battling against a dragon whose scaled wings represented cigarettes, petrol, tyres and other billboard advertising slogans which so incensed the preservationists (Plate 148).[14] The Council were not all against building *per se*: the *Face of the Land* book, which reproduced many of the photographs from the exhibition, celebrated many new, urban 20th-century constructions such as bridges, roads and factories as improvements on their Victorian predecessors, and aesthetically pleasing.[15] But, as David Matless has argued, their vision of the countryside extolled the 18th century with its ordered estates and landscaped parks (but of course ignored the oppression). They saw some modernism in architecture and landscaping as following this tradition, and approved. What they could not stand was the chaos of popular individualism (whereas writers like J. B. Priestley applauded it), nor the 'sham history' of mock-Tudor.[16] H. J. Massingham, who did not like much new, caught this last viewpoint with his opinion of Latimer,

> is now an Ideal Homes Exhibition of bogus and beading. There is one pigmy house of half-timber and brick with gables, dormers, porch, casement windows and gently rolling russet roof which represents this voluptuous corner with a felicity just short of Birket Fosterish sweetness.[17]

It was the wholesale 'invasion' of the countryside with building at random that was to cause the verbal baring of teeth and gnashing of jaws so evident in the publications of the CPRE and Clough Williams-Ellis. The desire was to keep the urban and rural areas separate but the reality was that the towns, their buildings and their occupants were creeping outwards at an alarming rate. The Metro-land dormitory settlements that we have described were one major element in this, but at least their estates were generally 'contained' and restricted to the areas adjacent to the line and the stations. Just as significant, and even more dramatic in its impact, was the 'sudden triumph, in the interwar period, of the internal combustion engine over all its rivals'. Harold Perkin in *The Age of the Automobile* described it thus: 'In the automobile age, the flexibility of the bus, the car and the goods vehicle enabled the city and the suburbs to burst like a poppy head, scattering its seeds into every available space ...'.[18]

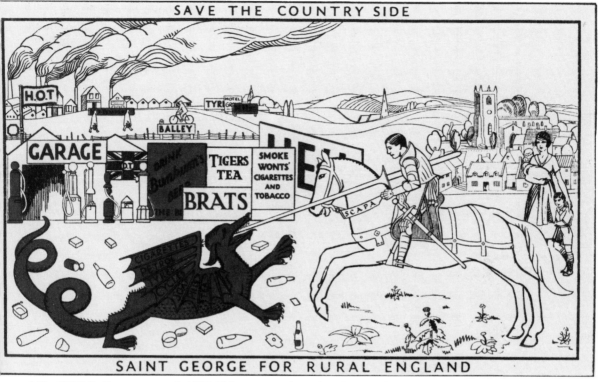

148. CPRE St George postcard, 1928. This was one of a series of postcards and posters provided by the CPRE as part of their 'Save the Countryside Campaign'.

The age of the car and bus

Prior to the 1920s motoring was a luxury enjoyed by a privileged few. In an article in June 1920 the Motor Owner visited Shirburn Castle.[19] These post-war years also saw the Chilterns used for the sport of hill-climb racing, with cars being tested on the steep inclines (Plate 149). Aston Hill above Halton was a popular venue, and Lionel Martin renamed his marque Aston Martin after his successes there. The post-war period saw the average price of the motor car drop substantially with mass production techniques, enabling a Ford 8 or Austin 7 to be purchased in the 1920s for just over £100. This meant that car ownership was within the range of a whole new group of middle-class families who delighted in their new-found freedom to travel. There was a twentyfold increase in car ownership, along with an extra half-million motorcycles, raising the total number of motor vehicles from 120,000 in 1919 to over two million in 1929. During the same period, the roads underwent radical improvements assisted by the post-war surplus of cheap labour. Trunk routes were widened and straightened, by-passes constructed and many country lanes were newly tarmacadammed, encouraging the motorist to venture deep into the countryside.

The private car was still not available to the majority of the working-class population, but this did not mean that they were kept off the roads. For them the countryside became accessible via the charabanc and the motor bus. The first motor bus service from Wycombe to Beaconsfield ran in 1908 (Plate 150), and the 1920s saw a huge expansion in the number of ordinary stage bus operators. These were mostly independents with five or fewer buses who

149. The Aston Hill Climb. One of Lionel Martin's cars raising the chalk dust at Aston Clinton, with the Coombe Hill monument visible on the horizon.

competed with larger municipal companies, Green Line and country express services and excursion coaches. In 1920-21 regular services connected places like Wycombe to central London. During this time it was the philosophy to have a network which placed almost every estate, village or suburb on a bus route. It was how families got to work, children to school and people went to the shops or the local cinema. Along with the motor car, buses were to extend the boundaries of rural settlements. In the 1930s London Transport did not just advertise rail access to the Chilterns: its poster art also promoted Green Line bus outings to places like the new Whipsnade Zoo (Plate 153).

Many preservationists saw these new people as an affront to the countryside they loved. The urbanites themselves who poured from the cars and charabancs were sometimes the targets for rather vicious class hatred. C. E. M. Joad, writing in *Britain and the Beast*, was appalled at the 'hordes of hikers cackling insanely in the woods', 'tents in meadows and girls in pyjamas dancing beside them to the strains of the gramophone', and 'fat girls in shorts, youths in gaudy ties and plus-fours'.[20] He also loathed the cars that 'decant their contents of whining children, nagging mothers and bored fathers'. Much more distress was created by the flotsam and jetsam that the motorised transport trailed in its wake: the road signs, the wayside cafés, and the scruffy petrol stations.

The problems are summed up by two new additions to the vocabulary of the day: ribbon development and bungaloid growth. *The Times* on 6 April 1925 wrote about ribbon development: 'Soon this green and pleasant land will only be glimpsed from our country roads through an almost continuous hedge of bungalows and houses'. Howard Marshall, also in *Britain and the Beast*, reinforced the view: 'and still the destruction spreads like a prairie fire. The gerry built bijou residences creep out along the roads. Beauty is sacrificed on the altar of the speeding motorist. The electric grid strides across the hillsides. A gimcrack civilisation crawls like a gigantic slug across the country, leaving a foul trail of slime behind it'. In the Chilterns the slug was ubiquitous. Rows of new houses were 'littering' the crest of Bledlow Ridge; High

Wycombe seen from the top of the hill was described by H. J. Massingham as a 'vast dustbin of houses'.[21]

Bungalows were singled out for a special degree of hatred. They came in many forms but the most disliked were those at the bottom of the housing ladder which could be erected quickly from pre-fabricated sections.[22] The worst travesty in the eyes of the critics was the new asbestos roofing tile coloured, according to Sheila Kaye Smith, 'a pink that can be seen nowhere else save in boiled crustaceans'. Bungalows were ideal for permanent housing and in their cheapest forms (like the 'cottabunga' or even converted railway carriages) were built as holiday homes and week-end retreats (Plate 154). They were inexpensive enough for thousands who had previously never owned a house, especially as cheap sites became available. Wooded hills on marginal land, the sort that was plentiful in the Chilterns, were particularly attractive and a truck carrying pre-fabricated sections could reach them easily.

S. P. B. Mais mourned the blight of plotlands and bungalows that sprang up on the Chiltern escarpment:

> The trouble begins, as it always does nowadays, where beauty can least bear disturbance. The whole side of the Chiltern escarpment that leads down to Aston Rowant is now honeycombed with hideous shacks thrown haphazard like splodges of mud against a hillside once covered with trees. The hut dwellers both get the view and spoil it.[23]

These hillside bungalows could be reached either from the little railway station down at Aston Rowant, or by the motor-coach service from Victoria coach station in London to Oxford via Stokenchurch, the way Mais himself arrived (Plate 155).

Most of these bungalows and plotlands arose from individual purchases of land or from farmers selling off plots. Tony Harman, in his farming autobiography, *Seventy Summers*, points

150. The motor bus near West Wycombe. This was the first scheduled motor bus from High Wycombe to Beaconsfield, in 1908, and advertises the photographer!

ORDNANCE SURVEY "ONE-INCH" MAP OF THE CHILTERNS

Price Three Shillings Net
Published by the Ordnance Survey Office,
SOUTHAMPTON

151. O.S. map cover for the Chilterns, 1932. Ellis Martin's evocative map cover design for the 1932 edition.

152. Metro-land booklet, 1921. This front cover was
designed to entice city dwellers with idyllic rural scenes.

153. Green Line to Whipsnade Zoo. London Transport in the
1930s had a poster campaign to advertise coach outings to the
Chilterns, and the new Whipsnade Zoo.

The **"COTTABUNGA"**
(Regd.)

THIS CHARMING BUNGALOW COTTAGE delivered, carriage paid, to any goods station in England or Wales, ready to erect, for · · · **£245 : 10** **nett.**
"COTTABUNGA" buildings may be seen dotted all over the Countryside, North—South—East—West, and are giving universal satisfaction. No better value at the price is possible, and if you would enjoy the comforts and luxury of this artistic residence this coming summer place your order NOW.

Our illustrated Catalogue, No. 103, containing full particulars and a full range of other Bungalows, Pavilions, Motor Houses, Chalets, etc., post free to any address.

BROWNE & LILLY, LTD.
THAMES SIDE, READING
Telegrams: Portable, Reading.   *'Phone: Reading 587*

154. Cottabunga. This was an advertisement for the kind of pre-fabricated bungalow that was sprouting up in many places throughout the Chilterns.

to the roadside near Orchard Leigh north of Chesham.[24] On the south side there are bungalows and houses with large plots, on land sold by Mr. Ford when grain prices fell after 1921. The north side, then farmed by the Mashes, remained as farmland because they grew fruit and vegetables and had a contract at Covent Garden. Above Marlow there were groups of plotlands in the two dry valleys of Marlow Bottom and Munday Dean. These were handled by London firms, and sold to ex-servicemen in 1920 as small-holdings, retirement and second homes. Some owners were commuters, and the writer George Woodcock spent part of his childhood there, recalling 'From early in the 1930s a group of men and women would cycle down out of the Bottom—an even larger group out of the Dean, to catch the 7.25 or the 7.58 up to Paddington, leaving their bikes at the station'.[25]

The ribbon development along the roadsides took advantage of the services that were already installed—electricity, water, service roads and so on. It took a great deal of persuasion before the 'Restriction of Ribbon Development Act' in 1935 stopped curbside buildings stringing out of every town and village. It insisted that a 220-ft. verge should be left, unless permission to do otherwise was granted. In spite of the influential preservationists' lobby, there was still a resistance to introduce the kind of legislation that could seriously control the plotlands, since it would interfere with traditional rights of property. Instead, the war intervened and had the effect of freezing the boundaries. By the end of it real advances in planning legislation were on the drawing board, and the clock had been stopped. Unfortunately it was too late to turn it back and the long lament about the loss of both the rural landscape and its previous guardians continued. Clough Williams-Ellis summed up the views of his contemporaries: 'We were fools in a fool's paradise. That comfortable society has been shattered—exploded by petrol in a million obedient engines'.[26]

The speed of change in the inter-war period caught much of society napping, not least the regulatory bodies. The Second World War was to impose a very long period of wakefulness and time to reflect and survey the damage. The inter-war arguments had also revealed real conflicts between town and country, conflicts about values, public access and different aspirations. Whatever their good intentions, the preservationists often came over as snobbish and class-ridden. Tudor semis and asbestos bungalows gave a much improved life-style to their owners. Many bungalows gave youngsters summers in the country; they gave a refuge from London under bombing in 1940, and some became permanent homes. Today they have either rotted away, or been converted and upgraded to more desirable residences. Trees have matured

155. Bungalows and petrol station at Aston Rowant. This is the spot that so upset S. P. B. Mais. This photograph was taken in the early 1960s, but the garage and buildings have now gone.

and softened the scene. Three generations have grown up in Metro-land and beyond, enjoying the Chilterns landscape, and the sum of human happiness is undoubtedly greater for it.

Yet the Chilterns were badly hit and wounded, scarred by their share of ill-planned housing, ruined views, lost lanes and urban sprawl. For those who remembered the Hills before 1914, it must have been hard to take. Clough Williams-Ellis had been inspired to explore the Chilterns by reading R. L. Stevenson's essay on a Chiltern walk, and he later recalled Stevenson's description of Wendover:

> Wendover lay well down in the midst, with mountains of foliage about it. The great plain stretched away to northward, variegated near at hand with the quaint pattern of the fields, but growing ever more and more indistinct until it became a mere hurly-burly of trees and bright crescents of river, and snatches of slanting road, and finally melted away into the ambiguous cloud-land over the horizon.[27]

In 1933 he reflected despairingly: 'What, between them, have the Air Force and the civilian commuters left of Stevenson's picture?'[28]

Our answer, standing above Wendover today, must be, 'More than you allowed for, Mr. Williams-Ellis'. Time mellows disruption to the landscape, and even Joad (less of a fool than he sometimes appeared) admitted that people would learn to like the roads as he liked the railways. The Chilterns were spared wholesale devastation as much development could be absorbed and 'hidden' by the dissected wooded landscape, and some areas were still too remote at that time. Thousands of acres were spared because they remained in the hands of large private estates and were managed in the time-honoured fashion. Much of the region south of the A40 was spared, most notably the lovely Wormsley valley, owned by the Fane family.

156. The ruin of Bix church. The old medieval church at Bix Bottom, well outside the village, was subsequently replaced by a new church in Bix itself and the fitments removed. The ruined church is tucked in a beautiful secret valley.

157. The Stonor valley. The upper Stonor valley, remaining wholly unspoilt, is an example of the remoter parts of the Chilterns that were always in the hands of large estates.

158. Meadow flowers in the Chilterns. The variety of species in the BBONT reserve at Aston Clinton includes the Bee Orchid, the Fragrant Orchid, and the Pyramidal Orchid, as well as many other chalkland flowers.

159. Bungalow near Hughenden. This 1930s 'snap' was captioned 'Uncle Rheuben's bungalow', and was typical of the period.

With the benefit of hindsight the overall balance-sheet can be be drawn in the black. However, the period highlighted and left unresolved all the problems of countryside planning, housing growth and transport that the Chilterns have had to wrestle with since then.

Chapter Thirteen

The Changing Countryside

Farming Change

Chiltern farming in the last 70 years has seen both depression and boom, with conflicting impacts on the landscape. The agricultural depression which began in late Victorian times persisted until 1939 and the Second World War. There was a minor reversal towards the end of the 1914-18 War, when British food imports were threatened by German submarines. The government encouraged arable by the 1917 Corn Production Act, but the conversion only took effect in 1918, and the repeal of the Act in 1921 led to a collapse in grain prices. The tumbling down to grass therefore continued: in Great Missenden parish the lowest point was reached in 1937 with only 40 per cent of the farming acreage under arable, and tillages below 30 per cent.[1] These years saw a down-at-heel, unkempt Chiltern landscape, with weed-ridden fields and overgrown hedges.

This was all changed by the outbreak of war in 1939. There was none of the dilatory reaction seen in 1914-18. Very quickly a great plough-up campaign, backed up by orders and requisitions, turned large areas back to arable. Land-girls and prisoners-of-war helped till the land. In Missenden the arable expanded back to 65 per cent by 1943. Most of the new arable had been fields laid down to grass since 1875. Some, however, was on old downland or commons, land either never ploughed or not for a very long time. On the plateau top at Russell's Water, for instance, 139 acres of the Common were requisitioned and cultivated, and the same happened to 240 acres of Berkhamsted Common.[2] At Grangelands, above Great Kimble, scarp grazing land was taken under the plough. Some of the more marginal attempts only lasted a few years, but unlike the previous post-war experience there was no wholesale reversal back to pasture after 1945.

Instead of withdrawing arable support, the 1947 Agricultural Act instituted a system of guaranteed prices for the farmer. This was the basis for farming expansion and prosperity in Britain until it was replaced by the CAP or Common Agricultural Policy, with membership of the European Community in 1973. Both policies kept farmers' incomes high, and created incentives to greater and more efficient production. These last 40 years have seen the great mechanisation of farming. In 1939 tractors were not commonplace; after 1945 combine harvesters and other equipment became widespread. New hybrid varieties, chemical fertilisers and pesticides led to massive increases in yields. The intensity of the new 'agri-business' depended less on farm labour than on capital. These high years of farming, and especially the CAP system, led to grain surpluses, 'milk lakes' and 'beef mountains', and the last decade has seen a questioning of the costs and rationality of this type of farming. Now farmers are being encouraged to reduce the output they strove to increase, to 'set aside' land for non-production. These changes raise issues of the whole role of farming in the Chiltern countryside, and we shall look at them in our final chapter. Here we shall trace out three strands in the way these farming and rural changes have affected the Chiltern landscape and ecology, before turning to these present-day issues of conservation and planning.

160. Open downland on Ivinghoe Beacon. Sheep grazing on this famous landmark has kept bushes and scrub at bay, and gives us the downland turf which elsewhere has been disappearing.

161. Old flowering cherry tree. A magnificent and very old coppiced wild cherry marking part of an ancient hedgerow in Pednor valley.

162. Harvest time, between Little Missenden and Holmer Green. Modern farming with its weed-free fields and mechanised baling, but still with a Chilterns profile of hedged field and beech hanger.

163. Sheep in Aston Clinton ragpits. BBONT sheep flock on this reserve during midwinter.

Chalk Downlands and Neglected Commons

The long rural and arable decline from 1875 to 1940 destroyed the farming role of many Chiltern scarp-pastures and commons. The practice of grazing on the downland and folding on the Vale arable declined, and the landscape began to change in various ways. Where the grazing was simply reduced or ceased, then scrub began to colonise, followed by trees and woodland. Where the land was ploughed up, either for arable or to sow improved grasses for permanent grazing at a higher stocking-rate, the old chalk grassland was equally transformed.[3]

Either way, an ancient and fragile ecosystem was being lost. Traditional chalk downlands have an amazingly rich and colourful flora, which in turn attract and host a wide variety of insects and butterflies. The chalk soils are poor in nutrients, and the sheep nibble down and hold back the stronger, more competitive grasses, allowing the flowers to flourish. Take away the sheep, or 'improve' the grass with artificial fertiliser, and this fragile system is gone, and is extremely difficult to re-create. Amongst the chalk downland species are the many wild orchids, which flower in May to July. Some rarities like the military and monkey orchids are only found on a few sites, but fragrant, pyramidal and bee orchids are more widespread. Other delights are the gentians, the little vetches (such as the horseshoe vetch on which the caterpillar of the chalkhill blue butterfly feeds), and the rare but beautiful purple of the pasque-flower.[4] Of this Oliver Rackham comments: 'It is quite robust; it survives picnicking and lack of grazing; but it is instantly destroyed by ploughing and never returns'.[5] Across all the English chalklands, this traditional downland has been ravaged, and the Chilterns are no exception. The more northerly Chilterns have probably suffered most from ploughing and improvement, and here the only remaining old downland is left clinging to the steeper and less accessible sections of the scarp-edge. A number of fine sites survive at Knocking Hoe, Totternhoe Knolls and the Barton Hills in Bedfordshire, and at Pitstone and Ivinghoe Beacon. Even on Pitstone Hill, however, the economics of grazing have led to improvement of the grass on the summit. The rarer species, and the old anthills so indicative of traditional grassland, are now restricted to the steeper slopes.

South of the Tring Gap, downland has faced the same problems, but neglect, rather than 'improvement', has been more frequent. The scarp is higher and steeper, so improvement is less attractive. More land here has therefore been left to revert to scrub, and adjacency to the woods of the plateau has aided this colonisation. One needs the evidence of old photographs and postcards to recapture just how open and bald the Chiltern tops were at the turn of the century. All along—at Coombe Hill, Whiteleaf Cross, Bledlow and Beacon Hill, Lewknor— the wood and scrubs have crept forward on the summit and invaded the scarp sides. It has been a long process, and still continues. The rabbit population helped to keep it at bay, but myxomatosis after 1954 removed this check (at least until recently).

A. S. Watt studied this colonisation in the early 1930s, and identified two types of succession (though later ecologists would complicate this).[6] On the drier, shallower, steeper slopes, juniper scrub colonised. These bushes then gave shelter to the beech seedlings, which later grew into beech woodland. Where there was more shelter and slightly deeper soils, hawthorn bushes were the coloniser, followed by ash seedlings, ash wood and finally beech. Juniper bushes used to be a common sight on chalk downland, but farmers have burnt and ploughed them over much of the English chalk.[7] On these steep escarpment slopes they have often flourished, with excellent colonies at Beacon Hill. Unfortunately protecting the wood seedlings leads to their own demise, for they cannot survive in the shade. Dead juniper is, however, slow to decay and dessicated bushes can be found within these woods they fostered, as at Windsor Hill above Risborough.

164. The changes on Coombe Hill, Wendover, *c.*1913. The old postcard shows how open Coombe Hill was when it was still grazed downland. Since 1913 the scarp has changed dramatically, with scrub and trees enveloping the slopes. The second photograph, taken from Butlers Cross, shows the changes which have occurred all round the hill.

165. The Wormsley Valley. This valley, unpenetrated by public roads, remained in the Fane family until the 1980s, when they sold it to J. P. Getty II, who has not only renovated and extended the house, but also ensured the preservation of this secluded Chiltern valley. (See Hart-Davis, 1991.)

The Chiltern heaths and commons have faced similar colonisation by scrub and wood. Grazing and woodfuel-cutting declined, often earlier than on the chalk downlands. These open spaces were on the acidic soils of the clay-with-flints or patches of Reading Beds, with a different flora to the chalk. Here reduction of grazing soon lead to ling, heather or bracken colonising and growing. These are succeeded by scrub, oak and beech woods. These woods, like Naphill, are widely regarded as some of the most valuable ecologically, with their diverse structure and good ground flora. Yet the heaths are disappearing under this growth, and they have attracted less attention than their downland compatriots. The exception is the renowned

166. Hardings Wood. This Chiltern meadow and the ancient woodland (which belongs to local conservationist Richard Mabey) have just escaped the line of the new A41 bypass.

167. Stonor House, home to the Stonor family for 800 years. The house has a Tudor T-shape, but the windows were remodelled in the 18th century. The chapel and parts of the house are medieval.

Burnham Beeches, maintained by the City of London. Some of the commons in more built-up areas are kept reasonably open by mowing (as at Gerrards Cross), but many are vanishing, like Ipsden Heath, Chesham Bois Common and the fascinating extent of Turville Heath and Summer Heath, where old Samuel Rockall used to wood-bodge.

Farming Landscapes

The rundown Chiltern farms of the 1930s have long gone, and with them have gone long-standing features of the Chiltern landscape. The agri-business has demanded a new efficiency in the scale and management of farming. Farms have been amalgamated, with redundant buildings sold off for homes. Old barns, no longer needed for grain storage, have also been converted into houses and workshops. But the most visible changes have been in the fields themselves—their boundaries and their very colour.

Mechanisation of farming, especially the combine harvesters, made very small fields a real nuisance. The result was hedgerow destruction, most obvious on the more open, loamy North Chilterns where arable farming was most profitable. It also occurred in the extreme south-west on the 'Ipsden Prairies', as Lionel Brett called them.[8] Here late enclosure generated

168. Harvesting at Whiteleaf, Princes Risborough, in 1910. This traditional rural scene also shows the openness of the scarp around Whiteleaf Cross at that time.

large fields and fewer hedges in the first place. Tony Harman of Chesham recalls how he was one of the first to begin this in the War, arranging a demonstration of hedge removal for the Ministry of Agriculture in 1944.[9] The big field he created by bulldozing six little fields (and they were small) into one can be seen on the left as you drive from Ashley Green to Chesham via Lye Green. Most of the Chiltern hedgerows were not recent creations, but part of the ancient countryside, some relics of the woodland itself, and their antiquity cannot be remade. Many other hedgerows have died by neglect rather than deliberate murder. Without the farm labour to maintain them, they have become overgrown, hacked back rather than relaid, and inadvertently poisoned. Yet it is in only a few parts of the Hills that all this has gone the way of East Anglia. Although many miles of boundaries have gone, the majority remain and the Chiltern topography of slope and bottom places limits on what can be done.

Intensive farming has also altered the colour of the Chiltern landscape. There are new pressures for farmers to grow different crops in response to changes in consumer tastes and European Community policy. Currently there are subsidies to encourage the growing of a variety of oilseeds, and these are reflected in new colours. The brilliant-yellow oilseed rape has been visibly on the increase throughout the nation. More recently, since 1987, there has been an incentive scheme to grow flax, both for linseed and for fibre. More and more Chiltern fields can be seen shrouded in the pale-blue haze of this flax in full bloom. Fertilisers make the sown grassland a vivid green, contrasting with the more subdued hues of old chalk downland. Fields sown with a crop are simply that crop: a wheat-field is just wheat (or almost), a hay-crop is just sown grass. The plethora of other species that got in with the sown-seed or sowed themselves naturally are largely a thing of the past, eliminated by seed-selection and selective weed-killers. The former diversity of corn-flowers, poppies and other species was much reduced, as were the old unploughed banks around the field edges which sustained a mass of flowers. Like the hedgerow, such species hosted a varied insect and butterfly population. None of these things completely vanished, but it is difficult for children of the 1980s to know just how different the fields were in the early 1950s before the great industrialisation of farming took effect. Capital-intensive farming produces very simple, but highly efficient, ecosystems, and maintains them artificially. Traditional farming was part of a more diverse ecosystem, and the price of high yields has been the loss of that scenic and ecological diversity in the landscape.

The Chiltern Woodlands
The beechwoods of the Hills have had their own set of problems this century. The previous century had seen their conversion to high forest, and the decline of the bodger and therefore of the Chiltern Selection System meant that woods were over-maturing. Their composition was too even-aged, with a closed canopy preventing seedling regeneration and creating a rather bleak ground-cover. Only the best timber was being taken, and much second-rate wood was left rather than being cut early. Heavy demands in both World Wars for rifle butts and plywood for aircraft took their toll, witnessed first by the felling of the Rothschild beechwoods above Halton. The unhealthy state of many beechwoods was recognised in the 1920s, and brought out clearly in the early aerial surveys of Ray Bourne.[10]

In a purely biological sense, a tract of senile wood is not a problem. When the trees rot or are brought down by storms like those in 1987 and 1990, the natural process of succession would lead through bush and scrub to new trees and broad-leafed wood. It would be a very long-term process, and, with the sheer number of Chiltern mature beechwoods, would be unacceptable in either scenic or economic terms. Some form of management, such as produced the beechwoods, is necessary.

During much of this century woodland policy has meant conifer plantations. First introduced as nursery crops, to protect the early stages of beech in late 19th-century plantations, the conifer dominated forestry for a long time. It was faster-growing and more profitable. After clear-felling the old woodland, regular rows of conifers were planted and, although thinning took place, the objective was an even-aged stand that would in its turn be clear-felled and replaced. Above Halton the beechwoods (first felled by the army) were replaced by the Forestry Commission's fir trees, which were also planted on former downland. The dilemma was that most Chiltern woods remained unmanaged, but those that were involved a change in the character of the landscape, to one more alien and less scenically attractive. After the Forestry Commission acquired Queen Wood, a mature beechwood at Christmas Common near Watlington, in 1947, they began a 'Chiltern Project' in 1951. Large acreages were clear-felled, but the long-term goal was to grow new beechwood. This was achieved by planting conifers to protect and nurse new seedlings, gradually thinning the conifers. The policy still involved years of conifer-dominated scenery, but the Project signalled the first beginnings of a new philosophy.[11] However, for the most part conifers continued to dominate forestry until the 1980s.

One problem has been confused public and forestry objectives, and changing views on the nature of woodland. The history of ancient woodland has only quite recently become widely-known and appreciated, thanks largely to Oliver Rackham and George Peterken. The new emphasis is on natural regeneration and diversity of age rather than planting. 1972 has been identified as the low-point for ancient woodland, and we can see this change in discussion of Chiltern policy. The Chilterns Standing Conference's 1971 *A Plan for the Chilterns* suggested an enlightened programme of felling in small blocks but allowing full replacement over 30 years, together with targets for beech or other broad-leaved trees per acre.[12] With widespread woodland owners' support, it aimed for healthy and scenically-attractive beech woods. Yet it contained no discussion at all of ancient woodland, reflecting the climate of the times.

Conservation in the Chilterns

Just as the spread of inter-war suburbia provoked movements to preserve the countryside from urban sprawl, so the changes in farming and forestry stimulated groups to press for environmental and nature conservation within the countryside. Whilst the larger-scale environmental movement is quite recent, some of these moves go back to the beginning of the century.

The value and importance of sites within the Chilterns was recognised early.[13] The scarp-edge sites where downland and beechwood met were the first. The Society for the Promotion of Nature Reserves (SPNR) was formed in 1912, led by the Hon. N. C. Rothschild, brother of Lord Rothschild. Chiltern sites like Beacon Hill (now referred to as Aston Rowant) and Pulpit Hill, Kimble, were included on lists of potential national reserves from 1915. The National Trust was actively acquiring sites at Coombe Hill (1918), Ivinghoe Beacon, Berkhamsted Common and Frithsden Beeches (1926-28). The researches of ecologists and their role in encouraging the setting up of nature reserves also promoted Chiltern sites. A. S. Watt's studies gave the Chiltern beechwoods and scarp a scientific prominence, and Sir Arthur Tansley discussed them at length in his major work *The British Islands and their Vegetation* (1939).[14] Another leading ecologist, E. J. (later Sir Edward) Salisbury came from Hertfordshire, where his work on scrub was amongst the first to show how it arose from arable and heath colonisation, rather than from woodland retrogression.[15] All three were involved in various nature reserve committees, and Tansley and Watt wrote a memorandum on the Chiltern sites for the Huxley Committee in June 1946.[16] They identified five climax vegetation types and four patterns of scrub succession, suggesting that eight of the types could be safeguarded by designating three national nature reserves in the Hills: Beacon Hill, Pulpit Hill and Lodge Wood.

The Nature Conservancy, with Tansley as its first Chairman, was set up in 1949 to give scientific and conservation advice. It started the process of designating national nature reserves (NNR) and then sites of special scientific interest (SSSI). Although there had been suggestions that the Chilterns should be a National Park this category was really reserved for wilder, more remote areas. However, there was recognition that the whole scarp section, and not just individual sites, was worthy of conservation. In the whole series of advisory reports in the 1940s, the Chilterns were shaded in as a potential 'conservation area'. It was not, however, until 1964 that 309 square miles (497 square kilometres) of the Hills were made an Area of Outstanding Natural Beauty by the National Parks Commission (now the Countryside Commission).

These conservation issues became more complicated, raising questions about 'nature' and the aims of conservation. Preserving a few special sites to keep rare species in existence was clear enough, but species live in habitats, ecosystems that are not at all 'natural' in the Chilterns, but man-made and historically specific. Conservation meant management, replicating the traditional grazing of the downland. At the Aston Rowant reserve, experiments have tried a whole range of grazing intensities and types, to hold successions at different points. Similarly, the Berkshire, Buckinghamshire and Oxfordshire Naturalists' Trust (BBONT), which owns or manages a large number of reserves, has its own flock of sheep that are moved around the different sites (Plate 163). The Chilterns now have a large number of SSSIs and several NNRs, but it was recognised early that the sum was more than the individual sites—a whole landscape was worth conserving. This was particularly true of the Chilterns because the topography broke up the 'best' sites into separate niches or islands. None of these were ecologically unique, but put together they formed a rich and diverse ecology, exactly what one would expect for the Chilterns.[17] These considerations widened the debate to consider scenic beauty and the amenity value of the sites. The Chiltern countryside had to be set against urban and economic needs, bringing together town and country. These wider issues are the theme of our final chapter.

Chapter Fourteen

The Chilterns Today

The Chiltern landscape today is buffeted between the claims of town and country, the needs of commuter, rambler, farmer and naturalist. Within the highly-populated south-east and so close to London, the Chilterns are in an especially exposed position. Yet there is today a heightened and growing sense of the Chilterns as 'place' and a distinctive landscape to be conserved and enhanced. This final chapter examines some of the issues and dilemmas facing the region, and the role of a historical understanding of the region and its landscape history.

Urban Growth

To discuss the present dilemmas facing the Chilterns we need to step backwards in time and examine how the planners picked up the pieces from the inter-war chaos of London's sprawl. Although some moves had been made before 1939, the really significant steps came with the need to reconstruct London after the war. The two most important were the 1944 *Greater London Plan* and the 1947 Town and Country Planning Act.

The 1944 Plan was the brainchild of Patrick Abercrombie, by then 65.[1] It remains a masterpiece, described by Peter Hall as having 'extraordinary cartoon-like simplicity, which concealed great subtlety'.[2] Abercrombie looked at the big picture, setting London in its geographical context with his outer zone including most of the Chilterns, and the *Plan* includes photographs of Burnham Common, Chiltern beech-hangers and the Chess at Latimer. A central concept in the *Plan* was the Green Belt, a ring 5-10 miles wide around London's suburban ring, where further urban growth would be banned, thus stopping the formless sprawl ever outwards. Within inner London there would be major rebuilding, then overspill and growth would be located in a series of new and expanded towns in the outer ring beyond the Green Belt. The 1947 Town and Country Planning Act gave planners real teeth to implement such ideas by transferring development rights from individuals to the local authorities. For the first time refusing planning permission did not involve paying out huge compensation claims to aggrieved applicants, and building could now be monitored and controlled more closely.

The full working through of these policies took time, a long time, and much of the formal approval of Green Belt proposals and County Structure plans took until the late 1950s or even 1960s. Immediately after 1947, the planners used their new powers to channel growth, albeit often in an *ad hoc* way. The worst excesses of new ribbon development and 'bungaloid growth' were soon stopped. For the various planning authorities in the Chilterns the problem was that only their south-eastern fringes were in the London Green Belt: London's expansion jumped over this and into their laps. This was, of course, anticipated by Abercrombie and his successors, though—like most experts since—they failed to forecast the sheer scale of population and housing growth in the south-east over the next 40 years.[3] Several of the new and expanded towns designed to take this leap-frogging growth were around the edges of the Chilterns. Hertfordshire had seen the first two experiments in the 'Garden City' ideal, at Letchworth and

Welwyn. Now Welwyn became an official 'New Town' together with Hatfield, Hemel Hempstead and Stevenage. Other growth went into existing centres, notably High Wycombe, Dunstable and Luton. All had experienced industrial growth in the inter-war period—Wycombe with its furniture industry and engineering and Luton and Dunstable with Vauxhall car production (started in 1907) and engineering. Now this was continued as both jobs and homes were decentralised from London.

The pressures for growth were such that they had to be accommodated. It was not simply the numbers but also the rising expectation of a better home and way of life. Within the Chilterns there was a lot of expansion of existing market and suburban towns and 'infilling' along and around the 1930s building. Some of this may now be regarded as unfortunate, making more of 'eyesores' along valley sides, but it was hard, perhaps impossible, for planners to reject them all. Much fault can be found with post-war planning, but one only has to contemplate the fate of the Chilterns without such measures to see just how much was achieved.

By the 1960s it was clear that the need for growth and housing was not decreasing. Underestimates in the original planning meant that most of the expansion had gone into the suburban towns rather than the planned centres. Peter Hall's *London 2000* (1963), *The South East Study* (1964) and then the *Strategic Plan for the South East* (1970) each proposed a new scale of thinking, expanding Abercrombie's vision. Another generation of new and expanded towns was required, out beyond the confines of Abercrombie's Greater London region. To the north-west this meant beyond the Chiltern escarpment. One of Hall's suggested new towns was at Princes Risborough.[4] Actual expansion came at Aylesbury, and then in north Bucks. at Milton Keynes. To the south-west Reading and the M4 Corridor attracted enormous developments, and Reading expanded across the Thames into the south Chilterns.

The Chilterns: Area of Natural Beauty

This new scale of thinking finally provoked the government and others to think about the Chilterns as a region, one of the largest rural and environmentally-attractive areas within London's orbit. In 1964 a large part of the Chilterns was designated an Area of Outstanding Natural Beauty (AONB). The area defined was inevitably restricted, and considerably smaller than the more comprehensive view taken in this book. The scarp and adjacent plateau woodlands and valleys are the heart of the AONB, and the boundary weaves around to exclude all the major towns. It also excludes those dip-slope areas where Chiltern character gradually fades away, as in Buckinghamshire south of Beaconsfield and the Chalfonts. Only small portions of Bedfordshire and Hertfordshire were included (scarp-edge areas) and none of the region north of the A5 (and M1) and east of Luton that was traditionally seen as Chiltern country, like Kings Walden and Codicote. The Countryside Commission rightly had to maintain rigorous (and consistent) criteria, and some of these areas had always been somewhat marginal and doubtful. They had also lost some of what they had: south Buckinghamshire to suburbia (however pleasant) and parts of Hertfordshire to development and agri-business. In the late 1980s the Commission reviewed and revised the AONB boundaries.

The purpose of the AONB was 'to conserve and enhance natural beauty', and the designation meant more rigorous criteria for development. Much of the zone (and Chiltern areas outside it) was already county or metropolitan green belt, but AONB status gave a further level of protection. Planning authority remained with the county and (after 1974) new district authorities. The Chilterns were, however, the first AONB to set up a coordinating group, the Chilterns Standing Conference, in 1967. This group produced *A Plan for the Chilterns* four years later.[5] For the first time the Chilterns were being considered as a whole—give or take

169. Hedge removal at Codicote. Standing trees and a few remnants are evidence enough of former hedges, removed to accommodate modern machinery.

arguments over boundary lines. In the same period the Chiltern Society was established as an amenity society to look after the interests of the region (comprehensively defined).

Just what to conserve and enhance in the Chilterns under the terms 'natural beauty' or 'scenic attractiveness'(and the Countryside Commission uses both terms) needs careful consideration. The well-known conservationist and writer Richard Mabey is a Chilterns' resident. He touched on this issue in his book *The Common Ground*.[6] He quotes the effusive comments of William Cobbett about the Chiltern scenery between Hemel Hempstead and Redbourn: 'And thus you go from field to field (on foot or on horseback), the sort of corn, the sort of underwood and timber, the shape and size of the fields, the height of the hedge-rows, the height of the trees, all continually varying. Talk of *pleasure-grounds* indeed!'[7]

Mabey then laments that today the 'continually varying' has changed to 'continually uniform', and suggests that although this area still looks like a traditional farming landscape, we should be careful about confusing 'landscape' with superficial scenery. As a conservationist, he makes us aware that the issues we are dealing with are more than surface deep. Any attempt to formulate a policy for the region immediately has to consider many conflicting views and pressures.

Countryside Conflicts
The increasing encirclement of the Chilterns heartland by new and expanding towns puts special pressures on the region, and with it temptation to retreat behind the wagons and fight

off all Indian attacks. Even if housing and industrial development within the Hills was resisted, the surrounding network of towns meant increased demands for water, roads and recreation.

The demands for water have gained a high profile in the last few years as hosepipe bans have brought the problems into our back yards. Increased abstractions from rivers and bore holes have combined with several years of low rainfall to cause severe water shortages in the Chilterns. The most obvious expression of the demand outstripping supply has been the shrinking and drying up of Chiltern rivers. Chalk streams, or bournes, by their nature flow erratically with heads that migrate up and down the valley and sections which disappear. The climatic conditions alter their length and their volume of water, but the current low levels are unprecedented. The worrying factor is that the level of abstraction has outstripped the capacity of aquifers to recharge themselves, and unless the trend is reversed these dried-up rivers will remain at best as occasional trickles. Estimates suggest that we have increased our demands for water by 70 per cent in the last 30 years, and water authorities have been at liberty to progressively increase their abstraction rates to meet these demands. Today we pay the price. The Misbourne has the highest profile amongst Chiltern 'lost rivers', with the backing of a powerful campaign. Once it totalled 16 miles in length and was a fast-flowing stream with pools large enough to swim in, and with

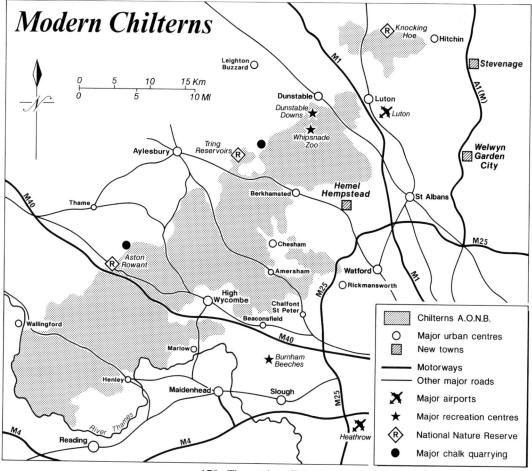

170. The modern Chilterns.

enough water to feed Shardeloes lake. Now it struggles to flow for three miles. The Chess, the Wye, the Ver and the Bulbourne are similarly dwindling, and along with them the rich chalk-stream ecology and traditional watercress beds that fed on their pure water. The National Rivers Authority and local water authorities have already started to implement short-term plans, but restoring all these rivers requires long-term solutions with a range of measures and huge amounts of money. Tomorrow we will count the cost.

New roads through the Chilterns almost inevitably damage the countryside, but they have been necessary, both for local traffic and because, as in the turnpike, canal and railway eras, the Hills lay between London and the midlands. The 1960s saw the M1 carve through the east Chilterns and the escarpment at Luton, and then the M40 to Oxford. This was a classic case of conflicting values. Such a road was much needed to replace the old road through Gerrards Cross, Beaconsfield and High Wycombe. The route chosen involved a great cutting through the scarp at Lewknor. Nor was this just any part of the scarp: the motorway sliced through an ancient wood (Hailey Wood) and part of the prime ecological site of Beacon Hill—not the most vital part, but damaging a dry valley. It runs, in fact, between the prime nature reserve and the best 'secret valley' (Wormsley) in the Hills, before descending to slice through the old fields of Lewknor, cutting across the lands shown on the 1598 map. Many still hate the cutting, but it speeds traffic on its way to Oxford and the Midlands, and greatly improves the quality of life in all the towns and villages now off the route. Similarly the A41 by-pass of Tring cut through Tring Park, but it has returned previously-choked Tring to a pleasant country town, and gives the passing motorist a very attractive piece of scenery. The extension to by-pass Berkhamsted and Kings Langley also slices through some ancient woodland, old enclosed countryside, and the ancient common at Boxmoor, but will bring similar benefits. There are gains and losses which are difficult to balance.

Roads, and increasing car ownership, not only speed traffic through the Hills, but bring traffic to them. The Hills have become a major amenity and recreation centre for the towns and cities around them, as well as for London itself. Ten thousand people now live within the AONB, but well over half a million live within two miles and nearly 10 million within 25 miles.[8] This creates intense pressures on the 'honeypot' locations, notably the car-parks on open downland: Dunstable Downs country park receives 850,000 visitors a year, 300,000 more than the most popular National Park sites.[9] As well as wanting access to the countryside, the woods, villages and footpaths, this population also wants sports and commercial recreation: golf courses, horse and pony clubs, leisure centres and theme parks.

It is important that the Chilterns AONB meets some of these recreational needs. Planning restrictions on new housing and types of housing have made house-prices high in the region. 'Rationing by price' is what green belts and AONB status often achieve. Many families will never be able to afford to live in such an area, or buy a second-home there, and the planning we all approve of has curtailed the chance of weekends in 'Uncle Rheuben's bungalow'. There is no apparent solution to this. Development must be restricted, but the leisure needs of those living around the Chilterns need to be on the agenda.

The 1971 *Plan for the Chilterns* recognised all these conflicts, together with many more. Given that urban and industrial development could be controlled, perhaps the most acute was between scenic amenity and farming. Agriculture and forestry were the prime land-uses in the AONB, yet the economic pressures there were often working against the AONB's goals: conifer plantations, destruction of old chalk grassland, hedgerow destruction and the loss of diversity in the landscape. In sorting out these countryside conflicts the AONB's terms (and hence the Chiltern Standing Conference) give primacy to the 'preservation of beauty'. Where recreation does not clash too severely with this, or with wildlife and natural conservation, then its needs can be met. This meant that free-ranging activities like rambling were approved, but general leisure facilities were to be met outside the AONB. The 1971 *Plan* was, however, rather defensive on agriculture and forestry: 'the development of agriculture and changing farming techniques must inevitably result in some changes ... but some aspects of the most utilitarian economic advantage may have to be sacrificed to policy No. (i) [preservation of beauty]'.[10]

Now, 20 years on, the *Plan* is being revised, in new circumstances and a new climate. In 1988 a new woodland policy was developed, and in 1991-92 the Standing Conference began the preparation of a new management plan, and the Countryside Commission funded a landscape appraisal by Land Use Consultants.[11] A prime aspect of the new circumstances is change in agriculture.

The New Agriculture
The difficulties of the Common Agricultural Policy have placed agriculture at something of a crossroads. The spiralling milk and grain surpluses have led to quotas and incentives to stop producing rather than incentives to increase output. This brings new problems, but also new opportunities to regions such as the Chilterns. Rather than the taxpayer subsidising farmers to 'damage' the countryside in the cause of higher yields, there is the opportunity to use subsidy and incentive to aid AONB policies. This is new territory, and the opportunities could yet be mirages, but the climate has changed rapidly. It will be compulsory to set aside at least 15 per cent of the farm holding, on a rotating basis. The results can be seen in the disused fields, often bright with poppies and other flowers emerging from the seed-bank in the soil. Much of the incentive is toward non-agricultural uses, such as horse-riding and cross-country courses, golf courses, some of which conflict with AONB policy. Other UK government policies point the way to more useful diversification. Designation of Environmentally-Sensitive Areas or ESAs and the Countryside Stewardship Scheme encourage farming with environmental objectives: the re-creation of chalk downland, and new broad-leaved woodland. Very recently the government has decided to fund the conservation of hedgerows. It is early days, and farmers rightly fear for their incomes, but a new partnership may be in the making.

In this new context, the Countryside Commission has seen the Chilterns as a test-bed, both nationally and internationally. The Smart-Anderson Report on AONB planning mentioned the Chilterns Standing Conference's impressive technical and policy record, singling out the 1988 woodland policy in particular, whilst a Countryside Commission spokesman recently noted: 'The UK has an international reputation for protecting "cultural landscapes". The Chilterns are well placed to act as a "demonstration model"'.[12]

Cultural Landscapes
It is time to examine just what is being conserved and enhanced. Discussion of Areas of Natural Beauty has subtly shifted from 'natural' to 'scenic' to 'landscape character', explicitly recognising the human and historical element in the landscapes. The basic geology and relief on which the landscape resides are natural, as are wild flowers and fauna being protected. The overall character is a cultural landscape, the product of human interference and management over centuries. Such landscapes are not just a legacy from the past, but something we construct, by valuing some aspects, recognising survivals and interpreting them.

The Chilterns provide a set-piece example of this changing perspective. The 1971 *Plan* grants the role of man's influence, though it puts it in terms that 'the appearance of the area probably results as much from the 18th and 19th century Inclosure Awards as from Nature itself'.[13] This is something of a travesty of landscape history in the Chilterns (but repeated in a 1991 document). Apart from archaeological sites, there is little discussion of historical legacy in landscape as such. Elsewhere, though, there is a thoughtful history of the Chiltern woodland, and a new perspective appears in the 1988 Woodlands Policy.[14] Between 1971 and 1988 'ancient woodland' and its character entered the language, and the Nature Conservancy produced preliminary maps (work confirmed by 1990). Much Chiltern woodland was now seen as 'ancient semi-natural woodland' with much transformed into high beechwood. As we have seen, this was not just a historical fact, detectable in old documents, but still traceable on the ground in old boundaries, flora and the trees themselves. Woodland conservation in the Chilterns could now mean recovering and reconstructing something of the more diverse earlier woodland, not just preserving the high beechwoods. The choice was not between tall dark beechwood or tall dark conifers. By careful management (which meant small group fellings, encouragement of natural regeneration and varied replanting), it should be possible to bring out, and literally unearth, more of the ancient woodland character. The 1988 Policy is a major step forward—though it recognises that there are economic problems about such management—and it also presses the case that non-ancient, secondary woodland on chalk downland and old wood pasture should be conserved.

Making Places

The distinctive character of the Chilterns is ultimately founded on its geology and relief: the chalk skeleton, the mantle of plateau drift and clay-with-flints, the dramatic scarp and the dissected dry valleys with their secluded 'bottoms'. But the landscape we see today is very much a human landscape, its features made, preserved and remade through the centuries. That cultural imprint runs deep: it is not primarily a product of the 18th and 19th centuries, for this is ancient countryside, with deep lanes, parish boundaries and old fields that may date back to Anglo-Saxon times or even earlier. Much of the countryside was shaped by medieval or early modern times, and it is this imposition of old, enclosed fields and lanes winding in and out, and up and down, that make the Chilterns so distinctive. Other dimensions are more recent, such as the high beechwoods, and they have already become part of the perceived regional character.

The regional distinctiveness of the Chilterns was probably most pronounced in the 17th and 18th centuries, after the open-fields within the Hills had been enclosed, but before the great age of Parliamentary Enclosure in the Vale and along the Thames. Its unity of character later began to crumble somewhat, as parts of the region reacted differently to the great agricultural depression of late Victorian times. The more rolling landscape of the northern Chilterns remained arable, but the long-term result was the removal of hedges and the creation of large grain prairies by modern agri-business. These areas retained the tradition of Chilterns arable, but lost the diverse landscape associated with the tradition. Most of these northerly areas have been refused AONB status, but they retain many Chiltern features and the task of planners and conservationists must now be to try to sustain and enhance these Chiltern features that remain.

The southern Chilterns have seen less overall change in their landscape character. Ironically this is partly due to the way they moved into dairying as a response to the agricultural depression. Dairying was very different from the traditional arable husbandry of the Chilterns, but it had preserved more of the traditional landscape than has arable farming. Dairying does not require such large fields, and there has been less ravaging of hedges and the farming scene.

The Stonor valley is a prime example of this (Plates 107, 167 and 171). The landscape we see today is a legacy of many historical periods, continually being adapted and changed, but not so violently as to destroy the threads that link its character to the past. The Anglo-

171. The Stonor valley from the air in 1985, showing many elements of 'ancient countryside'. Stonor village lies in the centre, with Stonor House to the east (right-hand side). To the west are the ancient Park and Doyley Woods. The old Anglo-Saxon boundary described in the Pyrton charter is still the county boundary here, running around the east of Stonor Park, then descending from the hills on the right-hand edge of the photograph to the Stonor-Henley road. It can be clearly seen in present lanes and field-boundaries. Fields have been amalgamated since the 1725 survey, but the old outlines can be seen. 'Mousalls' is the field on the extreme bottom of the picture, on the east side of the road to Henley, and 'Stomperhill' is the partly-wooded area immediately south-east of the village. The aerial view also distinguishes the types of woodland: high beech crowns and rows of conifers.

Saxon boundary charter for this detached part of Pyrton parish can still be followed across the landscape. The Stonor family have been at Stonor since the 12th century, one of the longest family lines in the country. There were medieval open-fields in this valley, but they had all been enclosed by the time of Thomas Stonor's detailed estate map of 1725.[15] Since then there have been field amalgamations, and hedgerows removed, but these have been restrained. On average groups of two to three fields on the 1725 map have been thrown together. The ancient fields were, however, very small, and there is still a hedged appearance. Fields can be traced back to a 1476 survey. Mousalls and Stomperhill are mentioned then, and can still be seen south and east of Stonor village. Great and Little Mousalls have been thrown together, and parts of Stomperhill have been wooded. On the west side of the valley, the ancient woodland of Park Wood and Doyley Wood, mentioned in late medieval records, remains, though it has been transformed to high beechwood. To the south-west, parts of Maidensgrove Scrubs have remained old coppice, and serviced the Nettlebed kilns throughout the 19th century. The valley also has its conifers, as at Stonor Park where over-mature beech at the ancient Kilridge Wood was clear-felled and firs planted. In the valley fields there are dairy cows as well as arable, and poppy-rich 'set aside' fields have appeared.

We can enjoy such landscapes without understanding the history—human and ecological— that created and maintained them. Yet our appreciation can be greatly enhanced by such understanding. Enjoyment of a country lane is increased when we know it is an Anglo-Saxon boundary or an old turnpike road, and can spot the medieval wood-bank and the flowers of ancient woods. Moreover, public and planning decisions on what to conserve and enhance do require historical understanding. Otherwise we walk blindly into the future. 'Heritage' is something we make from the materials the past has left us, and we cannot avoid selection and interpretation.

Our interpretation has been the story of this book. Like many others, much of our initial stimulus to study landscape history came from W. G. Hoskins' classic *Making of the English Landscape*.[16] Hoskins rediscovered a whole dimension of history, yet he suffered from a deep pessimism, writing in his last chapter, 'Let us turn away and contemplate the past before all is lost to the vandals'. We do not share his deep pessimism. The present century has seen very dramatic change in the Chilterns, and much has been damaged. Yet the Hills have absorbed it well, and their essential character remains. More today can enjoy—and celebrate—that landscape than ever before. The Chilterns remain very vulnerable, and the task is to conserve and enhance their qualities.

In facing these issues a renewed vision of the Chilterns is emerging, recognising that they are intimately related (as they always have been) to their surroundings and to London, but maintain their own sense of identity. The distinctive landscape has been historically split between four counties, reducing this overall identity. There is a growing sense of the Chilterns as 'place'. That sense is important both for preserving the character and taking opportunities to enhance it. If our book has traced the roots of that identity, and helped to promote such a sense, then it will have succeeded.

Chapter Notes

In these chapter notes manuscript sources are given in full: books and articles are given by author and date, which can then be located in the alphabetical list of References.

Manuscript Abbreviations:

BL	British Library (formerly British Museum)
Bodl	Bodleian Library, Oxford University
BRO	Buckinghamshire Record Office
ORO	Oxfordshire Record Office
PRO	Public Record Office

Chapter 1
1. Blythe (1986), 122
2. Esposito (1917). The original hoax is in*The Monthly Magazine* (1802) 13, 447-50
3. Smith, L. J. (1907), vol.2, 112
4. Mead (1954)
5. Elvey, G. R. (1977)
6. Oschinsky (1971), 323 [*Walter* c.49]
7. Petrie (1926)
8. Davies, A. M. (1951-52)
9. Stevenson (1907)
10. Roberts, C. (1934, 1935, 1936, 1938)
11. Thomas (1913), 154
12. Chenevix Trench (1973)
13. Home (1925), 21
14. Baines (1981a)
15. Young, A. [Arthur] (1804)
16. Betjeman (1960), 56

Chapter 2
1. Dyer (1978); Sampson (1978)
2. Wymer (1968)
3. Loveday (1962)
4. Peel (1950), 14
5. Ollier and Thomasson (1957)
6. Evans, J. G. (1975), 64
7. Farley (1978), 614
8. Stainton (1989)
9. Head (1955)
10. Head (1974)
11. Matthews (1964, 1976)
12. Dyer and Hales (1962)
13. Childe and Smith (1954)
14. Head (1955, 1974); Dyer (1959)
15. Bodl: Gough MS 47 [Delafield's *History of Stokenchurch*]
16. Evans, J. G. (1966, 1972); Evans and Valentine (1974)
17. Evans and Valentine (1974)
18. Cunliffe (1991)
19. Saunders (1971)

20. Richardson and Young (1951); Harding (1972)
21. Evans, J. G. (1966, 1972)
22. Hawkes (1940)
23. Dyer and Hales (1962)
24. Cotton and Frere (1968), 203
25. BL: Harley MS 3688, at end. Not printed in Jenkins (1938, 1955, 1962), but see Hughes (1931), 295
26. Crawford (1931); Dyer (1963); Bradley (1968); Davis, J. (1981)
27. Plot (1672), 324
28. Dyer (1961)
29. Davis and Evans (1984)

Chapter 3
1. Cunliffe (1991); Frere (1987); Millett (1990); Stead and Rigby (1989)
2. Stead (1967)
3. Wheeler and Wheeler (1936); see also Saunders (1982)
4. Hunn (1980)
5. Branigan (1985)
6. Case (1958)
7. Branigan (1985)
8. Neal, Wardle and Hunn (1990)
9. Branigan (1985), 105
10. Taylor (1983)
11. Bell (1983)
12. Wheeler and Wheeler (1936); Frere (1972, 1983, 1984)
13. Viatores (1964)
14. Branigan (1967, 1968, 1971a, 1973, 1985)
15. Neal (1976); St. Joseph (1965)
16. Branigan (1985), 105
17. Branigan (1967, 1971b)
18. Branigan (1985), 135
19. Orna (1976); also *Britannia* v (1974), 438; vi (1975), 257; vii (1976), 338-39
20. Thompson (1957)
21. Branigan (1971b)

22. Branigan (1971b)
23. Frere (1983), 24
24. Frere, personal communication, 28 February 1992
25. Esmonde Cleary (1989), 172
26. Wheeler and Wheeler (1936) 35
27. Buchan (1916)

Chapter 4
1. Gelling (1979), but see also Baines (1984a)
2. Farley (1976); Baines (1984a)
3. Matthews, Hawkes and others (1985)
4. Meaney (1964), 59
5. Matthews, Hawkes and others (1985)
6. Stenton (1975), 27; see also Sims-Williams (1983)
7. Hawkes (1986), 86
8. Gelling (1978); on -ham, see Cox (1972-73)
9. Cox (1975-76); Gelling (1976)
10. Frere (1966), 98
11. Davis, K. R. (1982)
12. Frere (1987), 369
13. Davies, W and Vierck, H. (1974); BL: Harley 3271 f6v
14. Baines (1981b, 1984)
15. Bailey (1989), 111
16. Chenevix Trench (1973); Baines (1984a, 1984b)
17. Seebohm (1883)
18. Baines, in Branigan (1971a), 192; Baines(1984a), 126-27
19. Chenevix Trench (1973)
20. Collett (1926), 247; Beddoe (1885)
21. Stonor (1951), 8 and 358
22. Cole (1982, 1985, 1989, 1990); see also Gelling (1984)
23. Baines (1981a); Davies, A. M. (1949)
24. Gelling (1976); Blair (1989); Hooke (1985)

25. Sawyer (1983)
26. Blair (1988a, 1988b)
27. Cam (1944)
28. Sawyer (1968), no.217; BL: Cotton Tiberius A xiii f28v-29v and f195-196.
29. Hooke (1985)
30. Blair (1989), 98
31. Chenevix Trench (1973)
32. Rowley (1973), 5
33. Lobel (1964), 2
34. Davies, A. M. (1949)
35. Newnham Murren: Grundy (1933), 39-42; Sawyer (1868), no.738; BL: Harley 596 f17v-18v. Bensington: Sawyer (1968), no.887; BL: Cotton Claudius B vi, f98v-99v.
36. Baines (1981a); Gelling (1953-54)
37. Baines (1981b); Reed(1979)
38. Lennard (1959)

Chapter 5
1. Darby and Campbell (1962)
2. Sellar and Yeatman (1930)
3. Seebohm (1883); Gray (1915)
4. Fox (1981, 1984); Williamson (1988)
5. Fox (1981), 96-97; Fowler (1926), 252; BL: Harley MS 1885 f7-8
6. Williamson (1988)
7. Harvey (1965)
8. Roden (1965), 236-270; Roden (1966)
9. Beresford (1953), 6
10. For a useful comparision with Kentish downland (rather than Weald), see Everett (1986)
11. Gray (1915), 401
12. Roden (1965-1973)
13. Campbell (1990)
14. Roden (1970), 61
15. Chenevix Trench (1973); Davies, A. M. (1949); Baines (1981a)
16. Hale (1858); Roden (1965), 296-301
17. Talbot (1959)
18. Roden (1965), 128-131; Roden (1970), 60-63
19. Vollans (1959), Jenkins (1938, 1955, 1962)
20. Casselden (1986, 1987)
21. Jenkins (1938), 154-55; Vollans (1959); BL: Harley 3688 f45r
22. Kosminsky (1956); Ulyanov (1966, 1971, 1972)
23. Kosminsky (1956), 128 and 143 ('peculiar')
24. Fox (1984)
25. Chibnall (1966),
26. Power and Campbell (1992); Campbell, Galloway and Murphy (1992)
27. Dyer, C. C. (1989), 54
28. Roden (1965,), 174-175; Roden

(1969b), 234; BL: Stowe 849
29. Chenevix Trench (1978), 418; Jenkins (1955), no.311
30. Ulyanov (1966)
31. Lobel (1964), 225; Salter (1935), 408
32. Roden (1965), 159-205; Levett (1938); Slota (1984, 1988); BL: Stowe MS 849
33. Roden (1965), 236-70; Roden(1966)
34. Young, A. [Alison] (1964), 271
35. Holt, R. (1988); Bloch(1967)
36. Ault (1972), 61
37. Oschinsky (1971), 277 [*Seneschausy*, c.38]
38. Ault (1972), 91, 113-14, 173-74
39. Ault (1972), 91, 107
40. Fox (1986)
41. Dahlman (1980)
42. BL: MS Stowe 849, f91-91v and f104
43. Roden (1965), 141-145
44. Roden (1965), Appendices F and G, 391-419; Slota (1988)
45. Holt, R. (1988)
46. Jenkins (1935), 42
47. Langdon (1986),
48. Oschinsky (1971), 319 [*Walter*, c.36]
49. Oschinsky (1971), 319 [*Walter*, c.41]
50. Chibnall (1966); Cornwall (1975)
51. Campbell (1988); later quote at 198
52. Reed (1978), Postles (1987)
53. Farmer (1991), 336
54. Beresford (1967)
55. Power (1941), 113; Lloyd (1977), 56
56. Ashford (1960)
57. Keene (1989); Galloway and Murphy (1991); Campbell, Galloway and Murphy (1992)
58. Postles (1984), Farmer (1991)
59. Holt, N. R. (1964), 153 and 156; Farmer (1991), 368
60. Ashford (1960)
61. Davis, R. H. C. (1973)
62. Farmer (1991), 353
63. Gras (1915), 164-165; Farmer (1991), 371-72; Roden (1966)
64. Kingsford (1919)

Chapter 6
1. Campbell (1990)
2. Kershaw (1973)
3. Titow (1962, 1972)
4. Kershaw (1973); Roden (1965); BL: MS Stowe 849 f43v
5. Baker (1966, 1970)
6. Baker (1970), 15
7. Roden (1970); Ashford (1960)
8. Elvey E. M. (1961), 32
9. Roden (1970), 66
10. Roden (1970), 67; *Register of*

Edward the Black Prince, iv (1933), 342
11. Harvey (1991), 676
12. Elvey E. M. (1961), 33
13. Preece (1990c), 15
14. Anon (1981); Riley (1867-69), vol. 3
15. Beresford (1953, 1954)
16. Beresford (1954), 231
17. Glennie (1983), 25-51
18. Roden (1970), 68. Oxwik: Roden (1965), 181; BL: MS Stowe 849, f89-89v
19. Johnson and Fenley (1971-74); Hughes (1931)
20. Chambers (1973)
21. Lobel (1964), 210-33; Allison et al. (1965)
22. Elvey E. M. (1961), 37-39
23. Roden (1965), 329-30
24. Cornwall (1970, 1988)
25. Roberts, E. (1974)
26. Bond, Gosling and Rhodes (1980); Stebbing, Rhodes and Meller (1980)
27. Money and Smith (1973); Turner, H. L. (1972); Fletcher (1975)
28. Evans, R. W. (1987)
29. Johnson and Fenley (1974)

Chapter 7
1. Darby and Campbell (1962), 211; Rackham (1980), 111-27
2. Rackham (1980), 123
3. Riley (1867-69)
4. Fitzstephen (*c.*1180)
5. *Calendar of Ancient Deeds* vi (1915, PRO), 168 c5065; see also Roden (1968), 62
6. Roden (1965,1966)
7. Lobel (1964), 166
8. Roden (1968), 64
9. PRO: C 47/37/5; Preece (1987, 1987-88, 1990a)
10. Roden (1965), 259
11. Lobel (1964), 166
12. Jenkins (1938), 68-69; BL: Harley 3688 f24v-25r
13. Kingsford (1919), vol.2, 141, no.307
14. Calendar of Ancient Deeds vi (1915, PRO), 245, c5623
15. Fowler (1926); BL: Harley 1885 f76v
16. Rackham (1990), 145
17. Jenkins (1938), 122-23; BL: Harley 3688 f37v
18. Hanley (1987)
19. Lobel (1964), 106
20. PRO: C 133/95
21. Hassall (1951)
22. Preece(1987, 1987-88, 1990a)
23. Prince (1954, 1959)
24. Lobel (1964), 230; PRO: E 36/157, 14-15
25. Kingsford (1919), vol.2, 19, no.176

26. Pavry and Knocker (1957-58), 170
27. Peterken (1981)
28. Mansfield (1952)
29. La Sueur (1955)
30. Bowen (1977, 1980); Harding and Rose (1986)
31. Roden (1965), 306-235
32. *Register of Edward the Black Prince*, iv (1933)
33. Rackham (1980), 325-26

Chapter 8
1. Cornwall (1959), 265
2. Hartley, D. (1931), 178-82
3. Roden (1965), 51060; Roden (1969a), 119
4. BRO: D/MH/28/2; see Roden (1965), 69-75; Roden (1973); Owen (1984)
5. Munby (1977), 168-69
6. Lobel (1964), 105
7. Gibson (1989); Havinden (1961a)
8. Dils (1987); Gras(1915)
9. PRO: SP 12/198, item 27
10. Blome (1673); see Dils (1987)
11. Kussmaul (1990)
12. Bodl: Gough MS 47 [Delafield's *History of Stokenchurch*], f173
13. Blith (1652)
14. Havinden (1961a); Glennie (1983, 1988a, 1988b)
15. Glennie (1983, 1988b)
16. Glennie (1988b), 150
17. Havinden (1961a), 255
18. Young, A. [Arthur] (1813), 119
19. Havinden (1965); Lobel (1964), 31
20. Ellis (1733), preface, ii
21. Ellis (1733), quotes at 2, 19 and 3
22. Bodl: Gough MS 47 [Delafield's *History of Stokenchurch*], f174
23. Ellis (1733), 26
24. Quoted in Bell (1956), 107
25. Ellis (1733), 20 and 4
26. Lucas (1892); Mead (1962)
27. Lucas (1892), quotes at 178, 255, 281-82, 327, 232, 187
28. Dils (1987)
29. Ashford (1960), 203
30. Elliman (1987)
31. Ashford (1960), 215
32. Prince (1954, 1959)
33. Kemp (1967)
34. Stroud (1975); Prince (1959)
35. Stroud (1962); Prince (1959)
36. Repton (1803), 61

Chapter 9
1. Baker (1932)
2. Lambert (1953)
3. quoted in Starey and Viccars (1992), 76
4. Pawson (1977)

5. Pawson (1977), 246, quoting *Journal of House of Commons*
6. Lobel (1964), 16
7. Bodl: MS Ad A262 [William Bayzard, 'Coaching In and Out of Oxford from 1820 to 1840 by A Chip off the old Block, with Anecdotes and Reminiscences in his 75 years'], 35-36
8. Quoted in Briers (1939)
9. Chibnall (1963)
10. Godber (1969), 316-17
11. Roberts, C. (1936), 44
12. Homer (1767), 6
13. Lambert (1953), 225
14. ORO: CH/S/II/i/1 [Stokenchurch to Woodstock Trust Minute Book 1740-93]
15. Hart (1975)
16. Faulkner (1972, 1975)
17. Richardson, A. (1969); Ware (1989)
18. Priest (1810), 338
19. Lambert (1953), 267-68
20. Faulkner (1975)
21. Evans, J. (1955)
22. Boyle (1848), 20
23. Simmons (1961), 7
24. quoted in Page, W. (1908), 104
25. Simmons (1961), 6
26. Scott (1907)
27. Cockman (1972, 1974); Coles (1980); Oppitz (1991)
28. Kirkland (1956); Christiansen (1981)
29. Coles (1980)
30. Bagwell (1974), 109
31. Disraeli (1845)
32. Whetham (1964-65)

Chapter 10
1. Rackham (1980), 167
2. *Calendar of Patent Rolls*, 16 August 1559
3. Prior (1981)
4. Bodl: MS Top Oxon d.46; Dils (1987); Mansfield (1952), 129
5. Defoe (1724-27)
6. Plot (1672), 267
7. BRO: D/D/14/55 and D/D/14/56 [Dashwood Deeds]
8. BRO: D/MH/30 [Hampden Wood Books; 30/4 is 1695-99]
9. Bodl: MS Top Oxon c404 172-75
10. Bodl: MS Top Oxon c206 107-16
11. Mansfield (1952), 22-42
12. Lobel (1964), 166, quoting Stonor Muniments
13. Bodl: MS Top Oxon c446, 11; MS Top Oxon c206, 124
14. Commissioners of Land Revenue (1792)
15. Ellis (1733), 93
16. Langley (1797), 1
17. Young, A. [Arthur] (1813), 221
18. BRO: D/MH/30; Mansfield

(1952), 123
19. Commissioners of Land Revenue (1792), 70
20. James and Malcolm (1794), 41
21. Collins (1989)
22. Mansfield (1952), 146
23. James and Malcolm (1794); Langley (1797), 9; Priest (1810), 225
24. McCreath (1986); Beckett (1985)
25. Mayes (1960); Sparkes (1989)
26. North (1882)
27. Sheahan (1862), 920
28. McCreath (1986)
29. Stokenchurch: quoted by Mansfield (1952), 131
30. Massingham (1940); for Stoke Row, see Baker (1959)
31. Peterken (1981)
32. Preece (1987, 1990b)
33. Peterken (1981), 74-76
34. Watt (1934)

Chapter 11
1. Tate (1978); Turner, M. E. (1980); for Bucks., see Turner, M. E. (1973)
2. Lobel (1964), 105-6; ORO: Lewknor Inclosure Award
3. Young, A. [Arthur] (1813), 103
4. Turner, M. E. (1973), 197-208; BRO: Princes Risborough and Monks Risborough Enclosure Papers
5. BRO: IR/M/1/7
6. Bond, Gosling and Rhodes (1980); Stebbing, Rhodes and Meller (1980)
7. Hay and Hay (1971), 120-21
8. Owen (1984), quoting BRO: D42/c28/1
9. Jackson, C. C. (1977)
10. Hoskins and Stamp (1963)
11. Whybrow (1934)
12. Thirsk (1961)
13. Palliser (1864); Spenceley (1973)
14. Pepys Diary, May 21 1663: Palliser (1864), 314
15. Defoe (1727), 332
16. Langley (1797)
17. Buck (1978)
18. Horn (1974, 1991)
19. Buck (1981)
20. Cole, A. S. (1892)
21. Gróf (1988), 14-19
22. Gibbs (1885)
23. Gróf (1988)
24. Horn and Horn (1983)
25. Greenwood (1883), 28
26. Gróf (1988)
27. Thorburn (1989)
28. Gróf (1988), 84
29. Children's Employment Commission (1864), 201
30. Buckinghamshire Federation of Women's Institutes (1975), 20-21

31. Lobel (1964), 231
32. Casselden (1987)
33. Starey and Viccars (1992), 153-57
34. Greening Lamborn 91936); Baines (1981a)
35. Coppock (1960a, 1961)
36. Prince (1981), 20
37. Coppock (1961), Whetham (1964-65)
38. Baker (1937), 182
39. Coppock (1957, 1961)
40. Ellis (1738), 65-70
41. Coppock (1961, 16)

Chapter 12
1. See Edwards and Pigram (1977, 1979, 1983); Jackson, A. A. (1986)
2. *Metro-land* (1987 reprint), 37 and 38.
3. Lowerson (1980)
4. Page, H. E. (1937)
5. Jackson A. A. (1973, 1976)
6. Betjeman (1978), 231
7. Coppock (1964)
8. Jackson A. A. (1973)
9. Lean and Pettit (n.d.)
10. Sheail (1981)
11. Trevelyan (1929)
12. Jeans (1990)
13. Williams-Ellis (1928; 1937)
14. Matless (1990b)
15. Peach and Carrington (1930)
16. Matless (1990a)

17. Massingham (1940), 106
18. Perkin (1976), 135 and 147
19. *Motor Owner* (1920)
20. In Williams-Ellis (1937), 72-73; Jeans (1991)
21. Massingham (1940), 73
22. King (1984)
23. In Williams-Ellis (1937), 213
24. Harman (1986)
25. Hardy and Wood (1984), 184
26. Williams-Ellis, in Peach and Carrington (1930)
27. Stevenson (1907), 140
28. Williams-Ellis, in CPRE [Penn Branch] (1933), 105

Chapter 13
1. Coppock (1957)
2. Hoskins and Stamp (1963)
3. Smith C. J. (1980)
4. Smith C. J. (1980)
5. Rackham (1986), 342; Wells (1968); Wells and Barling (1971)
6. Watt (1923, 1934)
7. Ward (1973)
8. Brett (1965)
9. Harman (1986)
10. Bourne (1931); Robbins (1931)
11. Forestry Commission (1961)
12. Chilterns Standing Conference (1971)
13. Sheail (1976, 1987)
14. Tansley (1939)
15. Salisbury (1918)

16. Sheail (1976), 153
17. Ratcliffe (1978); Peterken (1981)

Chapter 14
1. Abercrombie (1945)
2. Hall (1989), 36
3. Hall (1989)
4. Hall (1963)
5. Chilterns Standing Conference (1971)
6. Mabey (1980), 111; Mabey (1990)
7. Cobbett (1830)
8. Chilterns Standing Conference (1971)
9. Chilterns Standing Conference (1991, 1992)
10. Chilterns Standing Conference (1971), 73-74
11. Chilterns Standing Conference (1988, 1991, 1992)
12. Smart and Anderson (1990); Heynes in Chilterns Standing Conference (1992)
13. Chilterns Standing Conference (1971), 9; Chilterns Standing Conference (1991), 3
14. Chilterns Standing Conference (1988); see also Hornby (1987)
15. The 1725 map is displayed in Stonor House; the details are given in Ulyanov (1972)
16. Hoskins (1955)

References

Abercrombie, P. 1945 *Greater London Plan 1944*. London: HMSO.

Allen, R.C. 1992 *Enclosure and the Yeoman*. Oxford: Clarendon Press.

Allison, K.J., Beresford, M.W. and Hurst, J.G. 1965 *The Deserted Villages of Oxfordshire*. Leicester: Leicester University Department of English Local History, Occasional Paper 17.

Anon (ed.) 1981 *The Peasant's Revolt in Hertfordshire: The Rising and its Background*. Hertford: Hertfordshire Publications (Hertfordshire Library Service)

Ashford, L.J. 1960 *The History of the Borough of High Wycombe, from its origins to 1880*. London: Routledge and Kegan Paul.

Ault, W.O. 1972 *Open-Field Farming in Medieval England. A Study in Village By-Laws*. London: George Allen and Unwin.

Avery, B.W. 1964 *The Soils and Land Use of the District around Aylesbury and Hemel Hempstead. Memoirs of the Soil Survey of Great Britain*. London: HMSO.

Bagwell, P.S. 1974 *The Transport Revolution from 1770*. London: B.T.Batsford.

Bailey, K. 1989 'The Middle Saxons', in Bassett, S. (ed), *The Origins of Anglo-Saxon Kingdoms*, 108-22. Leicester: Leicester University Press.

Baines, A.H.J. 1981a 'Turville, Radenore and the Chiltern Feld', *Records of Buckinghamshire* 23, 4-22.

Baines, A.H.J. 1981b 'The boundaries of Monk's Risborough', *Records of Buckinghamshire* 23, 76-101.

Baines, A.H.J. 1983 'The Lady Elgiva, St.Aethwold and the Linslade charter of 966', *Records of Buckinghamshire* 25, 110-38.

Baines, A.H.J. 1984a 'Anglo-Saxon Buckinghamshire: the evolution of a duality in the cultural landscape'. Unpublished Ph.D. thesis, The Open University.

Baines, A.H.J. 1984b 'Cholesbury-cum-St.Leonards: a modern perambulation of ancient boundaries', *Records of Buckinghamshire* 26, 131-34.

Baker, A.R.H. 1966 'Evidence in the Nonarum Inquisitiones of contracting arable lands in England during the early fourteenth century', *Economic History Review*, series 2, 19, 518-32.

Baker, A.R.H. 1970 'Contracting arable lands in 1341', *Bedfordshire Historical Record Society* 39, 7-18.

Baker, J.H. 1932 *The Story of the Chiltern Heathlands*. Reading: Jas Golder.

Baker, J.H. 1937 *Land of the Gap*. Oxford: Basil Blackwell.

Baker, J.H. 1959 *The Ipsden Country*. Reading: William Smith.

Beckett, I.F.W. (ed) 1985 *The Buckinghamshire Posse Comitatus of 1798*. Aylesbury: Buckinghamshire Record Society, 22.

Beddoe, J. 1885 *The Races of Britain*. Bristol: J.W. Arrowsmith.

Bell, M. 1983 'Valley sediments as evidence of prehistoric land-use on the South Downs', *Proceedings of the Prehistoric Society*, 49, 119-50.

Bell, V. 1956 *To Meet Mr.Ellis. Little Gaddesden in the Eighteenth Century*. London: Faber.

Beresford, M.W. 1953 'Glebe terriers and open-field Buckinghamshire. Part II', *Records of Buckinghamshire* 16, 5-28.

Beresford, M.W. 1954 *The Lost Villages of England*. London: Lutterworth Press.

Beresford, M.W. 1967 *New Towns of the Middle Ages*. London: Lutterworth Press.

Betjeman, J. 1960 *Summoned by Bells*. London: John Murray.

Betjeman, J. 1978 *The Best of Betjeman*, selected by J.Guest. London: Penguin.

Blair, J. 1988a *Minsters and Parish Churches: The Local Church in Transition 950-1200*. Oxford: Oxford Committee for Archaeology.

Blair, J. 1988b 'Minster churches in the landscape', in Hooke, D. (ed) *Anglo-Saxon Settlements*, 35-58. Oxford: Basil Blackwell.

Blair, J. 1989 'Frithuwold's kingdom and the origins of Surrey', in Bassett, S. (ed) *The Origins of Anglo-Saxon Kingdoms*, 97-107. Leicester: Leicester University Press.

Blith, W. 1652 *The English Improver Improved*. London: John Wright.

Bloch, M. 1967 'The advent and triumph of the watermill', in *Land and work in Medieval Europe: Selected Papers*, 136-68. London: Routledge & Kegan Paul.

Blome, R. 1673 *Britannia*. London: Thomas Roycroft for R.Blome.

Blythe, R. 1986 *Divine Landscapes*. Harmondsworth: Viking.

Bond, J., Gosling, S. and Rhodes J. 1980 *Oxfordshire Brickmakers*. Woodstock, Oxford: Oxford Museums Service Publication 14.

Bourne, R. 1931 *Regional Survey, and its relation to stocktaking of the agricultural and forest resources of the British Empire.* Oxford: Clarendon Press.

Bowen, H.J.M. 1977 'Indicators of old forest', *Reading Naturalist* 29, 2-8.

Bowen, H.J.M. 1980 'A lichen flora of Berkshire, Buckinghamshire and Oxfordshire', *Lichenologist* 12, 199-237.

Boyle, T. 1848 *Hope for the Canals, Showing the evil of Amalgamations with Railways to Public and Private Interest.* London.

Bradley, R. 1968 'The South Oxfordshire Grim's Ditch and its significance', *Oxoniensia* 33, 1-12.

Branigan, K. 1967 'The distribution and development of Romano-British occupation in the Chess Valley', *Records of Buckinghamshire* 18, 136-49.

Branigan, K. 1968 'Romano-British rural settlement in the western Chilterns', *Archaeological Journal* 124, 129-59.

Branigan, K. 1969 'The Romano-British villa at Saunderton reconsidered', *Records of Buckinghamshire* 18, 261-76.

Branigan, K. 1971a *Latimer: Belgic, Roman and Dark Age and early modern farms.* Chesham: Chess Valley Archaeological and Historical Society.

Branigan, K 1971b 'Pavements and poverty in the Chiltern villas', *Britannia* 2, 109-16.

Branigan, K. 1973 *Town and Country: Verulamium and the Roman Chilterns.* Bourne End: Spur Books.

Branigan, K. 1985 *The Catuvellauni.* Gloucester: Alan Sutton.

Brett, L. 1965 *Landscape in Distress.* London: The Architectural Press.

Briers, P.M. 1939 *History of Nuffield.* Oxford: privately published (Lord Nuffield)

Buck, A. 1978 'Middlemen in the Bedfordshire Lace industry', *Bedfordshire Historical Record Society* 57, 31-58.

Buck, A. 1981 *Thomas Lester, his Lace and the East Midlands Industry 1820-1905.* Carlton, Bedford: Ruth Bean.

Buchan, J. 1916 *The Power House.* Edinburgh & London: W. Blackwood & sons.

Buckinghamshire Federation of Women's Institutes 1975 *A Pattern of Hundreds.* Chalfont St Giles: Richard Sadler Ltd.

Burn, J.S. 1861 *A History of Henley-on-Thames.* London: Longman.

Cam, H. 1944 *Liberties and Communities in Medieval England.* Cambridge: Cambridge University Press.

Campbell, B.M.S. 1988 'The diffusion of vetches in medieval England', *Economic History Review*, 2nd series, 41, 193-208.

Campbell, B.M.S. 1990 'People and land in the Middle Ages, 1066-1500', in Dodgshon, R.A. and Butlin, R.A. (eds), *An Historical Geography of England and Wales* (2nd Edition), 69-121. London: Academic Press.

Campbell, B.M.S., Galloway, J.A. and Murphy, M. 1992 'Rural land-use in the metropolitan hinterland, 1270-1339: the evidence of the Inquisitiones Post Mortem', *Agricultural History Review* 40, 1-22.

Case, H. 1958 'A late Belgic burial at Watlington', *Oxoniensia* 23, 139-41.

Casselden, P 1986 'Chartridge and Pednor hedgerows: a landscape study. Part 1', *Records of Buckinghamshire* 28, 182-210.

Casselden, P. 1987 'Chartridge and Pednor hedgerows: a landscape study. Part 2', *Records of Buckinghamshire* 29, 133-59.

Chambers, R.A. 1973 'A deserted medieval farmstead at Sadler's Wood, Lewknor', *Oxoniensia* 38, 146-67.

Chenevix Trench, J. 1973 'Coleshill and the settlement of the Chilterns', *Records of Buckinghamshire* 19, 241-58.

Chenevix Trench, J. 1978 'Fields and farms in a hilltop village', *Records of Buckinghamshire* 20, 410-30.

Chenevix Trench, J. 1983 'The houses of Coleshill: the social anatomy of a seventeenth century village', *Records of Buckinghamshire* 25, 61-109.

Chibnall, A.C (ed) 1966 *Early Taxation Returns.* Buckinghamshire Record Society 14. Welwyn Garden City: Broadwater Press.

Chibnall, J. 1963 'The roads of Buckinghamshire with special reference to turnpike roads'. Unpublished M.Sc. thesis, University of London.

Childe, V.G. and Smith, I.F. 1954 'The excavation of a Neolithic barrow on Whiteleaf Hill, Bucks', *Proceedings of the Prehistoric Society* 20, 212-30.

Children's Employment Commission. 1864 *Second Report of the Children's Employment Commission.* Parliamentary Papers, 1864, vol. 22.

Chilterns Standing Conference 1971 *A Plan for the Chilterns.* Aylesbury: Chilterns Standing Conference.

Chilterns Standing Conference 1988 *A Plan for the Chilterns: Woodland Policy.* Aylesbury: Chilterns Standing Conference.

Chilterns Standing Conference 1991 *The Chilterns Area of Outstanding Natural Beauty. A Statement of Intent.* Aylesbury: Chilterns Standing Conference.

Chilterns Standing Conference 1992 *The Chilterns...What Future?* Proceedings of a Seminar, 1 July 1992.

Christiansen, R. 1981 *Thames and Severn: A Regional History of the Railways of Great Britain*, volume 13. Newton Abbot: David and Charles.

Cobbett, W. 1830 *Rural Rides.* London.

Cockman, F.G. 1972 'The railway era in Buckinghamshire', *Records of Buckinghamshire* 19 (2), 156-168.

Cockman, F.G. 1974 *The Railway Age in Bedfordshire.* Bedford: Bedford Historical Record Society, 53.

Cole, A. 1982 'Topography, hydrology, and place-names in the chalklands of southern England: cumb and denu', *Nomina* 6, 73-87.

Cole, A. 1985 'Topography, hydrology, and place-names in the chalklands of southern England: *funta, -ewiell and -ewielm', *Nomina* 9, 3-19.

Cole, A. 1989 'The meaning of the OE place-name element ora', *Journal of the English Place-Name Society* 21, 15-22.

Cole, A. 1990 'The origin, distribution and use of the place-name element ora and its relationship to the element ofer',

Journal of the English Place-Name Society 22, 27-41.

Cole, A.S. 1892 *Report on Northampton, Bucks. and Beds. Lace-Making, 1891*. London: Department of Science and Art.

Coles, C.R.L. 1980 *Railways through the Chilterns*. London: Ian Allan.

Collett, A. 1926 *The Changing Face of England*. London: Nisbet & Co.

Collins, E.J.T. 1989 'The coppice and underwood trades', in Mingay, G.E. (ed), *The Agrarian History of England and Wales, volume VI 1750-1850*, 485-501. Cambridge: Cambridge University Press.

Commissioners of Land Revenue 1792 *The Eleventh Report of the Commissioners appointed to enquire into the State and Condition of the Woods, Forests, and Land Revenue of the Crown*. London: House of Commons Paper 4322.

Coppock, J.T. 1957 'The changing arable in the Chilterns 1875-1951', *Geography* 42, 217-29.

Coppock, J.T. 1959 'The Chilterns as an Area of Outstanding Natural Beauty', *Journal of the Town Planning Institute* 45, 137-41.

Coppock, J.T. 1960a 'The agricultural geography of the Chilterns, 1870-1951'. Unpublished Ph.D. thesis, University of London.

Coppock, J.T. 1960b 'Farms and fields in the Chilterns', *Erdkunde* 14, 134-46.

Coppock, J.T. 1961 'Agricultural changes in the Chilterns, 1875-1900,' *Agricultural History Review* 9, 1-16.

Coppock, J.T. 1964 'Dormitory settlements around London', in Coppock, J.T. and Prince, H.C. (eds), *Greater London*, 265-91. London: Faber & Faber.

Coppock, J.T. 1968. *The Chilterns*. Sheffield: The Geographical Association (Landscapes through Maps, 4).

Cornwall, J. 1959 'An Elizabethan census', *Records of Buckinghamshire* 16 (4), 258-73.

Cornwall, J. 1970 'English population in the early sixteenth century', *Economic History Review*, 2nd series, 33, 32-44.

Cornwall, J. 1975. 'Medieval peasant farmers', *Records of Buckinghamshire* 20, 57-75.

Cornwall, J.C.K. 1988 *Wealth and Society in Early Sixteenth Century England*. London: Routledge & Kegan Paul.

Cotton, M.A. and Frere, S.S. 1968 'Ivinghoe Beacon excavations 1963-1965', *Records of Buckinghamshire* 18, 187-260.

Cox, B. 1972-73 'The significance of the distribution of English place-names in -ham in the midlands and East Anglia', *Journal of the English Place-Name Society* 5, 15-73.

Cox, B. 1975-76 'The place-names of the earliest English records', *Journal of the English Place-Name Society* 8, 12-66.

CPRE (Council for the Preservation of Rural England) 1929 *The Thames Valley from Cricklade to Staines*. London: University of London Press.

CPRE (Penn Branch) 1933 *'The Penn Country of Buckinghamshire*, London: Council for the Preservation of Rural England.

Crawford, O.G.S. 1931 'The Chiltern Grim's Ditches', *Antiquity* 5, 161-71, 291-314, 370.

Cunliffe, B. 1991 (3rd edn) *Iron Age Communities in Britain*. London: Routledge.

Dahlman, C.J. 1980 *The Open Field System and Beyond*. Cambridge: Cambridge University Press.

Darby, H.C. and Campbell, E.M.J. (eds) 1962 *The Domesday Geography of South-East England*. Cambridge: Cambridge University Press.

Davies, A.M. 1949. 'Abefeld and Ackhamstead: two lost places', *Records of Buckinghamshire* 15, 166-77.

Davies, A.M. 1951-52 'The hundreds of Buckinghamshire and Oxfordshire', *Records of Buckinghamshire* 16, 231-49.

Davies, A.M. and Baines, A.H.J. 1953 'A preliminary study of the sarsen and pudding-stone blocks of the Chilterns', *Proceedings of the Geologists' Association of London* 64, 1-9.

Davies, W. and Vierck, H. 1974 'The contexts of the Tribal Hidage: social aggregates and settlement patterns', *Fruhmittelalterliche Studien* 8, 223-93.

Davis, J. 1981 'Grim's Ditch in Buckinghamshire and Hertfordshire', *Records of Buckinghamshire* 23, 23-31.

Davis, J. and Evans, J.G. 1984 'Grim's Ditch, Ivinghoe', *Records of Buckinghamshire* 26, 1-10.

Davis, K Rutherford, 1982 *Britons and Saxons. The Chiltern Region 400-700*. Chichester: Phillimore.

Davis, R. 1794 *A General View of the Agriculture of the County of Oxford*. London: Board of Agriculture.

Davis, R.H.C. 1973 'The ford, the river and the city', *Oxoniensia* 38, 258-67.

Defoe, D. 1724-27 *A Tour thro' the Whole Island of Great Britain, divided into circuits or journeys*. 3 vols. London: G.Strahan. [Everyman edition, 1962, by Dent, London]

Defoe, D. 1726-27 *The Compleat English Tradesman*. 2 vols. London: Charles Rivington.

Dils, J.A. 1987 'Henley and the river trade in the pre-industrial period', *Oxfordshire Local History* 2(6), 182-92.

Disraeli, B. 1845 *Sybil; or, The Two Nations*. London: Henry Colburn.

Dyer, C.C. 1989 'The retreat from marginal land': the growth and decline of medieval rural settlements, in Aston, M., Austin, D., and Dyer, C. (eds), *The Rural Settlements of Medieval England*, 45-57. Oxford: Basil Blackwell.

Dyer, J.F. 1959 'Barrows of the Chilterns', *Archaeological Journal* 116, 1-24.

Dyer, J.F. 1961 'Dray's ditches, Bedfordshire, and early Iron Age territorial boundaries in the eastern Chilterns', *Antiquaries Journal* 41, 32-43.

Dyer, J.F. 1963 'The Chiltern Grim's Ditch', *Antiquity* 37, 46-49.

Dyer, J. 1978 'Worthington George Smith', in *Worthington George Smith and Other Studies, presented to Joyce Godber*, 141-79. Bedford: Bedfordshire Historical Record Society, 57.

Dyer, J.F. and Hales, A.J. 1962 'Pitstone Hill—a study on field archaeology', *Records of Buckinghamshire* 17, 49-54.

Edwards, D. and Pigram, R. 1977 *Metro Memories*. (1988 edition) London: Bloomsbury Books.

Edwards, D. and Pigram, R. 1979 *The Romance of Metro-land*. (1988 edition) London: Bloomsbury Books.

Edwards, D. and Pigram, R. 1983 *The Golden Years of the Metropolitan Railway.* (1988 ed.)London: Bloomsbury
Eland, G. 1911 *The Chilterns and the Vale.* London: Longmans, Green & Co.
Elliman, P.D. 1987 'Glassmaking in Henley-on-Thames in the 17th century', *Henley Archaeological and Historical Group Journal*, 5, 2-15.
Ellis, W. 1733 *Chiltern and Vale Farming Explained.* London.
Ellis, W. 1738 *The Timber-Tree Improved.* London.
Elvey, E.M. 1961 'The Abbot of Missenden's estates at Chalfont St Giles', *Records of Buckinghamshire* 17, 20-40.
Elvey, G.R. 1977 'Walter of Henley reconsidered', *Records of Buckinghamshire* 20 (3), 470-77.
Emery, F.V. 1974 *The Oxfordshire Landscape.* London: Hodder and Stoughton.
Esmonde Cleary, A.S. 1989 *The Ending of Roman Britain.* London: B.T.Batsford.
Esposito, M. 1917 'The letters of Brunetto Latino. A nineteenth-century literary hoax', *Modern Languages Review* 12, 59-63.
Evans, J. 1955 *The Endless Web. John Dickinson & Co. Ltd 1804-1954.* London: Jonathan Cape.
Evans, J.G. 1966 'Late-glacial and post-glacial subaerial deposits at Pitstone, Buckinghamshire', *Proceedings of the Geological Association,* 77, 347-64.
Evans, J.G. 1972 *Land Snails in Archaeology.* London: Academic Press.
Evans, J.G. 1975 *The Environment of Early Man in the British Isles.* London: Paul Elek.
Evans, J.G. and Valentine, K.W.G. 1974 'Ecological changes induced by prehistoric man at Pitstone', *Buckinghamshire, Journal of Archaeological Science* 1, 343-351.
Evans, R.W. 1987 'A gazetteer of cruck buildings in Buckinghamshire', *Records of Buckinghamshire* 29, 205-10.
Everitt, A. 1986 *Continuity and Colonization. The Evolution of Kentish Settlement.* Leicester: Leicester University Press.
Farley, M. 1976 'Saxon and Medieval Walton, Aylesbury: excavations 1973-4', *Records of Buckinghamshire* 20, 153-290.
Farley, M. 1978 'Excavations at Low Farm, Fulmer, Bucks. 1: The Mesolithic occupation', *Records of Buckinghamshire* 20 (4), 601-16.
Farley, M. 1979 'A bell-pit or chalk well at Lane End', *Records of Buckinghamshire* 21, 135-40.
Farmer, D.L. 1991 'Marketing the produce of the countryside, 1200-1500', in Miller, E. (ed), *The Agrarian History of England and Wales,* vol.III 1348-1500, 324-429. Cambridge: Cambridge University Press.
Faulkner, A.H. 1972 *The Grand Junction Canal.* Newton Abbot: David & Charles.
Faulkner, A.H. 1987 *The Grand Union Canal in Hertfordshire.* Stevenage: Hertfordshire Publications.
Fenwick, C.C. 1983 'The English poll taxes of 1377, 1379 and 1381. A critical examination of the returns'. Unpublished Ph.D. thesis, London School of Economics, University of London.
Fitzstephen, W. (*c.*1180) *Vita Sancti Thomae Cantuariensis Archiepiscopi,* edited by J. Sparke (1723). London: Bowyn.
Fletcher, J. 1975 'The medieval hall at Lewknor', *Oxoniensia* 40, 247-53.
Forestry Commission 1961 *Forestry and Mature Beech. Chilterns: Queen Wood.* London: Forestry Commission.
Fowler, G.H.(ed) 1926 *A Digest of the Charters Preserved in the Cartulary of the Priory of Dunstable.* Apsley Guise: Bedfordshire Historical Record Society, 10.
Fox, H.S.A. 1981 'Approaches to the adoption of the Midland system', in Rowley, T. (ed), *The Origins of Open-field Agriculture,* 64-111. London: Croom Helm.
Fox, H.S.A. 1984 'Some ecological dimensions of medieval field systems', in Biddick, K. (ed), *Archaeological Approaches to Medieval Europe*, 119-58. Kalamazoo, Michigan: Western Michigan University (Studies in Medieval Culture 18, Medieval Institute Publications).
Fox, H.S.A. 1986 'The alleged transformation from two-field to three-field systems in medieval England', *Economic History Review,* 2nd series, 39, 526-48.
Frere, S.S. 1966 'The end of towns in Roman Britain', in Wacher, J.S. (ed), *The Civitas Capitals of Roman Britain,* 87-100. Leicester: Leicester University Press.
Frere, S.S. 1972 *Verulamium Excavations, 1.* London: Report of the Research Committee, Society of Antiquaries of London, 28.
Frere, S.S. 1983 *Verulamium Excavations, 2.* London: Report of the Research Committee, Society of Antiquaries of London, 41.
Frere, S.S. 1984 *Verulamium Excavations, 3.* Oxford: Oxford University University Committee for Archaeology, 1.
Frere, S.S. 1987 (3rd edn) *Britannia. A History of Roman Britain.* London: Routledge & Kegan Paul.
Galloway, J.A. and Murphy, M. 1991 'Feeding the city: medieval London and its agrarian hinterland', *The London Journal* 16, 3-14.
Gelling, M. 1953-54 *The Place-Names of Oxfordshire.* 2 vols. Cambridge: Cambridge University Press.
Gelling, M. 1976 *The Place-Names of Berkshire,* volume 3. Nottingham: English Place-Name Society.
Gelling, M. 1979 *Early Charters of the Thames Valley.* Leicester: Leicester University Press.
Gelling, M. 1978 *Signposts to the Past.* London: Dent.
Gelling, M. 1984 *Place-Names in the Landscape.* London: Dent
Gibbs, R. 1885 *A History of Aylesbury.* Aylesbury: R.Gibbs
Gibson, R. 1985 'A farm in the Chilterns', *Oxfordshire Local History* 2(3), 94-98.
Gibson, R.E. 1989 'Continuity and change in a Chiltern Parish: Harpsden 1586-1879'. Unpublished dissertation for joint degree in Archaeology and History, University of Reading.
Glennie, P.D. 1983 'A commercialising agrarian region: late medieval and early modern Hertfordshire'. Unpublished Ph.D. thesis, University of Cambridge.

Glennie, P.D. 1988a 'Continuity and change in Hertfordshire agriculture, 1550-1700: I - patterns of agricultural production', *Agricultural History Review* 36, 55-75.

Glennie, P.D. 1988b 'Continuity and change in Hertfordshire agriculture, 1550-1700: II - trends in crop yields and their determinants', *Agricultural History Review* 36, 145-61.

Godber, J. 1969 *History of Bedfordshire 1066-1888.* Bedford: Bedfordshire County Council.

Gras, N.S.B. 1915 *The Evolution of the English Corn Market.* Cambridge, Massachussetts: Harvard University Press.

Gray, H.L. 1915 *English Field Systems.* Cambridge, Massachussetts: Harvard University Press.

Greening Lamborn, E.A. 1936 'The churches of Bix', *Oxoniensia*, 1, 129-39.

Greenwood, J. 1883 *On the tramp.* London: Diprose and Bateman.

Gróf, L.L. 1988 *Children of Straw. The Story of a Vanished Craft and Industry in Bucks, Herts, Beds and Essex.* Buckingham: Barracuda Books.

Grundy, G.B. 1933 *Saxon Oxfordshire. Charters and Ancient Highways.* Oxford: Oxfordshire Record Society, volume 15.

Hale, W. (ed) 1858 *The Domesday of St.Paul's of the Year M.CC.XXII.* London: Camden Society Publications, 69.

Hall, P. 1963 *London 2000.* London: Faber and Faber.

Hall, P. 1989 *London 2001.* London: Unwin Hyman.

Hanley, H.A. 1975 'Population and mobility in Buckinghamshire, 1578-1583', *Local Population Studies* 15, 33-39.

Hanley, H.A. 1987 'The inclosure of Pitstone Common Wood in 1612', *Records of Buckinghamshire* 29, 175-204.

Harding, D.W. 1972 *The Iron Age in the Upper Thames Basin.* Oxford: Clarendon Press.

Harding, P.T. and Rose, F. 1986 *Pasture-woodlands in lowland Britain. Monks Wood,* Huntingdon: Institute of Terrestrial Ecology, NERC.

Hardy, D. and Ward, C. 1984 *Arcadia for all. The legacy of a makeshift landscape.* London and New York: Mansell.

Harman, T. 1986 *Seventy Summers.* London: BBC Publications.

Hart, H.W. 1975 'Henley-on-Thames: pre-railway road services', *Journal of the Railway and Canal History Society,* 21, 50-54.

Hart-Davis, D. 1991 'Waking the white ghost', *Country Life,* April 4, 82-85.

Hartley, D. (ed) 1931 *Thomas Tusser. His Good Points of Husbandry.* London: Country Life.

Hartley, F.D. 1953 'The agricultural geography of the Chilterns c1840', unpublished M.A. thesis, University of London.

Harvey, P.D.A. 1965 *A Medieval Oxfordshire Village: Cuxham 1240-1400.* Oxford: Oxford University Press.

Harvey, P.D.A. 1991 'The Home Counties', in Miller, E. (ed) *The Agrarian History of England and Wales*: volume III 1348-1500, 106-19 and 254-68 and 662-79. Cambridge: Cambridge University Press.

Hassall, W.O. 1951 'Hillwork', *Oxoniensia* 16, 89-90.

Havinden, M.A. 1961a 'The rural economy of Oxfordshire, 1580-1730', unpublished B.Litt thesis, University of Oxford.

Havinden, M.A. 1961b 'Agricultural progress in open-field Oxfordshire', *Agricultural History Review* 9, 73-83.

Havinden, M.A. 1965 'Review of Lobel, M.D. (ed), A History of the County of Oxford, volume 8', *Agricultural history Review* 13, 61-63.

Hawkes, C.F.C. 1940 'A site of the Late Bronze-Early Iron Age transition at Totternhoe, Beds', *The Antiquaries Journal* 20, 487-91.

Hawkes, S.C. 1986 'The early Saxon period', in Briggs, G., Cook, J. and Rowley,T. (eds), *The Archaeology of the Oxford Region,* 64-108. Oxford: Dept. of External Studies, University of Oxford.

Hay, D. and Hay J. 1971 *Hilltop Villages of the Chilterns.* London and Chichester: Phillimore.

Head, J.F. 1955 *Early Man in South Buckinghamshire.* Bristol: John Wright.

Head, J.F. 1974 'An important early valley route through the Chilterns', *Records of Buckinghamshire* 19, 422-28.

Hinton, D.A. and Rowley, T. (eds) 1973 'Excavations on the route of the M40', *Oxoniensia* 38, 1-183.

Holt, N.R. 1964 *The Pipe Roll of the Bishopric of Winchester 1210-1211.* Manchester: Manchester University Press.

Holt, R. 1988 *The Mills of Medieval England.* Oxford: Basil Blackwell.

Home, G. 1925 *Through the Chilterns to the Fens.* London: J.M.Dent.

Homer, H. 1767 *An Enquiry into the Means of Preserving and Improving the Public Roads of this Kingdom.* London.

Horn, C.A. and Horn, P. 1983 'The social structure of an "industrial" community: Ivinghoe in Buckinghamshire in 1871', *Local Population Studies* 31, 9-20.

Horn. P. 1971 'The Buckinghamshire straw plait trade in Victorian England', *Records of Buckinghamshire* 19, 42-54.

Horn, P. 1974 'Child workers in the pillow lace and straw plait trades of Victorian Buckinghamshire and Bedfordshire', *The Historical Journal* 17, 779-96.

Horn, P. 1991 *Victorian Countrywomen.* Oxford: Basil Blackwell.

Hornby, R. 1987 'Nature conservation in Chiltern woodlands—a Nature Conservancy Council view', *Quarterly Journal of Forestry* 31, 116-21.

Hoskins, W.G. 1955 *The Making of the English Landscape.* London: Hodder and Stoughton.

Hoskins, W.G. and Stamp, L.D. 1963 *The Common Lands of England and Wales* (New Naturalist series). London: Collins.

Hughes, M.W. 1931 'Grimsditch and Cuthwulf's expedition to the Chilterns in A.D.571', *Antiquity* 5, 291-314.

Hunn, J.R. 1980 'The earthworks at Prae Wood', *Britannia* 11, 21-30.

Hussey, T. 1987 'Hedgerow history', *The Local Historian* 17, 327-42.

Jackson, A.A. 1973 *Semi-detached London.* London: George Allen & Unwin.

Jackson, A.A. 1986 *London's Metropolitan Railway*. Newton Abbot: David & Charles.

Jackson, C.C. 1977 *Radnage*. Radnage: published by author.

James, W. and Malcolm, J. 1794 *A General View of the Agriculture of the County of Buckingham*. London: Board of Agriculture.

Jeans, D.N. 1990 'Planning and the myth of the English countryside, in the inter-war period', *Rural History* 1, 249-64.

Jenkins, J.G. 1935 *A History of the Parish of Penn in the county of Buckingham*. London: Saint Catherine's Press.

Jenkins, J.G. 1938 *The Cartulary of Missenden Abbey, Part I*. Publication No.2, Records Branch of Buckinghamshire Archaeological Society. Aylesbury & London: Buckinghamshire Archaeological Society.

Jenkins, J.G. 1955 *The Cartulary of Missenden Abbey, Part II*. Publication of Buckinghamshire Records Society 10 (for 1946). Twitchells Ends, Jordans: the author.

Jenkins, J.G. 1962 *The Cartulary of Missenden Abbey, Part III*. Publication no. 12, Buckinghamshire Record Society. London: Historical Manuscripts Commission.

Johnson, I and Fenley, P. 1974 'Grange Farm, Widmer End', *Records of Buckinghamshire* 19 (4), 449-56.

Keene, D. 1989 'Medieval London and its region', *London Journal* 14, 99-111.

Kemp, B. 1967 *Sir Francis Dashwood. An Eighteenth-Century Independent*. London: Macmillan.

Kershaw, I. 1973 'The Great Famine and agrarian crisis in England 1315-1322', *Past and Present* 59, 3-50.

King, A.D. 1984 *The Bungalow*. London: Routledge & Kegan Paul.

Kingsford, C.L. (ed.) 1919 *The Stonor Letters and Papers, 1290-1483*. 2 vols. London: Royal Historical Society (Camden series publications 29 and 30)

Kirkland, R.K. 1956 'The Watlington & Princes Risborough Railway', *Railway Magazine* 102, 355-61.

Kosminsky, E.A. 1956 *Studies in the Agrarian History of England in the Thirteenth Century*. Oxford: Basil Blackwell.

Kussmaul, A. 1990 *A General View of the Rural Economy of England 1538-1840*. Cambridge: Cambridge University Press.

Lambert, A.M. 1953 'Oxfordshire about 1800 AD: A study in human geography'. Unpublished Ph.D. thesis, University of London.

Langdon, J. 1986 *Horses, Oxen and Technological Innovation. The Use of Draught Animals in English Farming from 1066 to 1500*. Cambridge: Cambridge University Press.

Langley, T. 1797 *History and Antiquities of the Hundred of Desborough, and Deanery of Wycombe in Buckinghamshire*. London: R.Faulder.

La Sueur, A.D.C. 1955 *Burnham Beeches*. London: Corporation of the City of London.

Lean, G. and Pettit, C.E. no date (c.1928) *High on the Chiltern Hills [Totteridge]*. Totteridge, High Wycombe: the authors.

Lennard, R.V. 1959 *Rural England, 1086-1135: A study of social and agrarian conditions*. Oxford: Oxford University Press.

Levett, A.E. 1938 *Studies in Manorial History*. Oxford: Clarendon Press.

Lloyd, T.H. 1977 *The English Wool Trade in the Middle Ages*. Cambridge: Cambridge University Press.

Lobel, M.D. (ed) 1964 *A History of the County of Oxford*, volume 8. London: Oxford University Press.

Loveday, J. 1962 'Plateau deposits of the southern Chiltern Hills', *Proceedings of the Geologists' Association of London* 73, 83-102.

Lowerson, J. 1980 'Battles for the countryside', in Gloversmith, F. (ed), *Class, Culture and Social Change*, 258-80. Brighton: Harvester Press.

Lucas, J. (translator) 1892 *Kalm's Account of his visit to England on his way to America in 1748*. London: Macmillan.

Mabey, R. 1980 *The Common Ground*. London: Hutchinson.

Mabey, R. 1990 *Home Country*. London: Random Century.

McCreath, N. 1986 'The impact of the industrial revolution on selected aspects of the furniture industry in High Wycombe borough, Buckinghamshire, 1750-1900', unpublished B.Sc.dissertation, Department of Geography, University of Bristol.

Mansfield, A.J. 1952 'The historical geography of the woodlands of the southern Chilterns, 1600-1947', unpublished M.Sc. thesis, University of London.

Marren, P. 1992 *The Wild Woods. A regional guide to Britain's ancient woodland*. Newton Abbot: David & Charles.

Massingham, H.J. 1940 *Chiltern Country*. London: B.T.Batsford.

Matless, D. 1990a 'Ages of English design: preservation, modernism and tales of their history, 1926-1939', *Journal of Design History* 3, 203-12.

Matless, D. 1990b 'Definitions of England 1928-1939', *Built Environment* 16, 179-91.

Matthews, C.L. 1964 *Ancient Dunstable*. Dunstable: Manshead Archaeological Society (Revised edition, 1989).

Matthews, C.L. 1976 *Occupation Sites on a Chiltern Ridge. Part 1: Neolithic, Bronze Age and Early Iron Age*. Oxford: British Archaeological Reports 2.

Matthews, C.L., Hawkes, S.C. and others 1985 'Early Saxon settlements and burials on Puddlehill, near Dunstable, Bedfordshire', *Anglo-Saxon Studies in Archaeology and History* 4, 59-115.

Mawer, A. and Stenton, F.M. 1925 *The Place-Names of Buckinghamshire*. Cambridge: Cambridge University Press (English Place-Name Society 11).

Mayes, L.J. 1960 *The History of Chairmaking in High Wycombe*. London: Routledge and Kegan Paul.

Mead, W.R. 1954 'Ridge and furrow in Buckinghamshire', *Geographical Journal* 120, 34-42.

Mead, W.R. 1962 'Pehr Kalm in the Chilterns', *Acta Geographica* (Helsinki) 17 (1), 2-33.

Mead, W.R. 1966 'The study of field boundaries', *Geographische Zeitschrift* 54, 101-12.

Meaney, A. 1964 *A Gazetteer of Early Anglo-Saxon Burial Sites*. London: George Allen & Unwin.

Metro-land 1987 *Metro-land* (1932 edition). Reprinted, with introduction by O.Green. Harpenden: Oldcastle Books.

Miller, E. and Hatcher, J.1978 *Medieval England: Rural Society and Economic change 1086-1348*. London: Longman.

Millett, M. 1990 *The Romanization of Britain. An Essay in Archaeological Interpretation*. Cambridge: Cambridge University Press.

Money, M.C.J. and Smith, J.T. 1973 'The Great Barn', Lewknor: the architectural evidence, *Oxoniensia* 38, 339-45.

Motor Owner 1920 'Motor Owner visits Shirburn Castle', *Motor Owner*, June 1920, 33-36.

Munby, L. 1977 *The Hertfordshire Landscape*. London: Hodder and Stoughton.

Neal, D.S. 1976 'Northchurch, Boxmoor, and Hemel Hempstead Station: the excavation of three Roman buildings in the Bulbourne Valley', *Hertfordshire Archaeology* 4, 1-135.

Neal, D.S., Wardle, A., and Hunn, J. 1990 *Excavation of the Iron Age, Roman and medieval settlement at Gorhambury, St.Albans*. English Heritage: Archaeological Report 14. London: Historical Buildings & Monuments Commission for England.

North, B. (1882) *Autobiography of Benjamin North*. Aylesbury: Samuels.

North, J.D. 1976 *Richard of Wallingford*. 3 volumes. Oxford: Clarendon Press.

Oliver, J.L. 1966 *The development and structure of the furniture industry*. Oxford: Pergamon Press.

Ollier, C.D. and Thomasson, A.J. 1957 'Asymmetrical valleys of the Chiltern Hills', *Geographical Journal* 123, 71-80.

Oppitz, L. 1991 *Chiltern Railways Remembered*. Newbury: Countryside Books.

Orna, B. 1976 'A native town at Berkhamsted', *Current Archaeology* 5, 139.

Oschinsky, D. 1971 *Walter of Henley and other treatises on estate management and accounting*. Oxford: Clarendon Press.

Owen, J. 1984 'Hill and Vale: a comparison of the effects of enclosure in Buckinghamshire, 1550 to 1865', unpublished B.A. thesis, Department of Geography, University of Cambridge.

Page, H.E. 1937 *Rambles in the Chiltern Country*. Paddington, London: Great Western Railway.

Page, W. (ed) 1908 *Victoria County History of Buckinghamshire, volume 2*. London: Archibald Constable.

Palliser, F.B. 1864 *History of Lace*. London: Sampson Low, Son & Marston.

Pavry, F.H. and Knocker, G.M. 1957-58 'The Mount, Princes Risborough, Buckinghamshire', *Records of Buckinghamshire* 16, (3), 141-78.

Pawson, E. 1977 *Transport and Economy: the Turnpike Roads of Eighteeenth Century Britain*. London: Academic Press.

Peach, H.H. and Carrington, N.L. 1930 *The Face of the Land*. London: George Allen and Unwin.

Peel, J.H.B. 1950 *The Chilterns*. London: Paul Elek.

Perkin, H. 1976 *The Age of the Automobile*. London: Quartet.

Peterken, G.F. 1981 *Woodland Conservation and Management*. London: Chapman and Hall.

Petrie, F. 1926 *The Hill Figures of England*. London: Royal Anthropological Institute.

Plot, R. 1672 *The Natural history of Oxfordshire*. Oxford: The Theatre.

Postles, D. 1984 'Customary carrying services', *The Journal of Transport History*, 3rd series, 5, 1-15.

Postles, D. 1987 'Markets for rural produce in Oxfordshire, 1086-1350', *Midland History* 12, 14-26.

Power, E. 1941 *The Wool Trade in English Medieval History*. Oxford: Oxford University Press.

Power, J.P. and Campbell, B.M.S. 1992 'Cluster analysis and the classification of medieval demesne-farming systems', *Transactions of the Institute of British Geographers* (New Series) 17, 227-45.

Preece, P.G. 1987 'Firewood from the Oxfordshire Chilterns', *Arboricultural Journal* 11, 227-35.

Preece, P.G. 1987-88 'Woodmen of the Oxfordshire Chilterns 1300-1800', *Folk Life* 26, 70-77.

Preece, P.G. 1990a 'Medieval woods in the Oxfordshire Chilterns', *Oxoniensia* 55, 55-72.

Preece, P.G. 1990b 'Wood products from the Oxfordshire Chilterns before 1830', *The Local Historian* 20 (2), 73-79.

Preece, P.G. 1990c 'The Black Death in Woodcote?' *South Oxfordshire Archaeological Group Bulletin* 45, 15-16.

Priest, St.John 1810 *General View of the Agriculture of the County of Buckingham*. London: Board of Agriculture.

Prince, H.C. 1954 'Landscape Gardens in the Chilterns'. Unpublished M.A. thesis, University of London.

Prince, H.C. 1959 'Parkland in the Chilterns', *Geographical Review* 49, 18-31.

Prior, M. 1981 'The accounts of Thomas West of Wallingford, a 16th-century trader on the Thames', *Oxoniensia* 46, 73-93.

Prior, M. 1982 *Fisher Row. Fishermen, Bargemen and Canal Boatmen in Oxford, 1500-1800*. Oxford: Oxford University Press.

Rackham, O. 1980 *Ancient Woodland*. London: Edward Arnold.

Rackham, O. 1986 *The History of the Countryside*. London: Dent.

Rackham, O. 1988 (2nd edn) *Trees and Woodlands in the British Landscape*. London: Dent.

Ratcliffe, D. (ed) 1977 *A Nature Conservation Review*. 2 vols. Cambridge: Cambridge University Press.

Reed, M. 1978 'Markets and fairs in medieval Buckinghamshire', *Records of Buckinghamshire* 20, 563-85.

Reed, M. 1979a 'Buckinghamshire Anglo-Saxon estate boundaries', in Gelling, M., *The Early Charters of the Thames Valley*, 168-87. Leicester: Leicester University Press.

Reed, M. 1979b *The Buckinghamshire Landscape*. London: Hodder and Stoughton.

Repton, H. 1803 *Observations on the Theory and Practice of Landscape Gardening etc.* London: J.Taylor.

Richardson, A. 1969 'Water supplies to Tring Summit', *Journal of the Railway and Canal Society* 15, April, 21-27 and 54-62.

Richardson, K.M. and Young, A. 1951 'An Iron Age site on the Chilterns', *Antiquaries Journal* 31, 132-48.

Riley, H.T. (ed) 1867-69 *Gesta Abbatum Monasteri Sancti Albani, by Thomas Walsingham*. 3 vols. London: Longman, Green.

Robbins, C.R. 1931 'An economic aspect of regional survey', *Journal of Ecology* 19, 25-33.

Roberts, C. 1934 *Gone Rustic*. London: Hodder & Stoughton.

Roberts, C. 1935 *Gone Rambling*. London: Hodder & Stoughton.

Roberts, C. 1936 *Gone Afield*. London: Hodder & Stoughton.

Roberts, C. 1938 *The Pilgrim Cottage Omnibus*. London: Hodder & Stoughton.

Roberts, E. 1974 'Totternhoe stone and flint in Hertfordshire churches', *Medieval Archaeology* 18, 66-89.

Robinson, M. and Wilson R. 1987 'A survey of environmental archaeology in the South Midlands', in Keeley, H.C.M. (ed.) *Environmental Archaeology. A Regional Review,* 16-100. London: Historic Buildings and Monuments Commission for England (English Heritage Occasional Paper 1).

Roden, D. 1965 'Studies in Chiltern field systems'. Unpublished Ph.D. thesis, University of London.

Roden, D. 1966 'Field systems in Ibstone, a township of the south-west Chilterns, during the later middle ages', *Records of Buckinghamshire* 18, 43-58.

Roden, D. 1967 'Inheritance customs and succession to land in the Chiltern Hills in the thirteenth and early fourteenth centuries', *Journal of British Studies* 7, 1-11.

Roden, D. 1968 'Woodland and its management in the medieval Chilterns', *Forestry* 41, 59-71.

Roden, D. 1969a 'Enclosure in the Chiltern Hills', *Geografiska Annaler* 52B, 115-26.

Roden, D. 1969b 'Fragmentation of farms and fields in the Chiltern Hills thirteenth century and later', *Medieval Studies* 31, 225-38.

Roden, D. 1969c 'Demesne farming in the Chiltern Hills', *Agricultural History* Review 17, 9-23.

Roden, D. 1970 'Changing settlement in the Chiltern Hills before 1850', *Folk Life* 8, 57-71.

Roden, D. 1973 'Field systems of the Chiltern Hills and their environs', in Baker, A.R.H. and Butlin, R.A. (eds), *Studies of Field Systems in the British Isles*, 325-76. Cambridge: Cambridge University Press.

Rotuli Hundredorum 1818 *Rotuli Hundredorum temp. Hen. III & Edw. I in Turr' Lond'*. London: House of Commons.

Rowley, R.T. 1973. 'The archaeology of the M40', *Oxoniensia* 38, 1-5.

St Joseph, J.K. 1965 'Air reconnaissance in Britain 1961-1964', *Journal of Roman Studies* 55, 485-501.

Salisbury, E.J. 1918 'The ecology of scrub in Hertfordshire: a study of colonisation', *Transactions of the Hertfordshire Naturalists' Field Club* 17, 53-64.

Salter, H.E. (ed) 1935 *Cartulary of Oseney Abbey*, volume 4. Oxford: Oxford Historical Society, volume 47.

Sampson, C.G. 1978 *Paleoecology and Archaeology of an Acheulian Site at Caddington, England*. Dallas: Department of Anthropology, Southern Methodist University.

Saunders, C. 1971 'The Pre-Belgic Iron Age in the central and western Chilterns', *Archaeological Journal* 128, 1-30.

Saunders, C. 1982 'Some thoughts on the oppida at Wheathampstead and Verulamium', *Hertfordshire Archaeology* 8, 31-39.

Sawyer, P.H. 1968 *Anglo-Saxon Charters: An Annotated List and Bibliography*. London: Royal Historical Society.

Sawyer, P.H. 1983 'The royal tun in pre-Conquest England', in Wormald, P. (ed) *Ideal and Reality in Frankish and Anglo-Saxon Society,* 273-99. Cambridge: Cambridge University Press.

Scott, W.J. 1907 'How the West Midland railway tried to come to London', *Railway Magazine* 21, 314-16.

Seebohm, F. 1883 *The English Village Community*. London: Longman, Green & Co.

Sellar, W.J. and Yeatman, R.J. 1930 *1066 and All That*. London: Methuen.

Sheahan, J.J. 1862 *History and Topography of Buckinghamshire*. London: Longman.

Sheail, J. 1976 *Nature in Trust. The History of Nature Conservation in Britain*. Glasgow: Blackie.

Sheail, J. 1981 *Rural Conservation in Inter-war Britain*. Oxford: Clarendon Press.

Sheail, J. 1987 *Seventy-five Years in Ecology: the British Ecological Society*. Oxford: Blackwell Scientific Publications.

Simmons, J. 1961 *The Railways of Britain*. London: Routledge & Kegan Paul.

Sims-Williams, P. 1983 'The settlement of England in Bede and the Chronicle', *Anglo-Saxon England* 12, 1-41.

Slota, L.A. 1984 'The land market on the St.Albans manors of Park and Codicote 1237-1399', unpublished Ph.D. thesis, University of Michigan.

Slota, L.A. 1988 'Law, land transfer, and lordship on the estates of St.Albans Abbey in the thirteenth and fourteenth centuries', *Law and History Review* 6, 119-38.

Smart, G. and Anderson, M. 1990 *Planning and management of areas of outstanding natural beauty*. Cheltenham: Countryside Commission, Paper 295.

Smith, C.J. 1980 *Ecology of the English Chalk*. London: Academic Press.

Smith, L.T. (ed) 1907 *The Itinerary of John Leland in or about the years 1535-1543*. Parts I-V. (5 vols) London: George Bell & Sons.

Sparkes, I.G. 1989 *Wycombe Chairmakers in Camera*. Buckingham: Quotes.

Spenceley, G.F.R. 1973 'The origins of the English pillow lace industry', *Agricultural History Review* 21, 81-93.

Stainton, B. 1989 'Excavation of an early prehistoric site at Stratford's Yard, Chesham', *Records of Buckinghamshire* 31, 49-74.

Starey, C.J.H. and Viccars, P.G. (eds) 1992 *Stokenchurch in Perspective*. Horsleys Green, High Wycombe: STARVIC.

Stead, I.M. 1967 'A La Tene III burial at Welwyn Garden City', *Archaeologia* 101, 1-62.

Stead, I.M. and Rigby, V. 1989 *Verulamium: the King Harry Lane site*. London: Archaeological Report 12, English Heritage.

Stebbing, N., Rhodes, J. and Meller, M. 1980 *Oxfordshire Potters*. *Woodstock*, Oxford: Oxford Museums Service Publication13.

Stevenson, R.L. 1907 'An autumn effect', in *The Works of Robert Louis Stevenson*, volume XX, 129-150. London: Cassell.

Stonor, R.J. 1951 *Stonor: A Catholic Sanctuary in the Chilterns from the Fifth Century till Today*. Newport: R.H.Johns.

Stroud, D. 1962 *Humphry Repton*. London: Country Life.

Stroud, D. 1975 *Capability Brown*. London: Faber & Faber.

Talbot, C.H. (ed.) 1959 *The Life of Christina of Markyate; a twelfth-century recluse*. Oxford: Clarendon Press.

Tansley, A.G. 1939 *The British Islands and their Vegetation*. Cambridge: Cambridge University Press.

Tate, W.E. 1978 *A Domesday of English enclosure acts and awards*. Edited with an introduction by M.E.Turner. Reading: The University Library.

Taylor, C.C. 1983 *Village and Farmstead. A history of rural settlement in England*. London: George Philip.

Thirsk, J. 1961 'Industries in the countryside', in Fisher, F.J. (ed), *Essays in the Economic and Social History of Tudor and Stuart England,* 70-88. Cambridge: Cambridge University Press.

Thomas, E. 1913 *The Icknield Way*. London: Constable.

Thompson, R.D. 1957 'The Roman villa site at Little Kimble', unpublished report; copy in Buckinghamshire County Museum.

Thorburn, D. 1989 'Gender, work and schooling in the plaiting villages', *The Local Historian* 19, 107-13.

Titow, J.Z. 1962 'Land and population on the bishop of Winchester's estates, 1209-1350', unpublished Ph.D. thesis, University of Cambridge.

Titow, J.Z. 1969 *English Rural Society 1200-1350*. London: George Allen and Unwin.

Titow, J.Z. 1972 *Winchester Yields. A Study in Medieval Agricultural Productivity*. Cambridge: Cambridge University Press.

Trevelyan, G.M. 1929 *Must England's beauty perish?* London:Faber & Gwyer

Turner, H.L. 1972 '"The Great Barn", Lewknor: the documentary evidence', *Oxoniensia* 37, 187-91.

Turner, M.E. 1973 'Some social and economic considerations of parliamentary enclosure in Buckinghamshire, 1738-1865'. Unpublished Ph.D. thesis, University of Sheffield.

Turner, M.E. 1980 *English Parliamentary Enclosure*. Folkestone: Wm Dawson.

Ulyanov, Y.R. 1966 'Oksfordshirskii manor Uotlington v 1086-1300 gg [Watlington Manor, Oxfordshire, 1086-1300]' *Srednie Veka* 29, 28-69.

Ulyanov, Y.R. 1971 and 1972 'Obrazovanie i evolyutsiya strukturi manora Stonor v xiv-xv vv [The genesis and structural evolution of the Stonor Manor in the 14th and 15th centuries]' *Srednie Veka* 34, 117-44 and 35, 154-73.

Viatores, The 1964 *Roman Roads in the South-East Midlands*. London: Victor Gollancz.

Vollans, E.C. 1959 'The evolution of farmlands in the central Chilterns in the twelfth and thirteenth centuries', *Transactions and Papers of the Institute of British Geographers* 26, 197-214.

Ward, L.K. 1973 'The conservation of juniper. I. Present status of juniper in southern England', *Journal of Applied Ecology* 10, 165-88.

Ware, M.E. 1989 *Britain's Lost Waterways*. Ashbourne, Derbyshire: Moorland Publishing.

Watt, A.S. 1923 'On the ecology of British beechwoods, with special reference to their regeneration', *Journal of Ecology* 11, 1-48.

Watt, A.S. 1934 'The vegetation of the Chiltern Hills, with special reference to the beechwoods and their seral relationships', *Journal of Ecology* 22, 230-70 and 445-507.

Wells, T.C.E. 1968 'Land use changes affecting *Pulsatilla vulgaris* in England', *Biological Conservation* 1, 37-44.

Wells, T.C.E. and Barling, D.M. 1971. 'Biological flora of the British Isles: *Pulsatilla vulgaris*', *Journal of Ecology* 59, 275-92.

Wheeler, R.E.M. and Wheeler, T.V. 1936 *Verulamium: a Belgic and two Roman cities*. London: Report of the Research Committee of the Society of Antiquaries of London, 11.

Whetham, E.H. 1964-65 'The London milk trade', *Economic History Review* (2nd series) 17, 369-80.

Whitehand, J.W.R. 1967 'Traditional building materials in the Chilterns', *Oxoniensia* 32, 1-9.

Whybrow, C.H. 1934 *The History of Berkhamsted Common*. London: Commons, Open Spaces and Footpath Preservation Society.

Williams-Ellis, C. 1928 *England and the Octopus*. London: Geoffrey Bles.

Williams-Ellis, C. (ed) 1937 *Britain and the Beast*. London: J.M.Dent.

Williamson, T.M. 1988 'Explaining regional landscapes: woodland and champion in southern and eastern England', *Landscape History*, 10, 5-13.

Wordie, J.R. 1984 'The South: Oxfordshire, Buckinghamshire, Berkshire, Wiltshire, and Hampshire', in Thirsk, J. (ed), *The Agrarian History of England and Wales*, volume V 1640-1750: I Regional Farming Systems, 317-57. Cambridge: Cambridge University Press.

Wymer, J.J. 1968 *Lower Palaeolithic Archaeology in Britain, as represented by the Thames Valley*. London: John Baker.

Young A. [Alison] 1964 'Bledlow: I Land tenures and the three-field system', *Records of Buckinghamshire* 17 (4), 266-85.

Young, A. [Arthur] 1804 *General View of the Agriculture of Hertfordshire*. London: Board of Agriculture.

Young, A. [Arthur] 1813 *General View of the Agriculture of Oxfordshire*. London: Board of Agriculture.

General Index

Index of Place Names

Note: county names (Bedfordshire, Buckinghamshire, Hertfordshire, Oxfordshire) are not indexed, nor are there entries for the cities of London and Oxford.